Practical Business Math Procedures

Practical Business Math Procedures

Brief Ninth Edition

JEFFREY SLATER
North Shore Community College
Danvers, Massachusetts

Boston   Burr Ridge, IL   Dubuque, IA   New York   San Francisco   St. Louis
Bangkok   Bogotá   Caracas   Kuala Lumpur   Lisbon   London   Madrid   Mexico City
Milan   Montreal   New Delhi   Santiago   Seoul   Singapore   Sydney   Taipei   Toronto

 **McGraw-Hill Irwin**

Chapter opening photos: Chapter 1: Keith Brofsky/Getty Images. Chapter 2: PhotoLink/Getty Images. Chapter 3: The McGraw-Hill Companies, John Flournoy photographer. Chapter 4: Steve Cole/Photodisc Red/Getty Images. Chapter 5: Photodisc/Getty Images. Chapter 6: Image Source Pink/Getty Images. Chapter 7: Photodisc Red/Getty Images. Chapter 8: Teri Stratford. Chapter 9: Ryan McVay/Getty Images. Chapter 10: Tony Freeman/Photoedit. Chapter 11: Courtesy Bank of Internet USA. Chapter 12: Tony Freeman/Photoedit.

The Wall Street Journal articles republished by permission of The Wall Street Journal, Dow Jones & Company, Inc. All Rights Reserved Worldwide.

Chapter 2, page 34: article reprinted by permission of the Associated Press.

Kiplinger's articles reprinted by permission of *Kiplinger's Personal Finance* magazine. Chapter 1: December 2006. Chapter 2: May 2006. Chapter 3: February 2007. Chapter 4: December 2006. Chapter 5: February 2007. Chapter 6: June 2005. Chapter 7: February 2007. Chapter 8: May 2006. Chapter 9: June 2006. Chapter 10: December 2006. Chapter 11: May 2006. Chapter 12: January 2006.

PRACTICAL BUSINESS MATH PROCEDURES BRIEF NINTH EDITION

This book is printed on acid-free paper.

3 4 5 6 7 8 9 0 DOW/DOW 0 9

ISBN   978-0-07-327849-0 (student edition)
MHID   0-07-327849-1 (student edition)
ISBN   978-0-07-327867-4 (teacher's edition)
MHID   0-07-327867-X (teacher's edition)

Editorial director: *Stewart Mattson*
Executive editor: *Richard T. Hercher, Jr.*
Developmental editor: *Katie Jones*
Senior marketing manager: *Sankha Basu*
Senior project manager: *Susanne Riedell*
Senior production supervisor: *Debra R. Sylvester*
Design manager: *Kami Carter*
Senior photo research coordinator: *Jeremy Cheshareck*
Photo researcher: *Teri Stratford*
Lead media project manager: *Brian Nacik*
Media project manager: *Matthew Perry*
Cover design: *Kami Carter*
Interior design: *Kami Carter*
Typeface: *10/12 Times Roman*
Compositor: *Aptara*
Printer: *R. R. Donnelley*

Library of Congress Cataloging-in-Publication Data

Slater, Jeffrey, 1947-
    Practical business math procedures / Jeffrey Slater. — Brief 9th ed.
        p. cm.
    Includes index.
    ISBN-13: 978-0-07-327849-0 (student ed. : alk. paper)
    ISBN-10: 0-07-327849-1 (student ed. : alk. paper)
    ISBN-13: 978-0-07-327867-4 (teacher's ed. : alk. paper)
    ISBN-10: 0-07-327867-X (teacher's ed. : alk. paper)
    1. Business mathematics—Problems, exercises, etc. I. Title.
HF5694.S57 2008b
650.01'513—dc22
                                2007031153

Dedication

Just for Matthew, Mia, Samuel, Gracie,
Mabel, and Maggie
Love
PaPa Jeff

ROADMAP TO SUCCESS

How to use this book and the Total Slater Learning System.

Step 1: **Each chapter broken down into Learning Units. You should read one learning unit at a time.**

How do I know if I understand it?

- Try the practice quiz. All the worked out solutions are provided. If you still have questions, watch the author on your DVD (comes with your text) and work each problem out.

- Need more practice? Try the extra practice quiz provided. Check figures are at the end of the chapter. Your instructor has worked out solutions if needed.

- Go on to next Learning Unit in chapter.

Step 2: **Review the "Chapter Organizer" at the end of the chapter.**

How do I know if I understand it?

- Cover over the second or third column and see if you can explain the key points or the examples.

Step 3: **Do assigned problems at the end of the chapter (or Appendix A). These may include discussion questions, drill, word problems, challenge problems, video cases, as well as projects from the Business Math Scrapbook and Kiplinger's magazine.**

Can I check my homework?

- Appendix B has check figures for all the odd-numbered problems.

Step 4: **Take the Summary Practice Test.**

Can I check my progress?

- Appendix B has check figures for all problems.

What do I do if I do not match check figures?

- Review the video tutorial on the student DVD—the author works out each problem.

To aid you in studying the book, I have developed the following color code:

 Blue: Movement, cancellations, steps to solve, arrows, blueprints

 Gold: Formulas and steps

 Green: Tables and forms

 Red: Key items we are solving for

If you have difficulty with any text examples, pay special attention to the red and the blue. These will help remind you what you are looking for as well as what the procedures are.

FEATURES

Features students have told me have helped them the most.

Blueprint Aid Boxes

For the first eight chapters (not in Chapter 4), blueprint aid boxes are available to help you map out a plan to solve a word problem. I know that often the hardest thing to do in solving word problems is where to start. Use the blueprint as a model to get started.

Business Math Handbook

This reference guide contains all the tables found in the text. It makes homework, exams, etc. easier to deal with than flipping back and forth through the text. Also included is calculator reference guides with advice on how to use different calculators.

Chapter Organizer

At the end of each chapter is a quick reference guide called the Chapter Organizer and Study Guide. Key points, formulas, and examples are provided. A list of vocabulary terms is also included, as well as Check Figures for Extra Practice Quizzes. All have page references. (A complete glossary is found at the end of the text.) Think of the chapter organizer as your set of notes and use it as a reference when doing homework problems, and to review before exams.

DVD-ROM

The DVD packaged with the text includes practice quizzes, links to Web sites listed in the Business Math Internet Resource Guide, the Excel® templates, PowerPoint, videocases, and tutorial videos—which cover all the Learning Unit Practice Quizzes and Summary Practice Tests.

The Business Math Web site

Visit the site at www.mhhe.com/slater9e and find the Internet Resource Guide with hot links, tutorials, practice quizzes, and other study materials useful for the course.

Video Cases

There are seven video cases applying business math concepts to real companies such as Hotel Monaco, Louisville Slugger, American President Lines, Washburn Guitars, Online Banking, Buycostume.com, and Federal Signal Corporation. Video clips are included on the student DVD. Some background case information and assignment problems incorporating information on the companies are included at the end of Chapters 6, 7, 8, 9, and 11.

Business Math Scrapbook

At the end of each chapter you will find clippings from *The Wall Street Journal* and various other publications. These articles will give you a chance to use the theory provided in the chapter to apply to the real world. It allows you to put your math skills to work.

Group activity: Personal Finance, a Kiplinger Approach

In each chapter you can debate a business math issue based on a *Kiplinger's Personal Finance* magazine article that is presented. This is great for critical thinking, as well as improving your writing skills.

Spreadsheet Templates

Excel® templates are available for selected end-of-chapter problems. You can run these templates as is or enter your own data. The templates also include an interest table feature that enables you to input any percentage rate and any terms. The program will then generate table values for you.

Cumulative Reviews

At the end of Chapter 8 are word problems that test your retention of business math concepts and procedures. Check figures for *all* cumulative review problems are in Appendix B.

Acknowledgments

Academic Experts, Contributors

Anthony Aiken	Doug Dorsey	Ken Koerber	Dana Richardson
Justin Barclay	Acie Earl	Jennifer Lopez	Denver Riffe
Cheryl Bartlett	Rick Elder	Bruce MacLean	David Risch
Ben Bean	Marsha Faircloth	Lynda Mattes	Joel Sacramento
George Bernard	Tony Franco	Jon Matthews	Naim Saiti
Don Boyer	Bob Grenowski	Loretta McAdam	Ellen Sawyer
Gilbert Cohen	Victor Hall	Jean McArthur	Tim Samolis
Laura Coliton	Frank Harber	Sharon Meyer	Marguerite Savage
Judy Connell	James Hardman	Norma Montague	Warren Smock
Ronald Cooley	Helen Harris	Christine Moreno	Ray Sparks
Kathleen Crall	Ron Holm	Fran Okoren	William Tusang
Patrick Cunningham	William Hubert	Roy Peterson	Jennifer Wilbanks
John Davis	Christy Isakson	Cindy Phipps	Andrea Williams
Tamra Davis	Elizabeth Klooster	Anthony Ponder	Beryl Wright
James DeMeuse	Libby Kurtz	Joseph Reihling	Denise Wooten

Company/*Applications*

Chapter 1

Home Depot—*Problem solving*

Girl Scouts—*Reading, writing, and rounding numbers*

McDonald's—*Rounding*

Tootsie Roll—*Rounding all the way*

Toyota, Honda, Saturn—*Rounding*

Hershey—*Subtraction of whole numbers*

Chapter 2

M&M's/Mars—*Fractions and multiplication*

Wal-Mart—*Type of fractions*

TiVo—*Subraction of fractions*

M&M's/Mars—*Multiplying and dividing fractions*

Target, MinuteClinic, RediClinic—*Healthcare*

Exotic Car Share—*Fractional ownership*

Chapter 3

McDonald's—*Currency application*

M&M's/Mars—*Fractional decimal conversion*

Apple—*Decimal applications in foreign currency*

Cingular, T-Mobile—*Cost of phone calls*

Burberry, Tiffany—*Currency application*

Chapter 4

Bank of America—*Personal finance*

Continental, Amazon—*E-checks*

J.P. Morgan Chase—*Online banking*

eBay—*Online banking*

PayPal—*Online banking*

PNC Financial—*Online banking*

Visa, Mastercard—*Electronic bill paying*

Volkswagon—*Banking application*

Chapter 5

Calvin Klein, Burberry—*Unknown*

Stanley Consultants—*Workforce*

Snickers—*Solving for the Unknown*

Disney—*Solving for the Unknown*

American Quarter Coach—*Personal finance*

Yacht Smart—*Personal finance*

Chapter 6

Capital One Financial—*Cost of ATMs*

Ford—*Percents*

Dell, Apple, Gateway—*Percents*

HP, NEC, Sony, IBM—*Percents*

M&M's/Mars—*Percent, percent increase and decrease*

Kellogg—*Converting decimals to percents*

Wal-Mart—*Percent increase, decrease*

USA Today, The Wall Street Journal—Portion, base, rate

The New York Times, The Washington Post—Portion, base, rate

Chicago Tribune, Houston Chronicle—Portion, base, rate

UPS—*Portion, base, rate*

Chapter 7

Google, Overstock, AOL—*Online retailers*

Randall Scott Cycle, Condor Golf—*Discounts*

Lighting Galleries of Sarasota—*Discounts*

DHL, UPS—*Freight*

FedEx—*Freight*

Comcast, AT&T, Time Warner—*Personal finance*

Chapter 8

Disney, Payless Shoe Source—*Licensing*

Levi-Strauss, Target—*Markup*

H&M, GAP, French Connection, Wal-Mart—*Sourcing*

John Hancock—*Long-term care*

Bennigan's—*Markup*

Chapter 9

Delta Airlines—*Paycuts*

Fed Express—*Independent contractors*

Chapter 10

Federal Deposit Insurance Company—*Liability*

J.P. Morgan Chase, Citigroup—*Late Payment charges*

Bank of America—*Late payment charges*

Data Trac—*Cheaper loans*

Digital Equipment Corp.—*Cheaper loans*

Pentagon Federal Credit Union—*Cheaper loans*

Chapter 11

Bank of Internet, Citibank, E-Loan, Prosper.com—*Borrowing online*

Saks Inc.—*Notes*

Small Business Administration—*Line of credit*

U.S. Treasury—*Buying treasuries online*

Chapter 12

American Express, Bank of America—*Saving cash*

Bankrate.com—*Interest rates*

Contents

CHAPTER 1

Whole Numbers; How to Dissect and Solve Word Problems

Quick Fix

Insuring a Child in College

■ **The Problem:** You want to avoid paying $1,000 or more for college health insurance for your university-bound child.

■ **The Solution:** Most group and individual health insurance will cover dependents up to the age of 23 years old—in some cases 25—as long as they are enrolled full time at an accredited college or university.

To receive that extension, you or your employer has to send the insurer a form stating your child's college and semester course load. Insurers usually require a copy of a transcript or a receipt from a bursar's office, but some will accept just your signature. You have to repeat that process annually. Most big insurers have student-coverage forms available online.

If you have a health-maintenance organization and the college is out of state, make sure the plan's service area covers that region. Students not enrolled in university health plans may have to pay in advance to use the campus facilities, but most insurers will reimburse you.

—*Paola Singer*

LEARNING UNIT OBJECTIVES

LU 1–1: Reading, Writing, and Rounding Whole Numbers

- Use place values to read and write numeric and verbal whole numbers *(p. 3)*.
- Round whole numbers to the indicated position *(pp. 4–5)*.
- Use blueprint aid for dissecting and solving a word problem *(p. 6)*.

LU 1–2: Adding and Subtracting Whole Numbers

- Add whole numbers; check and estimate addition computations *(p. 8)*.
- Subtract whole numbers; check and estimate subtraction computations *(pp. 9–10)*.

LU 1–3: Multiplying and Dividing Whole Numbers

- Multiply whole numbers; check and estimate multiplication computations *(pp. 12–13)*.
- Divide whole numbers; check and estimate division computations *(pp. 14–15)*.

People of all ages make personal business decisions based on the answers to number questions. Numbers also determine most of the business decisions of companies. For example, click on your computer, go to the website of a company such as Home Depot and note the importance of numbers in the company's business decision-making process.

The following *Wall Street Journal* clipping "Home Depot Plans Gas-Mart Format in Four-Store Test" announces plans to test convenience stores with gasoline stations located in parking lots of four of its Nashville, Tennessee, stores:

Home Depot Plans Gas-Mart Format In Four-Store Test

By DESIREE J. HANFORD
Dow Jones Newswires

Home Depot Inc. will test convenience stores located in the parking lots of four of its Nashville, Tenn., stores this year and could expand the pilot to other markets.

The Atlanta-based home-improvement retailer plans to test convenience stores with gasoline stations starting in December, spokeswoman Paula Smith said. The stores will have items typically found in convenience stores, such as milk and soda, and prepackaged items for breakfast, lunch and dinner, she said. Some of the locations will have car washes.

Wall Street Journal © 2005

Companies often follow a general problem-solving procedure to arrive at a change in company policy. Using Home Depot as an example, the following steps illustrate this procedure:

Step 1.	State the problem(s).	Growth strategy is to continue drive for top-line growth.
Step 2.	Decide on the best methods to solve the problem(s).	Add convenience stores to adjacent Home Depot stores (some with car washes).
Step 3.	Does the solution make sense?	Good use of unproductive space, and customers can save time shopping.
Step 4.	Evaluate the results.	Home Depot will evaluate the four-store test cases.

Your study of numbers begins with a review of basic computation skills that focuses on speed and accuracy. You may think, "But I can use my calculator." Even if your instructor allows you to use a calculator, you still must know the basic computation skills. You need these skills to know what to calculate, how to interpret your calculations, how to make estimates to recognize errors you made in using your calculator, and how to make calculations when you do not have a calculator. (The Student Solutions Manual and Study Guide and the text website explain how to use calculators.)

The United States' numbering system is the **decimal system** or *base 10 system*. Your calculator gives the 10 single-digit numbers of the decimal system—0, 1, 2, 3, 4, 5, 6, 7, 8, and 9. The center of the decimal system is the **decimal point**. When you have a number with a decimal point, the numbers to the left of the decimal point are **whole numbers** and the numbers to the right of the decimal point are decimal numbers (discussed in Chapter 3). When you have a number *without* a decimal, the number is a whole number and the decimal is assumed to be after the number.

This chapter discusses reading, writing, and rounding whole numbers; adding and subtracting whole numbers; and multiplying and dividing whole numbers.

Learning Unit 1–1: Reading, Writing, and Rounding Whole Numbers

Girl Scout cookies are baked throughout the year. More than 200 million boxes of cookies are produced annually. This means that approximately 2 billion, 400 million cookies are produced. Numerically, we can write this as 2,400,000,000.

Now let's begin our study of whole numbers.

Mona Sullivan, Courtesy Girl Scouts USA

Reading and Writing Numeric and Verbal Whole Numbers

The decimal system is a *place-value system* based on the powers of 10. Any whole number can be written with the 10 digits of the decimal system because the position, or placement, of the digits in a number gives the value of the digits.

To determine the value of each digit in a number, we use a place-value chart (Figure 1.1) that divides numbers into named groups of three digits, with each group separated by a comma. To separate a number into groups, you begin with the last digit in the number and insert commas every three digits, moving from right to left. This divides the number into the named groups (units, thousands, millions, billions, trillions) shown in the place-value chart. Within each group, you have a ones, tens, and hundreds place. Keep in mind that the leftmost group may have fewer than three digits.

In Figure 1.1, the numeric number 1,605,743,891,412 illustrates place values. When you study the place-value chart, you can see that the value of each place in the chart is 10 times the value of the place to the right. We can illustrate this by analyzing the last four digits in the number 1,605,743,891,412 :

$$1,412 = (1 \times 1,000) + (4 \times 100) + (1 \times 10) + (2 \times 1)$$

So we can also say, for example, that in the number 745, the "7" means seven hundred (700); in the number 75, the "7" means 7 tens (70).

To read and write a numeric number in verbal form, you begin at the left and read each group of three digits as if it were alone, adding the group name at the end (except the last units group and groups of all zeros). Using the place-value chart in Figure 1.1, the number 1,605,743,891,412 is read as one trillion, six hundred five billion, seven hundred forty-three million, eight hundred ninety-one thousand, four hundred twelve. You do not read zeros. They fill vacant spaces as placeholders so that you can correctly state the number values. Also, the numbers twenty-one to ninety-nine must have a hyphen. And most important, when you read or write whole numbers in verbal form, do not use the word *and*. In the decimal system, *and* indicates the decimal, which we discuss in Chapter 3.

By reversing this process of changing a numeric number to a verbal number, you can use the place-value chart to change a verbal number to a numeric number. Remember that you must keep track of the place value of each digit. The place values of the digits in a number determine its total value.

Before we look at how to round whole numbers, we should look at how to convert a number indicating parts of a whole number to a whole number. We will use the Girl Scout cookies as an example.

FIGURE 1.1

Whole number place-value chart

Whole Number Groups

Trillions				Billions				Millions				Thousands				Units			
Hundred trillions	Ten trillions	Trillions	Comma	Hundred billions	Ten billions	Billions	Comma	Hundred millions	Ten millions	Millions	Comma	Hundred thousands	Ten thousands	Thousands	Comma	Hundreds	Tens	Ones (units)	Decimal Point
	1	,	6	0	5	,	7	4	3	,	8	9	1	,	4	1	2	.	

The 2,400,000,000 Girl Scout cookies could be written as 2.4 billion cookies. This amount is two billion plus four hundred million of an additional billion. The following steps explain how to convert these decimal numbers into a regular whole number:

CONVERTING PARTS OF A MILLION, BILLION, TRILLION, ETC., TO A REGULAR WHOLE NUMBER
Step 1. Drop the decimal point and insert a comma.
Step 2. Add zeros so the leftmost digit ends in the word name of the amount you want to convert. Be sure to add commas as needed.

EXAMPLE   Convert 2.4 billion to a regular whole number.

Step 1. 2.4 billion

2,4   Change the decimal point to a comma.

Step 2. 2,400,000,000   Add zeros and commas so the whole number indicates billion.

Rounding Whole Numbers

Many of the whole numbers you read and hear are rounded numbers. Government statistics are usually rounded numbers. The financial reports of companies also use rounded numbers. All rounded numbers are *approximate* numbers. The more rounding you do, the more you approximate the number.

Rounded whole numbers are used for many reasons. With rounded whole numbers you can quickly estimate arithmetic results, check actual computations, report numbers that change quickly such as population numbers, and make numbers easier to read and remember.

Numbers can be rounded to any identified digit place value, including the first digit of a number (rounding all the way). To round whole numbers, use the following three steps:

ROUNDING WHOLE NUMBERS
Step 1. Identify the place value of the digit you want to round.
Step 2. If the digit to the right of the identified digit in Step 1 is 5 or more, increase the identified digit by 1 (round up). If the digit to the right is less than 5, do not change the identified digit.
Step 3. Change all digits to the right of the rounded identified digit to zeros.

EXAMPLE 1   Round 9,362 to the nearest hundred.

Step 1. 9,362   The digit 3 is in the hundreds place value.

Step 2.   The digit to the right of 3 is 5 or more (6). Thus, 3, the identified digit in Step 1, is now rounded to 4. You change the identified digit only if the digit to the right is 5 or more.

9,462

Step 3. 9,400   Change digits 6 and 2 to zeros, since these digits are to the right of 4, the rounded number.

By rounding 9,362 to the nearest hundred, you can see that 9,362 is closer to 9,400 than to 9,300.

We can use the following *Wall Street Journal* clipping "Food for Thought" to illustrate rounding to the nearest hundred. For example, rounded to the nearest hundred, the 560 calories of Big Mac rounds to 600 calories, whereas the 290 calories of McDonald's Egg McMuffin rounds to 300 calories.

The McGraw-Hill Companies, John Flournoy photographer

Food for Thought

Nutrition information for some items on McDonald's menu:

	CALORIES	FAT(g)
Big Mac	560	30
Filet-O-Fish	400	18
Cheeseburger	310	12
Grilled Chicken Classic Sandwich	420	9
Medium French Fries	350	16
Chicken McNuggets (6)	250	15
Creamy Ranch Sauce (1.5 oz)	200	21
Cobb Salad w/Grilled Chicken	280	11
Newman's Own Cobb Dressing	120	9
Fruit & Walnut Salad	310	13
Egg McMuffin	290	11
Bacon, Egg & Cheese McGriddles	450	21
Fruit 'n Yogurt Parfait	160	2
Baked Apple Pie	250	11
Medium Coke	210	0

Source: the company

Wall Street Journal © 2005

Next, we show you how to round to the nearest thousand.

EXAMPLE 2 Round 67,951 to the nearest thousand.

Step 1. 67,951 The digit 7 is in the thousands place value.

Step 2. → Digit to the right of 7 is 5 or more (9). Thus, 7, the identified digit in Step 1, is now rounded to 8.

68,951

Step 3. 68,000 Change digits 9, 5, and 1 to zeros, since these digits are to the right of 8, the rounded number.

By rounding 67,951 to the nearest thousand, you can see that 67,951 is closer to 68,000 than to 67,000.

Now let's look at **rounding all the way.** To round a number all the way, you round to the first digit of the number (the leftmost digit) and have only one nonzero digit remaining in the number.

EXAMPLE 3 Round 7,843 all the way.

Step 1. 7,843 Identified leftmost digit is 7.

Step 2. → Digit to the right of 7 is greater than 5, so 7 becomes 8.

8,843

Step 3. 8,000 Change all other digits to zeros.

Rounding 7,843 all the way gives 8,000.

Remember that rounding a digit to a specific place value depends on the degree of accuracy you want in your estimate. For example, 24,800 rounds all the way to 20,000 because the digit to the right of 2 is less than 5. This 20,000 is 4,800 less than the original 24,800. You would be more accurate if you rounded 24,800 to the place value of the identified digit 4, which is 25,000.

Before concluding this unit, let's look at how to dissect and solve a word problem.

How to Dissect and Solve a Word Problem

As a student, your author found solving word problems difficult. Not knowing where to begin after reading the word problem caused the difficulty. Today, students still struggle with word problems as they try to decide where to begin.

Solving word problems involves *organization* and *persistence.* Recall how persistent you were when you learned to ride a two-wheel bike. Do you remember the feeling of success you experienced when you rode the bike without help? Apply this persistence to word problems.

Do not be discouraged. Each person learns at a different speed. Your goal must be to FINISH THE RACE and experience the success of solving word problems with ease.

To be organized in solving word problems, you need a plan of action that tells you where to begin—a blueprint aid. Like a builder, you will refer to this blueprint aid constantly until you know the procedure. The blueprint aid for dissecting and solving a word problem follows. Note that the blueprint aid serves an important function—**it decreases your math anxiety.**

Blueprint Aid for Dissecting and Solving a Word Problem

The facts	Solving for?	Steps to take	Key points

Now let's study this blueprint aid. The first two columns require that you *read* the word problem slowly. Think of the third column as the basic information you must know or calculate before solving the word problem. Often this column contains formulas that provide the foundation for the step-by-step problem solution. The last column reinforces the key points you should remember.

It's time now to try your skill at using the blueprint aid for dissecting and solving a word problem.

Teri Stratford

The Word Problem On the 100th anniversary of Tootsie Roll Industries, the company reported sharply increased sales and profits. Sales reached one hundred ninety-four million dollars and a record profit of twenty-two million, five hundred fifty-six thousand dollars. The company president requested that you round the sales and profit figures all the way.

Study the following blueprint aid and note how we filled in the columns with the information in the word problem. You will find the organization of the blueprint aid most helpful. Be persistent! You *can* dissect and solve word problems! When you are finished with the word problem, make sure the answer seems reasonable.

The facts	Solving for?	Steps to take	Key points
Sales: One hundred ninety-four million dollars. *Profit:* Twenty-two million, five hundred fifty-six thousand dollars.	Sales and profit rounded all the way.	Express each verbal form in numeric form. Identify leftmost digit in each number.	Rounding all the way means only the left-most digit will remain. All other digits become zeros.

Steps to solving problem

1. Convert verbal to numeric.
   One hundred ninety-four million dollars ⟶ $194,000,000
   Twenty-two million, five hundred fifty-six thousand dollars ⟶ $ 22,556,000

2. Identify leftmost digit of each number.

$194,000,000 $22,556,000

3. Round.

$200,000,000 $20,000,000

Note that in the final answer, $200,000,000 and $20,000,000 have only one nonzero digit.

Remember that you cannot round numbers expressed in verbal form. You must convert these numbers to numeric form.

Now you should see the importance of the information in the third column of the blueprint aid. When you complete your blueprint aids for word problems, do not be concerned if the order of the information in your boxes does not follow the order given in the text boxes. Often you can dissect a word problem in more than one way.

Your first Practice Quiz follows. Be sure to study the paragraph that introduces the Practice Quiz.

LU 1–1   PRACTICE QUIZ

Complete this **Practice Quiz** to see how you are doing

At the end of each learning unit, you can check your progress with a Practice Quiz. If you had difficulty understanding the unit, the Practice Quiz will help identify your area of weakness. Work the problems on scrap paper. Check your answers with the worked-out solutions that follow the quiz. Ask your instructor about specific assignments and the videos available on your DVD for each chapter Practice Quiz.

1. Write in verbal form:
  a. 7,948   **b.** 48,775   **c.** 814,410,335,414

2. Round the following numbers as indicated:

Nearest ten	Nearest hundred	Nearest thousand	Rounded all the way
a. 92	**b.** 745	**c.** 8,341	**d.** 4,752

3. Kellogg's reported its sales as five million, one hundred eighty-one thousand dollars. The company earned a profit of five hundred two thousand dollars. What would the sales and profit be if each number were rounded all the way? (*Hint:* You might want to draw the blueprint aid since we show it in the solution.)

✓ **Solutions**

1. a. Seven thousand, nine hundred forty-eight
  b. Forty-eight thousand, seven hundred seventy-five
  c. Eight hundred fourteen billion, four hundred ten million, three hundred thirty-five thousand, four hundred fourteen

2. a. 90   **b.** 700   **c.** 8,000   **d.** 5,000

3. Kellogg's sales and profit:

The facts	Solving for?	Steps to take	Key points
Sales: Five million, one hundred eighty-one thousand dollars. *Profit:* Five hundred two thousand dollars.	Sales and profit rounded all the way.	Express each verbal form in numeric form. Identify leftmost digit in each number.	Rounding all the way means only the leftmost digit will remain. All other digits become zeros.

Steps to solving problem

1. Convert verbal to numeric.
  Five million, one hundred eighty-one thousand ————————————➤ $5,181,000
  Five hundred two thousand ————————————————————➤ $ 502,000

2. Identify leftmost digit of each number.
  $5,181,000 $502,000

3. Round.
  $5,000,000 $500,000

LU 1–1a	EXTRA PRACTICE QUIZ

Need more practice? Try this **Extra Practice Quiz** (check figures in Chapter Organizer, p. 19)

1. Write in verbal form:
   a. 8,682   **b.** 56,295   **c.** 732,310,444,888

2. Round the following numbers as indicated:

Nearest ten	Nearest hundred	Nearest thousand	Rounded all the way
a. 43	**b.** 654	**c.** 7,328	**d.** 5,980

3. Kellogg's reported its sales as three million, two hundred ninety-one thousand dollars. The company earned a profit of four hundred five thousand dollars. What would the sales and profit be if each number were rounded all the way?

Learning Unit 1–2: Adding and Subtracting Whole Numbers

Did you know that the cost of long-term care in nursing homes varies in different locations? The following *Wall Street Journal* clipping "Costly Long-Term Care" gives the daily top 10 rates and lowest 10 rates of long-care costs reported in various cities. For example, note the difference in daily long-term care costs between Alaska and Shreveport, Louisiana:

$$\begin{array}{lr}\text{Alaska:} & \$561 \\ \text{Sherveport:} - & 99 \\ \hline & \$462 \end{array}$$

Costly Long-Term Care

The average daily rate for a private room in a nursing home is $192. The highest and lowest rates were reported in:

TOP 10

Alaska[1]	$561
Stamford, Conn.	331
New York	312
San Francisco	293
Boston	284
Hartford, Conn.	277
Worcester, Mass.	272
Washington, D.C.	260
Rochester, N.Y.	251
Bridgewater, N.J.	244

LOWEST 10

Shreveport, La.	$99
New Orleans	107
Kansas City. Mo.	129
Little Rock, Ark.	131
St. Louis	131
Birmingham, Ala.	133
Chicago	136
Charleston, S.C.	138
Salt Lake City	138
Wichita, Kan.[2]	142

[1]Statewide [2]Tied with Jackson, Miss., and Billings, Mont.

Source: MetLife Mature Market Institute

Wall Street Journal © 2006

If you may have long-term nursing care in your future or in the future of someone in your family, be sure to research the cost (and conditions) of long-term care in various locations.

This unit teaches you how to manually add and subtract whole numbers. When you least expect it, you will catch yourself automatically using this skill.

Addition of Whole Numbers

To add whole numbers, you unite two or more numbers called **addends** to make one number called a **sum,** *total,* or *amount.* The numbers are arranged in a column according to their place values—units above units, tens above tens, and so on. Then, you add the columns of numbers from top to bottom. To check the result, you re-add the columns from bottom to top. This procedure is illustrated in the steps that follow.

ADDING WHOLE NUMBERS
Step 1. Align the numbers to be added in columns according to their place values, beginning with the units place at the right and moving to the left (Figure 1.1).
Step 2. Add the units column. Write the sum below the column. If the sum is more than 9, write the units digit and carry the tens digit.
Step 3. Moving to the left, repeat Step 2 until all place values are added.

EXAMPLE

Adding top bottom	2 1 1 1,362 5,913 8,924 + 6,594 22,793	Checking bottom to to top	**Alternate check** Add each column as a separate total and then combine. The end result is the same.

1,362
5,913
8,924
+ 6,594
13
18
2 6
20
22,793

How to Quickly Estimate Addition by Rounding All the Way

In Learning Unit 1–1, you learned that rounding whole numbers all the way gives quick arithmetic estimates. Using the following *Wall Street Journal* clipping "Hottest Models," note how you can round each number all the way and the total will not be rounded all the way. Remember that rounding all the way does not replace actual computations, but it is helpful in making quick commonsense decisions.

Hottest Models

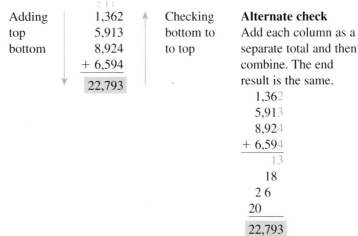

Model	Days on Lot	Average Price	Rounded all the way
Toyota Prius	5	$25,365	$ 30,000
Scion tC	9	$18,278	20,000
Scion xB	10	$15,834	20,000
BMW 7 Series	13	$80,507	80,000
Scion xA	14	$14,532	10,000
Lexus RX 400h	14	$50,131	50,000
Honda Odyssey	16	$31,001	30,000
Toyota Corolla	16	$16,290	20,000
Mazda MX-5	17	$25,380	30,000
Lexus RX 330	17	$39,467	40,000
Saturn VUE	17	$22,553	+ 20,000
			$350,000

Rounding all the way means each number has only one nonzero digit.

Note: The final answer could have more than one nonzero digit since the total is not rounded all the way.

Subtraction of Whole Numbers

Subtraction is the opposite of addition. Addition unites numbers; subtraction takes one number away from another number. In subtraction, the top (largest) number is the **minuend.** The number you subtract from the minuend is the **subtrahend,** which gives you the **difference** between the minuend and the subtrahend. The steps for subtracting whole numbers follow.

SUBTRACTING WHOLE NUMBERS
Step 1. Align the minuend and subtrahend according to their place values.
Step 2. Begin the subtraction with the units digits. Write the difference below the column. If the units digit in the minuend is smaller than the units digit in the subtrahend, borrow 1 from the tens digit in the minuend. One tens digit is 10 units.
Step 3. Moving to the left, repeat Step 2 until all place values in the subtrahend are subtracted.

EXAMPLE   The following *Wall Street Journal* clipping "Big Bills Ahead" illustrates the subtraction of whole numbers:

Big Bills Ahead
A look at average long-term-care costs in 2004

■ Private Nursing Home
Daily rate: $192
Highest rate: Alaska—$561
Lowest rate: Shreveport, La.—$99

■ Assisted-Living Facility
Monthly rate: $2,524
Highest rate: Stamford, Conn.—$4,327
Lowest rate: Miami—$1,340

■ Home-Health Aide
Hourly rate: $18
Highest rate: Hartford, Conn.—$28
Lowest rate: Jackson, Miss.—$13

Source: MetLife Inc.

What is the difference in cost between the Stamford, Connecticut, and the Miami, Florida, assisted-living facilities? As shown below, you can use subtraction to arrive at the $2,987 difference.

$$\begin{array}{r} \overset{\scriptstyle 12}{} \\ 3\ \overset{\scriptstyle 2}{\cancel{3}}\ 12 \\ \$4,\cancel{327} \quad \leftarrow \text{Minuend (larger number)} \\ -1,340 \quad \leftarrow \text{Subtrahend} \\ \hline \$2,987 \quad \leftarrow \text{Difference} \end{array}$$

Check $2,987
              $\underline{+1,340}$
              $4,327

In subtraction, borrowing from the column at the left is often necessary. Remember that 1 ten = 10 units, 1 hundred = 10 tens, and 1 thousand = 10 hundreds.

Step 1. In the above example, the 0 in the subtrahend of the rightmost column (ones or units column) can be subtracted from the 7 in the minuend to give a difference of 7. This means we do not have to borrow from the tens column at the left. However, in the tens column, we cannot subtract 4 in the subtrahend from 2 in the minuend, so we move left and borrow 1 from the hundreds column. Since 1 hundred = 10 tens, we have 10 + 2, or 12 tens in the minuend. Now we can subtract 4 tens in the subtrahend from 12 tens in the minuend to give us 8 tens in the difference.

Step 2. Since we borrowed 1 hundred from our original 3 hundred, we now have 2 hundred in the minuend. The 3 hundred in the subtrahend will not subtract from the 2 hundred in the minuend, so again we must move left. We take 1 thousand from the 4 thousand in the thousands column. Since 1 thousand is 10 hundreds, we have 10 + 2, or 12 hundreds in the hundreds column. The 3 hundred in the subtrahend subtracted from the 12 hundred in the minuend gives us 9 hundred in the difference. The 1 thousand in the subtrahend subtracted from the 3 thousand in the minuend gives 2 thousand. Our total difference between the subtrahend $1,340 and the minuend $4,327 is $2,987 as proved in the check.

Checking subtraction requires adding the difference ($2,987) to the subtrahend ($1,340) to arrive at the minuend ($4,327). The Stamford, Connecticut, assisted-living facility costs $2,987 more than the Miami, Florida, assisted-living facility.

How to Dissect and Solve a Word Problem

Accurate subtraction is important in many business operations. In Chapter 4 we discuss the importance of keeping accurate subtraction in your checkbook balance. Now let's check your progress by dissecting and solving a word problem.

The Word Problem Hershey's produced 25 million Kisses in one day. The same day, the company shipped 4 million to Japan, 3 million to France, and 6 million throughout the United States. At the end of that day, what is the company's total inventory of Kisses? What is the inventory balance if you round the number all the way?

The facts	Solving for?	Steps to take	Key points
Produced: 25 million. *Shipped:* Japan, 4 million; France, 3 million; United States, 6 million.	Total Kisses left in inventory. Inventory balance rounded all the way.	Total Kisses produced − Total Kisses shipped = Total Kisses left in inventory.	Minuend − Subtrahend = Difference. Rounding all the way means rounding to last digit on the left.

Steps to solving problem

1. Calculate the total Kisses shipped.

$$\begin{array}{r} 4,000,000 \\ 3,000,000 \\ +\ 6,000,000 \\ \hline 13,000,000 \end{array}$$

2. Calculate the total Kisses left in inventory.

$$\begin{array}{r} 25,000,000 \\ -\ 13,000,000 \\ \hline 12,000,000 \end{array}$$

3. Rounding all the way.

Identified digit is 1. Digit to right of 1 is 2, which is less than 5. *Answer:* 10,000,000.

The Practice Quiz that follows will tell you how you are progressing in your study of Chapter 1.

Teri Stratford

LU 1–2 | **PRACTICE QUIZ**

Complete this **Practice Quiz** to see how you are doing

1. Add by totaling each separate column:

   $$\begin{array}{r} 8,974 \\ 6,439 \\ +\ 16,941 \end{array}$$

2. Estimate by rounding all the way (do not round the total of estimate) and then do the actual computation:

   $$\begin{array}{r} 4,241 \\ 8,794 \\ +\ 3,872 \end{array}$$

3. Subtract and check your answer:

   $$\begin{array}{r} 9,876 \\ -\ 4,967 \end{array}$$

4. Jackson Manufacturing Company projected its year 2003 furniture sales at $900,000. During 2003, Jackson earned $510,000 in sales from major clients and $369,100 in sales from the remainder of its clients. What is the amount by which Jackson over- or underestimated its sales? Use the blueprint aid, since the answer will show the completed blueprint aid.

✓ **Solutions**

1.
$$\begin{array}{r} 14 \\ 14 \\ 2\ 2 \\ 20 \\ \hline 22,354 \end{array}$$

2.

Estimate	Actual
4,000	4,241
9,000	8,794
+ 4,000	+ 3,872
17,000	16,907

3.
$$\begin{array}{r} {}^{8\ 18\,6\,16} \\ \cancel{9,876} \\ -\ 4,967 \\ \hline 4,909 \end{array}$$

Check
$$\begin{array}{r} 4,909 \\ +\ 4,967 \\ \hline 9,876 \end{array}$$

4. Jackson Manufacturing Company over- or underestimated sales:

The facts	Solving for?	Steps to take	Key points
Projected 2003 sales: $900,000. *Major clients:* $510,000. *Other clients:* $369,100.	How much were sales over- or underestimated?	Total projected sales − Total actual sales = Over- or underestimated sales.	Projected sales (minuend) − Actual sales (subtrahend) = Difference.

Steps to solving problem

1. Calculate total actual sales.

$510,000
+ 369,100
$879,100

2. Calculate overestimated or underestimated sales.

$900,000
− 879,100

$ 20,900 (overestimated)

LU 1–2a **EXTRA PRACTICE QUIZ**

Need more practice? Try this **Extra Practice Quiz** (check figures in Chapter Organizer, p. 19)

1. Add by totaling each separate column:
    9,853
    7,394
   +8,843

2. Estimate by rounding all the way (do not round the total of estimate) and then do the actual computation:
    3,482
    6,981
   +5,490

3. Subtract and check your answer:
    9,787
   −5,968

4. Jackson Manufacturing Company projected its year 2008 furniture sales at $878,000. During 2008, Jackson earned $492,900 in sales from major clients and $342,000 in sales from the remainder of its clients. What is the amount by which Jackson over- or underestimated its sales?

Learning Unit 1–3: Multiplying and Dividing Whole Numbers

At the beginning of Learning Unit 1–2, you learned how you would save $462 on the purchase of daily long-term care in a Shreveport, Louisiana, nursing home instead of in an Alaska nursing home.

If you stay in the Alaska and Shreveport nursing homes for 5 days, the Alaska nursing home would cost you $2,805, but the Shreveport nursing home would cost you $495, and you would save $2,310:

Alaska: $561 × 5 = $2,805
Shreveport: 99 × 5 = −   495
                            $2,310

If you divide $2,310 by 5, you will get the $462 difference in price between Alaska and Shreveport as shown at the beginning of Learning Unit 1–2.

This unit will sharpen your skills in two important arithmetic operations—multiplication and division. These two operations frequently result in knowledgeable business decisions.

Multiplication of Whole Numbers—Shortcut to Addition

From calculating your purchase of 5 days of long-term care in Shreveport, you know that multiplication is a *shortcut to addition:*

$$\$99 \times 5 = \$495 \quad \text{or} \quad \$99 + \$99 + \$99 + \$99 + \$99 = \$495$$

Before learning the steps used to multiply whole numbers with two or more digits, you must learn some multiplication terminology.

Note in the following example that the top number (number we want to multiply) is the **multiplicand.** The bottom number (number doing the multiplying) is the **multiplier.** The final number (answer) is the **product.** The numbers between the multiplier and the product are **partial products.** Also note how we positioned the partial product 2090. This number is the result of multiplying 418 by 50 (the 5 is in the tens position). On each line in the partial products, we placed the first digit directly below the digit we used in the multiplication process.

EXAMPLE

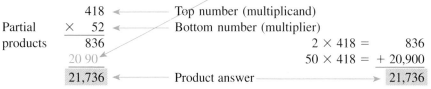

```
                418  ←————————  Top number (multiplicand)
   Partial    ×   52  ←————————  Bottom number (multiplier)
   products      836                        2 × 418 =        836
               20 90                       50 × 418 =  + 20,900
              ─────────
              21,736  ←————— Product answer ————————→   21,736
```

We can now give the following steps for multiplying whole numbers with two or more digits:

MULTIPLYING WHOLE NUMBERS WITH TWO OR MORE DIGITS
Step 1. Align the multiplicand (top number) and multiplier (bottom number) at the right. Usually, you should make the smaller number the multiplier.
Step 2. Begin by multiplying the right digit of the multiplier with the right digit of the multiplicand. Keep multiplying as you move left through the multiplicand. Your first partial product aligns at the right with the multiplicand and multiplier.
Step 3. Move left through the multiplier and continue multiplying the multiplicand. Your partial product right digit or first digit is placed directly below the digit in the multiplier that you used to multiply.
Step 4. Continue Steps 2 and 3 until you have completed your multiplication process. Then add the partial products to get the final product.

Checking and Estimating Multiplication

We can check the multiplication process by reversing the multiplicand and multiplier and then multiplying. Let's first estimate 52×418 by rounding all the way.

EXAMPLE

```
        50  ←——    52
   ×  400  ←—  × 418
   ─────────     ─────
   20,000         416
                   52
                 20 8
                ───────
                21,736
```

By estimating before actually working the problem, we know our answer should be about 20,000. When we multiply 52 by 418, we get the same answer as when we multiply 418×52—and the answer is about 20,000. Remember, if we had not rounded all the way, our estimate would have been closer. If we had used a calculator, the rounded estimate would have helped us check the calculator's answer. Our commonsense estimate tells us our answer is near 20,000—not 200,000.

Before you study the division of whole numbers, you should know (1) the multiplication shortcut with numbers ending in zeros and (2) how to multiply a whole number by a power of 10.

MULTIPLICATION SHORTCUT WITH NUMBERS ENDING IN ZEROS
Step 1. When zeros are at the end of the multiplicand or the multiplier, or both, disregard the zeros and multiply.
Step 2. Count the number of zeros in the multiplicand and multiplier.
Step 3. Attach the number of zeros counted in Step 2 to your answer.

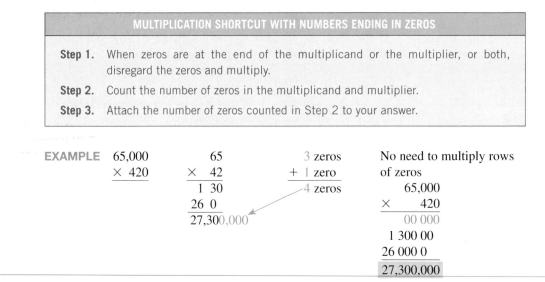

EXAMPLE

$$
\begin{array}{r}
65{,}000 \\
\times\ 420 \\
\end{array}
\qquad
\begin{array}{r}
65 \\
\times\ 42 \\
\hline
1\ 30 \\
26\ 0 \\
\hline
27{,}300{,}000 \\
\end{array}
\qquad
\begin{array}{r}
3\ \text{zeros} \\
+\ 1\ \text{zero} \\
\hline
4\ \text{zeros} \\
\end{array}
$$

No need to multiply rows of zeros

$$
\begin{array}{r}
65{,}000 \\
\times\ \ \ \ \ 420 \\
\hline
00\ 000 \\
1\ 300\ 00 \\
26\ 000\ 0 \\
\hline
27{,}300{,}000 \\
\end{array}
$$

MULTIPLYING A WHOLE NUMBER BY A POWER OF 10
Step 1. Count the number of zeros in the power of 10 (a whole number that begins with 1 and ends in one or more zeros such as 10, 100, 1,000, and so on).
Step 2. Attach that number of zeros to the right side of the other whole number to obtain the answer. Insert comma(s) as needed every three digits, moving from right to left.

EXAMPLE

$99 \times 10\ \ \ = 990\ \ \ = \boxed{990}$ ←—Add 1 zero

$99 \times 100\ \ = 9{,}900\ \ = \boxed{9{,}900}$ ←—Add 2 zeros

$99 \times 1{,}000 = 99{,}000 = \boxed{99{,}000}$ ←—Add 3 zeros

When a zero is in the center of the multiplier, you can do the following:

EXAMPLE

$$
\begin{array}{r}
658 \\
\times\ \ 403 \\
\hline
1\ 974 \\
263\ 2\square \\
\hline
\boxed{265{,}174} \\
\end{array}
\qquad
\begin{array}{r}
3 \times 658 = \ \ \ \ \ 1{,}974 \\
400 \times 658 = +\ 263{,}200 \\
\hline
\boxed{265{,}174} \\
\end{array}
$$

Division of Whole Numbers

Division is the reverse of multiplication and a time-saving shortcut related to subtraction. For example, in the introduction to this learning unit, you determined that you would save $2,310 by staying for 5 days in a nursing home in Shreveport, Louisiana, versus Alaska. If you subtract $462—the difference between the cost of Alaska and Shreveport—5 times from the difference of $2,310, you would get to zero. You can also multiply $462 times 5 to get $2,310. Since division is the reverse of multiplication, you can say that $2,310 ÷ 5 = $462.

Division can be indicated by the common symbols ÷ and $\overline{)}$, or by the bar — in a fraction and the forward slant / between two numbers, which means the first number is divided by the second number. Division asks how many times one number (**divisor**) is contained in another number (**dividend**). The answer, or result, is the **quotient.** When the divisor (number used to divide) doesn't divide evenly into the dividend (number we are dividing), the result is a **partial quotient,** with the leftover amount the **remainder** (expressed as fractions in later chapters). The following example illustrates *even division* (this is also an example of *long division* because the divisor has more than one digit).

EXAMPLE
$$
\begin{array}{r}
18 \leftarrow \text{Quotient} \\
\text{Divisor} \longrightarrow 15\overline{)270} \leftarrow \text{Dividend} \\
\underline{15} \\
120 \\
\underline{120}
\end{array}
$$

This example divides 15 into 27 once with 12 remaining. The 0 in the dividend is brought down to 12. Dividing 120 by 15 equals 8 with no remainder; that is, even division. The following example illustrates *uneven division with a remainder* (this is also an example of *short division* because the divisor has only one digit).

EXAMPLE
$$
\begin{array}{r}
24 \text{ R1} \leftarrow \text{Remainder} \\
7\overline{)169} \\
\underline{14} \\
29 \\
\underline{28} \\
1
\end{array}
$$

Check

(7 × 24) + 1 = 169

Divisor × Quotient + Remainder = Dividend

Note how doing the check gives you assurance that your calculation is correct. When the divisor has one digit (short division) as in this example, you can often calculate the division mentally as illustrated in the following examples:

EXAMPLES
$$
\begin{array}{cc}
108 & 16 \text{ R6} \\
8\overline{)864} & 7\overline{)118}
\end{array}
$$

Next, let's look at the value of estimating division.

Estimating Division

Before actually working a division problem, estimate the quotient by rounding. This estimate helps check the answer. The example that follows is rounded all the way. After you make an estimate, work the problem and check your answer by multiplication.

EXAMPLE
$$
\begin{array}{r}
36 \text{ R111} \\
138\overline{)5,079} \\
\underline{4\ 14} \\
939 \\
\underline{828} \\
111
\end{array}
$$

Estimate
$$
\begin{array}{r}
50 \\
100\overline{)5,000}
\end{array}
$$

Check
$$
\begin{array}{r}
138 \\
\times\ \ 36 \\
\hline
828 \\
4\ 14 \\
\hline
4,968 \\
+\ \ 111 \leftarrow \text{Add remainder} \\
\hline
5,079
\end{array}
$$

Now let's turn our attention to division shortcuts with zeros.

Division Shortcuts with Zeros

The steps that follow show a shortcut that you can use when you divide numbers with zeros.

DIVISION SHORTCUT WITH NUMBERS ENDING IN ZEROS
Step 1. When the dividend and divisor have ending zeros, count the number of ending zeros in the divisor.
Step 2. Drop the same number of zeros in the dividend as in the divisor, counting from right to left.

Note the following examples of division shortcut with numbers ending in zeros. Since two of the symbols used for division are ÷ and $\overline{)}$, our first examples show the zero shortcut method with the ÷ symbol.

EXAMPLES

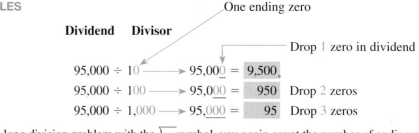

One ending zero

Dividend **Divisor**

Drop 1 zero in dividend

$95{,}000 \div 10 \longrightarrow 95{,}00\underline{0} = \boxed{9{,}500}$

$95{,}000 \div 100 \longrightarrow 95{,}0\underline{00} = \boxed{950}$ Drop 2 zeros

$95{,}000 \div 1{,}000 \longrightarrow 95{,}\underline{000} = \boxed{95}$ Drop 3 zeros

In a long division problem with the $\overline{)}$ symbol, you again count the number of ending zeros in the divisor. Then drop the same number of ending zeros in the dividend and divide as usual.

EXAMPLE

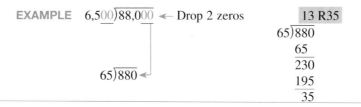

$6{,}5\underline{00})\overline{88{,}0\underline{00}}$ ← Drop 2 zeros

$65)\overline{880}$ ←

$$
\begin{array}{r}
13 \text{ R35} \\
65)\overline{880} \\
\underline{65} \\
230 \\
\underline{195} \\
35
\end{array}
$$

You are now ready to practice what you learned by dissecting and solving a word problem.

How to Dissect and Solve a Word Problem

The blueprint aid that follows will be your guide to dissecting and solving the following word problem.

The Word Problem Dunkin' Donuts sells to four different companies a total of $3,500 worth of doughnuts per week. What is the total annual sales to these companies? What is the yearly sales per company? (Assume each company buys the same amount.) Check your answer to show how multiplication and division are related.

The facts	Solving for?	Steps to take	Key points
Sales per week: $3,500. *Companies:* 4.	Total annual sales to all four companies. Yearly sales per company.	Sales per week × Weeks in year (52) = Total annual sales. Total annual sales ÷ Total companies = Yearly sales per company.	Division is the reverse of multiplication.

Steps to solving problem

1. Calculate total annual sales. $3,500 × 52 weeks = $182,000

2. Calculate yearly sales per company. $182,000 ÷ 4 = $45,500

Check

$45,500 × 4 = $182,000

It's time again to check your progress with a Practice Quiz.

LU 1–3 PRACTICE QUIZ

Complete this **Practice Quiz** to see how you are doing

DVD

1. Estimate the actual problem by rounding all the way, work the actual problem, and check:

Actual	Estimate	Check
3,894		
× 18		

2. Multiply by shortcut method:
   77,000
   × 1,800

3. Multiply by shortcut method:
   95 × 10,000

4. Divide by rounding all the way, complete the actual calculation, and check, showing remainder as a whole number.
   26)5,325

5. Divide by shortcut method:
   4,000)96,000

6. Assume General Motors produces 960 Chevrolets each workday (Monday through Friday). If the cost to produce each car is $6,500, what is General Motors' total cost for the year? Check your answer.

✓ Solutions

1.

Estimate	Actual	Check
4,000	3,894	8 × 3,894 = 31,152
× 20	× 18	10 × 3,894 = + 38,940
80,000	31 152	70,092
	38 94	
	70,092	

2. 77 × 18 = 1,386 + 5 zeros = 138,600,000   **3.** 95 + 4 zeros = 950,000

4.

Rounding	Actual	Check
166 R20	204 R21	26 × 204 = 5,304
30)5,000	26)5,325	+ 21
3 0	5 2	5,325
2 00	125	
1 80	104	
200	21	
180		
20		

5. Drop 3 zeros = 4)96   (24)

6. General Motors' total cost per year:

The facts	Solving for?	Steps to take	Key points
Cars produced each workday: 960. Workweek: 5 days. Cost per car: $6,500.	Total cost per year.	Cars produced per week × 52 = Total cars produced per year. Total cars produced per year × Total cost per car = Total cost per year.	Whenever possible, use multiplication and division shortcuts with zeros. Multiplication can be checked by division.

Steps to solving problem

1. Calculate total cars produced per week.   5 × 960 = 4,800 cars produced per week

2. Calculate total cars produced per year.   4,800 cars × 52 weeks = 249,600 total cars produced per year

3. Calculate total cost per year.   249,600 cars × $6,500 = $1,622,400,000 (multiply 2,496 × 65 and add zeros)

Check

$1,622,400,000 ÷ 249,600 = $6,500 (drop 2 zeros before dividing)

LU 1–3a   EXTRA PRACTICE QUIZ

Need more practice? Try this
Extra Practice Quiz (check
figures in Chapter Organizer,
p. 19)

1. Estimate the actual problem by rounding all the way, work the actual problem, and
   check:

Actual	Estimate	Check
4,938		
× 19		

2. Multiply by shortcut method: 3. Multiply by shortcut method:

   86,000   86 × 10,000
   × 1,900

4. Divide by rounding all the way, complete the actual calculation, and check, showing
   remainder as a whole number.

   26)6,394

5. Divide by the shortcut method:

   3,000)99,000

6. Assume General Motors produces 850 Chevrolets each workday (Monday through Friday). If the cost to produce each car is $7,000, what is General Motors's total cost for the
   year? Check your answer.

CHAPTER ORGANIZER AND STUDY GUIDE
WITH CHECK FIGURES FOR EXTRA PRACTICE QUIZZES

Topic	Key point, procedure, formula	Example(s) to illustrate situation
Reading and writing numeric and verbal whole numbers, p. 3	Placement of digits in a number gives the value of the digits (Figure 1.1). Commas separate every three digits, moving from right to left. Begin at left to read and write number in verbal form. Do not read zeros or use *and*. Hyphenate numbers twenty-one to ninety-nine. Reverse procedure to change verbal number to numeric.	462 → Four hundred sixty-two 6,741 → Six thousand, seven hundred forty-one
Rounding whole numbers, p. 4	1. Identify place value of the digit to be rounded. 2. If digit to the right is 5 or more, round up; if less than 5, do not change. 3. Change all digits to the right of rounded identified digit to zeros.	643 to nearest ten 4 in tens place value. 3 is not 5 or more Thus, 643 rounds to 640.
Rounding all the way, p. 5	Round to first digit of number. One nonzero digit remains. In estimating, you round each number of the problem to one nonzero digit. The final answer is not rounded.	468,451 → 500,000 The 5 is the only nonzero digit remaining.
Adding whole numbers, p. 8	1. Align numbers at the right. 2. Add units column. If sum more than 9, carry tens digit. 3. Moving left, repeat Step 2 until all place values are added. Add from top to bottom. Check by adding bottom to top or adding each column separately and combining.	$\begin{matrix}&\overset{1}{6}5\\+&47\\\hline&112\end{matrix}$ $\begin{matrix}&12\\+&10\\\hline&112\end{matrix}$ Checking sum of each digit

(continues)

CHAPTER ORGANIZER AND STUDY GUIDE
WITH CHECK FIGURES FOR EXTRA PRACTICE QUIZZES (concluded)

Topic	Key point, procedure, formula	Example(s) to illustrate situation
Subtracting whole numbers, p. 9	1. Align minuend and subtrahend at the right. 2. Subtract units digits. If necessary, borrow 1 from tens digit in minuend. 3. Moving left, repeat Step 2 until all place values are subtracted. Minuend less subtrahend equals difference.	**Check** $$\begin{array}{r} 5\,18 \\ \cancel{685} \\ -492 \\ \hline 193 \end{array} \qquad \begin{array}{r} 193 \\ +492 \\ \hline 685 \end{array}$$
Multiplying whole numbers, p. 12	1. Align multiplicand and multiplier at the right. 2. Begin at the right and keep multiplying as you move to the left. First partial product aligns at the right with multiplicand and multiplier. 3. Move left through multiplier and continue multiplying multiplicand. Partial product right digit or first digit is placed directly below digit in multiplier. 4. Continue Steps 2 and 3 until multiplication is complete. Add partial products to get final product. **Shortcuts:** (a) When multiplicand or multiplier, or both, end in zeros, disregard zeros and multiply; attach same number of zeros to answer. If zero in center of multiplier, no need to show row of zeros. (b) If multiplying by power of 10, attach same number of zeros to whole number multiplied.	$$\begin{array}{r} 223 \\ \times\ 32 \\ \hline 446 \\ 6\ 69 \\ \hline 7{,}136 \end{array}$$ a. $\begin{array}{r} 48{,}000 \\ \times\quad 40 \end{array}$ $\begin{array}{r} 48 \\ 4 \end{array}$ 3 zeros $+1$ zero $1{,}920{,}000$ ◄4 zeros $\begin{array}{r} 524 \\ \times\ 206 \\ \hline 3\ 144 \\ 104\ 8 \\ \hline 107{,}944 \end{array}$ b. $14 \times 10 = \boxed{140}$ (attach 1 zero) $14 \times 1{,}000 = \boxed{14{,}000}$ (attach 3 zeros)
Dividing whole numbers, p. 14	1. When divisor is divided into the dividend, the remainder is less than divisor. 2. Drop zeros from dividend right to left by number of zeros found in the divisor. Even division has no remainder; uneven division has a remainder; divisor with one digit is short division; and divisor with more than one digit is long division.	1. $\begin{array}{r} \boxed{5\ R6} \\ 14\overline{)76} \\ 70 \\ \hline 6 \end{array}$ 2. $5{,}000 \div 100\ \ = 50 \div 1 = \boxed{50}$ $5{,}000 \div 1{,}000 = 5 \div 1 = \boxed{5}$
KEY TERMS	addends, *p. 8* decimal point, *p. 2* decimal system, *p. 2* difference, *p. 9* dividend, *p. 14* divisor, *p. 14*	minuend, *p. 9* multiplicand, *p. 13* multiplier, *p. 13* partial products, *p. 13* partial quotient, *p. 14* product, *p. 13*	quotient, *p. 14* remainder, *p. 14* rounding all the way, *p. 5* subtrahend, *p. 9* sum, *p. 8* whole number, *p. 2*
CHECK FIGURE FOR EXTRA PRACTICE QUIZZES WITH PAGE REFERENCES	LU 1–1a (p. 8) 1. A. Eight thousand, six hundred eighty-two; B. Fifty-six thousand, two hundred ninety-five; C. Seven hundred thirty two billion, three hundred ten million, four hundred forty-four thousand, eight hundred eighty-eight 2. A. 40; B. 700; C. 7,000; D. 6,000 3. 3,000,000; 400,000	LU 1–2a (p. 12) 1. 26,090 2. 15,000; 15,953 3. 3,819 4. 43,100 (over)	LU 1–3a (p. 18) 1. 100,000; 93,822 2. 163,400,000 3. 860,000 4. 255 R19 5. 33 6. $1,547,000,000

Critical Thinking Discussion Questions

1. List the four steps of the decision-making process. Do you think all companies should be required to follow these steps? Give an example.

2. Explain the three steps used to round whole numbers. Pick a whole number and explain why it should not be rounded.

3. How do you check subtraction? If you were to attend a movie, explain how you might use the subtraction check method.

4. Explain how you can check multiplication. If you visit a local supermarket, how could you show multiplication as a short-cut to addition?

5. Explain how division is the reverse of multiplication. Using the supermarket example, explain how division is a timesaving shortcut related to subtraction.

1–71. Matty Kaminsky, the bookkeeper for Maggie's Real Estate, and his manager are concerned about the company's telephone bills. Last year the company's average monthly phone bill was $34. Matty's manager asked him for an average of this year's phone bills. Matty's records show the following:

January	$ 34	July	$ 28
February	60	August	23
March	20	September	29
April	25	October	25
May	30	November	22
June	59	December	41

What is the average of this year's phone bills? Did Matty and his manager have a justifiable concern?

1–72. The Associated Press reported that bankruptcy filings were up for the first three months of the year. Filings reached 366,841 in the January–March period, the highest ever for a first quarter, up from 312,335 a year earlier. How much was the increase in quarterly filings?

1–73. On Monday, True Value Hardware sold 15 paint brushes at $3 each, 6 wrenches at $5 each, 7 bags of grass seed at $3 each, 4 lawn mowers at $119 each, and 28 cans of paint at $8 each. What were True Value's total dollar sales on Monday?

1–74. While redecorating, Pete Allen went to Sears and bought 125 square yards of commercial carpet. The total cost of the carpet was $3,000. How much did Pete pay per square yard?

1–75. Washington Construction built 12 ranch houses for $115,000 each. From the sale of these houses, Washington received $1,980,000. How much gross profit (Sales − Costs = Gross profit) did Washington make on the houses?

The four partners of Washington Construction split all profits equally. How much will each partner receive?

CHALLENGE PROBLEMS

1–76. The *St. Paul Pioneer Press* reported that after implementing a new parking service called e-Park, the Minneapolis–St. Paul International Airport reduced the number of its parking garage cashiers. E-Park is expected to allow the airport to cut 35 parking cashiers from its force of 130. Cashiers make about $11 an hour plus benefits. For a 40-hour week, **(a)** what has been the yearly cost of salaries? and **(b)** what will be the savings in labor costs for a year?

1–77. Paula Sanchez is trying to determine her 2009 finances. Paula's actual 2008 finances were as follows:

Income:		Assets:	
Gross income	$69,000	Checking account	$ 1,950
Interest income	450	Savings account	8,950
Total	$69,450	Automobile	1,800
		Personal property	14,000
Expenses:		Total	$26,700
Living	$24,500	Liabilities:	
Insurance premium	350		
Taxes	14,800	Note to bank	4,500
Medical	585	Net worth	$22,200 ($26,700 − $4,500)
Investment	4,000		
Total	$44,235		

Net worth = Assets − Liabilities
            (own)   (owe)

Paula believes her gross income will double in 2009 but her interest income will decrease $150. She plans to reduce her 2009 living expenses by one-half. Paula's insurance company wrote a letter announcing that her insurance premiums would triple in 2009. Her accountant estimates her taxes will decrease $250 and her medical costs will increase $410. Paula also hopes to cut her investments expenses by one-fourth. Paula's accountant projects that her savings and checking accounts will each double in value. On January 2, 2009, Paula sold her automobile and began to use public transportation. Paula forecasts that her personal property will decrease by one-seventh. She has sent her bank a $375 check to reduce her bank note. Could you give Paula an updated list of her 2009 finances? If you round all the way each 2008 and 2009 asset and liability, what will be the difference in Paula's net worth?

1. Translate the following verbal forms to numbers and add. *(p. 3)*

   a. Four thousand, eight hundred thirty-nine

   b. Seven million, twelve

   c. Twelve thousand, three hundred ninety-two

2. Express the following number in verbal form. *(p. 3)*

   9,622,364

3. Round the following numbers. *(p. 4)*

Nearest ten	Nearest hundred	Nearest thousand	Round all the way
a. 68	b. 888	c. 8,325	d. 14,821

4. Estimate the following actual problem by rounding all the way, work the actual problem, and check by adding each column of digits separately. *(pp. 5, 8)*

Actual	Estimate	Check
1,886		
9,411		
+ 6,395		

5. Estimate the following actual problem by rounding all the way and then do the actual multiplication. *(pp. 5, 12)*

Actual	Estimate
8,843	
× 906	

6. Multiply the following by the shortcut method. *(p. 14)*

   829,412 × 1,000

7. Divide the following and check the answer by multiplication. *(p. 15)*

   Check

   39)‾14,800

8. Divide the following by the shortcut method. *(p. 15)*

   6,000 ÷ 60

9. Ling Wong bought a $299 ipod that was reduced to $205. Ling gave the clerk 3 $100 bills. What change will Ling receive? *(p. 9)*

10. Sam Song plans to buy a $16,000 Ford Saturn with an interest charge of $4,000. Sam figures he can afford a monthly payment of $400. If Sam must pay 40 equal monthly payments, can he afford the Ford Saturn? *(p. 14)*

11. Lester Hal has the oil tank at his business filled 20 times per year. The tank has a capacity of 200 gallons. Assume **(a)** the price of oil fuel is $3 per gallon and **(b)** the tank is completely empty each time Lester has it filled. What is Lester's average monthly oil bill? Complete the following blueprint aid for dissecting and solving the word problem. *(pp. 6, 12, 15)*

The facts	Solving for?	Steps to take	Key points

Steps to solving problem

Saving the world with FRENCH FRIES

Interview by Jessica Anderson

PHOTOGRAPH BY REENA BAMMI

Justin Carven's business sells kits that let diesel cars run on vegetable oil.

A typical fuel tank holds 15 gallons. Where do people get that much vegetable oil? Most of our customers are using recycled cooking oil from restaurants.

So I can get all the fuel I need at the local fast-food joint? Restaurants can produce as much as 100 gallons of waste oil per week, which they're willing to give away. Plus, the converted vehicles have one tank for diesel and one for vegetable oil–so you have backup fuel.

How far will a tank take me? Vegetable oil is similar to diesel. Many diesel cars get 40 miles per gallon, so a tank should take you 600 miles.

Will my car smell like fries? It will smell like food cooking, but not what was cooked in that oil.

How much does the kit cost? It starts at $795 and includes a manual and all the parts to install it yourself. To have a professional install it will run $500 to $1,000.

Is using your kit a violation of the Clean Air Act? Any aftermarket automotive product must go through an evaluation process with the Environmental Protection Agency to be certified–we're in the process of doing that.

Could customers be fined in the meantime? The EPA has never fined anyone for using vegetable oil.

How many kits have you sold? We've sold about 3,000 conversion kits since I founded the business six years ago. Sales broke $1 million last year.

What are the benefits? Besides cheap fuel, there are incredible environmental benefits. You're putting less carbon dioxide into the atmosphere than plants take out.

Is this a step toward curing our "addiction to oil"? I believe so. It's still going to be an addiction; it's just going to be an addiction to something a bit healthier for us. [For more information, go to www.greasecar.com.] ◖

BUSINESS MATH ISSUE

Vegetable oil will not solve our oil problem.

1. List the key points of the article and information to support your position.
2. Write a group defense of your position using math calculations to support your view.

Slater's Business Math Scrapbook

with Internet Application
Putting Your Skills to Work

PROJECT A
Show the math using the shortcut method of multiplication to prove the million dollars.

Pipe Dream / *By Gwendolyn Bounds*

How Selling Pixels May Yield a Million Bucks

IT WAS JUST a few months ago that 21-year-old Alex Tew of Great Britain was stumped about how to pay for college. He'd filled a notebook with ideas before jotting down this simple, if rather audacious, query to himself: How Can I Become a Millionaire?

In the annals of entrepreneurship, what followed is an instructional tale of how a brainstorm, coupled with the Internet's powerful word-of-mouth culture, can set a trend in motion with lightning speed. Mr. Tew says his strategy was to find an idea simple to understand and cheap to set up, with a catchy name that would garner attention online, where he gained experience from having free-lanced as a Web designer for a few years.

Ultimately, his solution amounted to making money via Internet advertising—but with a twist. Instead of selling banner ads, text links or splashy videolike ads that fill a screen, Mr. Tew opted to hawk the simplest graphical denominator of a computer screen: the pixel. A pixel is a tiny dot of light and color, and each screen has tens of thousands of them.

Mr. Tew created a home page, www.milliondollarhomepage.com, where he divided the screen into 10,000 small squares of 100 pixels each. His plan: to sell the pixels for $1 a piece, with a minimum order of 100 pixels. In each space, buyers could put a graphical ad of their choosing that links

*Alex Tew sells tiny ad spaces on his Web page (inset) and has **generated $623,800** toward his $1 million goal.*

to their own site when clicked on. The end result is a cluttered collage of ads in various shapes and colors all amassed on a single digital billboard. (Mr. Tew doesn't charge his advertisers anything when a visitor clicks on the ads.)

Mr. Tew pledged to keep the site up for at least five years and to close the page when his goal of one million dollars was reached. "I had to think big," he says.

The notion seemed absurd. Who would want to advertise on an unknown site that had no target audience, no track record of attracting visitors or even the slightest brand recognition?

But as with many gimmicks, its newness gave it legs, as did Mr. Tew's shrewd marketing. He first roped his friends and family into buying pixels and placing ads to make the page seem legitimate. He then began touting his site, and himself, to bloggers, who wrote about his crazy idea and linked to the site, which directed traffic his way. The media in Britain picked up on his efforts, fueling more visitors.

Within two weeks of the site's Aug. 26 launch Mr. Tew says he sold $40,000 in ads. More important, the traffic numbers started gaining attention among the U.S. Internet community.

Internet Projects: See text Web site (www.mhhe.com/slater9e) and The Business Math Internet Resource Guide.

CHAPTER 2

Fractions

Lifestyle Changes Could Prevent Almost Half of Cancer Deaths

By KRISTEN GERENCHER

SAN FRANCISCO—As many as half of cancer deaths could be prevented if more people made lifestyle changes such as avoiding smoking and excessive sun exposure, eating nutritiously and getting regular exercise and recommended health screenings, according to a study from the American Cancer Society.

Whether due to socioeconomic or personal challenges, many people have trouble following common health precautions, said Vilma Cokkinides, co-author of the report and program director of risk-factor surveillance for the American Cancer Society in Atlanta.

"What's astonishing is how small the numbers are in terms of the population actually doing these things," Ms. Cokkinides said. "It's a disconnect....The awareness that theoretically half [of cancer deaths] could be prevented hasn't gotten in the mindset."

Smoking is the biggest sticking point because it increases the risk of many kinds of cancer, not just lung, and is expected to

kill 170,000 this year. About a third of the 564,830 expected cancer deaths in 2006 will be related to poor diets, physical inactivity and obesity, which itself causes many chronic illnesses, the report said.

Americans have been receiving the antitobacco message for decades, but one in five adults still lights up. Despite calls for better nutrition and more physical activity to maintain a healthy weight, waistlines are growing dangerously wider. And few people do enough to protect their skin from the sun's harmful rays, leading to high rates of skin cancer.

People also fail to follow commonly recommended screenings based on age, family and medical history to catch cancer in its earliest, most treatable phases, the study said.

The ability to keep up with recommended screenings for colorectal, cervical and breast cancer—where evidence of effective treatment and reduced chance of death is greatest—is largely dependent on whether people have health insurance, Ms. Cokkinides said. "It's perhaps the single most important determinant."

LEARNING UNIT OBJECTIVES

LU 2–1: Types of Fractions and Conversion Procedures

LU 2–2: Adding and Subtracting Fractions

LU 2–3: Multiplying and Dividing Fractions

The following two *Wall Street Journal* clippings "Product Piracy Rises in China, U.S. Says" and "Fruitcake Makers See a Way to Boost Sales: Slice the Serving Size" illustrate the use of fractions. For example, from the first clipping you learn that almost two-thirds ($\frac{2}{3}$) of all seizures of fake products come from China.

Product Piracy Rises In China, U.S. Says

Associated Press

SHANGHAI—Illegal copying of music, movies and other goods by Chinese product pirates is rising despite Beijing's promises to stamp it out, U.S. officials said.

Almost two-thirds of all seizures of fake products by U.S. Customs officials come from China, and despite stronger laws and pledges to crack down the problem has been getting worse, they said.

Associated Press © 2005

Fruitcake Makers See A Way to Boost Sales: Slice the Serving Size

By JANE ZHANG

EVEN FRUITCAKE bakers count calories now: Four of them recently petitioned the Food and Drug Administration to cut the serving size for fruitcake by two-thirds.

Wall Street Journal © 2005

Now let's look at Milk Chocolate M&M's® candies as another example of using fractions.

As you know, M&M's® candies come in different colors. Do you know how many of each color are in a bag of M&M's®? If you go to the M&M's website, you learn that a typical bag of M&M's® contains approximately 17 brown, 11 yellow, 11 red, and 5 each of orange, blue, and green M&M's®.[1]

The 1.69-ounce bag of M&M's® shown here contains 55 M&M's®. In this bag, you will find the following colors:

18 yellow	9 blue	6 brown
10 red	7 orange	5 green

55 pieces in the bag

The number of yellow candies in a bag might suggest that yellow is the favorite color of many people. Since this is a business math text, however, let's look at the 55 M&M's® in terms of fractional arithmetic.

Of the 55 M&M's® in the 1.69-ounce bag, 5 of these M&M's® are green, so we can say that 5 parts of 55 represent green candies. We could also say that 1 out of 11 M&M's® is green. Are you confused?

For many people, fractions are difficult. If you are one of these people, this chapter is for you. First you will review the types of fractions and the fraction conversion procedures. Then you will gain a clear understanding of the addition, subtraction, multiplication, and division of fractions.

---

[1]Off 1 due to rounding.

Learning Unit 2–1: Types of Fractions and Conversion Procedures

This chapter explains the parts of whole numbers called **fractions.** With fractions you can divide any object or unit—a whole—into a definite number of equal parts. For example, the bag of 55 M&M's® shown at the beginning of this chapter contains 6 brown candies. If you eat only the brown M&M's®, you have eaten 6 parts of 55, or 6 parts of the whole bag of M&M's®. We can express this in the following fraction:

6 is the **numerator,** or top of the fraction. The numerator describes the number of equal parts of the whole bag that you ate.

55 is the **denominator,** or bottom of the fraction. The denominator gives the total number of equal parts in the bag of M&M's®.

Before reviewing the arithmetic operations of fractions, you must recognize the three types of fractions described in this unit. You must also know how to convert fractions to a workable form.

Types of Fractions

Wal-Mart Buys Stake in Retailer In Latin America

By Ann Zimmerman

Wal-Mart Stores Inc., in another move to expand its international holdings, said it purchased a one-third stake in Central America's largest retailer.

Wal-Mart didn't disclose how much it paid for the stake in **Central American Retail Holding** Co., which it purchased from Dutch retailer **Royal Ahold** NV. The Bentonville, Ark., retailer said the deal includes an agreement to eventually buy additional interest in the company "toward achieving majority ownership."

This is Wal-Mart's first store expansion into Central America, although the retailer said it directly imports more than $350 million in goods—mostly apparel—from Guatemala, Honduras, El Salvador, Nicaragua and Costa Rica.

Wall Street Journal © 2005

When you read the *Wall Street Journal* clipping "Wal-Mart Buys Stake in Retailer in Latin America," you see that Wal-Mart is buying a one-third ($\frac{1}{3}$) stake in Central America's largest retailer. The fraction $\frac{1}{3}$ is a proper fraction.

PROPER FRACTIONS
A **proper fraction** has a value less than 1; its numerator is smaller than its denominator.

EXAMPLES $\dfrac{1}{2}, \dfrac{1}{10}, \dfrac{1}{12}, \dfrac{1}{3}, \dfrac{4}{7}, \dfrac{9}{10}, \dfrac{12}{13}, \dfrac{18}{55}$

IMPROPER FRACTIONS
An **improper fraction** has a value equal to or greater than 1; its numerator is equal to or greater than its denominator.

EXAMPLES $\dfrac{14}{14}, \dfrac{7}{6}, \dfrac{15}{14}, \dfrac{22}{19}$

MIXED NUMBERS
A **mixed number** is the sum of a whole number greater than zero and a proper fraction.

EXAMPLES $\quad 5\frac{1}{6}, 5\frac{9}{10}, 8\frac{7}{8}, 33\frac{5}{6}, 139\frac{9}{11}$

Conversion Procedures

In Chapter 1 we worked with two of the division symbols ($\div$ and $\overline{)}$). The horizontal line (or the diagonal) that separates the numerator and the denominator of a fraction also indicates division. The numerator, like the dividend, is the number we are dividing into. The denominator, like the divisor, is the number we use to divide. Then, referring to the 6 brown M&M's® in the bag of 55 M&M's® ($\frac{6}{55}$) shown at the beginning of this unit, we can say that we are dividing 55 into 6, or 6 is divided by 55. Also, in the fraction $\frac{3}{4}$, we can say that we are dividing 4 into 3, or 3 is divided by 4.

Working with the smaller numbers of simple fractions such as $\frac{3}{4}$ is easier, so we often convert fractions to their simplest terms. In this unit we show how to convert improper fractions to whole or mixed numbers, mixed numbers to improper fractions, and fractions to lowest and highest terms.

Converting Improper Fractions to Whole or Mixed Numbers

Business situations often make it necessary to change an improper fraction to a whole number or mixed number. You can use the following steps to make this conversion:

CONVERTING IMPROPER FRACTIONS TO WHOLE OR MIXED NUMBERS
Step 1. Divide the numerator of the improper fraction by the denominator.
Step 2. **a.** If you have no remainder, the quotient is a whole number.
b. If you have a remainder, the whole number part of the mixed number is the quotient. The remainder is placed over the old denominator as the proper fraction of the mixed number.

EXAMPLES

$$\frac{15}{15} = 1 \qquad \frac{16}{5} = 3\frac{1}{5} \qquad \begin{array}{r} 3\text{ R}1 \\ 5\overline{)16} \\ \underline{15} \\ 1 \end{array}$$

Converting Mixed Numbers to Improper Fractions

By reversing the procedure of converting improper fractions to mixed numbers, we can change mixed numbers to improper fractions.

CONVERTING MIXED NUMBERS TO IMPROPER FRACTIONS
Step 1. Multiply the denominator of the fraction by the whole number.
Step 2. Add the product from Step 1 to the numerator of the old fraction.
Step 3. Place the total from Step 2 over the denominator of the old fraction to get the improper fraction.

EXAMPLE $\quad 6\frac{1}{8} = \frac{(8 \times 6) + 1}{8} = \frac{49}{8}$ ←—Note that the denominator stays the same.

Converting (Reducing) Fractions to Lowest Terms

When solving fraction problems, you always reduce the fractions to their lowest terms. This reduction does not change the value of the fraction. For example, in the bag of M&M's®, 5 out of 55 were green. The fraction for this is $\frac{5}{55}$. If you divide the top and bottom of the fraction by 5, you have reduced the fraction to $\frac{1}{11}$ without changing its value. Remember, we said in the chapter introduction that 1 out of 11 M&M's® in the bag of 55 M&M's® represents green candies. Now you know why this is true.

To reduce a fraction to its lowest terms, begin by inspecting the fraction, looking for the largest whole number that will divide into both the numerator and the denominator without leaving a remainder. This whole number is the **greatest common divisor,** which cannot be zero. When you find this largest whole number, you have reached the point where the fraction is reduced to its **lowest terms.** At this point, no number (except 1) can divide evenly into both parts of the fraction.

REDUCING FRACTIONS TO LOWEST TERMS BY INSPECTION

Step 1. By inspection, find the largest whole number (greatest common divisor) that will divide evenly into the numerator and denominator (does not change the fraction value).

Step 2. Now you have reduced the fraction to its lowest terms, since no number (except 1) can divide evenly into the numerator and denominator.

EXAMPLE $\dfrac{24}{30} = \dfrac{24 \div 6}{30 \div 6} = \dfrac{4}{5}$

Using inspection, you can see that the number 6 in the above example is the greatest common divisor. When you have large numbers, the greatest common divisor is not so obvious. For large numbers, you can use the following step approach to find the greatest common divisor:

STEP APPROACH FOR FINDING GREATEST COMMON DIVISOR

Step 1. Divide the smaller number (numerator) of the fraction into the larger number (denominator).

Step 2. Divide the remainder of Step 1 into the divisor of Step 1.

Step 3. Divide the remainder of Step 2 into the divisor of Step 2. Continue this division process until the remainder is a 0, which means the last divisor is the greatest common divisor.

EXAMPLE

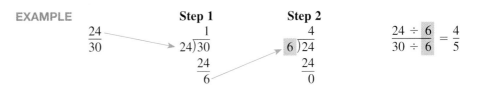

Reducing a fraction by inspection is to some extent a trial-and-error method. Sometimes you are not sure what number you should divide into the top (numerator) and bottom (denominator) of the fraction. The following reference table on divisibility tests will be helpful. Note that to reduce a fraction to lowest terms might result in more than one division.

	2	3	4	5	6	10
Will divide evenly into number if	Last digit is 0, 2, 4, 6, 8.	Sum of the digits is divisible by 3.	Last two digits can be divided by 4.	Last digit is 0 or 5.	The number is even and 3 will divide into the sum of the digits.	The last digit is 0.
Examples	$\dfrac{12}{14} = \dfrac{6}{7}$	$\dfrac{36}{69} = \dfrac{12}{23}$ $3 + 6 = 9 \div 3 = 3$ $6 + 9 = 15 \div 3 = 5$	$\dfrac{140}{160} = \dfrac{1(40)}{1(60)}$ $= \dfrac{35}{40} = \dfrac{7}{8}$	$\dfrac{15}{20} = \dfrac{3}{4}$	$\dfrac{12}{18} = \dfrac{2}{3}$	$\dfrac{90}{100} = \dfrac{9}{10}$

Converting (Raising) Fractions to Higher Terms

Later, when you add and subtract fractions, you will see that sometimes fractions must be raised to **higher terms.** Recall that when you reduced fractions to their lowest terms, you looked for the largest whole number (greatest common divisor) that would divide evenly into both the numerator and the denominator. When you raise fractions to higher terms, you do the opposite and multiply the numerator and the denominator by the same whole number. For example, if you want to raise the fraction $\frac{1}{4}$, you can multiply the numerator and denominator by 2.

EXAMPLE $\dfrac{1}{4} \times \dfrac{2}{2} = \dfrac{2}{8}$

The fractions $\frac{1}{4}$ and $\frac{2}{8}$ are **equivalent** in value. By converting $\frac{1}{4}$ to $\frac{2}{8}$, you only divided it into more parts.

Let's suppose that you have eaten $\frac{4}{7}$ of a pizza. You decide that instead of expressing the amount you have eaten in 7ths, you want to express it in 28ths. How would you do this?

To find the new numerator when you know the new denominator (28), use the steps that follow.

RAISING FRACTIONS TO HIGHER TERMS WHEN DENOMINATOR IS KNOWN
Step 1. Divide the *new* denominator by the *old* denominator to get the common number that raises the fraction to higher terms.
Step 2. Multiply the common number from Step 1 by the old numerator and place it as the new numerator over the new denominator.

EXAMPLE $\dfrac{4}{7} = \dfrac{?}{28}$

Step 1. Divide 28 by 7 = 4.

Step 2. Multiply 4 by the numerator 4 = 16.

Result:

$$\dfrac{4}{7} = \dfrac{16}{28} \quad \left(\textit{Note: This is the same as multiplying } \dfrac{4}{7} \times \dfrac{4}{4}. \right)$$

Note that the $\frac{4}{7}$ and $\frac{16}{28}$ are equivalent in value, yet they are different fractions.

Now try the following Practice Quiz to check your understanding of this unit.

LU 2–1   PRACTICE QUIZ

Complete this **Practice Quiz** to see how you are doing

1. Identify the type of fraction—proper, improper, or mixed:

   a. $\dfrac{4}{5}$ **b.** $\dfrac{6}{5}$ **c.** $19\dfrac{1}{5}$ **d.** $\dfrac{20}{20}$

2. Convert to a mixed number:

   $\dfrac{160}{9}$

3. Convert the mixed number to an improper fraction:

   $9\dfrac{5}{8}$

4. Find the greatest common divisor by the step approach and reduce to lowest terms:

   a. $\dfrac{24}{40}$ **b.** $\dfrac{91}{156}$

5. Convert to higher terms:

   a. $\dfrac{14}{20} = \dfrac{}{200}$ **b.** $\dfrac{8}{10} = \dfrac{}{60}$

✓ **Solutions**

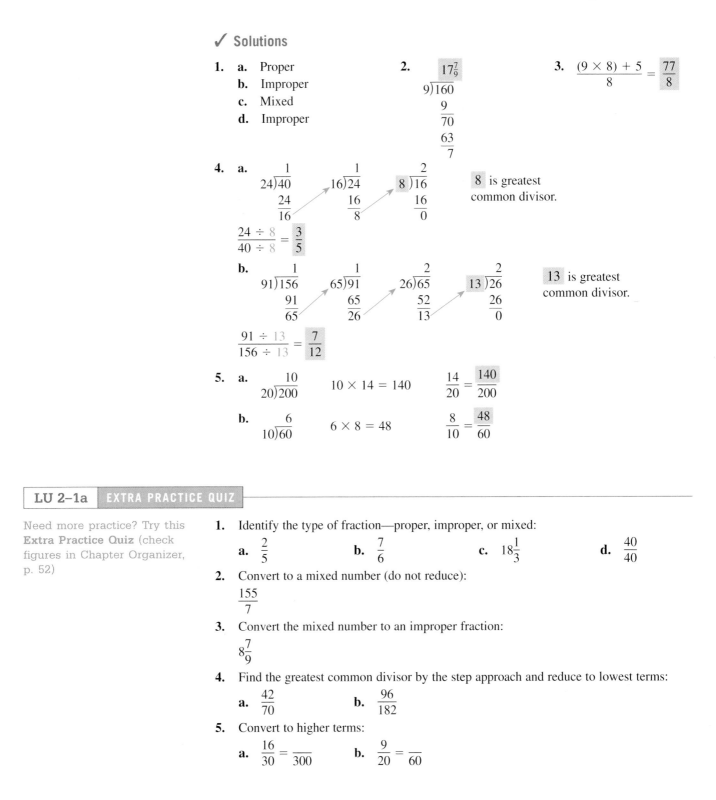

1. a. Proper
    b. Improper
    c. Mixed
    d. Improper

2. $17\frac{7}{9}$
    $9\overline{)160}$
    $\quad\underline{9}$
    $\quad70$
    $\quad\underline{63}$
    $\quad\ 7$

3. $\dfrac{(9 \times 8) + 5}{8} = \dfrac{77}{8}$

4. a.
    $24\overline{)40}$ $16\overline{)24}$ $8\overline{)16}$ **8** is greatest
    $\ \underline{24}$ $\ \underline{16}$ $\ \underline{16}$ common divisor.
    $\ 16$ $\ \ 8$ $\ \ 0$

    $\dfrac{24 \div 8}{40 \div 8} = \dfrac{3}{5}$

    b.
    $91\overline{)156}$ $65\overline{)91}$ $26\overline{)65}$ $13\overline{)26}$ **13** is greatest
    $\ \underline{91}$ $\ \underline{65}$ $\ \underline{52}$ $\ \underline{26}$ common divisor.
    $\ 65$ $\ 26$ $\ 13$ $\ \ 0$

    $\dfrac{91 \div 13}{156 \div 13} = \dfrac{7}{12}$

5. a.
    $20\overline{)200}^{\,10}$ $10 \times 14 = 140$ $\dfrac{14}{20} = \dfrac{140}{200}$

    b.
    $10\overline{)60}^{\,6}$ $6 \times 8 = 48$ $\dfrac{8}{10} = \dfrac{48}{60}$

LU 2–1a EXTRA PRACTICE QUIZ

Need more practice? Try this **Extra Practice Quiz** (check figures in Chapter Organizer, p. 52)

1. Identify the type of fraction—proper, improper, or mixed:
    a. $\dfrac{2}{5}$ b. $\dfrac{7}{6}$ c. $18\dfrac{1}{3}$ d. $\dfrac{40}{40}$

2. Convert to a mixed number (do not reduce):
    $\dfrac{155}{7}$

3. Convert the mixed number to an improper fraction:
    $8\dfrac{7}{9}$

4. Find the greatest common divisor by the step approach and reduce to lowest terms:
    a. $\dfrac{42}{70}$ b. $\dfrac{96}{182}$

5. Convert to higher terms:
    a. $\dfrac{16}{30} = \dfrac{}{300}$ b. $\dfrac{9}{20} = \dfrac{}{60}$

Learning Unit 2–2: Adding and Subtracting Fractions

TiVo Slashes Recorder Price In Half, to $50

Latest Cut Is Made to Fend Off Competition From Cable Giants; Comparing the Monthly Costs

By NICK WINGFIELD

FACED WITH growing competition from powerful rivals with cheaper products, TiVo Inc. sharply cut the prices on its digital video recorders.

Wall Street Journal © 2005

The *Wall Street Journal* clipping "TiVo Slashes Recorder Price in Half, to $50" states that TiVo cut the price of its recorder in half $(\frac{1}{2})$. Since a whole is $\frac{2}{2}$ $(\frac{2}{2} = 1)$, you can determine the new selling price of the recorder by subtracting the numerator of the fraction $\frac{1}{2}$ from the numerator of the fraction $\frac{2}{2}$. You can make this subtraction because you are working with *like fractions*—fractions with the same denominators. Then you can prove that you are correct by adding the numerators of the fractions $\frac{1}{2}$ and $\frac{1}{2}$.

In this unit you learn how to add and subtract fractions with the same denominators (**like fractions**) and fractions with different denominators (**unlike fractions**). We have also included how to add and subtract mixed numbers.

Addition of Fractions

When you add two or more quantities, they must have the same name or be of the same denomination. You cannot add 6 quarts and 3 pints unless you change the denomination of one or both quantities. You must either make the quarts into pints or the pints into quarts. The same principle also applies to fractions. That is, to add two or more fractions, they must have a **common denominator.**

Adding Like Fractions

In our TiVo clipping at the beginning of this unit we stated that because the fractions had the same denominator, or a common denominator, they were *like fractions*. Adding like fractions is similar to adding whole numbers.

ADDING LIKE FRACTIONS
Step 1. Add the numerators and place the total over the original denominator.
Step 2. If the total of your numerators is the same as your original denominator, convert your answer to a whole number; if the total is larger than your original denominator, convert your answer to a mixed number.

EXAMPLE $\dfrac{1}{7} + \dfrac{4}{7} = \boxed{\dfrac{5}{7}}$

The denominator, 7, shows the number of pieces into which some whole was divided. The two numerators, 1 and 4, tell how many of the pieces you have. So if you add 1 and 4, you get 5, or $\frac{5}{7}$.

Adding Unlike Fractions

Since you cannot add *unlike fractions* because their denominators are not the same, you must change the unlike fractions to *like fractions*—fractions with the same denominators. To do this, find a denominator that is common to all the fractions you want to add. Then look for the **least common denominator (LCD).**[2] The LCD is the smallest nonzero whole number into which all denominators will divide evenly. You can find the LCD by inspection or with prime numbers.

---

[2]Often referred to as the *lowest common denominator.*

Finding the Least Common Denominator (LCD) by Inspection The example that follows shows you how to use inspection to find an LCD (this will make all the denominators the same).

EXAMPLE $\dfrac{3}{7} + \dfrac{5}{21}$

Inspection of these two fractions shows that the smallest number into which denominators 7 and 21 divide evenly is 21. Thus, 21 is the LCD.

You may know that 21 is the LCD of $\frac{3}{7} + \frac{5}{21}$, but you cannot add these two fractions until you change the denominator of $\frac{3}{7}$ to 21. You do this by building (raising) the equivalent of $\frac{3}{7}$, as explained in Learning Unit 2–1. You can use the following steps to find the LCD by inspection:

Step 1. Divide the new denominator (21) by the old denominator (7): $21 \div 7 = 3$.

Step 2. Multiply the 3 in Step 1 by the old numerator (3): $3 \times 3 = 9$. The new numerator is 9.

Result:

$$\frac{3}{7} = \frac{9}{21}$$

Now that the denominators are the same, you add the numerators.

$$\frac{9}{21} + \frac{5}{21} = \frac{14}{21} = \frac{2}{3}$$

Note that $\frac{14}{21}$ is reduced to its lowest terms $\frac{2}{3}$. Always reduce your answer to its lowest terms.

You are now ready for the following general steps for adding proper fractions with different denominators. These steps also apply to the following discussion on finding LCD by prime numbers.

ADDING UNLIKE FRACTIONS
Step 1. Find the LCD.
Step 2. Change each fraction to a like fraction with the LCD.
Step 3. Add the numerators and place the total over the LCD.
Step 4. If necessary, reduce the answer to lowest terms.

Finding the Least Common Denominator (LCD) by Prime Numbers When you cannot determine the LCD by inspection, you can use the prime number method. First you must understand prime numbers.

PRIME NUMBERS
A **prime number** is a whole number greater than 1 that is only divisible by itself and 1. The number 1 is not a prime number.

EXAMPLES   2, 3, 5, 7, 11, 13, 17, 19, 23, 29, 31, 37, 41, 43

Note that the number 4 is not a prime number. Not only can you divide 4 by 1 and by 4, but you can also divide 4 by 2.

A whole number that is greater than 1 and is only divisible by itself and 1 has become a source of interest to some people. These people are curious as to what is the largest known prime number. The accompanying newspaper clipping answers this question. This number, of course, is the known number at the time of the writing of this clipping. Probably by the time you become impressed with this large prime number, someone will have discovered a larger prime number.

EXAMPLE $\dfrac{1}{3} + \dfrac{1}{8} + \dfrac{1}{9} + \dfrac{1}{12}$

Step 1. Copy the denominators and arrange them in a separate row.

3 8 9 12

Step 2. Divide the denominators in Step 1 by prime numbers. Start with the smallest number that will divide into at least two of the denominators. Bring down any number that is not divisible. Keep in mind that the lowest prime number is 2.

$$2 \underline{\smash{\big/}\ 3\quad 8\quad 9\quad 12}$$
$$\ 3\quad 4\quad 9\quad 6$$

Note: The 3 and 9 were brought down, since they were not divisible by 2.

Step 3. Continue Step 2 until no prime number will divide evenly into at least two numbers.

Note: The 3 is used, since 2 can no longer divide evenly into at least two numbers.

$$2 \underline{\smash{\big/}\ 3\quad 8\quad 9\quad 12}$$
$$2 \underline{\smash{\big/}\ 3\quad 4\quad 9\quad 6}$$
$$3 \underline{\smash{\big/}\ 3\quad 2\quad 9\quad 3}$$
$$\ 1\quad 2\quad 3\quad 1$$

Step 4. To find the LCD, multiply all the numbers in the divisors (2, 2, 3) and in the last row (1, 2, 3, 1).

$$\boxed{2 \times 2 \times 3} \times \boxed{1 \times 2 \times 3 \times 1} = \boxed{72}\ \text{(LCD)}$$

Divisors × Last row

Step 5. Raise each fraction so that each denominator will be 72 and then add fractions.

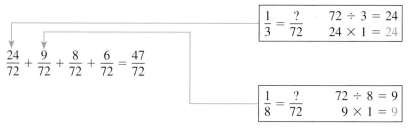

$$\frac{24}{72} + \frac{9}{72} + \frac{8}{72} + \frac{6}{72} = \frac{47}{72}$$

$$\boxed{\frac{1}{3} = \frac{?}{72} \qquad \begin{array}{l} 72 \div 3 = 24 \\ 24 \times 1 = 24 \end{array}}$$

$$\boxed{\frac{1}{8} = \frac{?}{72} \qquad \begin{array}{l} 72 \div 8 = 9 \\ 9 \times 1 = 9 \end{array}}$$

The above five steps used for finding LCD with prime numbers are summarized as follows:

FINDING LCD FOR TWO OR MORE FRACTIONS
Step 1. Copy the denominators and arrange them in a separate row.
Step 2. Divide the denominators by the smallest prime number that will divide evenly into at least two numbers.
Step 3. Continue until no prime number divides evenly into at least two numbers.
Step 4. Multiply all the numbers in divisors and last row to find the LCD.
Step 5. Raise all fractions so each has a common denominator and then complete the computation.

Adding Mixed Numbers

The following steps will show you how to add mixed numbers:

ADDING MIXED NUMBERS
Step 1. Add the fractions (remember that fractions need common denominators, as in the previous section).
Step 2. Add the whole numbers.
Step 3. Combine the totals of Steps 1 and 2. Be sure you do not have an improper fraction in your final answer. Convert the improper fraction to a whole or mixed number. Add the whole numbers resulting from the improper fraction conversion to the total whole numbers of Step 2. If necessary, reduce the answer to lowest terms.

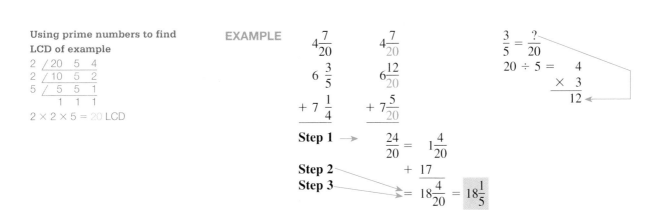

Using prime numbers to find LCD of example

2 / 20 5 4
2 / 10 5 2
5 / 5   5 1
    1   1 1

$2 \times 2 \times 5 = 20$ LCD

EXAMPLE

$$4\frac{7}{20} \qquad 4\frac{7}{20}$$
$$6\frac{3}{5} \qquad 6\frac{12}{20}$$
$$+ 7\frac{1}{4} \qquad + 7\frac{5}{20}$$

Step 1 $\rightarrow \qquad \dfrac{24}{20} = 1\dfrac{4}{20}$

Step 2 $\qquad\qquad + 17$

Step 3 $\qquad\qquad = 18\dfrac{4}{20} = \boxed{18\dfrac{1}{5}}$

$$\frac{3}{5} = \frac{?}{20}$$
$$20 \div 5 = \quad 4$$
$$\times \ 3$$
$$12$$

Subtraction of Fractions

The subtraction of fractions is similar to the addition of fractions. This section explains how to subtract like and unlike fractions and how to subtract mixed numbers.

Subtracting Like Fractions

To subtract like fractions, use the steps that follow.

SUBTRACTING LIKE FRACTIONS
Step 1. Subtract the numerators and place the answer over the common denominator.
Step 2. If necessary, reduce the answer to lowest terms.

EXAMPLE $\qquad \dfrac{9}{10} - \dfrac{1}{10} = \dfrac{8 \div 2}{10 \div 2} = \boxed{\dfrac{4}{5}}$

$\qquad\qquad\qquad\qquad\quad \uparrow \qquad\quad \uparrow$

$\qquad\qquad\qquad$ Step 1 $\quad$ Step 2

Subtracting Unlike Fractions

Now let's learn the steps for subtracting unlike fractions.

SUBTRACTING UNLIKE FRACTIONS
Step 1. Find the LCD.
Step 2. Raise the fraction to its equivalent value.
Step 3. Subtract the numerators and place the answer over the LCD.
Step 4. If necessary, reduce the answer to lowest terms.

EXAMPLE

$$\frac{5}{8} \qquad \frac{40}{64}$$
$$-\frac{2}{64} \qquad -\frac{2}{64}$$
$$\qquad\qquad \frac{38}{64} = \boxed{\frac{19}{32}}$$

By inspection, we see that LCD is 64.
Thus $64 \div 8 = 8 \times 5 = 40$.

Subtracting Mixed Numbers

When you subtract whole numbers, sometimes borrowing is not necessary. At other times, you must borrow. The same is true of subtracting mixed numbers.

SUBTRACTING MIXED NUMBERS	
When Borrowing Is Not Necessary	*When Borrowing Is Necessary*
Step 1. Subtract fractions, making sure to find the LCD.	**Step 1.** Make sure the fractions have the LCD.
Step 2. Subtract whole numbers.	**Step 2.** Borrow from the whole number of the minuend (top number).
Step 3. Reduce the fraction(s) to lowest terms.	**Step 3.** Subtract the whole numbers and fractions.
	Step 4. Reduce the fraction(s) to lowest terms.

EXAMPLE   Where borrowing is not necessary: Find LCD of 2 and 8. LCD is 8.

$$6\frac{1}{2}$$ $$6\frac{4}{8}$$
$$-\frac{3}{8}$$ $$-\frac{3}{8}$$
$$\overline{\phantom{6\frac{1}{8}}}$$ $$\overline{6\frac{1}{8}}$$

EXAMPLE   Where borrowing is necessary:

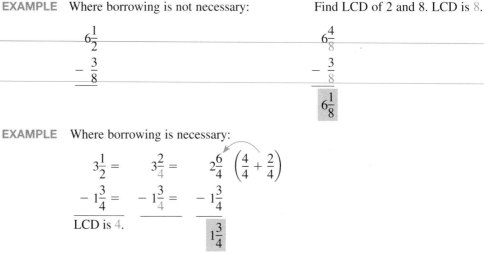

$$3\frac{1}{2} = \qquad 3\frac{2}{4} = \qquad 2\frac{6}{4} \left(\frac{4}{4} + \frac{2}{4}\right)$$
$$-1\frac{3}{4} = \qquad -1\frac{3}{4} = \qquad -1\frac{3}{4}$$
$$\overline{\text{LCD is } 4.} \qquad\qquad\qquad \overline{1\frac{3}{4}}$$

Since $\frac{3}{4}$ is larger than $\frac{2}{4}$, we must borrow 1 from the 3. This is the same as borrowing $\frac{4}{4}$. A fraction with the same numerator and denominator represents a whole. When we add $\frac{4}{4} + \frac{2}{4}$, we get $\frac{6}{4}$. Note how we subtracted the whole number and fractions, being sure to reduce the final answer if necessary.

How to Dissect and Solve a Word Problem

Let's now look at how to dissect and solve a word problem involving fractions.

The Word Problem The Albertsons grocery store has $550\frac{1}{4}$, total square feet of floor space. Albertsons' meat department occupies $115\frac{1}{2}$ square feet, and its deli department occupies $145\frac{7}{8}$ square feet. If the remainder of the floor space is for groceries, what square footage remains for groceries?

The facts	Solving for?	Steps to take	Key points
Total square footage: $550\frac{1}{4}$ sq. ft. *Meat department:* $115\frac{1}{2}$ sq. ft. *Deli department:* $145\frac{7}{8}$ sq. ft.	Total square footage for groceries.	Total floor space − Total meat and deli floor space = Total grocery floor space.	Denominators must be the same before adding or subtracting fractions. $\frac{8}{8} = 1$ Never leave improper fraction as final answer.

Steps to solving problem

1. Calculate total square footage of the meat and deli departments.

Meat: $115\frac{1}{2} = \quad 115\frac{4}{8}$
Deli: $+145\frac{7}{8} = +145\frac{7}{8}$
$$\overline{260\frac{11}{8} = 261\frac{3}{8} \text{ sq. ft.}}$$

2. Calculate total grocery square footage.

$$550\tfrac{1}{4} = \quad 550\tfrac{2}{8} = \quad 549\tfrac{10}{8}$$

$$-\;261\tfrac{3}{8} = \; -\;261\tfrac{3}{8} = \; -\;261\tfrac{3}{8} \quad \left(\tfrac{2}{8} + \tfrac{8}{8}\right)$$

$$\boxed{288\tfrac{7}{8}}\text{ sq. ft.}$$

Check

$$261\tfrac{3}{8}$$
$$+\;288\tfrac{7}{8}$$
$$549\tfrac{10}{8} = 550\tfrac{2}{8} = 550\tfrac{1}{4}\text{ sq. ft.}$$

Note how the above blueprint aid helped to gather the facts and identify what we were looking for. To find the total square footage for groceries, we first had to sum the areas for meat and deli. Then we could subtract these areas from the total square footage. Also note that in Step 1 above, we didn't leave the answer as an improper fraction. In Step 2, we borrowed from the 550 so that we could complete the subtraction.

It's your turn to check your progress with a Practice Quiz.

LU 2–2	PRACTICE QUIZ

Complete this **Practice Quiz** to see how you are doing

1. Find LCD by the division of prime numbers:

12, 9, 6, 4

2. Add and reduce to lowest terms if needed:

  a. $\dfrac{3}{40} + \dfrac{2}{5}$ **b.** $2\tfrac{3}{4} + 6\tfrac{1}{20}$

3. Subtract and reduce to lowest terms if needed:

  a. $\dfrac{6}{7} - \dfrac{1}{4}$ **b.** $8\tfrac{1}{4} - 3\tfrac{9}{28}$ **c.** $4 - 1\tfrac{3}{4}$

4. Computerland has $660\tfrac{1}{4}$ total square feet of floor space. Three departments occupy this floor space: hardware, $201\tfrac{1}{8}$ square feet; software, $242\tfrac{1}{4}$ square feet; and customer service, _____ square feet. What is the total square footage of the customer service area? You might want to try a blueprint aid, since the solution will show a completed blueprint aid.

✓ Solutions

1.
```
2 / 12  9  6  4
2 /  6  9  3  2
3 /  3  9  3  1
     1  3  1  1
```
   $LCD = 2 \times 2 \times 3 \times 1 \times 3 \times 1 \times 1 = \boxed{36}$

2. **a.** $\dfrac{3}{40} + \dfrac{2}{5} = \dfrac{3}{40} + \dfrac{16}{40} = \boxed{\dfrac{19}{40}}$

  $\left(\begin{array}{c} \dfrac{2}{5} = \dfrac{?}{40} \\[4pt] 40 \div 5 = 8 \times 2 = 16 \end{array}\right)$

  b.
  $$2\tfrac{3}{4} \qquad 2\tfrac{15}{20}$$
  $$+\,6\tfrac{1}{20} \qquad +\,6\tfrac{1}{20}$$
  $$8\tfrac{16}{20} = \boxed{8\tfrac{4}{5}}$$

  $\dfrac{3}{4} = \dfrac{?}{20}$

  $20 \div 4 = 5 \times 3 = 15$

3. **a.**
  $$\dfrac{6}{7} = \dfrac{24}{28}$$
  $$-\,\dfrac{1}{4} = -\,\dfrac{7}{28}$$
  $$\boxed{\dfrac{17}{28}}$$

  b.
  $$8\tfrac{1}{4} = \quad 8\tfrac{7}{28} = \quad 7\tfrac{35}{28} \qquad \left(\tfrac{28}{28} + \tfrac{7}{28}\right)$$
  $$-\,3\tfrac{9}{28} = -\,3\tfrac{9}{28} = -\,3\tfrac{9}{28}$$
  $$4\tfrac{26}{28} = \boxed{4\tfrac{13}{14}}$$

  c.
  $$3\tfrac{4}{4}$$
  $$-\,1\tfrac{3}{4}$$
  $$\boxed{2\tfrac{1}{4}}$$

  Note how we showed the 4 as $3\tfrac{4}{4}$.

4. Computerland's total square footage for customer service:

The facts	Solving for?	Steps to take	Key points
Total square footage: $660\frac{1}{4}$ sq. ft. *Hardware:* $201\frac{1}{8}$ sq. ft. *Software:* $242\frac{1}{4}$ sq. ft.	Total square footage for customer service.	Total floor space − Total hardware and software floor space = Total customer service floor space.	Denominators must be the same before adding or subtracting fractions.

Steps to solving problem

1. Calculate the total square footage of hardware and software.

$$201\frac{1}{8} = \quad 201\frac{1}{8} \text{ (hardware)}$$
$$+\, 242\frac{1}{4} = +\, 242\frac{2}{8} \text{ (software)}$$
$$\overline{\qquad\qquad 443\frac{3}{8}}$$

2. Calculate the total square footage for customer service.

$$660\frac{1}{4} = \quad 660\frac{2}{8} = 659\frac{10}{8} \text{ (total square footage)}$$
$$-\,443\frac{3}{8} = -\,443\frac{3}{8} = -\,443\frac{3}{8} \text{ (hardware plus software)}$$
$$\overline{\qquad\qquad\qquad\qquad 216\frac{7}{8}} \text{ sq. ft. (customer service)}$$

LU 2–2a | **EXTRA PRACTICE QUIZ**

Need more practice? Try this **Extra Practice Quiz** (check figures in Chapter Organizer, p. 52)

1. Find the LCD by the division of prime numbers:
    10, 15, 9, 4

2. Add and reduce to lowest terms if needed:
    a. $\dfrac{2}{25} + \dfrac{3}{5}$ **b.** $3\dfrac{3}{8} + 6\dfrac{1}{32}$

3. Subtract and reduce to lowest terms if needed:
    a. $\dfrac{5}{6} - \dfrac{1}{3}$ **b.** $9\dfrac{1}{8} - 3\dfrac{7}{32}$ **c.** $6 - 1\dfrac{2}{5}$

4. Computerland has $985\frac{1}{4}$ total square feet of floor space. Three departments occupy this floor space: hardware, $209\frac{1}{8}$ square feet; software, $382\frac{1}{4}$ square feet; and customer service, _____ square feet. What is the total square footage of the customer service area?

Learning Unit 2–3: Multiplying and Dividing Fractions

The following recipe for Coconutty "M&M's"® Brownies makes 16 brownies. What would you need if you wanted to triple the recipe and make 48 brownies?

Coconutty "M&M's"® Brownies

6 squares (1 ounce each) semi-sweet chocolate
½ cup (1 stick) butter
¾ cup granulated sugar
2 large eggs
1 tablespoon vegetable oil
1 teaspoon vanilla extract
1¼ cups all-purpose flour
3 tablespoons unsweetened cocoa powder
1 teaspoon baking powder
½ teaspoon salt
1½ cups "M&M's"® Chocolate Mini Baking Bits, divided
Coconut Topping (recipe follows)

Preheat oven to 350°F. Grease 8 × 8 × 2-inch pan; set aside. In small saucepan combine chocolate, butter, and sugar over low heat; stir constantly until smooth. Remove from heat; let cool. In bowl beat eggs, oil, and vanilla; stir in chocolate mixture until blended. Stir in flour, cocoa powder, baking powder, and salt. Stir in 1 cup "M&M's"® Chocolate Mini Baking Bits. Spread batter in prepared pan. Bake 35 to 40 minutes or until toothpick inserted in center comes out clean. Cool. Prepare a coconut topping. Spread over brownies; sprinkle with $\frac{1}{2}$ cup "M&M's"® Chocolate Mini Baking Bits.

In this unit you learn how to multiply and divide **fractions.**

Multiplication of Fractions

Multiplying fractions is easier than adding and subtracting fractions because you do not have to find a common denominator. This section explains the multiplication of proper fractions and the multiplication of mixed numbers.

MULTIPLYING PROPER FRACTIONS[3]
Step 1. Multiply the numerators and the denominators.
Step 2. Reduce the answer to lowest terms or use the cancellation method.

First let's look at an example that results in an answer that we do not have to reduce.

EXAMPLE $\dfrac{1}{7} \times \dfrac{5}{8} = \dfrac{5}{56}$

In the next example, note how we reduce the answer to lowest terms.

EXAMPLE $\dfrac{5}{1} \times \dfrac{1}{6} \times \dfrac{4}{7} = \dfrac{20}{42} = \dfrac{10}{21}$ Keep in mind $\dfrac{5}{1}$ is equal to 5.

We can reduce $\frac{20}{42}$ by the step approach as follows:

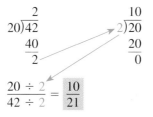

We could also have found the greatest common divisor by inspection.

$$\frac{20 \div 2}{42 \div 2} = \boxed{\frac{10}{21}}$$

As an alternative to reducing fractions to lowest terms, we can use the **cancellation** technique. Let's work the previous example using this technique.

EXAMPLE $\dfrac{5}{1} \times \dfrac{1}{\cancel{6}_3} \times \dfrac{\cancel{4}^2}{7} = \dfrac{10}{21}$ 2 divides evenly into 4 twice and into 6 three times.

Note that when we cancel numbers, we are reducing the answer before multiplying. We know that multiplying or dividing both numerator and denominator by the same number gives an equivalent fraction. So we can divide both numerator and denominator by any number that divides them both evenly. It doesn't matter which we divide first. Note that this division reduces $\frac{10}{21}$ to its lowest terms.

Multiplying Mixed Numbers

The following steps explain how to multiply mixed numbers:

MULTIPLYING MIXED NUMBERS
Step 1. Convert the mixed numbers to improper fractions.
Step 2. Multiply the numerators and denominators.
Step 3. Reduce the answer to lowest terms or use the cancellation method.

[3]You would follow the same procedure to multiply improper fractions.

EXAMPLE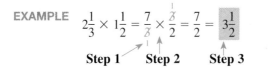

Step 1   Step 2   Step 3

Division of Fractions

When you studied whole numbers in Chapter 1, you saw how multiplication can be checked by division. The multiplication of fractions can also be checked by division, as you will see in this section on dividing proper fractions and mixed numbers.

Dividing Proper Fractions

The division of proper fractions introduces a new term—the **reciprocal.** To use reciprocals, we must first recognize which fraction in the problem is the divisor—the fraction that we divide by. Let's assume the problem we are to solve is $\frac{1}{8} \div \frac{2}{3}$. We read this problem as "$\frac{1}{8}$ divided by $\frac{2}{3}$." The divisor is the fraction after the division sign (or the second fraction). The steps that follow show how the divisor becomes a reciprocal.

DIVIDING PROPER FRACTIONS
Step 1. Invert (turn upside down) the divisor (the second fraction). The inverted number is the *reciprocal.*
Step 2. Multiply the fractions.
Step 3. Reduce the answer to lowest terms or use the cancellation method.

Do you know why the inverted fraction number is a reciprocal? Reciprocals are two numbers that when multiplied give a product of 1. For example, 2 (which is the same as $\frac{2}{1}$) and $\frac{1}{2}$ are reciprocals because multiplying them gives 1.

EXAMPLE $\frac{1}{8} \div \frac{2}{3}$ $\frac{1}{8} \times \frac{3}{2} = \boxed{\frac{3}{16}}$

Dividing Mixed Numbers

Now you are ready to divide mixed numbers by using improper fractions.

DIVIDING MIXED NUMBERS
Step 1. Convert all mixed numbers to improper fractions.
Step 2. Invert the divisor (take its reciprocal) and multiply. If your final answer is an improper fraction, reduce it to lowest terms. You can do this by finding the greatest common divisor or by using the cancellation technique.

EXAMPLE $8\frac{3}{4} \div 2\frac{5}{6}$

Step 1. $\dfrac{35}{4} \div \dfrac{17}{6}$

Step 2. $\dfrac{35}{\underset{2}{\cancel{4}}} \times \dfrac{\overset{3}{\cancel{6}}}{17} = \dfrac{105}{34} = 3\dfrac{3}{34}$ Here we used the cancellation technique.

How to Dissect and Solve a Word Problem

The Word Problem   Jamie Slater ordered $5\frac{1}{2}$ cords of oak. The cost of each cord is $150. He also ordered $2\frac{1}{4}$ cords of maple at $120 per cord. Jamie's neighbor, Al, said that he would share the wood and pay him $\frac{1}{5}$ of the total cost. How much did Jamie receive from Al?

Note how we filled in the blueprint aid columns. We first had to find the total cost of all the wood before we could find Al's share—$\frac{1}{5}$ of the total cost.

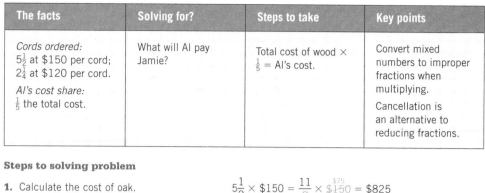

The facts	Solving for?	Steps to take	Key points
Cords ordered: $5\frac{1}{2}$ at \$150 per cord; $2\frac{1}{4}$ at \$120 per cord. *Al's cost share:* $\frac{1}{5}$ the total cost.	What will Al pay Jamie?	Total cost of wood $\times$ $\frac{1}{5}$ = Al's cost.	Convert mixed numbers to improper fractions when multiplying. Cancellation is an alternative to reducing fractions.

Steps to solving problem

1. Calculate the cost of oak.

$$5\frac{1}{2} \times \$150 = \frac{11}{2} \times \$\overset{\$75}{\cancel{150}} = \$825$$

2. Calculate the cost of maple.

$$2\frac{1}{4} \times \$120 = \frac{9}{4} \times \$\overset{\$30}{\cancel{120}} = +270$$

$$\overline{\$1,095} \text{ (total cost of wood)}$$

3. What Al pays.

$$\frac{1}{5} \times \$\overset{\$219}{\cancel{1,095}} = \boxed{\$219}$$

You should now be ready to test your knowledge of the final unit in the chapter.

LU 2–3 **PRACTICE QUIZ**

Complete this **Practice Quiz** to see how you are doing

1. Multiply (use cancellation technique):

   a. $\dfrac{4}{8} \times \dfrac{4}{6}$ **b.** $35 \times \dfrac{4}{7}$

2. Multiply (do not use canceling; reduce by finding the greatest common divisor):

   $\dfrac{14}{15} \times \dfrac{7}{10}$

3. Complete the following. Reduce to lowest terms as needed.

   a. $\dfrac{1}{9} \div \dfrac{5}{6}$ **b.** $\dfrac{51}{5} \div \dfrac{5}{9}$

4. Jill Estes bought a mobile home that was $8\frac{1}{8}$ times as expensive as the home her brother bought. Jill's brother paid \$16,000 for his mobile home. What is the cost of Jill's new home?

✓ Solutions

1. **a.** $\dfrac{\cancel{4}}{\cancel{8}} \times \dfrac{\cancel{4}}{\cancel{6}} = \boxed{\dfrac{1}{3}}$ **b.** $\overset{5}{\cancel{35}} \times \dfrac{4}{\cancel{7}} = \boxed{20}$

2. $\dfrac{14}{15} \times \dfrac{7}{10} = \dfrac{98 \div 2}{150 \div 2} = \boxed{\dfrac{49}{75}}$

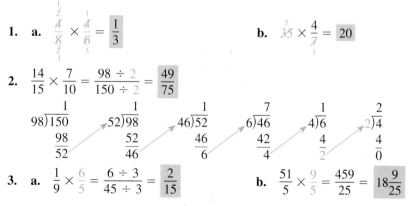

3. **a.** $\dfrac{1}{9} \times \dfrac{6}{5} = \dfrac{6 \div 3}{45 \div 3} = \boxed{\dfrac{2}{15}}$ **b.** $\dfrac{51}{5} \times \dfrac{9}{5} = \dfrac{459}{25} = \boxed{18\dfrac{9}{25}}$

4. Total cost of Jill's new home:

The facts	Solving for?	Steps to take	Key points
Jill's mobile home: $8\frac{1}{8}$ as expensive as her brother's. *Brother paid:* \$16,000.	Total cost of Jill's new home.	$8\frac{1}{8}$ $\times$ Total cost of Jill's brother's mobile home = Total cost of Jill's new home.	Canceling is an alternative to reducing.

Steps to solving problem

1. Convert 8⅛ to a mixed number. $\dfrac{65}{8}$

2. Calculate the total cost of Jill's home. $\dfrac{65}{8} \times \$\overset{\$2,000}{\cancel{16,000}} = \$130,000$

LU 2–3a | **EXTRA PRACTICE QUIZ**

Need more practice? Try this **Extra Practice Quiz** (check figures in Chapter Organizer, p. 52)

1. Multiply (use cancellation technique):

    a. $\dfrac{6}{8} \times \dfrac{3}{6}$ **b.** $42 \times \dfrac{1}{7}$

2. Multiply (do not use canceling; reduce by finding the greatest common divisor):

    $\dfrac{13}{117} \times \dfrac{9}{5}$

3. Complete the following. Reduce to lowest terms as needed.

    a. $\dfrac{1}{8} \div \dfrac{4}{5}$ **b.** $\dfrac{61}{6} \div \dfrac{6}{7}$

4. Jill Estes bought a mobile home that was $10\frac{1}{8}$ times as expensive as the home her brother brought. Jill's brother paid $10,000 for his mobile home. What is the cost of Jill's new home?

CHAPTER ORGANIZER AND STUDY GUIDE
WITH CHECK FIGURES FOR EXTRA PRACTICE QUIZZES

Topic	Key point, procedure, formula	Example(s) to illustrate situation
Types of fractions, p. 35	*Proper:* Value less than 1; numerator smaller than denominator. *Improper:* Value equal to or greater than 1; numerator equal to or greater than denominator. *Mixed:* Sum of whole number greater than zero and a proper fraction.	$\dfrac{3}{5}, \dfrac{7}{9}, \dfrac{8}{15}$ $\dfrac{14}{14}, \dfrac{19}{18}$ $6\frac{3}{8}, 9\frac{8}{9}$
Fraction conversions, p. 36	*Improper to whole or mixed:* Divide numerator by denominator; place remainder over *old* denominator. *Mixed to improper:* $\dfrac{\text{Whole number} \times \text{Denominator} + \text{Numerator}}{\text{Old denominator}}$	$\dfrac{17}{4} = \boxed{4\frac{1}{4}}$ $4\frac{1}{8} = \dfrac{32+1}{8} = \boxed{\dfrac{33}{8}}$
Reducing fractions to lowest terms, p. 37	1. Divide numerator and denominator by largest possible divisor (does not change fraction value). 2. When reduced to lowest terms, no number (except 1) will divide evenly into both numerator and denominator.	$\dfrac{18 \div 2}{46 \div 2} = \boxed{\dfrac{9}{23}}$
Step approach for finding greatest common denominator, p. 37	1. Divide smaller number of fraction into larger number. 2. Divide remainder into divisor of Step 1. Continue this process until no remainder results. 3. The last divisor used is the greatest common divisor.	$\dfrac{15}{65} \longrightarrow 15\overline{)65} \quad 5\overline{)15}$ $ \dfrac{60}{5} \qquad \dfrac{15}{0}$ 5 is greatest common divisor.
Raising fractions to higher terms, p. 38	Multiply numerator and denominator by same number. Does not change fraction value.	$\dfrac{15}{41} = \dfrac{?}{410}$ $410 \div 41 = 10 \times 15 = \boxed{150}$

(continues)

CHAPTER ORGANIZER AND STUDY GUIDE
WITH CHECK FIGURES FOR EXTRA PRACTICE QUIZZES (Continued)

Topic	Key point, procedure, formula	Example(s) to illustrate situation
Adding and subtracting like and unlike fractions, p. 40	When denominators are the same (like fractions), add (or subtract) numerators, place total over original denominator, and reduce to lowest terms. When denominators are different (unlike fractions), change them to like fractions by finding LCD using inspection or prime numbers. Then add (or subtract) the numerators, place total over LCD, and reduce to lowest terms.	$\frac{4}{9} + \frac{1}{9} = \boxed{\frac{5}{9}}$ $\frac{4}{9} - \frac{1}{9} = \frac{3}{9} = \boxed{\frac{1}{3}}$ $\frac{4}{5} + \frac{2}{7} = \frac{28}{35} + \frac{10}{35} = \frac{38}{35} = \boxed{1\frac{3}{35}}$
Prime numbers, p. 41	Whole numbers larger than 1 that are only divisible by itself and 1.	2, 3, 5, 7, 11
LCD by prime numbers, p. 42	1. Copy denominators and arrange them in a separate row. 2. Divide denominators by smallest prime number that will divide evenly into at least two numbers. 3. Continue until no prime number divides evenly into at least two numbers. 4. Multiply all the numbers in the divisors and last row to find LCD. 5. Raise fractions so each has a common denominator and complete computation.	$\frac{1}{3} + \frac{1}{6} + \frac{1}{8} + \frac{1}{12} + \frac{1}{9}$ $\begin{array}{r} 2\,\underline{/\,3\quad 6\quad 8\quad 12\quad 9} \\ 2\,\underline{/\,3\quad 3\quad 4\quad 6\quad 9} \\ 3\,\underline{/\,3\quad 3\quad 2\quad 3\quad 9} \\ 1\quad 1\quad 2\quad 1\quad 3 \end{array}$ $2 \times 2 \times 3 \times 1 \times 1 \times 2 \times 1 \times 3 = \boxed{72}$
Adding mixed numbers, p. 42	1. Add fractions. 2. Add whole numbers. 3. Combine totals of Steps 1 and 2. If denominators are different, a common denominator must be found. Answer cannot be left as improper fraction.	$1\frac{4}{7} + 1\frac{3}{7}$ Step 1: $\frac{4}{7} + \frac{3}{7} = \frac{7}{7}$ Step 2: $1 + 1 = 2$ Step 3: $2\frac{7}{7} = \boxed{3}$
Subtracting mixed numbers, p. 44	1. Subtract fractions. 2. If necessary, borrow from whole numbers. 3. Subtract whole numbers and fractions if borrowing was necessary. 4. Reduce fractions to lowest terms. If denominators are different, a common denominator must be found.	$12\frac{2}{5} - 7\frac{3}{5}$ $11\frac{7}{5} - 7\frac{3}{5}$ $= 4\frac{4}{5}$ Due to borrowing $\frac{5}{5}$ from number 12 $\frac{5}{5} + \frac{2}{5} = \frac{7}{5}$ The whole number is now 11.
Multiplying proper fractions, p. 47	1. Multiply numerators and denominators. 2. Reduce answer to lowest terms or use cancellation method.	$\frac{4}{\overset{}{\underset{1}{7}}} \times \frac{\overset{1}{7}}{9} = \frac{4}{9}$
Multiplying mixed numbers, p. 47	1. Convert mixed numbers to improper fractions. 2. Multiply numerators and denominators. 3. Reduce answer to lowest terms or use cancellation method.	$1\frac{1}{8} \times 2\frac{5}{8}$ $\frac{9}{8} \times \frac{21}{8} = \frac{189}{64} = \boxed{2\frac{61}{64}}$
Dividing proper fractions, p. 48	1. Invert divisor. 2. Multiply. 3. Reduce answer to lowest terms or use cancellation method.	$\frac{1}{4} \div \frac{1}{8} = \frac{1}{\underset{1}{4}} \times \frac{\overset{2}{8}}{1} = \boxed{2}$

(continues)

CHAPTER ORGANIZER AND STUDY GUIDE
WITH CHECK FIGURES FOR EXTRA PRACTICE QUIZZES (Concluded)

Topic	Key point, procedure, formula	Example(s) to illustrate situation
Dividing mixed numbers, p. 48	1. Convert mixed numbers to improper fractions. 2. Invert divisor and multiply. If final answer is an improper fraction, reduce to lowest terms by finding greatest common divisor or using the cancellation method.	$1\frac{1}{2} \div 1\frac{5}{8} = \frac{3}{2} \div \frac{13}{8}$ $= \frac{3}{2} \times \frac{\overset{4}{8}}{13}$ $= \frac{12}{13}$
KEY TERMS	Cancellation, *p. 47* Common denominator, *p. 40* Denominator, *p. 40* Equivalent, *p. 38* Fraction, *p. 35* Greatest common divisor, *p. 37*	Higher terms, *p. 38* Improper fraction, *p. 35* Least common denominator (LCD), *p. 40* Like fractions, *p. 40* Lowest terms, *p. 37* Mixed numbers, *p. 36*	Numerator, *p. 35* Prime numbers, *p. 41* Proper fractions, *p. 35* Reciprocal, *p. 48* Unlike fractions, *p. 40*
CHECK FIGURE FOR EXTRA PRACTICE QUIZZES WITH PAGE REFERENCES	LU 2–1a (p. 39) 1. a. P b. I c. M d. I 2. $22\frac{1}{7}$ 3. $\frac{79}{9}$ 4. a. 14; $\frac{3}{5}$ b.2; $\frac{48}{91}$ 5. a. 160; b. 27	LU 2–2a (p. 46) 1. 180 2. a. $\frac{17}{25}$ b. $9\frac{13}{32}$ 3. a. $\frac{1}{2}$ b. $5\frac{29}{32}$ c. $4\frac{3}{5}$ 4. $393\frac{7}{8}$ ft.	LU 2–3a (p. 50) 1. a. $\frac{3}{8}$ b. 6 2. 117; $\frac{1}{5}$ 3. a. $\frac{5}{32}$ b. $11\frac{31}{36}$ 4. $101,250

Note: For how to dissect and solve a word problem, see page 44.

Critical Thinking Discussion Questions

1. What are the steps to convert improper fractions to whole or mixed numbers? Give an example of how you could use this conversion procedure when you eat at Pizza Hut.

2. What are the steps to convert mixed numbers to improper fractions? Show how you could use this conversion procedure when you order doughnuts at Dunkin' Donuts.

3. What is the greatest common divisor? How could you use the greatest common divisor to write an advertisement showing that 35 out of 60 people prefer MCI to AT&T?

4. Explain the step approach for finding the greatest common divisor. How could you use the MCI–AT&T example in question 3 to illustrate the step approach?

5. Explain the steps of adding or subtracting unlike fractions. Using a ruler, measure the heights of two different-size cans of food and show how to calculate the difference in height.

6. What is a prime number? Using the two cans in question 5, show how you could use prime numbers to calculate the LCD.

7. Explain the steps for multiplying proper fractions and mixed numbers. Assume you went to Staples (a stationery superstore). Give an example showing the multiplying of proper fractions and mixed numbers.

15. A taste-testing survey of Zing Farms showed that $\frac{2}{3}$ of the people surveyed preferred the taste of veggie burgers to regular burgers. If 90,000 people were in the survey, how many favored veggie burgers? How many chose regular burgers? *(p. 48)*

16. Jim Janes, an employee of Enterprise Co., worked $9\frac{1}{4}$ hours on Monday, $4\frac{1}{2}$ hours on Tuesday, $9\frac{1}{4}$ hours on Wednesday, $7\frac{1}{2}$ hours on Thursday, and 9 hours on Friday. How many total hours did Jim work during the week? *(p. 41)*

17. JCPenney offered a $\frac{1}{3}$ rebate on its $39 hair dryer. Joan bought a J.C. Penney hair dryer. What did Joan pay after the rebate? *(p. 48)*

HEALTH | Retail kiosks offer routine services at a fraction of physician prices. *By Thomas M. Anderson*

CHECKUPS on the run

YOUR CHILD wakes up with an earache—and you take him to Target. You suspect your nagging cough may signal bronchitis, so you have it checked—at Wal-Mart. You don't need an appointment for either visit, the cost is a fraction of what you would have paid if you had cooled your heels in your doctor's office all morning, and your insurance might even cover it.

Walk-in clinics are coming soon to a retailer, pharmacy or grocery store near you. Minneapolis-based MinuteClinic, the country's largest chain of retail clinics, expects to have 250 facilities in 20 states by year-end.

Customers appreciate the convenience of one-stop shopping. Stores get a boost in sales of drugs and other health-related products. And patients and insurers save money as routine care, which accounts for one-fourth of U.S. health spending, moves out of doctor's offices and into settings with lower overhead.

At express medical clinics, one nurse practitioner usually runs the whole operation, from reception to diagnosis to prescription. A visit takes about 15 minutes per patient.

Retail clinics put a clear price tag on your health care. RediClinic, with kiosks in three Wal-Marts, charges a flat fee of $45 for all its basic services. A sore-throat checkup with a strep test costs $62 at a Minneapolis Minute-Clinic, compared with $109 at a doc-

● **MinuteClinic posts prices for services, which are often covered by insurance.**

tor's office, $125 at an urgent-care center and $406 at an emergency room, according to the Minnesota Council of Health Plans.

Clinics generally accept cash and major credit cards. You can be reimbursed with money you've contributed to an employer-sponsored flexible-spending account or to a health savings account, and now some health insurers are picking up the tab.

MinuteClinic, for example, has signed agreements with Aetna, Cigna and United-Healthcare. If you're covered by one of those insurers, you'll pay your plan's co-payment rather than the full cost of the clinic visit. Some employers, including Best Buy, Black & Decker and Carlson Cos., offer lower co-payments to encourage employees to use MinuteClinics.

Retail clinics generally won't treat children younger than 18 months old. If you're on multiple medications or are older than 65, it's better to visit an urgent-care center or your doctor's office. If you have chest pain, head straight for the emergency room.

Have questions about using a clinic? "Call your family doctor," advises Larry Fields, president of the American Academy of Family Physicians. "It's free."

BUSINESS MATH ISSUE

Retail clinics are a fad and will not solve the health care problem.

1. List the key points of the article and information to support your position.
2. Write a group defense of your position using math calculations to support your view.

PROJECT A

What is the total cost of a Bentley boat? Prove your answer using fractions.

Luxury yachts, cars and RVs are among the goods available for fractional ownership.

All 1/8 of This Could Be Yours

Fractional Ownership Moves Beyond Jets to Include Yachts, Bentleys, Even Deluxe RVs

By RON LIEBER

TRAVELING THE INTERSTATE like a rock star seemed like a swell idea to Tom Roegner until he began to do the math.

The motor coach itself would cost more than a quarter million dollars, insurance and storage fees were expensive, and the depreciation would be immediate and dramatic. So the retired banker from Palos Heights, Ill. did what bankers before him have been doing with jets for years: he bought himself a chunk of the vehicle instead.

Fractional ownership, where buyers purchase a share of an expensive asset and pay the seller fees to handle the scheduling and maintenance, is a fixture of the private jet industry and a growing force in the market for vacation properties. Now, this model of ownership is creeping into other asset classes, too.

Increasingly it is becoming possible to buy a piece of a yacht, a fancy sports car, or even a luxury recreational vehicle—and share the use of it with other owners. **Exotic Car Share**, based in the Chicago suburb of Palatine, Ill., is in the middle of parceling out pieces of a new Bentley Conti-

usual boats and cars: an explosives-detection device that eight owners could share. Price: $2,475 each.

Despite the recent activity, there is still only a handful of companies offering fractional ownership outside aviation and real estate. But buyers and sellers say the economic logic behind shares in jets and vacation properties applies to other luxury discretionary goods, too.

Fractional ownership has been around in one form or another for quite a while, starting of course with the long-running practice of groups of friends going in on boats and condos. In the 1990s, the business of selling shares of small jets and managing them grew rapidly; it gained further respect in 1998 when Warren Buffett's **Berkshire Hathaway** bought the aircraft-sharing company NetJets.

Wall Street Journal © 2005

Internet Projects: See text Web site (www.mhhe.com/slater9e) and The Business Math Internet Resource Guide.

63

CHAPTER 3

Decimals

LEARNING UNIT OBJECTIVES

LU 3–1: Rounding Decimals; Fraction and Decimal Conversions

- Explain the place values of whole numbers and decimals; round decimals *(pp. 65–67)*.

- Convert decimal fractions to decimals, proper fractions to decimals, mixed numbers to decimals, and pure and mixed decimals to decimal fractions *(pp. 67–70)*.

LU 3–2: Adding, Subtracting, Multiplying, and Dividing Decimals

- Add, subtract, multiply, and divide decimals *(pp. 71–73)*.

- Complete decimal applications in foreign currency *(p. 73)*.

- Multiply and divide decimals by shortcut methods *(p. 74)*.

What It Costs to Buy Health Insurance

What a healthy 30-year-old would pay monthly for the most affordable private insurance policy available in the 10 most- and least-expensive major cities.

■ The 10 Cheapest Cities		■ The 10 Most Costly Cities	
Long Beach, Cailf.	$54.00	New York	$334.09
Sacramento, Calif.	56.00	Boston	267.57
Fresno, Calif.	56.00	Miami	151.20
San Diego	57.00	Dallas	146.42
Columbus, Ohio	57.91	Houston	146.28
San Jose, Calif.	58.00	Seattle	143.00
San Francisco	58.00	San Juan, P.R.	133.00
Oakland, Calif.	58.00	Washington, D.C.	132.00
Mesa, Ariz.	58.74	Fort Worth, Texas	129.53
Tucson, Ariz.	58.77	New Orleans	126.11

Source: eHealthInsurance.com

Wall Street Journal © 2005

Are you looking to buy health insurance? As you can see from the *Wall Street Journal* clipping "What It Costs to Buy Health Insurance," health insurance is $280.09 cheaper in Long Beach, California, than in New York:

New York: $334.09
Long Beach: −   54.00
                $280.09

If you plan to move to another city, you might consider the cost of health insurance in that city. Also, remember that health insurance is a cost that continues to increase.

Chapter 2 introduced the 1.69-ounce bag of M&M's® shown in Table 3.1. In Table 3.1 (p. 66), the six colors in the 1.69-ounce bag of M&M's® are given in fractions and their values expressed in decimal equivalents that are rounded to the nearest hundredths.

This chapter is divided into two learning units. The first unit discusses rounding decimals, converting fractions to decimals, and converting decimals to fractions. The second unit shows you how to add, subtract, multiply, and divide decimals, along with some shortcuts for multiplying and dividing decimals. Added to this unit is a global application of decimals dealing with foreign exchange rates.

The increase in the United States of the cost of a stamp from $.39 to $.41 is indicated by decimals. If you think $.41 is high, compare this with Norway ($.87), Italy ($.73), Japan ($.57), and the United Kingdom ($.53). One of the most common uses of decimals occurs when we spend dollars and cents, which is a *decimal number*.

A **decimal** is a decimal number with digits to the right of a *decimal point*, indicating that decimals, like fractions, are parts of a whole that are less than one. Thus, we can interchange the terms *decimals* and *decimal numbers*. Remembering this will avoid confusion between the terms *decimal, decimal number,* and *decimal point*.

Learning Unit 3–1: Rounding Decimals; Fraction and Decimal Conversions

Remember to read the decimal point as *and*.

In Chapter 1 we stated that the **decimal point** is the center of the decimal numbering system. So far we have studied the whole numbers to the left of the decimal point and the parts of whole numbers called fractions. We also learned that the position of the digits in a whole number gives the place values of the digits (Figure 1.1, p. 3). Now we will study the position (place values) of the digits to the right of the decimal point (Figure 3.1, p. 66). Note that the words to the right of the decimal point end in *ths*.

You should understand why the decimal point is the center of the decimal system. If you move a digit to the left of the decimal point by place (ones, tens, and so on), *you increase its value 10 times for each place (power of 10)*. If you move a digit to the right of the decimal point by place (tenths, hundredths, and so on), *you decrease its value 10 times for each place*.

| TABLE | 3.1 |

Analyzing a bag of M&M's®

Sharon Hoogstraten

Color*	Fraction	Decimal
Yellow	$\frac{18}{55}$	.33
Red	$\frac{10}{55}$	.18
Blue	$\frac{9}{55}$	.16
Orange	$\frac{7}{55}$	.13
Brown	$\frac{6}{55}$	.11
Green	$\frac{5}{55}$	.09
Total	$\frac{55}{55} = 1$	1.00

*The color ratios currently given are a sample used for educational purposes. They do not represent the manufacturer's color ratios.

EXAMPLES $.06 ⟶ The 6 is in the hundred*ths* place value.

1.527 ⟶ The 5 is in the ten*ths* place value.

2.8394 ⟶ The 4 is in the ten thousand*ths* place value.

.33 ⟶ The thirty-three hundred*ths* represents the yellow M&M's® in our M&M's® bag of 55 M&M's®.

1.69 oz. ⟶ The one ounce and sixty-nine hundred*ths* of another ounce is the weight of our bag of M&M's®.

Do you recall from Chapter 1 how you used a place-value chart to read or write whole numbers in verbal form? To read or write decimal numbers, you read or write the decimal number as if it were a whole number. Then you use the name of the decimal place of the last digit as given in Figure 3.1. For example, you would read or write the decimal .0796 as seven hundred ninety-six ten thousandths (the last digit, 6, is in the ten thousandths place).

To read a decimal with four or fewer whole numbers, you can also refer to Figure 3.1. For larger whole numbers, refer to the whole-number place-value chart in Chapter 1 (Figure 1.1, p. 3). For example, from Figure 3.1 you would read the number 126.2864 as one hundred twenty-six and two thousand eight hundred sixty-four ten thousandths. Remember that the *and* is the decimal point.

Now let's round decimals. Rounding decimals is similar to the rounding of whole numbers that you learned in Chapter 1.

| FIGURE | 3.1 |

Decimal place-value chart

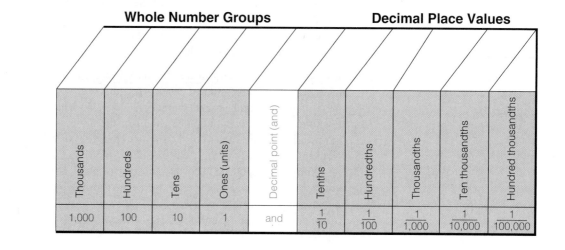

Whole Number Groups					Decimal Place Values				
Thousands	Hundreds	Tens	Ones (units)	Decimal point (and)	Tenths	Hundredths	Thousandths	Ten thousandths	Hundred thousandths
1,000	100	10	1	and	$\frac{1}{10}$	$\frac{1}{100}$	$\frac{1}{1,000}$	$\frac{1}{10,000}$	$\frac{1}{100,000}$

Rounding Decimals

From Table 3.1, you know that the 1.69-ounce bag of M&M's® introduced in Chapter 2 contained $\frac{18}{55}$, or .33, yellow M&M's®. The .33 was rounded to the nearest hundredth. **Rounding decimals** involves the following steps:

ROUNDING DECIMALS TO A SPECIFIED PLACE VALUE
Step 1. Identify the place value of the digit you want to round.
Step 2. If the digit to the right of the identified digit in Step 1 is 5 or more, increase the identified digit by 1. If the digit to the right is less than 5, do not change the identified digit.
Step 3. Drop all digits to the right of the identified digit.

Let's practice rounding by using the $\frac{18}{55}$ yellow M&M's® that we rounded to .33 in Table 3.1. Before we rounded $\frac{18}{55}$ to .33, the number we rounded was .32727. This is an example of a **repeating decimal** since the 27 repeats itself.

EXAMPLE   Round .3272727 to nearest hundredth.

Step 1.   .3272727   The identified digit is 2, which is in the hundredths place (two places to the right of the decimal point).

Step 2.   → The digit to the right of 2 is more than 5 (7). Thus, 2, the identified digit in Step 1, is changed to 3.

          .3372727

Step 3.   .33   Drop all other digits to right of the identified digit 3.

We could also round the .3272727 M&M's® to the nearest tenth or thousandth as follows:

Tenth		**or**	**Thousandth**	
.3272727 ⟶	.3		.3272727 ⟶	.327

OTHER EXAMPLES

Round to nearest dollar:	$166.39 ⟶	$166
Round to nearest cent:	$1,196.885 ⟶	$1,196.89
Round to nearest hundredth:	$38.563 ⟶	$38.56
Round to nearest thousandth:	$1,432.9981 ⟶	$1,432.998

The rules for rounding can differ with the situation in which rounding is used. For example, have you ever bought one item from a supermarket produce department that was marked "3 for $1" and noticed what the cashier charged you? One item marked "3 for $1" would not cost you $33\frac{1}{3}$ cents rounded to 33 cents. You will pay 34 cents. Many retail stores round to the next cent even if the digit following the identified digit is less than $\frac{1}{2}$ of a penny. In this text we round on the concept of 5 or more.

Fraction and Decimal Conversions

In business operations we must frequently convert fractions to decimal numbers and decimal numbers to fractions. This section begins by discussing three types of fraction-to-decimal conversions. Then we discuss converting pure and mixed decimals to decimal fractions.

Converting Decimal Fractions to Decimals

From Figure 3.1 you can see that a **decimal fraction** (expressed in the digits to the right of the decimal point) is a fraction with a denominator that has a power of 10, such as $\frac{1}{10}$, $\frac{17}{100}$, and $\frac{23}{1,000}$. To convert a decimal fraction to a decimal, follow these steps:

	CONVERTING DECIMAL FRACTIONS TO DECIMALS
Step 1.	Count the number of zeros in the denominator.
Step 2.	Place the numerator of the decimal fraction to the right of the decimal point the same number of places as you have zeros in the denominator. (The number of zeros in the denominator gives the number of digits your decimal has to the right of the decimal point.) Do not go over the total number of denominator zeros.

Now let's change $\frac{3}{10}$ and its higher multiples of 10 to decimals.

EXAMPLES

Verbal form	Decimal fraction	Decimal[1]	Number of decimal places to right of decimal point
a. Three tenths	$\frac{3}{10}$	.3	1
b. Three hundredths	$\frac{3}{100}$	.03	2
c. Three thousandths	$\frac{3}{1,000}$	.003	3
d. Three ten thousandths	$\frac{3}{10,000}$	.0003	4

Note how we show the different values of the decimal fractions above in decimals. The zeros after the decimal point and before the number 3 indicate these values. If you add zeros after the number 3, you do not change the value. Thus, the numbers .3 , .30 , and .300 have the same value. So 3 tenths of a pizza, 30 hundredths of a pizza, and 300 thousandths of a pizza are the same total amount of pizza. The first pizza is sliced into 10 pieces. The second pizza is sliced into 100 pieces. The third pizza is sliced into 1,000 pieces. Also, we don't need to place a zero to the left of the decimal point.

Converting Proper Fractions to Decimals

Recall from Chapter 2 that proper fractions are fractions with a value less than 1. That is, the numerator of the fraction is smaller than its denominator. How can we convert these proper fractions to decimals? Since proper fractions are a form of division, it is possible to convert proper fractions to decimals by carrying out the division.

	CONVERTING PROPER FRACTIONS TO DECIMALS
Step 1.	Divide the numerator of the fraction by its denominator. (If necessary, add a decimal point and zeros to the number in the numerator.)
Step 2.	Round as necessary.

EXAMPLES

$$\frac{3}{4} = 4\overline{)3.00} \quad .75$$
$$\frac{2\ 8}{20}$$
$$\frac{20}{}$$

$$\frac{3}{8} = 8\overline{)3.000} \quad .375$$
$$\frac{2\ 4}{60}$$
$$\frac{56}{40}$$
$$\frac{40}{}$$

$$\frac{1}{3} = 3\overline{)1.000} \quad .33\overline{3}$$
$$\frac{9}{10}$$
$$\frac{9}{10}$$
$$\frac{9}{1}$$

[1]From .3 to .0003, the values get smaller and smaller, but if you go from .3 to .3000, the values remain the same.

Note that in the last example $\frac{1}{3}$, the 3 in the quotient keeps repeating itself (never ends). The short bar over the last 3 means that the number endlessly repeats.

Converting Mixed Numbers to Decimals

A mixed number, you will recall from Chapter 2, is the sum of a whole number greater than zero and a proper fraction. To convert mixed numbers to decimals, use the following steps:

CONVERTING MIXED NUMBERS TO DECIMALS
Step 1. Convert the fractional part of the mixed number to a decimal (as illustrated in the previous section).
Step 2. Add the converted fractional part to the whole number.

EXAMPLE

$$8\frac{2}{5} = \textbf{(Step 1)} \quad 5\overline{)2.0} \begin{array}{c} .4 \\ \underline{} \\ 2\,0 \end{array} \quad \textbf{(Step 2)} = \begin{array}{c} 8.00 \\ \underline{+\ .40} \\ 8.40 \end{array}$$

Now that we have converted fractions to decimals, let's convert decimals to fractions.

Converting Pure and Mixed Decimals to Decimal Fractions

A **pure decimal** has no whole number(s) to the left of the decimal point (.43, .458, and so on). A **mixed decimal** is a combination of a whole number and a decimal. An example of a mixed decimal follows.

EXAMPLE 737.592 = Seven hundred thirty-seven and five hundred ninety-two thousandths

Note the following conversion steps for converting pure and mixed decimals to decimal fractions:

CONVERTING PURE AND MIXED DECIMALS TO DECIMAL FRACTIONS
Step 1. Place the digits to the right of the decimal point in the numerator of the fraction. Omit the decimal point. (For a decimal fraction with a fractional part, see examples **c** and **d** below.)
Step 2. Put a 1 in the denominator of the fraction.
Step 3. Count the number of digits to the right of the decimal point. Add the same number of zeros to the denominator of the fraction. For mixed decimals, add the fraction to the whole number.

If desired, you can reduce the fractions in Step 3.

EXAMPLES		Step 1	Step 2	Places	Step 3
a.	.3	$\dfrac{3}{}$	$\dfrac{3}{1}$	1	$\dfrac{3}{10}$
b.	.24	$\dfrac{24}{}$	$\dfrac{24}{1}$	2	$\dfrac{24}{100}$
c.	$.24\frac{1}{2}$	$\dfrac{245}{}$	$\dfrac{245}{1}$	3	$\dfrac{245}{1,000}$

Before completing Step 1 in example **c,** we must remove the fractional part, convert it to a decimal ($\frac{1}{2} = .5$), and multiply it by .01 ($.5 \times .01 = .005$). We use .01 because the 4 of .24 is in the hundredths place. Then we add $.005 + .24 = .245$ (three places to right of the decimal) and complete Steps 1, 2, and 3.

d.	$.07\frac{1}{4}$	$\dfrac{725}{}$	$\dfrac{725}{1}$	4	$\dfrac{725}{10,000}$

In example **d,** be sure to convert $\frac{1}{4}$ to .25 and multiply by .01. This gives .0025. Then add .0025 to .07, which is .0725 (four places), and complete Steps 1, 2, and 3.

$$\textbf{e.} \quad 17.45 \qquad \underline{45} \qquad \frac{45}{1} \qquad 2 \qquad \frac{45}{100} = 17\frac{45}{100}$$

Example **e** is a mixed decimal. Since we substitute *and* for the decimal point, we read this mixed decimal as seventeen and forty-five hundredths. Note that after we converted the .45 of the mixed decimals to a fraction, we added it to the whole number 17.

The Practice Quiz that follows will help you check your understanding of this unit.

LU 3–1	PRACTICE QUIZ

Complete this **Practice Quiz** to see how you are doing

DVD

Write the following as a decimal number.

1. Four hundred eight thousandths

Name the place position of the identified digit:

2. 6.82$\overset{\uparrow}{4}$1   **3.** 9.3$\overset{\uparrow}{9}$42

Round each decimal to place indicated:

	Tenth	**Thousandth**
4. .62768	**a.**	**b.**
5. .68341	**a.**	**b.**

Convert the following to decimals:

6. $\dfrac{9}{10,000}$ **7.** $\dfrac{14}{100,000}$

Convert the following to decimal fractions (do not reduce):

8. .819   **9.** 16.93   **10.** .05$\frac{1}{4}$

Convert the following fractions to decimals and round answer to nearest hundredth:

11. $\dfrac{1}{6}$ **12.** $\dfrac{3}{8}$ **13.** $12\frac{1}{8}$

✓ **Solutions**

1. .408 (3 places to right of decimal)

2. Hundredths   **3.** Thousandths

4. a. .6 (identified digit 6—digit to right less than 5)   **b.** .628 (identified digit 7—digit to right greater than 5)

5. a. .7 (identified digit 6—digit to right greater than 5)   **b.** .683 (identified digit 3—digit to right less than 5)

6. .0009 (4 places)   **7.** .00014 (5 places)

8. $\dfrac{819}{1,000}$ $\left(\dfrac{819}{1 + 3 \text{ zeros}}\right)$ **9.** $16\dfrac{93}{100}$

10. $\dfrac{525}{10,000}$ $\left(\dfrac{525}{1 + 4 \text{ zeros}} \dfrac{1}{4} \times .01 = .0025 + .05 = .0525\right)$

11. .16666 = .17   **12.** .375 = .38   **13.** 12.125 = 12.13

LU 3–1a	EXTRA PRACTICE QUIZ

Need more practice? Try this **Extra Practice Quiz** (check figures in Chapter Organizer, p. 78)

Write the following as a decimal number:

1. Three hundred nine thousandths

Name the place position of the identified digit:

2. 7.9$\overset{\uparrow}{3}$24   **3.** 8.36$\overset{\uparrow}{8}$2

Round each decimal to place indicated:

	Tenth	**Thousandth**
4. .84361	a.	b.
5. .87938	a.	b.

Convert the following to decimals:

6. $\dfrac{8}{10,000}$

7. $\dfrac{16}{100,000}$

Convert the following to decimal fractions (do not reduce):

8. .938   **9.** 17.95   **10.** $.03\frac{1}{4}$

Convert the following fractions to decimals and round answer to nearest hundredth:

11. $\dfrac{1}{8}$ **12.** $\dfrac{4}{7}$ **13.** $13\dfrac{1}{9}$

Learning Unit 3–2: Adding, Subtracting, Multiplying, and Dividing Decimals

People who are contemplating a career move to another city or state usually want to know the cost of living in that city or state. Also, you will hear retirees saying they are moving to another city or state because the cost of living is cheaper in this city or state. The following *Wall Street Journal* clipping "City by City" gives you some interesting statistics on the costs of various items in selected locations:

City by City

How the cost of living compares for selected locations (all amounts in U.S. dollars)

CITY	CUP OF COFFEE, WITH SERVICE	FAST-FOOD HAMBURGER MEAL	DRY CLEANING, MEN'S BLAZER	TOOTHPASTE, FLUORIDE, 4.2 OUNCES	2 MOVIE TICKETS, INT'L. RELEASE
Tokyo	$4.76	$5.99	$10.48	$2.02	$32.66
London	3.11	7.62	13.30	3.07	28.41
New York	3.30	5.75	8.80	3.12	20.00
Sydney	2.42	4.45	8.28	2.73	20.71
Chicago	2.10	4.99	9.99	3.23	18.00
San Francisco	3.52	5.29	6.50	2.48	19.50
Boston	2.90	4.39	5.25	2.05	18.00
Atlanta	1.71	3.70	5.95	2.24	16.00
Toronto	2.11	4.62	7.37	1.66	18.05
Rio de Janeiro	0.94	2.99	6.32	1.38	9.90

Source: Mercer Human Resource Consulting, 2004 Cost of Living Survey

Wall Street Journal © 2005

If you frequent coffee restaurants, you might want to check the cost of a cup of coffee with service in various locations. The "City by City" clipping helps you do this. For example, a cup of coffee with service costs $1.71 in Atlanta, while a cup of coffee with service costs $4.76 in Tokyo. The coffee with service in Atlanta saves you $3.05 per cup. If you drink 1 cup of coffee per day for a year in Atlanta, you would save $1,113.25.

Tokyo: $4.76
Atlanta: − 1.71
           $3.05 × 365 days = $1,113.25

This learning unit shows you how to add, subtract, multiply, and divide decimals. You also make calculations involving decimals, including decimals used in foreign currency.

Addition and Subtraction of Decimals

Since you know how to add and subtract whole numbers, to add and subtract decimal numbers you have only to learn about the placement of the decimals. The following steps will help you:

ADDING AND SUBTRACTING DECIMALS
Step 1. Vertically write the numbers so that the decimal points align. You can place additional zeros to the right of the decimal point if needed without changing the value of the number.
Step 2. Add or subtract the digits starting with the right column and moving to the left.
Step 3. Align the decimal point in the answer with the above decimal points.

EXAMPLES   Add 4 + 7.3 + 36.139 + .0007 + 8.22.

Whole number to the right of the last digit is assumed to have a decimal.

$$
\begin{array}{r}
4.0000 \\
7.3000 \\
36.1390 \\
.0007 \\
8.2200 \\
\hline
55.6597
\end{array}
$$

Extra zeros have been added to make calculation easier.

Subtract 45.3 − 15.273.

$$
\begin{array}{r}
{\scriptstyle 2\,9\,10} \\
45.\cancel{3}\cancel{0}\cancel{0} \\
-15.273 \\
\hline
30.027
\end{array}
$$

Subtract 7 − 6.9.

$$
\begin{array}{r}
{\scriptstyle 6\,10} \\
7.\cancel{0} \\
-6.9 \\
\hline
.1
\end{array}
$$

Multiplication of Decimals

The multiplication of decimal numbers is similar to the multiplication of whole numbers except for the additional step of placing the decimal in the answer (product). The steps that follow simplify this procedure.

MULTIPLYING DECIMALS
Step 1. Multiply the numbers as whole numbers ignoring the decimal points.
Step 2. Count and total the number of decimal places in the multiplier and multiplicand.
Step 3. Starting at the right in the product, count to the left the number of decimal places totaled in Step 2. Place the decimal point so that the product has the same number of decimal places as totaled in Step 2. If the total number of places is greater than the places in the product, insert zeros in front of the product.

EXAMPLES

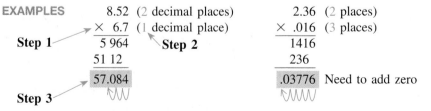

Step 1

Step 2

Step 3

$$
\begin{array}{r}
8.52 \\
\times\ 6.7 \\
\hline
5\,964 \\
51\,12 \\
\hline
57.084
\end{array}
$$
8.52 (2 decimal places)
× 6.7 (1 decimal place)

$$
\begin{array}{r}
2.36 \\
\times\ .016 \\
\hline
1416 \\
236 \\
\hline
.03776
\end{array}
$$
2.36 (2 places)
× .016 (3 places)

Need to add zero

Division of Decimals

If the divisor in your decimal division problem is a whole number, first place the decimal point in the quotient directly above the decimal point in the dividend. Then divide as usual. If the divisor has a decimal point, complete the steps that follow.

DIVIDING DECIMALS
Step 1. Make the divisor a whole number by moving the decimal point to the right.
Step 2. Move the decimal point in the dividend to the right the same number of places that you moved the decimal point in the divisor (Step 1). If there are not enough places, add zeros to the right of the dividend.
Step 3. Place the decimal point in the quotient above the new decimal point in the dividend. Divide as usual.

EXAMPLE

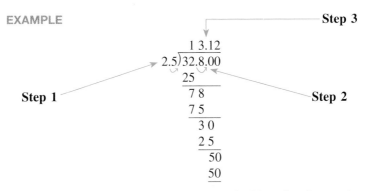

Stop a moment and study the above example. Note that the quotient does not change when we multiply the divisor and the dividend by the same number. This is why we can move the decimal point in division problems and always divide by a whole number.

Bargain Hunting

The dollar's fall creates deals for British shoppers in the U.S.

■ Apple iPod
(20GB: 5,000 songs)
New York City: **$299**

Wall Street Journal © 2004

Decimal Applications in Foreign Currency

The *Wall Street Journal* clipping "Bargain Hunting" showed the cost of an Apple iPod in New York City at $299. Using the updated currency table that follows, what would be the cost of the iPod in pounds? Check your answer.

Key Currency Cross Rates			Late New York Trading Wednesday, October 25, 2006				
	Dollar	**Euro**	**Pound**	**SFranc**	**Peso**	**Yen**	**CdnDlr**
Canada	1.1256	1.4194	2.1145	0.8906	.10471	.00946	...
Japan	119.02	150.08	223.58	94.168	11.071	...	105.737
Mexico	10.7504	13.5562	20.195	8.5057	...	.09032	9.5506
Switzerland	1.2639	1.5938	2.3742	...	.11757	.01062	1.1229
U.K.	.53230	.6713	...	.4212	.04952	.00447	.47293
Euro	.79300	...	1.4897	.62744	.07377	.00666	.70452
U.S.	...	1.2610	1.8785	.79120	.09302	.00840	.88840

Source: Reuters

Wall Street Journal © 2006

EXAMPLE

$$\$299 \times .53230 = \boxed{159.1577} \text{ pounds}$$

Check   159.1577 pounds × 1.8785 = $298.98 (cost of iPod in New York City)

Multiplication and Division Shortcuts for Decimals

The shortcut steps that follow show how to solve multiplication and division problems quickly involving multiples of 10 (10,100, 1,000, 10,000, etc.).

SHORTCUTS FOR MULTIPLES OF 10
Multiplication
Step 1. Count the zeros in the multiplier.
Step 2. Move the decimal point in the multiplicand the same number of places to the right as you have zeros in the multiplier.
Division
Step 1. Count the zeros in the divisor.
Step 2. Move the decimal point in the dividend the same number of places to the left as you have zeros in the divisor.

In multiplication, the answers are *larger* than the original number.

Ric Francis/AP Wide World

EXAMPLE If Toyota spends $60,000 for magazine advertising, what is the total value if it spends this same amount for 10 years? What would be the total cost?

$60,000 × 10 = $600,000   (1 place to the right)

OTHER EXAMPLES
6.89 × 10 = 68.9   (1 place to the right)

6.89 × 100 = 689.   (2 places to the right)

6.89 × 1,000 = 6,890.   (3 places to the right)

In division, the answers are *smaller* than the original number.

EXAMPLES
6.89 ÷ 10 = .689   (1 place to the left)

6.89 ÷ 100 = .0689   (2 places to the left)

6.89 ÷ 1,000 = .00689   (3 places to the left)

6.89 ÷ 10,000 = .000689   (4 places to the left)

Next, let's dissect and solve a word problem.

How to Dissect and Solve a Word Problem

The Word Problem May O'Mally went to Sears to buy wall-to-wall carpet. She needs 101.3 square yards for downstairs, 16.3 square yards for the upstairs bedrooms, and 6.2 square yards for the halls. The carpet cost $14.55 per square yard. The padding cost $3.25 per square yard. Sears quoted an installation charge of $6.25 per square yard. What was May O'Mally's total cost?

By completing the following blueprint aid, we will slowly dissect this word problem. Note that before solving the problem, we gather the facts, identify what we are solving for, and list the steps that must be completed before finding the final answer, along with any key points we should remember. Let's go to it!

The facts	Solving for?	Steps to take	Key points
Carpet needed: 101.3 sq. yd.; 16.3 sq. yd.; 6.2 sq. yd. *Costs:* Carpet, $14.55 per sq. yd.; padding, $3.25 per sq. yd.; installation, $6.25 per sq. yd.	Total cost of carpet	Total square yards × Cost per square yard = Total cost.	Align decimals. Round answer to nearest cent.

Steps to solving problem

1. Calculate the total number of square yards.

101.3
16.3
6.2
___
123.8 square yards

2. Calculate the total cost per square yard.

$14.55
3.25
6.25
___
$24.05

3. Calculate the total cost of carpet.

123.8 × $24.05 = $2,977.39

It's time to check your progress.

LU 3–2 **PRACTICE QUIZ**

Complete this **Practice Quiz** to see how you are doing

1. Rearrange vertically and add:
   14, .642, 9.34, 15.87321
2. Rearrange and subtract:
   28.1549 − .885
3. Multiply and round the answer to the nearest tenth:
   28.53 × 17.4
4. Divide and round to the nearest hundredth:
   2,182 ÷ 2.83

Complete by the shortcut method:

5. 14.28 × 100   6. 9,680 ÷ 1,000   7. 9,812 ÷ 10,000

8. Could you help Mel decide which product is the "better buy"?
   Dog food A: $9.01 for 64 ounces   **Dog food B:** $7.95 for 50 ounces

Round to the nearest cent as needed.

9. At Avis Rent-A-Car, the cost per day to rent a medium-size car is $39.99 plus 29 cents per mile. What will it cost to rent this car for 2 days if you drive 602.3 miles? Since the solution shows a completed blueprint, you might use a blueprint also.

10. A trip to Mexico cost 6,000 pesos. What would this be in U.S. dollars? Check your answer.

✓ **Solutions**

1. 14.00000
   .64200
   9.34000
   15.87321
   _____
   39.85521

2. 28.1549
   − .8850
   _____
   27.2699

3.   28.53
    × 17.4
    _____
    11 412
    199 71
    285 3
    _____
    496.422   = 496.4

4.   771.024 = 771.02
   2.83)218200.000
        1981
        ____
        2010
        1981
        ____
         290
         283
         ____
         7 00
         5 66
         ____
         1 340
         1 132

5. 14.28 = 1,428   6. 9.680 = 9.680   7. .9812 = .9812

8. **A:** $9.01 ÷ 64 = $.14   **B:** $7.95 ÷ 50 = $.16   Buy A.

9. Avis Rent-A-Car total rental charge:

The facts	Solving for?	Steps to take	Key points
Cost per day, $39.99. 29 cents per mile. Drove 602.3 miles. 2-day rental.	Total rental charge.	Total cost for 2 days' rental + Total cost of driving = Total rental charge.	In multiplication, count the number of decimal places. Starting from right to left in the product, insert decimal in appropriate place. Round to nearest cent.

Steps to solving problem

1. Calculate total costs for 2 days' rental. $39.99 × 2 = $79.98

2. Calculate the total cost of driving. $.29 × 602.3 = $174.667 = $174.67

3. Calculate the total rental charge.
$ 79.98
+ 174.67
$254.65

10. 6,000 × $.09302 = $558.12

Check $558.12 × 10.7504 = 6,000.01 pesos due to rounding

LU 3–2a   EXTRA PRACTICE QUIZ

Need more practice? Try this **Extra Practice Quiz** (check figures in Chapter Organizer, p. 78)

1. Rearrange vertically and add:
16, .831, 9.85, 17.8321

2. Rearrange and subtract:
29.5832 − .998

3. Multiply and round the answer to the nearest tenth:
29.64 × 18.2

4. Divide and round to the nearest hundredth:
3,824 ÷ 4.94

Complete by the shortcut method:

5. 17.48 × 100   **6.** 8,432 ÷ 1,000   **7.** 9,643 ÷ 10,000

8. Could you help Mel decide which product is the "better buy"?
Dog food A: $8.88 for 64 ounces   **Dog food B:** $7.25 for 50 ounces

Round to the nearest cent as needed:

9. At Avis Rent-A-Car, the cost per day to rent a medium-size car is $29.99 plus 22 cents per mile. What will it cost to rent this car for 2 days if you drive 709.8 miles?

10. A trip to Mexico costs 7,000 pesos. What would this be in U.S. dollars? Check your answer.

CHAPTER ORGANIZER AND STUDY GUIDE
WITH CHECK FIGURES FOR EXTRA PRACTICE QUIZZES

Topic	Key point, procedure, formula	Example(s) to illustrate situation
Identifying place value, p. 66	$10, 1, \frac{1}{10}, \frac{1}{100}, \frac{1}{1,000}$, etc.	.439 in thousandths place value
Rounding decimals, p. 67	1. Identify place value of digit you want to round. 2. If digit to right of identified digit in Step 1 is 5 or more, increase identified digit by 1; if less than 5, do not change identified digit. 3. Drop all digits to right of identified digit.	.875 rounded to nearest tenth = .9 Identified digit

(continues)

CHAPTER ORGANIZER AND STUDY GUIDE
WITH CHECK FIGURES FOR EXTRA PRACTICE QUIZZES (continued)

Topic	Key point, procedure, formula	Example(s) to illustrate situation
Converting decimal fractions to decimals, p. 68	1. Decimal fraction has a denominator with multiples of 10. Count number of zeros in denominator. 2. Zeros show how many places are in the decimal.	$\frac{8}{1,000} = .008$ $\frac{6}{10,000} = .0006$
Converting proper fractions to decimals, p. 68	1. Divide numerator of fraction by its denominator. 2. Round as necessary.	$\frac{1}{3}$ (to nearest tenth) = $.3$
Converting mixed numbers to decimals, p. 69	1. Convert fractional part of the mixed number to a decimal. 2. Add converted fractional part to whole number.	$6\frac{1}{4}$ $\frac{1}{4} = .25 + 6 = 6.25$
Converting pure and mixed decimals to decimal fractions, p. 69	1. Place digits to right of decimal point in numerator of fraction. 2. Put 1 in denominator. 3. Add zeros to denominator, depending on decimal places of original number. For mixed decimals, add fraction to whole number.	.984 (3 places) 1. $\frac{984}{}$ 2. $\frac{984}{1}$ 3. $\frac{984}{1,000}$
Adding and subtracting decimals, p. 71	1. Vertically write and align numbers on decimal points. 2. Add or subtract digits, starting with right column and moving to the left. 3. Align decimal point in answer with above decimal points.	Add 1.3 + 2 + .4 1.3 2.0 .4 3.7 Subtract 5 − 3.9 $\overset{4\ 10}{5.0}$ -3.9 1.1
Multiplying decimals, p. 72	1. Multiply numbers, ignoring decimal points. 2. Count and total number of decimal places in multiplier and multiplicand. 3. Starting at right in the product, count to the left the number of decimal places totaled in Step 2. Insert decimal point. If number of places greater than space in answer, add zeros.	2.48 (2 places) × .018 (3 places) 1 984 2 48 .04464
Dividing a decimal by a whole number, p. 73	1. Place decimal point in quotient directly above the decimal point in dividend. 2. Divide as usual.	$\begin{array}{r} 1.1 \\ 42\overline{)46.2} \\ 42 \\ \hline 42 \\ 42 \end{array}$
Dividing if the divisor is a decimal, p. 73	1. Make divisor a whole number by moving decimal point to the right. 2. Move decimal point in dividend to the right the same number of places as in Step 1. 3. Place decimal point in quotient above decimal point in dividend. Divide as usual.	$\begin{array}{r} 14.2 \\ 2.9\overline{)41.39} \\ 29 \\ \hline 123 \\ 116 \\ \hline 79 \\ 58 \\ \hline 21 \end{array}$

(continues)

CHAPTER ORGANIZER AND STUDY GUIDE
WITH CHECK FIGURES FOR EXTRA PRACTICE QUIZZES (concluded)

Topic	Key point, procedure, formula	Example(s) to illustrate situation
Shortcuts on multiplication and division of decimals, p. 74	When multiplying by 10, 100, 1,000, and so on, move decimal point in multiplicand the same number of places to the right as you have zeros in multiplier. For division, move decimal point to the left.	$4.85 \times 100 = $ 485 $4.85 \div 100 = $ .0485
KEY TERMS	Decimal, *p. 65* Mixed decimal, *p. 69* Rounding decimals, *p. 67* Decimal fraction, *p. 67* Pure decimal, *p. 69* Decimal point, *p. 65* Repeating decimal, *p. 67*	

CHECK FIGURES FOR EXTRA PRACTICE QUIZZES WITH PAGE REFERENCES	**LU 3–1a (p. 70)**
	 1. .309 8. $\frac{938}{1,000}$
	 2. Hundredths
	 3. Ten-thousandths 9. $17\frac{95}{100}$
	 4. A. .8
	    B. .844 10. $\frac{325}{10,000}$
	 5. A. .9
	    B. .879 11. .13
	 6. .0008 12. .57
	 7. .00016 13. 13.11
		LU 3–2a (p. 76)
		 1. 44.5131 6. 8.432
		 2. 28.5852 7. .9643
		 3. 539.4 8. Buy A $.14
		 4. 774.09 9. $216.14
		 5. 1,748 10. $651.14

Note: For how to dissect and solve a word problem, see page 74.

Critical Thinking Discussion Questions

1. What are the steps for rounding decimals? Federal income tax forms allow the taxpayer to round each amount to the nearest dollar. Do you agree with this?

2. Explain how to convert fractions to decimals. If 1 out of 20 people buys a Land Rover, how could you write an advertisement in decimals?

3. Explain why .07, .70, and .700 are not equal. Assume you take a family trip to Disney World that covers 500 miles. Show that $\frac{8}{10}$ of the trip, or .8 of the trip, represents 400 miles.

4. Explain the steps in the addition or subtraction of decimals. Visit a car dealership and find the difference between two sticker prices. Be sure to check each sticker price for accuracy. Should you always pay the sticker price?

Name _____ Date _____

DRILL PROBLEMS

Identify the place value for the following

3–1. 8.56932

3–2. 293.9438

Round the following as indicated:

	Tenth	Hundredth	Thousandth
3–3. .7582			
3–4. 4.9832			
3–5. 5.8312			
3–6. 6.8415			
3–7. 6.5555			
3–8. 75.9913			

Round the following to the nearest cent:

3–9. $4,822.775

3–10. $4,892.046

Convert the following types of decimal fractions to decimals (round to nearest hundredth as needed):

3–11. $\dfrac{9}{100}$

3–12. $\dfrac{3}{10}$

3–13. $\dfrac{91}{1,000}$

3–14. $\dfrac{910}{1,000}$

3–15. $\dfrac{64}{100}$

3–16. $\dfrac{979}{1,000}$

3–17. $14\dfrac{91}{100}$

Convert the following decimals to fractions. Do not reduce to lowest terms.

3–18. .3

3–19. .62

3–20. .006

3–21. .0125

3–22. .609

3–23. .825

3–24. .9999

3–25. .7065

Convert the following to mixed numbers. Do not reduce to the lowest terms.

3–26. 7.4

3–27. 28.48

3–28. 6.025

Write the decimal equivalent of the following:

3–29. Four thousandths

3–30. Three hundred three and two hundredths

3–31. Eighty-five ten thousandths

3–32. Seven hundred seventy-five thousandths

Rearrange the following and add:

3–33. .115, 10.8318, 4.7, 802.4811

3–34. .005, 2,002.181, 795.41, 14.0, .184

Rearrange the following and subtract:

3–35. 9.2 − 5.8

3–36. 7 − 2.0815

3–37. 3.4 − 1.08

Estimate by rounding all the way and multiply the following (do not round final answer):

3–38. 6.24×3.9

Estimate

3–39. $.413 \times 3.07$

Estimate

3–40. 675×1.92

Estimate

3–41. $4.9 \times .825$

Estimate

Divide the following and round to the nearest hundredth:

3–42. $.8931 \div 3$

3–43. $29.432 \div .0012$

3–44. $.0065 \div .07$

3–45. $7,742.1 \div 48$

3–46. $8.95 \div 1.18$

3–47. $2,600 \div .381$

Convert the following to decimals and round to the nearest hundredth:

3–48. $\dfrac{1}{8}$

3–49. $\dfrac{1}{25}$

3–50. $\dfrac{5}{6}$

3–51. $\dfrac{5}{8}$

Complete these multiplications and divisions by the shortcut method (do not do any written calculations):

3–52. $96.7 \div 10$

3–53. $258.5 \div 100$

3–54. $8.51 \times 1,000$

3–55. $.86 \div 100$

3–56. 9.015×100

3–57. 48.6×10

3–58. 750×10

3–59. $3,950 \div 1,000$

3–60. $8.45 \div 10$

3–61. $7.9132 \times 1,000$

WORD PROBLEMS

As needed, round answers to the nearest cent.

3–62. A Ford Explorer costs $ 30,000. What would be the cost in pounds in London? Use the currency table and check your answer.

3–63. Ken Griffey, Jr. got 7 hits out of 12 at bats. What was his batting average to the nearest thousandths place?

3–64. An article in *The Boston Globe* dated January 11, 2007 reported ticket prices for Rod Stewart's February 3rd concert at the TD Banknorth Garden at $125 per ticket. In addition to the price of a ticket, there is a $14.80 convenience charge, a $2.50 facility fee, and a $2.50 electronic delivery fee. Richard Evans purchased 4 tickets to the concert. What was Richard's total cost for the tickets?

3–65. At Wal-Mart, Alice Rose purchased 19.10 yards of ribbon. Each yard costs 89 cents. What was the total cost of the ribbon?

3–66. Douglas Noel went to Home Depot and bought 4 doors at $42.99 each and 6 bags of fertilizer at $8.99 per bag. What was the total cost to Douglas? If Douglas had $300 in his pocket, what does he have left to spend?

3–67. The stock of Intel has a high of $30.25 today. It closed at $28.85. How much did the stock drop from its high?

3–68. Ed Weld is traveling by car to a comic convention in San Diego. His company will reimburse him $.39 per mile. If Ed travels 906.5 miles, how much will Ed receive from his company?

3–69. Mark Ogara rented a truck from Avis Rent-A-Car for the weekend (2 days). The base rental price was $29.95 per day plus $14\frac{1}{2}$ cents per mile. Mark drove 410.85 miles. How much does Mark owe?

3–70. The *Houston Chronicle* on January 13, 2007 reported on Texans' ticket prices to be charged Texas football fans for the 2007 season. The average ticket price will be $60.63, an increase of $2.88 from last year. Before the 2006 season, 22 teams increased ticket prices. The average ticket price was $62.38 with the New England Patriots having the highest average ticket at $90.90 per game. **(a)** What was the price of ticket to a Texan game last year? **(b)** How much below the average is the Texans' ticket. **(c)** How much above the average are the Patriots tickets? **(d)** What is the average price between Texans' tickets and the Patriots' tickets? Round to the nearest hundredth.

3–71. Pete Allan bought a scooter on the Web for $99.99. He saw the same scooter in the mall for $108.96. How much did Pete save by buying on the Web?

3–72. Russell is preparing the daily bank deposit for his coffee shop. Before the deposit, the coffee shop had a checking account balance of $3,185.66. The deposit contains the following checks:

| No. 1 | $ 99.50 | No. 3 | $8.75 |
| No. 2 | 110.35 | No. 4 | 6.83 |

Russell included $820.55 in currency with the deposit. What is the coffee shop's new balance, assuming Russell writes no new checks?

3–73. The *Chattanooga Times/Free Press* ran a story on US Airways offering lower fares for Chattanooga, Tennessee–New York City flights. US Airways Express is offering a $190 round-trip fare for those who buy tickets in the next couple of weeks. Ticket prices had been running between $230 and $330 round-trip. Mark VanLoh, Airport Authority president, said the new fare is lower than the $219 ticket price offered by Southwest Airlines. How much would a family of four save using US Airways versus Southwest Airlines?

3–74. Randi went to Lowes to buy wall-to-wall carpeting. She needs 110.8 square yards for downstairs, 31.8 square yards for the halls, and 161.9 square yards for the bedrooms upstairs. Randi chose a shag carpet that costs $14.99 per square yard. She ordered foam padding at $3.10 per square yard. The carpet installers quoted Randi a labor charge of $3.75 per square yard. What will the total job cost Randi?

3–75. Art Norton bought 4 new Aquatred tires at Goodyear for $89.99 per tire. Goodyear charged $3.05 per tire for mounting, $2.95 per tire for valve stems, and $3.80 per tire for balancing. If Art paid no sales tax, what was his total cost for the 4 tires?

3–76. Shelly is shopping for laundry detergent, mustard, and canned tuna. She is trying to decide which of two products is the better buy. Using the following information, can you help Shelly?

Laundry detergent A	**Mustard A**	**Canned tuna A**
$2.00 for 37 ounces	$.88 for 6 ounces	$1.09 for 6 ounces

Laundry detergent B	**Mustard B**	**Canned tuna B**
$2.37 for 38 ounces	$1.61 for $12\frac{1}{2}$ ounces	$1.29 for $8\frac{3}{4}$ ounces

3–77. Roger bought season tickets for weekend games to professional basketball games. The cost was $945.60. The season package included 36 home games. What is the average price of the tickets per game? Round to the nearest cent. Marcelo, Roger's friend, offered to buy 4 of the tickets from Roger. What is the total amount Roger should receive?

3–78. A nurse was to give each of her patients a 1.32-unit dosage of a prescribed drug. The total remaining units of the drug at the hospital pharmacy were 53.12. The nurse has 38 patients. Will there be enough dosages for all her patients?

3–79. Audrey Long went to Japan and bought an animation cel of Mickey Mouse. The price was 25,000 yen. What is the price in U.S. dollars? Check your answer.

ADDITIONAL SET OF WORD PROBLEMS

3–80. On Monday, the stock of IBM closed at $88.95. At the end of trading on Tuesday, IBM closed at $94.65. How much did the price of stock increase from Monday to Tuesday?

3–81. Tie Yang bought season tickets to the Boston Pops for $698.55. The season package included 38 performances. What is the average price of the tickets per performance? Round to nearest cent. Sam, Tie's friend, offered to buy 4 of the tickets from Tie. What is the total amount Tie should receive?

3–82. Morris Katz bought 4 new tires at Goodyear for $95.49 per tire. Goodyear also charged Morris $2.50 per tire for mounting, $2.40 per tire for valve stems, and $3.95 per tire for balancing. Assume no tax. What was Morris's total cost for the 4 tires?

3–83. The *Denver Post* reported that Xcel Energy is revising customer charges for monthly residential electric bills and gas bills. Electric bills will increase $3.32. Gas bills will decrease $1.74 a month. (**a**) What is the resulting new monthly increase for the entire bill? (**b**) If Xcel serves 2,350 homes, how much additional revenue would Excel receive each month?

3–84. Steven is traveling to a computer convention by car. His company will reimburse him $.29 per mile. If Steven travels 890.5 miles, how much will he receive from his company?

3–85. Gracie went to Home Depot to buy wall-to-wall carpeting for her house. She needs 104.8 square yards for downstairs, 17.4 square yards for halls, and 165.8 square yards for the upstairs bedrooms. Gracie chose a shag carpet that costs $13.95 per square yard. She ordered foam padding at $2.75 per square yard. The installers quoted Gracie a labor cost of $5.75 per square yard in installation. What will the total job cost Gracie?

3–86. On February 1, 2007 *The Kansas City Star,* reported the Dow Jones Industrial Average rose 98.38 points from the previous day, and closed at 12,621.69. The blue-chip index set a trading high, at 12,657.02 and just missed the record of 12,621.77 points. (**a**) What were closing points on January 31, 2007? (**b**) This closing on February 1 was how many points from the record? (**c**) What were the average points from January 31, 2007's lowest to February 1, 2007's highest? Round to the nearest hundredth.

CHALLENGE PROBLEMS

3–87. The *Miami Herald* ran a story on Carnival Cruise's profit per share. For the third quarter, Carnival earned $734.3 million with 815.9 million shares of stock outstanding. Last year, earnings were $500.8 million, or 85 cents a share. (**a**) How much were the earnings per shareholder for the third quarter? Round to the nearest cent. (**b**) How many shareholders did Carnival Cruise have last year? Round to the nearest hundred thousands. Check your answers.

3–88. Jill and Frank decided to take a long weekend in New York. City Hotel has a special getaway weekend for $79.95. The price is per person per night, based on double occupancy. The hotel has a minimum two-night stay. For this price, Jill and Frank will receive $50 credit toward their dinners at City's Skylight Restaurant. Also included in the package is a $3.99 credit per person toward breakfast for two each morning.

Since Jill and Frank do not own a car, they plan to rent a car. The car rental agency charges $19.95 a day with an additional charge of $.22 a mile and $1.19 per gallon of gas used. The gas tank holds 24 gallons.

From the following facts, calculate the total expenses of Jill and Frank (round all answers to nearest hundredth or cent as appropriate). Assume no taxes.

Car rental (2 days):		Dinner cost at Skylight	$182.12
Beginning odometer reading	4,820	Breakfast for two:	
Ending odometer reading	4,940	Morning No. 1	24.17
Beginning gas tank: $\frac{3}{4}$ full.		Morning No. 2	26.88
Gas tank on return: $\frac{1}{2}$ full.			
Tank holds 24 gallons.			

 SUMMARY PRACTICE TEST

1. Add the following by translating the verbal form to the decimal equivalent. *(p. 71)*

Three hundred thirty-eight and seven hundred five thousandths
Nineteen and fifty-nine hundredths
Five and four thousandths
Seventy-five hundredths
Four hundred three and eight tenths

Convert the following decimal fractions to decimals. *(p. 68)*

2. $\dfrac{7}{10}$

3. $\dfrac{7}{100}$

4. $\dfrac{7}{1,000}$

Convert the following to proper fractions or mixed numbers. Do not reduce to the lowest terms. *(p. 68)*

5. .9

6. 6.97

7. .685

Convert the following fractions to decimals (or mixed decimals) and round to the nearest hundredth as needed. *(p. 68)*

8. $\dfrac{2}{7}$

9. $\dfrac{1}{8}$

10. $4\dfrac{4}{7}$

11. $\dfrac{1}{13}$

12. Rearrange the following decimals and add. *(p. 71)*

5.93,　11.862,　284.0382,　88.44

13. Subtract the following and round to the nearest tenth. *(p. 71)*

13.111 − 3.872

14. Multiply the following and round to the nearest hundredth. *(p. 72)*

7.4821 × 15.861

15. Divide the following and round to the nearest hundredth. *(p. 73)*

203,942 ÷ 5.88

Complete the following by the shortcut method. *(p. 74)*

16. 62.94 × 1,000

17. 8,322,249.821 × 100

18. The average pay of employees is $795.88 per week. Lee earns $820.44 per week. How much is Lee's pay over the average? *(p. 71)*

19. Lowes reimburses Ron $.49 per mile. Ron submitted a travel log for a total of 1,910.81 miles. How much will Lowes reimburse Ron? Round to the nearest cent. *(p. 72)*

20. Lee Chin bought 2 new car tires from Michelin for $182.11 per tire. Michelin also charged Lee $3.99 per tire for mounting, $2.50 per tire for valve stems, and $4.10 per tire for balancing. What is Lee's final bill? *(p. 72)*

21. Could you help Judy decide which of the following products is cheaper per ounce? *(p. 73)*

Canned fruit A　　　　　　　　　　　　**Canned fruit B**

$.37 for 3 ounces　　　　　　　　　　　　$.58 for $3\frac{3}{4}$ ounces

22. Paula Smith bought an iPod for 350 euros. What is this price in U.S. dollars? *(p. 73)*

23. Google stock traded at a high of $438.22 and closed at $410.12. How much did the stock fall from its high? *(p. 71)*

TRAVEL SLEUTH | You don't have to break the bank to phone home from the Alps. *By Sean O'Neill*

Call **U.S.** for less

During a recent trip to Germany and Austria, I called the States five times, using pay phones and charging my Visa card. I returned home to find a $105 bill for a 20-minute call and a $192 bill for all my other calls, which each lasted fewer than ten minutes. What might I have done differently? —**RAY TAYLOR**, *Bend, Ore.*

Ouch. Your credit card is one of many that charge sky-high rates for placing international phone calls. For your next trip, try this: If you own a cell phone, ask your wireless carrier if you can use it overseas for a low rate. Cingular (the nation's largest provider) and T-Mobile have adopted GSM technology, the standard for much of the world. If you own a relatively new phone and use one of these providers, you can usually place calls from overseas. Check first

with your provider, and ask to buy a temporary plan that will allow you to call home cheaply while traveling abroad. Cingular, for instance, lets many of its customers call home from several European countries at rates of about $1 a minute, plus a fee of about $6 for each month of travel.

Or buy a prepaid phone card that lets you call for rates of about 10 cents to 15 cents per minute. We like the $20 cards from Nobel (www.nobel.com) and $10 cards from OneSuite (www.onesuite.com). You can use any phone overseas, but note that a hotel phone may come with a high fee.

REBOOK FOR LESS

To get the lowest fares, I usually need to book air tickets well in advance. But my next trip will be to celebrate the birth of my granddaughter, and I can't know for sure the date I'll be

flying cross-country to New York City. How can I book a cheap ticket today that will let me change my flight dates later without paying hefty fees? —**CHARLES KUTTNER**, *Portland, Ore.*

Congratulations on becoming a grandparent. If you can make an educated guess about when you're most likely to travel, you'll save by booking early on a discount airline. In the best case, you'll have a cheap ticket and you'll arrive at the right time. In the worst case, you'll need to rebook, your new flight date will come with a higher round-trip fare—which is typical—and you'll have to pay the difference plus a rebooking fee.

But here's why booking with a discounter is a good idea, even if a discounter and a major airline offer similar advance ticket prices: You'll face lower 11th-hour fares *and* the rebooking fee will be smaller. Major carriers typically charge $100 to rebook, while top discounters charge less. Rebooking fees for ATA are $50 and for JetBlue, $30. Southwest doesn't charge a fee.

Given that you know the due date of your granddaughter, we suggest you book your trip from Portland to New York City now (more than a month ahead). You'll pay $403 before taxes and fees of $50 on JetBlue. In the past year on this route, fares booked just days before departure weren't much higher than $400 before taxes, says FareCompare.com, a site that gives you the lowest average fares available on most routes. We estimate you'll save between $75 and $300 by rebooking on JetBlue instead of a major airline.

What if no discounter serves your route? If you have to go with a major airline and you need to rebook, ask the agent to waive the rebooking fee when you call to change flight dates. Agents often have discretion to waive fees—but you'll always pay the difference between the old and new fare.

Have a money-related travel question? Write us at travelsleuth@kiplinger.com.

JULIETTE BORDA

BUSINESS MATH ISSUE

Prepaid phone cards do not really save you money.

1. List the key points of the article and information to support your position.
2. Write a group defense of your position using math calculations to support your view.

Slater's Business Math Scrapbook

with Internet Application

Putting Your Skills to Work

Revenue Search

In Latest Deal, Google Steps Further Into World of Old Media

Internet Giant Expands Role As an Advertising Broker; Automating Radio Sales

Next Target May Be Television

By KEVIN J. DELANEY

Google Inc. has brought in billions of dollars in revenue by brokering advertisements that appear on Web sites. Now it is taking its ad machine beyond the Internet in an ambitious quest to place ads in traditional media such as newspapers and radio.

The move could open enormous new markets to the search company. But it could also test the limits of Google's automated ad-placement technology that brought it more than $3 billion in online ad revenue in 2004.

Following the Money

Estimated U.S. spending on advertising for 2005, in billions:

TV	$55.4
Newspapers	$50.2
Direct Mail	$44.5
Magazines	$23.9
Radio	$20.6
Internet	$10.0
Outdoor	$5.7
Cinema	$0.4
Other	$45.8

Source: ZenithOptimedia

Wall Street Journal © 2006

	U.K. retail price (converted into dollars)	U.S. retail price
Burberry short raincoat	£465.00 ($914.14)	$695.00
iPod Nano special edition (8GB)	£169.00 ($332.24)	$249.00
Tiffany Lace bracelet	£6,775.00 ($13,318.97)	$9,800.00
Dior J'Adore 50ml	£39.50 ($77.65)	$58.00
Nintendo Wii	£179.99 ($353.84)	$249.99

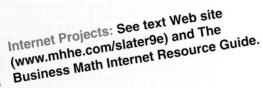

CHAPTER 4

Banking

LEARNING UNIT OBJECTIVES

LU 4–1: The Checking Account

- Define and state the purpose of signature cards, checks, deposit slips, check stubs, check registers, and endorsements (*pp. 89–91*).
- Correctly prepare deposit slips and write checks (*pp. 91–92*).

LU 4–2: Bank Statement and Reconciliation Process; Trends in Online Banking

- Define and state the purpose of the bank statement (*pp. 93–94*).
- Complete a check register and a bank reconciliation (*pp. 96–98*).
- Explain the trends in online banking (*pp. 98–100*).

Tricks Of the Trade

Money Adviser Pays Bills

Allison Shipley, an adviser to high-net-worth clients at PricewaterhouseCoopers' Private Company Services practice, once spent long hours in front of the computer reconciling the family checkbook. But Ms. Shipley freed herself from that with a simple strategy: She puts as many bills as possible on automatic bill paying using a single credit card. This way she not only saves time from writing checks (now just two a month), but she accrues credit-card reward points for a trip to Europe. For bills not covered by her card, Ms. Shipley has funds directly withdrawn from her checking account and sent to the companies, including her credit card. She spends a minute or two a day watching the running balances online to make sure they match the accounts' activity. She says she gets enough information about her family's spending from monthly statements. She prints online confirmations of bills paid and keeps them in separate files like car payments and electric bills.—*Sarah Tilton*

Wall Street Journal © 2005

Mark Lennihan/AP Wide World

Bank of America To Pay $2.5 Billion For China Foothold

Bank of America Corp., moving to make one of the largest single foreign investments to date in China's fast-changing banking sector, said it has reached a deal to buy a stake in **China Construction Bank** for $2.5 billion.

Wall Street Journal © 2005

Too often people think their bank is their best friend. You should remember that your bank is a business. The banking industry is very competitive. Note in the *Wall Street Journal* clipping "Bank of America to Pay $2.5 Billion for China Foothold" how quickly the banking sectors are changing all over the world to be more competitive.

An important fixture in today's banking is the **automatic teller machine (ATM).** The ability to get instant cash is a convenience many bank customers enjoy. However, more than half of the ATM customers do not like to deposit checks because they are afraid the checks will not be correctly deposited to their account. Bank of America, Bank One, and Wells Fargo are testing new ATMs that accept a check, scan the check, and print a receipt with a photographic image of the check. When these machines are widely available, they will eliminate the fear of depositing checks.

The effect of using an ATM card is the same as using a **debit card**—both transactions result in money being immediately deducted from your checking account balance. As a result, debit cards have been called enhanced ATM cards or *check cards.* Often banks charge fees for these card transactions. The frequent complaints of bank customers have made many banks offer their ATMs as a free service, especially if customers use an ATM in the same network as their bank. Some banks charge fees for using another bank's ATM.

Remember that the use of debit cards involves planning. As *check cards,* you must be aware of your bank balance every time you use a debit card. Also, if you use a credit card instead of a debit card, you can only be held responsible for $50 of illegal charges; and during the time the credit card company investigates the illegal charges, they are removed from your account. However, with a debit card, this legal limit only applies if you report your card lost or stolen within two business days.

We should add that debit cards are profitable for banks. When shopping, if you use a debit card that does not require a personal identification number, the store pays a fee to the bank that issued the card—usually from 1.4 to 2 cents on the dollar.

This chapter begins with a discussion of the checking account. You will follow Molly Kate as she opens a checking account for Gracie's Natural Superstore and performs her banking transactions. Pay special attention to the procedure used by Gracie's to reconcile its checking account and bank statement. This information will help you reconcile your checkbook records with the bank's record of your account. The chapter concludes by discussing how the trends in online banking may affect your banking procedures.

Learning Unit 4–1: The Checking Account

A **check** or **draft** is a written order instructing a bank, credit union, or savings and loan institution to pay a designated amount of your money on deposit to a person or an organization. Checking accounts are offered to individuals and businesses. Businesses may be charged $.39 per check received for a business transaction. Note that the business checking account usually receives more services than the personal checking account.

Most small businesses depend on a checking account for efficient record keeping. In this learning unit you will follow the checking account procedures of a newly organized small business. You can use many of these procedures in your personal check writing. You will also learn about e-checks—a new trend.

Opening the Checking Account

Molly Kate, treasurer of Gracie's Natural Superstore, went to Ipswich Bank to open a business checking account. The bank manager gave Molly a **signature card.** The signature card contained space for the company's name and address, references, type of account, and the signature(s) of the person(s) authorized to sign checks. If necessary, the bank will use the signature card to verify that Molly signed the checks. Some companies authorize more than one person to sign checks or require more than one signature on a check.

FIGURE 4.1 **FIGURE 4.1** Deposit slip

Preprinted numbers in magnetic ink identify bank number, routing and sorting of the check, and Gracie's Natural Superstore account number

The 53-7058 is taken from the upper right corner of the check from the top part of the fraction. This number is known as the American Bankers Association transit number. The 53 identifies the city or state where the bank is located and the 7058 identifies the bank.

Molly then lists on a **deposit slip** (or deposit ticket) the checks and/or cash she is depositing in her company's business account. The bank gave Molly a temporary check-book to use until the company's printed checks arrived. Molly also will receive *preprinted* checking account deposit slips like the one shown in Figure 4.1. Since the deposit slips are in duplicate, Molly can keep a record of her deposit. Note that the increased use of making deposits at ATM machines has made it more convenient for people to make their deposits.

Writing business checks is similar to writing personal checks. Before writing any checks, however, you must understand the structure of a check and know how to write a check. Carefully study Figure 4.2. Note that the verbal amount written in the check should

FIGURE 4.2 The structure of a check

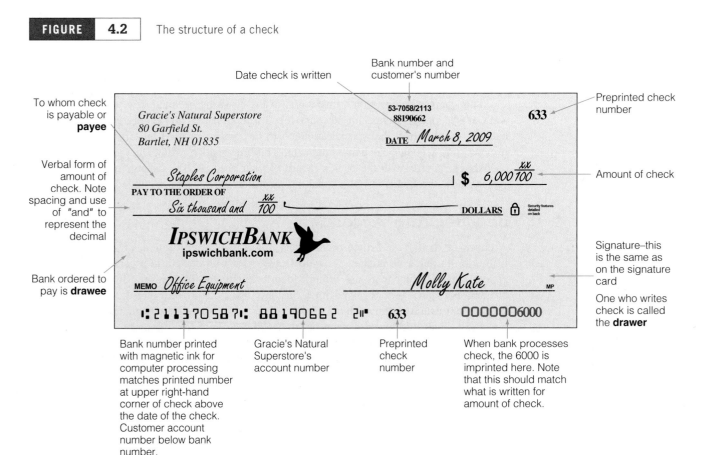

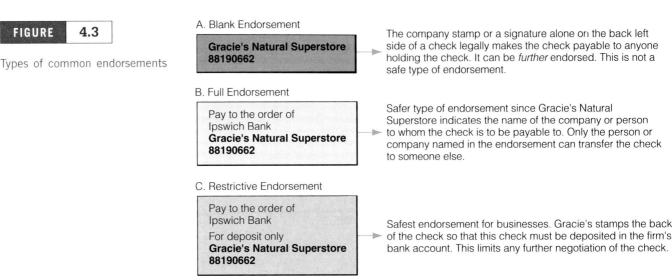

FIGURE   4.3

Types of common endorsements

A. Blank Endorsement

> **Gracie's Natural Superstore**
> **88190662**

The company stamp or a signature alone on the back left side of a check legally makes the check payable to anyone holding the check. It can be *further* endorsed. This is not a safe type of endorsement.

B. Full Endorsement

> Pay to the order of
> Ipswich Bank
> **Gracie's Natural Superstore**
> **88190662**

Safer type of endorsement since Gracie's Natural Superstore indicates the name of the company or person to whom the check is to be payable to. Only the person or company named in the endorsement can transfer the check to someone else.

C. Restrictive Endorsement

> Pay to the order of
> Ipswich Bank
> For deposit only
> **Gracie's Natural Superstore**
> **88190662**

Safest endorsement for businesses. Gracie's stamps the back of the check so that this check must be deposited in the firm's bank account. This limits any further negotiation of the check.

match the figure amount. If these two amounts are different, by law the bank uses the verbal amount. Also, note the bank imprint on the bottom right section of the check. When processing the check, the bank imprints the check's amount. This makes it easy to detect bank errors.

Using the Checking Account

Once the check is written, the writer must keep a record of the check. Knowing the amount of your written checks and the amount in the bank should help you avoid writing a bad check. Business checkbooks usually include attached **check stubs** to keep track of written checks. The sample check stub in the margin shows the information that the check writer will want to record. Some companies use a **check register** to keep their check records instead of check stubs. Figure 4.6 (p. 96) shows a check register with a ✔ column that is often used in balancing the checkbook with the bank statement (Learning Unit 4–2).

Gracie's Natural Superstore has had a busy week, and Molly must deposit its checks in the company's checking account. However, before she can do this, Molly must **endorse,** or sign, the back left side of the checks. Figure 4.3 explains the three types of check endorsements: **blank endorsement, full endorsement,** and **restrictive endorsement.** These endorsements transfer Gracie's ownership to the bank, which collects the money from the person or company issuing the check. Federal Reserve regulation limits all endorsements to the top $1\frac{1}{2}$ inches of the trailing edge on the back left side of the check.

After the bank receives Molly's deposit slip, shown in Figure 4.1 (p. 90), it increases (or credits) Gracie's account by $2,000. Often Molly leaves the deposit in a locked bag in a night depository. Then the bank credits (increases) Gracie's account when it processes the deposit on the next working day.

E-Checks—A New Trend

Before concluding this unit, let's look at a new trend using e-checks. In the *Wall Street Journal* clipping "Taking Rain Check on 'E-Checks,'" p. 92, we see that retailers are now trying to get your bank account number and "routing" number at the bottom of your checks so bills can be paid directly from your bank account when your bills are due.

Check Stub

It should be completed before the check is written.

No.	633		$	6000 $\frac{00}{100}$
March 8			20	*09*
To	*Staples Corp,*			
For	*Other Furniture*			

	DOLLARS	CENTS
BALANCE	*14,416*	*24*
AMT. DEPOSITED		
TOTAL	*14,416*	*24*
AMT. THIS CHECK	*6,000*	*00*
BALANCE FORWARD	*8,416*	*24*

Green Thumb / *By Ron Lieber*

Taking Rain Check on 'E-Checks'

More Retailers Ask for Your Bank-Account Info—Here's Why

RETAILERS NOW WANT to siphon money straight out of your bank account when you reach the checkout counter—a move that saves them money, but may cost you in other ways.

This process—known variously as e-check, ACH (which stands for automated clearing house) and direct debit—has been around for a number of years. It's common among utilities and others that send out monthly bills: They ask for your bank-account number and the "routing" number at the bottom of your checks, then withdraw what you owe when your bill's due.

Now, other retailers are getting into the game. Last month, **Amazon.com** Inc. began inviting customers to "pay directly from your bank account" as a payment option. Also in October, Stop&Shop, a unit of **Ahold** NV, started testing a system in 12 grocery stores that links customers' loyalty cards to their checking accounts. **Continental Airlines** has allowed e-check payments on its Web site for just over a year.

Check Mate

Some retailers now let customers give them bank-account information and have money withdrawn for purchases.

■ **Pluses:** It costs retailers less money; you don't need plastic to shop

■ **Minuses:** Can't earn rewards for using credit card or borrow against it to fund a shopping spree

Cash, e-check, or credit? Send your preferences to ron.lieber@wsj.com.

Wall Street Journal © 2005

Let's check your understanding of the first unit in this chapter.

LU 4–1 **PRACTICE QUIZ**

Complete this **Practice Quiz** to see how you are doing

Complete the following check and check stub for Long Company. Note the $9,500.60 balance brought forward on check stub No. 113. You must make a $690.60 deposit on May 3. Sign the check for Roland Small.

Date	Check no.	Amount	Payable to	For
June 5, 2009	113	$83.76	Angel Corporation	Rent

No. _113_ $ _____
_____ 20 ____
To _____
For _____

	DOLLARS	CENTS
BALANCE	9,500	60
AMT. DEPOSITED		
TOTAL		
AMT. THIS CHECK		
BALANCE FORWARD		

Long Company
22 Aster Rd.
Salem, MA 01970

No. 113

PAY
TO THE
ORDER
OF _____ $ _____

_____ 20 ____   5-13/110

_____ DOLLARS

IPSWICHBANK
ipswichbank.com

MEMO_____

⑆011000138⑆   14 0380 113

✓ Solution with page reference to check your progress

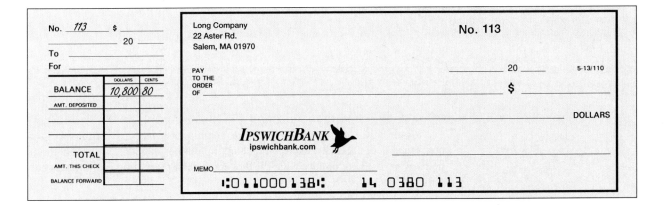

LU 4–1a	EXTRA PRACTICE QUIZ

Need more practice? Try this **Extra Practice Quiz** (check figures in Chapter Organizer, p. 101)

Complete the following check and stub for Long Company. Note the $10,800.80 balance brought forward on check stub No. 113. You must make an $812.88 deposit on May 3. Sign the check for Roland Small.

Date	**Check No.**	**Amount**	**Payable to**	**For**
July 8, 2009	113	$79.88	Lowe Corp	Advertising

Learning Unit 4–2: Bank Statement and Reconciliation Process; Trends in Online Banking

This learning unit is divided into two sections: (1) bank statement and reconciliation process, and (2) trends in online banking. The bank statement discussion will teach you why it was important for Gracie's Natural Superstore to reconcile its checkbook balance with the balance reported on its bank balance. Note that you can also use this reconciliation process in reconciling your personal checking account and avoiding the expensive error of an overdrawn account.

To introduce you to the "Trends in Online Banking" section, we have included the following *Wall Street Journal* clipping "Financial Institutions Give Cash to Induce Customers to Use Web-Based Services," p. 94. As you probably know, financial institutions favor online banking because it is less expensive for them.

Financial Institutions Give Cash to Induce Customers To Use Web-Based Services

By JENNIFER SARANOW

Financial institutions, eager to get more consumers to pay their bills online, are offering a new incentive: cash.

Citigroup Inc.'s Citibank introduced a promotion in October offering as much as $200 to new online bill-paying customers, depending on the number of bills they pay electronically. The promotion runs until the end of the year.

FAMILY FINANCE

At Wells Fargo & Co., customers in certain markets who are new to the service can get $10 if they pay at least one bill online by January. E*Trade Financial Corp. is paying $25 to customers who pay at least two bills online and hold specific types of accounts. Last month, J.P. Morgan Chase & Co. ran a sweepstakes where customers in select markets received a chance to win a grand prize of $5,000 if they paid bills electronically. Online bill-pay services allow individuals to transfer funds electronically from their accounts directly to a biller.

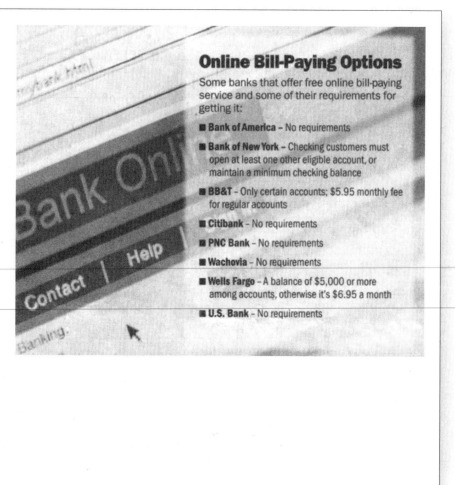

Online Bill-Paying Options

Some banks that offer free online bill-paying service and some of their requirements for getting it:

■ **Bank of America** – No requirements

■ **Bank of New York** – Checking customers must open at least one other eligible account, or maintain a minimum checking balance

■ **BB&T** – Only certain accounts; $5.95 monthly fee for regular accounts

■ **Citibank** – No requirements

■ **PNC Bank** – No requirements

■ **Wachovia** – No requirements

■ **Wells Fargo** – A balance of $5,000 or more among accounts, otherwise it's $6.95 a month

■ **U.S. Bank** – No requirements

Wall Street Journal © 2004

Would you bank online if you were given a cash incentive? Many customers are still concerned about security issues when banking online. In 2006, more than 40 million households were banking online, which leaves more than 60 million customers who do not bank online.

Bank Statement and Reconciliation Process

Each month, Ipswich Bank sends Gracie's Natural Superstore a **bank statement** (Figure 4.4, p. 95). We are interested in the following:

1. Beginning bank balance.

2. Total of all the account increases. Each time the bank increases the account amount, it *credits* the account.

3. Total of all account decreases. Each time the bank decreases the account amount, it *debits* the account.

4. Final ending balance.

Due to differences in timing, the bank balance on the bank statement frequently does not match the customer's checkbook balance. Also, the bank statement can show transactions that have not been entered in the customer's checkbook. Figure 4.5, p. 95, tells you what to look for when comparing a checkbook balance with a bank balance.

FIGURE 4.4

Bank statement

Ipswich Bank
1 Pleasant St.
Bartlett, NH 01835

Account Statement

Gracie's Natural Superstore
80 Garfield St.
Bartlett, NH 01835

Checking Account: 881900662

Checking Account Summary as of 3/31/09

Beginning Balance	Total Deposits	Total Withdrawals	Service Charge	Ending Balance
$13,112.24	$8,705.28	$9,926.00	$28.50	$11,863.02

Checking Accounts Transactions

Deposits	Date	Amount
Deposit	3/05	2,000.00
Deposit	3/05	224.00
Deposit	3/09	389.20
EFT leasing: Bakery dept.	3/18	1,808.06
EFT leasing: Meat dept.	3/27	4,228.00
Interest	3/31	56.02

Charges	Date	Amount
Service charge: Check printing	3/31	28.50
EFT: Health insurance	3/21	722.00
NSF	3/21	104.00

Checks			Daily Balance			
Number	Date	Amount	Date	Balance	Date	Balance
301	3/07	200.00	2/28	13,112.24	3/18	10,529.50
633	3/13	6,000.00	3/05	15,232.24	3/21	9,807.50
634	3/13	300.00	3/07	14,832.24	3/28	14,035.50
635	3/11	200.00	3/09	15,221.44	3/31	11,863.02
636	3/18	200.00	3/11	15,021.44		
637	3/31	2,200.00	3/13	8,721.44		

FIGURE 4.5

Reconciling checkbook with bank statement

Checkbook balance		Bank balance
+ EFT (electronic funds transfer)	− NSF check	+ Deposits in transit
+ Interest earned	− Online fees	− Outstanding checks
+ Notes collected	− Automatic payments*	± Bank errors
+ Direct deposits	− Overdrafts[†]	
− ATM withdrawals	− Service charges	
− Automatic withdrawals	− Stop payments[‡]	
	± Book errors[§]	

*Preauthorized payments for utility bills, mortgage payments, insurance, etc.
[†]**Overdrafts** occur when the customer has no overdraft protection and a check bounces back to the company or person who received the check because the customer has written a check without enough money in the bank to pay for it.
[‡]A stop payment is issued when the writer of check does not want the receiver to cash the check.
[§]If a $60 check is recorded at $50, the checkbook balance must be decreased by $10.

Gracie's Natural Superstore is planning to offer to its employees the option of depositing their checks directly into each employee's checking account. This is accomplished through the **electronic funds transfer (EFT)**—a computerized operation that electronically transfers funds among parties without the use of paper checks. Gracie's, who sublets space in the store, receives rental payments by EFT. Gracie's also has the bank pay the store's health insurance premiums by EFT.

To reconcile the difference between the amount on the bank statement and in the checkbook, the customer should complete a **bank reconciliation.** Today, many companies and home computer owners are using software such as Quicken and QuickBooks to complete their bank reconciliation. However, you should understand the following steps for manually reconciling a bank statement.

RECONCILING A BANK STATEMENT
Step 1. Identify the outstanding checks (checks written but not yet processed by the bank). You can use the ✓ column in the check register (Figure 4.6) to check the canceled checks listed in the bank statement against the checks you wrote in the check register. The unchecked checks are the outstanding checks.
Step 2. Identify the deposits in transit (deposits made but not yet processed by the bank), using the same method in Step 1.
Step 3. Analyze the bank statement for transactions not recorded in the check stubs or check registers (like EFT).
Step 4. Check for recording errors in checks written, in deposits made, or in subtraction and addition.
Step 5. Compare the adjusted balances of the checkbook and the bank statement. If the balances are not the same, repeat Steps 1–4.

Molly uses a check register (Figure 4.6) to keep a record of Gracie's checks and deposits. By looking at Gracie's check register, you can see how to complete Steps 1 and 2 above. The explanation that follows for the first four bank statement reconciliation steps will help you understand the procedure.

FIGURE 4.6

Gracie's Natural Superstore check register

		RECORD ALL CHARGES OR CREDITS THAT AFFECT YOUR ACCOUNT					
NUMBER	DATE 2007	DESCRIPTION OF TRANSACTION	PAYMENT/DEBIT (−)	✓	FEE (IF ANY) (−)	DEPOSIT/CREDIT (+)	BALANCE $ 12,912 24
	3/04	Deposit	$		$	$ 2,000 00	+ 2,000 00
							14,912 24
	3/04	Deposit				224 00	+ 224 00
							15,136 24
633	3/08	Staples Company	6,000 00	✓			− 6,000 00
							9,136 24
634	3/09	Health Foods Inc.	1,020 00	✓			− 1,020 00
							8,116 24
	3/09	Deposit				389 20	+ 389 20
							8,505 44
635	3/10	Liberty Insurance	200 00	✓			− 200 00
							8,305 44
636	3/18	Ryan Press	200 00	✓			− 200 00
							8,105 44
637	3/29	Logan Advertising	2,200 00	✓			− 2,200 00
							5,905 44
	3/30	Deposit				3,383 26	+ 3,383 26
							9,288 70
638	3/31	Sears Roebuck	572 00				− 572 00
							8,716 70
639	3/31	Flynn Company	638 94				− 638 94
							8,077 76
640	3/31	Lynn's Farm	166 00				− 166 00
							7,911 76
641	3/31	Ron's Wholesale	406 28				− 406 28
							7,505 48
642	3/31	Grocery Natural, Inc.	917 06				− 917 06
							86,588 42

REMEMBER TO RECORD AUTOMATIC PAYMENTS/DEPOSITS ON DATE AUTHORIZED.

Step 1. Identify Outstanding Checks

Outstanding checks are checks that Gracie's Natural Superstore has written but Ipswich Bank has not yet recorded for payment when it sends out the bank statement. Gracie's treasurer identifies the following checks written on 3/31 as outstanding:

No. 638	$572.00
No. 639	638.94
No. 640	166.00
No. 641	406.28
No. 642	917.06

Step 2. Identify Deposits in Transit

Deposits in transit are deposits that did not reach Ipswich Bank by the time the bank prepared the bank statement. The March 30 deposit of $3,383.26 did not reach Ipswich Bank by the bank statement date. You can see this by comparing the company's bank statement with its check register.

Step 3. Analyze Bank Statement for Transactions Not Recorded in Check Stubs or Check Register

The bank statement of Gracie's Natural Superstore (Figure 4.4, p. 95) begins with the deposits, or increases, made to Gracie's bank account. Increases to accounts are known as credits. These are the result of a **credit memo (CM).** Gracie's received the following increases or credits in March:

1. *EFT leasing:* $1,808.06 and $4,228.00.

   Each month the bakery and meat departments pay for space they lease in the store.

2. *Interest credited:* $56.02.

   Gracie's has a checking account that pays interest; the account has earned $56.02.

When Gracie's has charges against her bank account, the bank decreases, or debits, Gracie's account for these charges. Banks usually inform customers of a debit transaction by a **debit memo (DM).** The following items will result in debits to Gracie's account:

1. *Service charge:* $28.50   The bank charged $28.50 for printing Gracie's checks.
2. *EFT payment:* $722.   The bank made a health insurance payment for Gracie's.
3. *NSF check:* $104.   One of Gracie's customers wrote Gracie's a check for $104. Gracie's deposited the check, but the check bounced for **nonsufficient funds (NSF).** Thus, Gracie's has $104 less than it figured.

Step 4. Check for Recording Errors

The treasurer of Gracie's Natural Superstore, Molly Kate, recorded check No. 634 for the wrong amount—$1,020 (see the check register). The bank statement showed that check No. 634 cleared for $300. To reconcile Gracie's checkbook balance with the bank balance, Gracie's must add $720 to its checkbook balance. Neglecting to record a deposit also results in an error in the company's checkbook balance. As you can see, reconciling the bank's balance with a checkbook balance is a necessary part of business and personal finance.

Step 5. Completing the Bank Reconciliation

Now we can complete the bank reconciliation on the back side of the bank statement as shown in Figure 4.7 (p. 98). This form is usually on the back of a bank statement. If necessary, however, the person reconciling the bank statement can construct a bank reconciliation form similar to Figure 4.8 (p. 98).

FIGURE

Reconciliati...

of paper checks, some banks no longer return canceled checks. Instead, these banks use a **safekeeping** procedure involving holding the checks for a period of time, keeping microfilm copies of checks for at least a year, and returning a check or a photocopy for a small fee.

In 2003, a new piece of legislation known as Check 21 was signed into law. This legislation means that canceled checks can now be transferred electronically to customers rather than bundling them up and sending them through the mail. The electronic transfer of their canceled checks gives customers time to study all their canceled checks without the concern for safekeeping.

Role of Middlemen on the Internet

Have you ever made a purchase on eBay? eBay is a popular website for many people who use the company to buy and sell items at auction and also to buy and sell items outright.

After you make a purchase on eBay, you have the option to pay by check, credit card, or use PayPal. Many people use PayPal because they believe it is safer than their check or credit card. Here, you can see a partial Web screen of eBay with PayPal.

PayPal acts like a third person operating between eBay and the seller. Since PayPal performs a service, it charges customers a fee. Obviously, banks and credit unions object to letting PayPal dominate the field and handle these transactions for a fee. As a result, PayPal recently agreed to be purchased by eBay. In the next five years, banks hope to eliminate middlemen like PayPal. At that time you might be able to e-mail cash to Internet-enabled ATM machines or use a cell phone to send your money.

The Practice Quiz that follows will test your knowledge of the bank reconciliation process.

LU 4–2   **PRACTICE QUIZ**

FIGURE

Bank recor...

Complete this **Practice Quiz** to see how you are doing

Rosa Garcia received her February 3, 2009, bank statement showing a balance of $212.80. Rosa's checkbook has a balance of $929.15. The bank statement showed that Rosa had an ATM fee of $12.00 and a deposited check returned fee of $20.00. Rosa earned interest of $1.05. She had three outstanding checks: No. 300, $18.20; No. 302, $38.40; and No. 303, $68.12. A deposit for $810.12 was not on her bank statement. Prepare Rosa Garcia's bank reconciliation.

ROSA GARCIA					
Bank Reconciliation as of February 3, 2009					
Checkbook balance			**Bank balance**		
Rosa's checkbook balance		$929.15	Bank balance		$ 212.80
Add:			Add:		
Interest		1.05	Deposit in transit		810.12
		$930.20			$1,022.92
Deduct:			Deduct:		
Deposited check			Outstanding checks:		
returned fee	$20.00		No. 300	$18.20	
ATM	12.00	32.00	No. 302	38.40	
			No. 303	68.12	124.72
Reconciled balance		$898.20	Reconciled balance		$ 898.20

LU 4–2a   **EXTRA PRACTICE QUIZ**

Need more practice? Try this **Extra Practice Quiz** (check figures in Chapter Organizer, p. 101)

Earl Miller received his March 8, 2009, bank statement, which had a $300.10 balance. Earl's checkbook has a $1,200.10 balance. The bank statement showed a $15.00 ATM fee and a $30.00 deposited check returned fee. Earl earned $24.06 interest. He had three outstanding checks: No. 300, $22.88; No. 302, $15.90; and No. 303, $282.66. A deposit for $1,200.50 was not on his bank statement. Prepare Earl's bank reconciliation.

CHAPTER ORGANIZER AND STUDY GUIDE
WITH CHECK FIGURES FOR EXTRA PRACTICE QUIZZES

Topic	Key point, procedure, formula	Example(s) to illustrate situation
Types of endorsements, p. 91	*Blank:* Not safe; can be further endorsed.	Jones Co. 21-333-9
	Full: Only person or company named in endorsement can transfer check to someone else.	Pay to the order of Regan Bank Jones Co. 21-333-9
	Restrictive: Check must be deposited. Limits any further negotiation of the check.	Pay to the order of Regan Bank. For deposit only. Jones Co. 21-333-9

Bank reconciliation, p. 94	**Checkbook balance**
	+ EFT (electronic funds transfer)
	+ Interest earned
	+ Notes collected
	+ Direct deposits
	− ATM withdrawals
	− NSF check
	− Online fees
	− Automatic withdrawals
	− Overdrafts
	− Service charges
	− Stop payments
	± Book errors*
	CM—adds to balance
	DM—deducts from balance
	
	Bank balance
	+ Deposits in transit
	− Outstanding checks
	± Bank errors
	
	*If a $60 check is recorded as $50, we must decrease checkbook balance by $10.
		Checkbook balance
		Balance $800
		  − NSF 40
		    $760
		  − Service charge 4
		    $756
		
		Bank balance
		Balance $ 632
		  + Deposits in transit 416
		    $1,048
		  − Outstanding checks 292
		    $ 756

KEY TERMS	Automatic teller machine
	  (ATM), *p. 89*
	Bank reconciliation, *p. 96*
	Bank statement, *p. 95*
	Blank endorsement, *p. 91*
	Check, *p. 89*
	Check register, *p. 96*
	Check stub, *p. 91*
	Credit memo (CM), *p. 97*
	Debit card, *p. 89*
		Debit memo (DM), *p. 97*
		Deposit slip, *p. 90*
		Deposits in transit, *p. 97*
		Draft, *p. 89*
		Drawee, *p. 90*
		Drawer, *p. 90*
		Electronic funds transfer
		  (EFT), *p. 95*
		Endorse, *p. 91*
		Full endorsement, *p. 91*
		
		Nonsufficient funds (NSF),
		  p. 97
		Outstanding checks,
		  p. 97
		Overdrafts, *p. 95*
		Payee, *p. 90*
		Restrictive endorsement,
		  p. 91
		Safekeeping, *p. 100*
		Signature card, *p. 89*

CHECK FIGURES FOR EXTRA PRACTICE QUIZZES WITH PAGE REFERENCES	LU 4–1a (p. 93) Ending Balance Forward $11,533.80	LU 4–2a (p. 100) Reconciled Balance $1,179.16

Critical Thinking Discussion Questions

1. Explain the structure of a check. The trend in bank statements is not to return the canceled checks. Do you think this is fair?

2. List the three types of endorsements. Endorsements are limited to the top $1\frac{1}{2}$ inches of the trailing edge on the back left side of your check. Why do you think the Federal Reserve made this regulation?

3. List the steps in reconciling a bank statement. Today, many banks charge a monthly fee for certain types of checking accounts. Do you think all checking accounts should be free? Please explain.

4. What are some of the trends in online banking? Will we become a cashless society in which all transactions are made with some type of credit card?

No. _____ $ _____
_____ 20 _____
To _____
For _____

BALANCE	DOLLARS	CENTS
AMT. DEPOSITED		
TOTAL		
AMT. THIS CHECK		
BALANCE FORWARD		

PAYROLL.COM
1 LEDGER RD.
ST. PAUL, MN 55113

No. 191

PAY TO THE ORDER OF Compaq Corporation   12-15 20 09   5-13/110

$ 3,815, 99

three thousand eight fifteen and 99/100 _____ DOLLARS

IPSWICH BANK
ipswichbank.com

MEMO Computer equipment

⑈011000138⑈   25 11103 191

4–3. Using the check register in Problem 4–1 and the following bank statement, prepare a bank reconciliation for Lee.com.

BANK STATEMENT			
Date	**Checks**	**Deposits**	**Balance**
7/1 balance			$4,500.75
7/18	$133.50		4,367.25
7/19		$ 700.00	5,067.25
7/26	319.24		4,748.01
7/30	15.00 SC		4,733.01

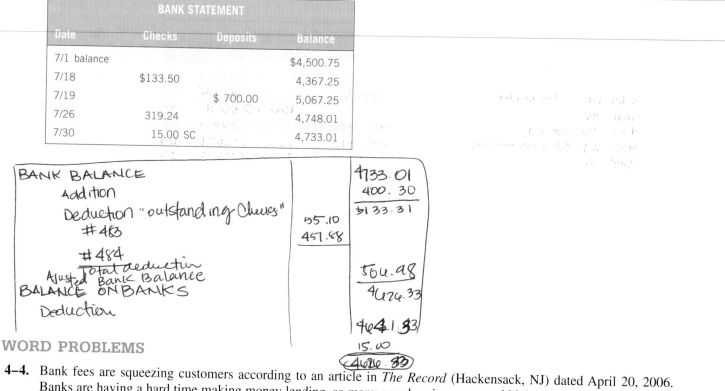

BANK BALANCE 4733.01
  Addition 400.30
  Deduction "outstanding Checks" 5133.31
    #483 .... 55.10
    #484 .... 457.88
    Total deduction
  Ajusted Bank Balance 564.98
BALANCE ON BANKS 4624.33
  Deduction
                                            4641.33
                                            15.00
                                        (4626.33)

WORD PROBLEMS

4–4. Bank fees are squeezing customers according to an article in *The Record* (Hackensack, NJ) dated April 20, 2006. Banks are having a hard time making money lending, so many are charging more and higher fees. Meanwhile, interest paid on interest-bearing checking accounts remains low. Kayla Siska received her bank statement from the Commerce Bank which increased its overdraft fee from $33 to $35. To avoid future overdraft fees and bounced-checks (NSF) fees, Kayla wants to make sure her checkbook is in balance. The following checks have not cleared the bank: No. 634, $58.30; No. 635, $108.75; and No. 637, $112.68. Her checkbook balance shows $695.23. She received $1.75 in interest. She also was charged a $35.00 overdraft fee. The bank shows a balance of $320.10. A $621.61 deposit was not recorded. Prepare Kayla's bank reconciliation.

4–9. Bank

Fa
ho
the
cle

4–5. In the February 2007 issue of *Consumer Reports Money Adviser* an article appeared, stating ATM surcharges and bounced-check fees have reached record highs. The report found the average bounced-check (NSF) fee was $27.40 up from $27.04 last spring. ATM fees rose 10 cents, to $1.64 since last fall's survey. Norman Rand uses his ATM several times a month. Norman received his June 2007 bank statement showing a balance of $835.38, the statement did not show a $178.79 deposit he had made. His checkbook balance shows $838.40. Check No. 234 for $88.70 and check No. 236 for $124.75 were outstanding. He had an ATM surcharge of $11.48 and had a bounced-check fee of $27.40. He received $1.20 in interest. Prepare Norman's bank reconciliation.

Handwritten work:

Donnas checkbook balance $806.94
Intrest: $2.68
M. Fee: $8.00
Rec. balance: $799.12

add: $765.69
deduct: $41.25

121.16
106.30
210.12
64.84
502.42

41.25
502.42
543.67

4–10. Care
The
refu
clea
Care

4–6. A local bank began charging $2.50 each month for returning canceled checks. The bank also has an $8.00 "maintenance" fee if a checking account slips below $750. Donna Sands likes to have copies of her canceled checks for preparing her income tax. She has received her bank statement with a balance of $535.85. Donna received $2.68 in interest and has been charged for the canceled checks and the maintenance fee. The following checks were outstanding: No. 94, $121.16; No. 96, $106.30; No. 98, $210.12; and No. 99, $64.84. A deposit of $765.69 was not recorded on Donna's bank statement. Her checkbook shows a balance of $806.94. Prepare Donna's bank reconciliation.

4–11. Lo
an
yo
ba
re
$6

4–7. *USA T*
checki
avoid
to a re
check
and a
shows
Check

4–8. John
that
mon
havi
men
che
elec
and

CHALLENGE PROBLEMS

4–12. Carolyn Crosswell, who banks in New Jersey, wants to balance her checkbook, which shows a balance of $985.20. The bank shows a balance of $1,430.33. The following transactions occurred: $135.20 automatic withdrawal to the gas company, $6.50 ATM fee, $8.00 service fee, and $1,030.05 direct deposit from the IRS. Carolyn used her debit card 5 times and was charged 45 cents for each transaction; she was also charged $3.50 for check printing. A $931.08 deposit was not shown on her bank statement. The following checks were outstanding: No. 235, $158.20; No. 237, $184.13; No. 238, $118.12; and No. 239, $38.83. Carolyn received $2.33 interest. Prepare Carolyn's bank reconciliation.

4–13. Melissa Jackson, bookkeeper for Kinko Company, cannot prepare a bank reconciliation. From the following facts, can you help her complete the June 30, 2009, reconciliation? The bank statement showed a $2,955.82 balance. Melissa's checkbook showed a $3,301.82 balance.

Melissa placed a $510.19 deposit in the bank's night depository on June 30. The deposit did not appear on the bank statement. The bank included two DMs and one CM with the returned checks: $690.65 DM for NSF check, $8.50 DM for service charges, and $400.00 CM (less $10 collection fee) for collecting a $400.00 non-interest-bearing note. Check No. 811 for $110.94 and check No. 912 for $82.50, both written and recorded on June 28, were not with the returned checks. The bookkeeper had correctly written check No. 884, $1,000, for a new cash register, but she recorded the check as $1,069. The May bank reconciliation showed check No. 748 for $210.90 and check No. 710 for $195.80 outstanding on April 30. The June bank statement included check No. 710 but not check No. 748.

 SUMMARY PRACTICE TEST

1. Walgreens has a $12,925.55 beginning checkbook balance. Record the following transactions in the check stubs provided. *(p. 91)*

   a. November 4, 2009, check No. 180 payable to Johnson and Johnson Corporation, $1,700.88 for drugs.

   b. $5,250 deposit—November 24.

   c. November 24, 2009, check No. 181 payable to Gillette Corporation, $825.55 merchandise.

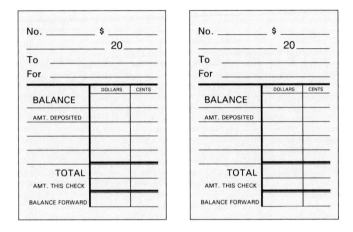

2. On April 1, 2009, Lester Company received a bank statement that showed a $8,950 balance. Lester showed an $8,000 checking account balance. The bank did not return check No. 115 for $750 or check No. 118 for $370. A $900 deposit made on March 31 was in transit. The bank charged Lester $20 for printing and $250 for NSF checks. The bank also collected a $1,400 note for Lester. Lester forgot to record a $400 withdrawal at the ATM. Prepare a bank reconciliation. *(p. 95)*

3. Felix Babic banks at Role Federal Bank. Today he received his March 31, 2009, bank statement showing a $762.80 balance. Felix's checkbook shows a balance of $799.80. The following checks have not cleared the bank: No. 140, $130.55; No. 149, $66.80; and No. 161, $102.90. Felix made a $820.15 deposit that is not shown on the bank statement. He has his $617.30 monthly mortgage payment paid through the bank. His $1,100.20 IRS refund check was mailed to his bank. Prepare Felix Babic's bank reconciliation. *(p. 95)*

4. On June 30, 2009, Wally Company's bank statement showed a $7,500.10 bank balance. Wally has a beginning checkbook balance of $9,800.00. The bank statement also showed that it collected a $1,200.50 note for the company. A $4,500.10 June 30 deposit was in transit. Check No. 119 for $650.20 and check No. 130 for $381.50 are outstanding. Wally's bank charges $.40 cents per check. This month, 80 checks were processed. Prepare a reconciled statement. *(p. 95)*

Personal Finance

CREDIT | Online banking is convenient but not foolproof. *By Joan Goldwasser*

Electronic bill-paying SNAFUS

WHEN EMILY and Greg Martinez moved from Philadelphia to Los Angeles earlier this year, they thought that transferring their online bank account would be a snap. They were wrong. Because they didn't notify Sprint in time, their monthly cell-phone bill was paid twice—once from their Philadelphia account and again from their new Los Angeles bank account.

Other online bill-payers have had bills that narrowly escaped being paid late, or weren't paid at all. One couple failed to notify Checkfree, their bill-paying service, that their mortgage lender had changed addresses. Their mortgage check was forwarded and ended up arriving on time. However, a young teacher wasn't so fortunate. He assumed that his car payments would be automatically debited from his checking account. But he neglected to sign the necessary documents, and after several missed payments, he had to scramble to fix the problem—after his car had been repossessed in the middle of the night.

If you're among the two-thirds of U.S. consumers who no longer worry about writing checks or running out of stamps thanks to automatic bill-paying services, you still need to monitor your bills. After you sign up with a vendor or your bank, review your account statements on a regular basis, advises Mike Herd of Nacha, the electronic-payments association. And make sure that your payee mailing addresses are up-to-date.

When you sign up for automatic bill-paying with an individual vendor or with your bank, you can generally decide whether you want the funds debited from your checking account or charged to a credit card. You can change the amount, or even cancel the payment, sometimes as late as the day before your bill is due.

If you have a problem with unauthorized payments—which happens to about 25 out of every 100,000 transactions, according to Nacha—be sure to notify your bank or credit-card company immediately. Nacha rules require the financial institution to reimburse your account if a transaction is unauthorized. Neither Visa nor MasterCard holds consumers liable for unintended charges to their accounts.

In a rare instance, automatic bill-paying can be too efficient. Take the case of the Canadian man who died in his Winnipeg apartment but wasn't discovered for nearly two years. No one noticed because all of his monthly bills had been paid on time.

● Because of an online glitch, Emily Martinez ended up overpaying her cell-phone bill.

DAN CHAVKIN

BUSINESS MATH ISSUE

In ten years everyone will pay bills online.

1. List the key points of the article and information to support your position.
2. Write a group defense of your position using math calculations to support your view.

Slater's Business Math Scrapbook

with Internet Application

Putting Your Skills to Work

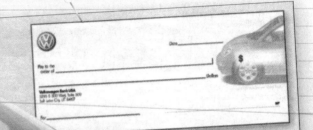

*Volkswagen is among the car companies and retailers that are expanding into **traditional banking areas**.*

PROJECT A
Visit the Toyota Motor Corp. Web site and check out the banking options they offer. Do you think retailers should be in the banking business?

PROJECT A
Visit the Toyota Motor Corp. Web site and check out the banking options they offer. Do you think retailers should be in the banking business?

Now Open: The Bank of VW

Auto Makers, Retailers Offer Checking Accounts and CDs; A $1,600 Rebate on Next Car

By JENNIFER SARANOW

THE NEXT TIME you are in the market for a Volkswagen, you may wind up with a certificate of deposit instead of a convertible.

From car makers to department stores, an increasing number of companies are getting into the consumer-banking business. While many long have offered limited financial products such as credit cards and auto loans, they now are increasingly expanding into more traditional banking areas, ranging from checking accounts to CDs.

This month, **Volkswagen of America** Inc.'s Volkswagen Bank USA plans to open an Internet bank, offering CDs and savings accounts to its Volkswagen and Audi customers online. By the first quarter of next year, the two-year-old affiliate—which currently offers only home-equity lines of credit, credit cards and auto financing—plans to roll out checking accounts.

Meanwhile, **Toyota Motor** Corp.'s Toyota Financial Services unit is developing a host of banking products, including money-market accounts, CDs and savings accounts.

Both **General Motors** Corp. and **BMW AG** already have U.S. banks offering personal banking products. **Nordstrom** Inc.'s Nordstrom Federal Savings Bank has offered a checking account, among other banking products, since 2001.

The moves come as retail banking is booming in the U.S. After the dot-com bubble burst, many consumers looking for safe investments put their money in banks. "The U.S. retail-banking industry has been terrifically profitable and very successful over the last half a dozen years. That is why you see retailers trying to get into retail banking," says Jim Eckenrode, vice president of banking and payments research at TowerGroup.

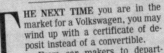
Internet Projects: See text Web site (www.mhhe.com/slater9e) and The Business Math Internet Resource Guide.

CHAPTER 5

Solving for the Unknown: A How-to Approach for Solving Equations

Why Suiting Up Will Cost More This Year

A menswear shake-up is changing the price equation for some popular suits; $50 extra for 'sweat guards'

By RAY A. SMITH

SOME SUIT BUYERS are going to have to tighten their belts this year—and it has nothing to do with a new fashion statement.

There's a shakeup in the suit business and it's prompting a big shift in the prices that have long distinguished a good suit from a cheap one. At the low end, the $200-$300 suit has gotten a major quality upgrade and is now bidding to compete with suits in the $500-$700 range. Meanwhile, some of the companies making those midrange suits are also trying to trade up, by offering features you might find in the made-to-measure segment, traditionally the province of higher-end names. For shoppers, the most obvious result of this jockeying: The standard suit from many established makers—everyone from Hart Schaffner Marx to Calvin Klein to Burberry—will cost between $50 and $100 more this fall.

Those suit makers say they have added touches that justify the higher prices. They include underarm guards that promise to prevent embarrassing sweat stains and an extra panel of fabric sewn into the chest area to make the suit feel less boxy. Some of the improvements are largely cosmetic, while others are more substantive—such as upgrading to super 120s wool, a finer, softer fabric that is starting to show up in some $700 suits but is more common in pricier menswear.

Higher prices aren't the only thing turning up on suits this fall. Shoppers will see lots of glen plaids and navy suits with pinstripes

Please Turn to Page P5, Column 1

LEARNING UNIT OBJECTIVES

LU 5–1: Solving Equations for the Unknown

- Explain the basic procedures used to solve equations for the unknown (*pp. 114–116*).
- List the five rules and the mechanical steps used to solve for the unknown in seven situations; know how to check the answers (*pp. 117–119*).

LU 5–2: Solving Word Problems for the Unknown

- List the steps for solving word problems (*p. 121*).
- Complete blueprint aids to solve word problems; check the solutions (*pp. 121–123*).

When you shop at Home Depot, have you noticed that Home Depot employs many older employees? Often you are greeted by an older employee. Older, experienced employees frequently are ready to answer customers' questions.

Traditionally, many employers have avoided hiring older people. Now this has changed. The following *Wall Street Journal* clipping "Gray Is Good: Employers Make Efforts to Retain Older, Experienced Workers" gives interesting facts about the hiring of older, experienced employees. Some companies are seeking employees 55 and over. Home Depot and Stanley Consultants are two examples. At Stanley Consultants about $\frac{1}{4}$ of the 1,100 employees are over 50. This means that 275 employees are over 50:

$$\frac{1}{4} \times 1,100 = 275$$

Gray Is Good: Employers Make Efforts To Retain Older, Experienced Workers

AT AGE 69, John Sayles retired as principal planner for **Stanley Consultants**, a civil-engineering firm. Or he thought he did.

A few months later, his employer tracked him down on a family vacation in Colorado and told him his skills were needed in Iraq. "I was dumfounded" but pleased to be asked, says Mr. Sayles. He spent the next two months working in the presidential palace in Baghdad, as part of a team of government contractors rebuilding the infrastructure. Mr. Sayles, who lives in the company's hometown of Muscatine, Iowa, is now 71, and still works part-time.

Traditionally, many employers have viewed older workers as inflexible, less productive than their younger colleagues, and more expensive because of higher salaries and health-care costs. When hard times force layoffs, older workers are often the first to get the ax. But now, many employers are at least giving lip service to retaining older workers. And a few are taking concrete steps to actually do so—seeking out older workers and retirees with needed skills, rooting out age bias, and setting up complex flexible work arrangements tailored to their needs.

For employers, the writing on the wall is hard to miss. Workers 55 and over are growing four times faster than the work force as a whole.

Some companies are recognizing that older workers are repositories of hard-to-replace knowledge critical to their businesses, says Eric Lesser, an associate partner in Cambridge, Mass., with IBM Business Consulting Services. As workers retire, companies worry about losing relationships with suppliers and distributors, as well as the ability to maintain aging equipment, such as plants, machinery or other gear built to past standards, he says.

In addition, as the work force ages, so do the customers, who often prefer to deal with older workers. At **Home Depot**, older employees serve as a powerful draw to baby-boomer shoppers by mirroring their knowledge and perspective, says Dennis Donovan, executive vice president, human resources, for the 2,000-store retailer. Similarly, **Westpac Banking** Corp., a big Australian financial-services concern, recruited 950 over-45 workers as financial planners, among other roles. Older clients, a spokeswoman says, prefer advisers with experience.

At Stanley Consultants, an 1,100-employee firm where more than one-fourth of employees are over 50, older workers are encouraged to continue part-time.

Wall Street Journal © 2005

Learning Unit 5–1 explains how to solve for unknowns in equations. In Learning Unit 5–2 you learn how to solve for unknowns in word problems. When you complete these learning units, you will not have to memorize as many formulas to solve business and personal math applications. Also, with the increasing use of computer software, a basic working knowledge of solving for the unknown has become necessary.

Learning Unit 5–1: Solving Equations for the Unknown

The Rose Smith letter at the top of the following page is based on a true story. Note how Rose states that the blueprint aids, the lesson on repetition, and the chapter organizers were important factors in the successful completion of her business math course.

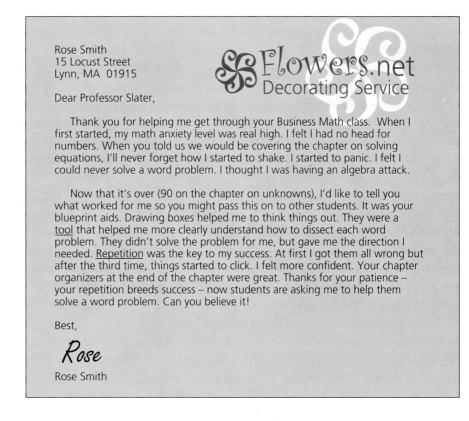

Rose Smith
15 Locust Street
Lynn, MA 01915

Flowers.net
Decorating Service

Dear Professor Slater,

Thank you for helping me get through your Business Math class. When I first started, my math anxiety level was real high. I felt I had no head for numbers. When you told us we would be covering the chapter on solving equations, I'll never forget how I started to shake. I started to panic. I felt I could never solve a word problem. I thought I was having an algebra attack.

Now that it's over (90 on the chapter on unknowns), I'd like to tell you what worked for me so you might pass this on to other students. It was your blueprint aids. Drawing boxes helped me to think things out. They were a tool that helped me more clearly understand how to dissect each word problem. They didn't solve the problem for me, but gave me the direction I needed. Repetition was the key to my success. At first I got them all wrong but after the third time, things started to click. I felt more confident. Your chapter organizers at the end of the chapter were great. Thanks for your patience – your repetition breeds success – now students are asking me to help them solve a word problem. Can you believe it!

Best,

Rose

Rose Smith

Many of you are familiar with the terms *variables* and *constants.* If you are planning to prepare for your retirement by saving only what you can afford each year, your saving is a *variable;* if you plan to save the same amount each year, your saving is a *constant.* Now you can also say that you cannot buy clothes by size because of the many variables involved. This unit explains the importance of mathematical variables and constants when solving equations.

Basic Equation-Solving Procedures

Do you wait for the after-Christmas sales to make your purchases? What happens when retailers have fewer inventories to sell after Christmas because they had a good Christmas season and discounted merchandise deeply before Christmas? This means it will be harder for customers to find bargains. The best bargains will be found in computers and clothes.

Navigating the New World Of Post-Christmas Sales

Strong season, gift cards change the equation;

Wall Street Journal © 2005

From the *Wall Street Journal* heading "Navigating the New World of Post-Christmas Sales," you can see that stores had a strong Christmas season. To have merchandise to sell, retailers offered large discounts to gift-card recipients with the hope that retailers could sell the gift-card recipients new, full-priced items. The heading also stated that gift cards change the equation. But no explanation is given on how the equation is changed or what the equation was before the change. The definition of an equation given in the next paragraph may suggest to you what is meant by "the equation."

Do you know the difference between a mathematical expression, equation, and formula? A mathematical **expression** is a meaningful combination of numbers and letters called *terms.* Operational signs (such as + or −) within the expression connect the terms to show a relationship between them. For example, $6 + 2$ or $6A - 4A$ are mathematical expressions. An **equation** is a mathematical statement with an equal sign showing that a mathematical expression on the left equals the mathematical expression on the right. An equation has an equal sign; an expression does not have an equal sign. A **formula** is an equation that expresses in symbols a general fact, rule, or principle. Formulas are shortcuts for expressing a word concept. For example, in Chapter 10 you will learn that the formula for simple interest is Interest (I) = Principal (P) × Rate (R) × Time (T). This means that when you see $I = P \times R \times T$, you recognize the simple interest formula. Now let's study basic equations.

As a mathematical statement of equality, equations show that two numbers or groups of numbers are equal. For example, $6 + 4 = 10$ shows the equality of an equation. Equations also use letters as symbols that represent one or more numbers. These symbols, usually a letter of the alphabet, are **variables** that stand for a number. We can use a variable even though we may not know what it represents. For example, $A + 2 = 6$. The variable A represents the number or **unknown** (4 in this example) for which we are solving. We distinguish variables from numbers, which have a fixed value. Numbers such as 3 or −7 are **constants** or **knowns,** whereas A and $3A$ (this means 3 times the variable A) are variables. So we can now say that variables and constants are *terms of mathematical expressions.*

Usually in solving for the unknown, we place variable(s) on the left side of the equation and constants on the right. The following rules for variables and constants are important.

VARIABLES AND CONSTANTS RULES
1. If no number is in front of a letter, it is a 1: $B = 1B$; $C = 1C$.
2. If no sign is in front of a letter or number, it is a +: $C = +C$; $4 = +4$.

You should be aware that in solving equations, the meaning of the symbols $+$, $-$, $\times$, and $\div$ has not changed. However, some variations occur. For example, you can also write $A \times B$ (A times B) as $A \cdot B$, $A(B)$, or AB. Also, A divided by B is the same as A/B. Remember that to solve an equation, you must find a number that can replace the unknown in the equation and make it a true statement. Now let's take a moment to look at how we can change verbal statements into variables.

Assume Dick Hersh, an employee of Nike, is 50 years old. Let's assign Dick Hersh's changing age to the symbol A. The symbol A is a variable.

Verbal statement	Variable A (age)
Dick's age 8 years ago	$A - 8$
Dick's age 8 years from today	$A + 8$
Four times Dick's age	$4A$
One-fifth Dick's age	$A/5$

FIGURE   5.1

Equality in equations

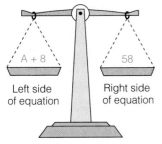

Left side
of equation

Right side
of equation

Dick's age in 8 years will equal 58.

To visualize how equations work, think of the old-fashioned balancing scale shown in Figure 5.1. The pole of the scale is the equals sign. The two sides of the equation are the two pans of the scale. In the left pan or left side of the equation, we have $A + 8$; in the right pan or right side of the equation, we have 58. To solve for the unknown (Dick's present age), we isolate or place the unknown (variable) on the left side and the numbers on the right. We will do this soon. For now, remember that to keep an equation (or scale) in balance, we must perform mathematical operations (addition, subtraction, multiplication, and division) to *both* sides of the equation.

SOLVING FOR THE UNKNOWN RULE
Whatever you do to one side of an equation, you must do to the other side.

How to Solve for Unknowns in Equations

This section presents seven drill situations and the rules that will guide you in solving for unknowns in these situations. We begin with two basic rules—the opposite process rule and the equation equality rule.

OPPOSITE PROCESS RULE
If an equation indicates a process such as addition, subtraction, multiplication, or division, solve for the unknown or variable by using the opposite process. For example, if the equation process is addition, solve for the unknown by using subtraction.

EQUATION EQUALITY RULE
You can add the same quantity or number to both sides of the equation and subtract the same quantity or number from both sides of the equation without affecting the equality of the equation. You can also divide or multiply both sides of the equation by the same quantity or number *(except zero)* without affecting the equality of the equation.   *To check your answer(s),* substitute your answer(s) for the letter(s) in the equation. The sum of the left side should equal the sum of the right side.

Drill Situation 1: Subtracting Same Number from Both Sides of Equation

Example	**Mechanical steps**	**Explanation**
$A + 8 = 58$	$A + 8 = 58$	8 is subtracted from *both* sides of equation to isolate variable A on the left.
Dick's age A plus 8 equals 58.	$\dfrac{-8 \quad -8}{A \quad = \boxed{50}}$	**Check**
		$50 + 8 = 58$
		$58 = 58$

Note: Since the equation process used *addition,* we use the opposite process rule and solve for variable A with *subtraction.* We also use the equation equality rule when we subtract the same quantity from both sides of the equation.

Drill Situation 2: Adding Same Number to Both Sides of Equation

Example	**Mechanical steps**	**Explanation**
$B - 50 = 80$	$B - 50 = 80$	50 is added to *both* sides to isolate variable B on the left.
Some number B less 50 equals 80.	$\dfrac{+50 \quad +50}{B \quad = \boxed{130}}$	**Check**
		$130 - 50 = 80$
		$80 = 80$

Note: Since the equation process used *subtraction,* we use the opposite process rule and solve for variable B with *addition.* We also use the equation equality rule when we add the same quantity to both sides of the equation.

Drill Situation 3: Dividing Both Sides of Equation by Same Number

Example	**Mechanical steps**	**Explanation**
$7G = 35$	$7G = 35$	By dividing both sides by 7, G equals 5.
Some number G times 7 equals 35.	$\dfrac{7G}{7} = \dfrac{35}{7}$	
	$G = \boxed{5}$	**Check**
		$7(5) = 35$
		$35 = 35$

Note: Since the equation process used *multiplication*, we use the opposite process rule and solve for variable *G* with *division*. We also use the equation equality rule when we divide both sides of the equation by the same quantity.

Drill Situation 4: Multiplying Both Sides of Equation by Same Number

Example	Mechanical steps	Explanation
$\dfrac{V}{5} = 70$	$\dfrac{V}{5} = 70$	By multiplying both sides by 5, *V* is equal to 350.
Some number *V* divided by 5 equals 70.	$5\left(\dfrac{V}{5}\right) = 70(5)$ $V = \boxed{350}$	**Check** $\dfrac{350}{5} = 70$ $70 = 70$

Note: Since the equation process used *division*, we use the opposite process rule and solve for variable *V* with *multiplication*. We also use the equation equality rule when we multiply both sides of the equation by the same quantity.

Drill Situation 5: Equation That Uses Subtraction and Multiplication to Solve Unknown

> **MULTIPLE PROCESSES RULE**
>
> When solving for an unknown that involves more than one process, do the addition and subtraction before the multiplication and division.

Example	Mechanical steps	Explanation
$\dfrac{H}{4} + 2 = 5$	$\dfrac{H}{4} + 2 = 5$	1. Move constant to right side by subtracting 2 from both sides.
When we divide unknown *H* by 4 and add the result to 2, the answer is 5.	$\dfrac{H}{4} + 2 = 5$ $\underline{-2 \quad -2}$ $\dfrac{H}{4} = 3$ $4\left(\dfrac{H}{4}\right) = 4(3)$ $H = \boxed{12}$	2. To isolate *H*, which is divided by 4, we do the opposite process and multiply 4 times *both* sides of the equation.
		Check $\dfrac{12}{4} + 2 = 5$ $3 + 2 = 5$ $5 = 5$

Drill Situation 6: Using Parentheses in Solving for Unknown

> **PARENTHESES RULE**
>
> When equations contain parentheses (which indicate grouping together), you solve for the unknown by first multiplying each item inside the parentheses by the number or letter just outside the parentheses. Then you continue to solve for the unknown with the opposite process used in the equation. Do the additions and subtractions first; then the multiplications and divisions.

Example	**Mechanical steps**	**Explanation**
$5(P - 4) = 20$	$5(P - 4) = \quad 20$	1. Parentheses tell us that everything inside parentheses is multiplied by 5. Multiply 5 by P and 5 by -4.
The unknown P less 4, multiplied by 5 equals 20.	$5P - 20 = \quad 20$ $\underline{\quad +20 \qquad +20}$ $\dfrac{\cancel{5}P}{\cancel{5}} = \dfrac{40}{5}$ $P = \quad 8$	2. Add 20 to both sides to isolate $5P$ on left. 3. To remove 5 in front of P, divide both sides by 5 to result in P equals 8.

Check

$5(8 - 4) = 20$
$5(4) = 20$
$20 = 20$

Drill Situation 7: Combining Like Unknowns

LIKE UNKNOWNS RULE
To solve equations with like unknowns, you first combine the unknowns and then solve with the opposite process used in the equation.

Example	**Mechanical steps**	**Explanation**
$4A + A = 20$	$4A + A = 20$ $\dfrac{\cancel{5}A}{\cancel{5}} = \dfrac{20}{5}$ $A = 4$	To solve this equation: $4A + 1A = 5A$. Thus, $5A = 20$. To solve for A, divide both sides by 5, leaving A equals 4.

Before you go to Learning Unit 5–2, let's check your understanding of this unit.

LU 5–1   PRACTICE QUIZ

Complete this **Practice Quiz** to see how you are doing

1. Write equations for the following (use the letter Q as the variable). Do not solve for the unknown.
   a. Nine less than one-half a number is fourteen.
   b. Eight times the sum of a number and thirty-one is fifty.
   c. Ten decreased by twice a number is two.
   d. Eight times a number less two equals twenty-one.
   e. The sum of four times a number and two is fifteen.
   f. If twice a number is decreased by eight, the difference is four.

2. Solve the following:
   a. $B + 24 = 60$ b. $D + 3D = 240$ c. $12B = 144$
   d. $\dfrac{B}{6} = 50$ e. $\dfrac{B}{4} + 4 = 16$ f. $3(B - 8) = 18$

✓ Solutions

1. a. $\dfrac{1}{2}Q - 9 = 14$ b. $8(Q + 31) = 50$ c. $10 - 2Q = 2$
    d. $8Q - 2 = 21$ e. $4Q + 2 = 15$ f. $2Q - 8 = 4$

2. a. $\begin{aligned} B + 24 &= -60 \\ \underline{-24} \quad &\underline{-24} \\ B \quad &= \quad 36 \end{aligned}$ b. $\dfrac{\cancel{4}D}{\cancel{4}} = \dfrac{240}{4}$
 $D = 60$ c. $\dfrac{\cancel{12}B}{\cancel{12}} = \dfrac{144}{12}$
 $B = 12$

d. $6\left(\dfrac{B}{6}\right) = 50(6)$

$B = \boxed{300}$

e.
$$\dfrac{B}{4} + 4 = 16$$
$$\phantom{\dfrac{B}{4}} \underline{-4 \quad -4}$$
$$\dfrac{B}{4} = 12$$
$$4\left(\dfrac{B}{4}\right) = 12(4)$$
$$B = \boxed{48}$$

f.
$$3(B - 8) = 18$$
$$3B - 24 = 18$$
$$\underline{+24 \quad +24}$$
$$\dfrac{3B}{3} = \dfrac{42}{3}$$
$$B = \boxed{14}$$

LU 5–1a   EXTRA PRACTICE QUIZ

Need more practice? Try this **Extra Practice Quiz** (check figures in Chapter Organizer, p. 127)

1. Write equations for the following (use the letter Q as the variable). Do not solve for the unknown.
   a. Eight less than one-half a number is sixteen.
   b. Twelve times the sum of a number and forty-one is 1,200.
   c. Seven decreased by twice a number is one.
   d. Four times a number less two equals twenty-four.
   e. The sum of three times a number and three is nineteen.
   f. If twice a number is decreased by six, the difference is five.

2. Solve the following:
   a. $B + 14 = 70$
   b. $D + 4D = 250$
   c. $11B = 121$
   d. $\dfrac{B}{8} = 90$
   e. $\dfrac{B}{2} + 2 = 16$
   f. $3(B - 6) = 18$

Learning Unit 5–2: Solving Word Problems for the Unknown

When you buy a candy bar such as a Snickers, you should turn the candy bar over and carefully read the ingredients and calories contained on the back of the candy bar wrapper. For example, on the back of the Snickers wrapper you will read that there are "170 calories per piece." You could misread this to mean that the entire Snickers bar has 170 calories. However, look closer and you will see that the Snickers bar is divided into three pieces, so if you eat the entire bar, instead of consuming 170 calories, you will consume 510 calories. Making errors like this could result in a weight gain that you cannot explain.

$$\frac{1}{3}S = 170 \text{ calories}$$

$$3\left(\frac{1}{3}S\right) = 170 \times 3$$

$$S = \boxed{510} \text{ calories per bar}$$

In this unit, we use blueprint aids in six different situations to help you solve for unknowns. Be patient and *persistent*. Remember that the more problems you work, the easier the process becomes. Do not panic! Repetition is the key. Study the five steps that follow. They will help you solve for unknowns in word problems.

SOLVING WORD PROBLEMS FOR UNKNOWNS
Step 1. Carefully read the entire problem. You may have to read it several times.
Step 2. Ask yourself: "What is the problem looking for?"
Step 3. When you are sure what the problem is asking, let a variable represent the unknown. If the problem has more than one unknown, represent the second unknown in terms of the same variable. For example, if the problem has two unknowns, Y is one unknown. The second unknown is $4Y$—4 times the first unknown.
Step 4. Visualize the relationship between unknowns and variables. Then set up an equation to solve for unknown(s).
Step 5. Check your result to see if it is accurate.

Word Problem Situation 1: Number Problems From the *Wall Street Journal* clipping "The Flagging Division," you can determine that Disney Stores reduced its product offerings by 1,600. Disney now has 1,800 product offerings. What was the original number of product offerings?

Bill Aron/PhotoEdit

The Flagging Division ...

A snapshot of the Disney Stores

- **NUMBER OF STORES:** 740
- **STORE VISITORS:** 250 million annually
- **LOCATIONS:** 11 countries including Britain, Australia and Japan
- **PRODUCTS:** Toys, costumes, apparel, jewelry, accessories, videos and games, among others
- **PRODUCT PLANS:** Each store will have 1,800 product offerings, down from 3,400 in the past. Focus on adults will be narrowed to sleepwear and parenting products.

Blueprint aid

Unknown(s)	Variable(s)	Relationship*
Original number of product offerings	P	$P - 1{,}600 = $ New offerings New offerings $= 1{,}800$

*This column will help you visualize the equation before setting up the actual equation.

Mechanical steps

$$
\begin{array}{rr}
P - 1{,}600 = & 1{,}800 \\
+ 1{,}600 & + 1{,}600 \\
\hline
P \qquad = & 3{,}400
\end{array}
$$

Explanation

The original offerings less $1{,}600 = 1{,}800$. Note that we added 1,600 to both sides to isolate P on the left. Remember, $1P = P$.

Check

$3{,}400 - 1{,}600 = 1{,}800$
$1{,}800 = 1{,}800$

Word Problem Situation 2: Finding the Whole When Part Is Known A local Burger King budgets $\frac{1}{8}$ of its monthly profits on salaries. Salaries for the month were $12,000. What were Burger King's monthly profits?

Blueprint aid

Unknown(s)	Variable(s)	Relationship
Monthly profits	P	$\frac{1}{8}P$ Salaries = $12,000

Mechanical steps

$$\frac{1}{8}P = \$12,000$$

$$8\left(\frac{P}{8}\right) = \$12,000(8)$$

$$P = \boxed{\$96,000}$$

Explanation

$\frac{1}{8}P$ represents Burger King's monthly salaries. Since the equation used division, we solve for P by multiplying both sides by 8.

Check

$$\frac{1}{8}(\$96,000) = \$12,000$$
$$\$12,000 = \$12,000$$

Word Problem Situation 3: Difference Problems ICM Company sold 4 times as many computers as Ring Company. The difference in their sales is 27. How many computers of each company were sold?

Blueprint aid

Unknown(s)	Variable(s)	Relationship
ICM	$4C$	$4C$
Ring	C	$-\,C$ 27

Note: If problem has two unknowns, assign the variable to smaller item or one who sells less. Then assign the other unknown using the same variable. *Use the same letter.*

Mechanical steps

$$4C - C = 27$$
$$\frac{3C}{3} = \frac{27}{3}$$
$$C = \boxed{9}$$

Ring = $\boxed{9}$ computers

ICM = 4(9)

$= \boxed{36}$ computers

Explanation

The variables replace the names ICM and Ring. We assigned Ring the variable C, since it sold fewer computers. We assigned ICM $4C$, since it sold 4 times as many computers.

Check

36 computers
-9
27 computers

Word Problem Situation 4: Calculating Unit Sales Together Barry Sullivan and Mitch Ryan sold a total of 300 homes for Regis Realty. Barry sold 9 times as many homes as Mitch. How many did each sell?

Blueprint aid

Unknown(s)	Variable(s)	Relationship
Homes sold:		
B. Sullivan	$9H$	$9H$
M. Ryan	H^*	$+\,H$ 300 homes

*Assign H to Ryan since he sold less.

Mechanical steps

$$9H + H = 300$$
$$\frac{10H}{10} = \frac{300}{10}$$
$$H = \boxed{30}$$

Ryan: $\boxed{30}$ homes

Sullivan: 9(30) = $\boxed{270}$ homes

Explanation

We assigned Mitch H, since he sold fewer homes. We assigned Barry $9H$, since he sold 9 times as many homes. Together Barry and Mitch sold 300 homes.

Check

30 + 270 = 300

Word Problem Situation 5: Calculating Unit and Dollar Sales (Cost per Unit) When Total Units Are Not Given Andy sold watches ($9) and alarm clocks ($5) at a flea market. Total sales were $287. People bought 4 times as many watches as alarm clocks. How many of each did Andy sell? What were the total dollar sales of each?

Blueprint aid

Unknown(s)	Variable(s)	Price	Relationship
Unit sales:			
Watches	4C	$9	36C
Clocks	C	5	+ 5C
			$287 total sales

Mechanical steps

$$36C + 5C = 287$$
$$\frac{41C}{41} = \frac{287}{41}$$
$$C = \boxed{7}$$

$\boxed{7}$ clocks
$4(7) = \boxed{28}$ watches

Explanation

Number of watches times $9 sales price plus number of alarm clocks times $5 equals $287 total sales.

Check

$$7(\$5) + 28(\$9) = \$287$$
$$\$35 + \$252 = \$287$$
$$\$287 = \$287$$

Word Problem Situation 6: Calculating Unit and Dollar Sales (Cost per Unit) When Total Units Are Given Andy sold watches ($9) and alarm clocks ($5) at a flea market. Total sales for 35 watches and alarm clocks were $287. How many of each did Andy sell? What were the total dollar sales of each?

Blueprint aid

Unknown(s)	Variable(s)	Price	Relationship
Unit sales:			
Watches	W*	$9	9W
Clocks	35 − W	5	+ 5(35 − W)
			$287 total sales

*The more expensive item is assigned to the variable first only for this situation to make the mechanical steps easier to complete.

Mechanical steps

$$9W + 5(35 - W) = 287$$
$$9W + 175 - 5W = 287$$
$$4W + 175 = 287$$
$$\frac{-175 \quad\quad -175}{\frac{4W}{4} = \frac{112}{4}}$$
$$W = \boxed{28}$$

Watches = $\boxed{28}$
Clocks = 35 − 28 = $\boxed{7}$

Explanation

Number of watches (*W*) times price per watch plus number of alarm clocks times price per alarm clock equals $287. Total units given was 35.

Check

$$28(\$9) + 7(\$5) = \$287$$
$$\$252 + \$35 = \$287$$
$$\$287 = \$287$$

Why did we use 35 − *W*? Assume we had 35 pizzas (some cheese, others meatball). If I said that I ate all the meatball pizzas (5), how many cheese pizzas are left? Thirty? Right, you subtract 5 from 35. Think of 35 − *W* as meaning one number.

Note in Word Problem Situations 5 and 6 that the situation is the same. In Word Problem Situation 5, we were not given total units sold (but we were told which sold better). In Word Problem Situation 6, we were given total units sold, but we did not know which sold better.

Now try these six types of word problems in the Practice Quiz. Be sure to complete blueprint aids and the mechanical steps for solving the unknown(s).

LU 5–2   PRACTICE QUIZ

Complete this **Practice Quiz** to see how you are doing

Situations

1. An L. L. Bean sweater was reduced $30. The sale price was $90. What was the original price?
2. Kelly Doyle budgets $\frac{1}{8}$ of her yearly salary for entertainment. Kelly's total entertainment bill for the year is $6,500. What is Kelly's yearly salary?
3. Micro Knowledge sells 5 times as many computers as Morse Electronics. The difference in sales between the two stores is 20 computers. How many computers did each store sell?
4. Susie and Cara sell stoves at Elliott's Appliances. Together they sold 180 stoves in January. Susie sold 5 times as many stoves as Cara. How many stoves did each sell?
5. Pasquale's Pizza sells meatball pizzas ($6) and cheese pizzas ($5). In March, Pasquale's total sales were $1,600. People bought 2 times as many cheese pizzas as meatball pizzas. How many of each did Pasquale sell? What were the total dollar sales of each?

6. Pasquale's Pizza sells meatball pizzas ($6) and cheese pizzas ($5). In March, Pasquale's sold 300 pizzas for $1,600. How many of each did Pasquale's sell? What was the dollar sales price of each?

✓ Solutions

1.

Unknown(s)	Variable(s)	Relationship
Original price	P^*	$P - \$30 =$ Sale price Sale price $= \$90$

*P = Orignal price.

Mechanical steps

$$P - \$30 = \$90$$
$$\underline{+ 30 \quad + 30}$$
$$P \qquad = \boxed{\$120}$$

2.

Unknown(s)	Variable(s)	Relationship
Yearly salary	S^*	$\frac{1}{8}S$ Entertainment $= \$6,500$

*S = Salary.

Mechanical steps

$$\frac{1}{8}S = \$6,500$$
$$8\left(\frac{S}{8}\right) = \$6,500(8)$$
$$S = \boxed{\$52,000}$$

3.

Unknown(s)	Variable(s)	Relationship
Micro	$5C^*$	$5C$
Morse	C	$\underline{-C}$
		20 computers

*C = Computers.

Mechanical steps

$$5C - C = 20$$
$$\frac{4C}{4} = \frac{20}{4}$$
$$C = \boxed{5} \text{ (Morse)}$$
$$5C = \boxed{25} \text{ (Micro)}$$

4.

Unknown(s)	Variable(s)	Relationship
Stoves sold:		
Susie	$5S^*$	$5S$
Cara	S	$\underline{+ S}$
		180 stoves

*S = Stoves.

Mechanical steps

$$5S + S = 20$$
$$\frac{6S}{6} = \frac{180}{6}$$
$$S = \boxed{30} \text{ (Cara)}$$
$$5S = \boxed{150} \text{ (Susie)}$$

5.

Unknown(s)	Variable(s)	Price	Relationship
Meatball	M	$6	$6M$
Cheese	$2M$	5	$\underline{+ 10M}$
			$1,600 total sales

Mechanical steps

$$6M + 10M = 1,600$$
$$\frac{16M}{16} = \frac{1,600}{16}$$
$$M = \boxed{100} \text{ (meatball)}$$
$$2M = \boxed{200} \text{ (cheese)}$$

Check

$$(100 \times \$6) + (200 \times \$5) = \$1,600$$
$$\$600 + \$1,000 = \$1,600$$
$$\$1,600 = \$1,600$$

6.

Unknown(s)	Variable(s)	Price	Relationship
Unit sales:			
Meatball	M^*	$6	$6M$
Cheese	$300 - M$	5	$\underline{+ 5(300 - M)}$
			$1,600 total sales

*We assign the variable to the most expensive to make the mechanical steps easier to complete.

Mechanical steps

$$6M + 5(300 - M) = 1,600$$
$$6M + 1,500 - 5M = 1,600$$
$$M + 1,500 = 1,600$$
$$\underline{- 1,500 \qquad - 1,500}$$
$$M = \boxed{100}$$

Meatball $= \boxed{100}$

Cheese $= 300 - 100 = \boxed{200}$

Check

$$100(\$6) + 200(\$5) = \$600 + \$1,000$$
$$= \$1,600$$

LU 5–2a EXTRA PRACTICE QUIZ

Need more practice? Try this
Extra Practice Quiz (check
figures in Chapter Organizer,
p. 127)

Situations

1. An L. L. Bean sweater was reduced $50. The sale price was $140. What was the original price?
2. Kelly Doyle budgets $\frac{1}{7}$ of her yearly salary for entertainment. Kelly's total entertainment bill for the year is $7,000. What is Kelly's yearly salary?
3. Micro Knowledge sells 8 times as many computers as Morse Electronics. The difference in sales between the two stores is 49 computers. How many computers did each store sell?
4. Susie and Cara sell stoves at Elliott's Appliances. Together they sold 360 stoves in January. Susie sold 2 times as many stoves as Cara. How many stoves did each sell?
5. Pasquale's Pizza sells meatball pizzas ($7) and cheese pizzas ($6). In March, Pasquale's total sales were $1,800. People bought 3 times as many cheese pizzas as meatball pizzas. How many of each did Pasquale sell? What were the total dollar sales of each?
6. Pasquale's Pizza sells meatball pizzas ($7) and cheese pizzas ($6). In March, Pasquale sold 288 pizzas for $1,800. What was the dollar sales price of each?

CHAPTER ORGANIZER AND STUDY GUIDE
WITH CHECK FIGURES FOR EXTRA PRACTICE QUIZZES

Solving for unknowns from basic equations	Mechanical steps to solve unknowns	Key point(s)
Situation 1: Subtracting same number from both sides of equation, p. 117	$D + 10 = 12$ $\underline{-10 \quad\quad -10}$ $D = 2$	Subtract 10 from both sides of equation to isolate variable D on the left. Since equation used addition, we solve by using opposite process—subtraction.
Situation 2: Adding same number to both sides of equation, p. 117	$L - 24 = 40$ $\underline{+24 \quad\quad +24}$ $L = 64$	Add 24 to both sides to isolate unknown L on left. We solve by using opposite process of subtraction—addition.
Situation 3: Dividing both sides of equation by same number, p. 117	$6B = 24$ $\dfrac{\cancel{6}B}{\cancel{6}} = \dfrac{24}{\cancel{6}}$ $B = 4$	To isolate B by itself on the left, divide both sides of the equation by 6. Thus, the 6 on the left cancels—leaving B equal to 4. Since equation used multiplication, we solve unknown by using opposite process—division.
Situation 4: Multiplying both sides of equation by same number, p. 118	$\dfrac{R}{3} = 15$ $\cancel{3}\left(\dfrac{R}{\cancel{3}}\right) = 15(3)$ $R = 45$	To remove denominator, multiply both sides of the equation by 3—the 3 on the left side cancels, leaving R equal to 45. Since equation used division, we solve unknown by using opposite process—multiplication.
Situation 5: Equation that uses subtraction and multiplication to solve for unknown, p. 118	$\dfrac{B}{3} + 6 = 13$ $\underline{-6 \quad\quad -6}$ $\dfrac{B}{3} = 7$ $\cancel{3}\left(\dfrac{B}{\cancel{3}}\right) = 7(3)$ $B = 21$	1. Move constant 6 to right side by subtracting 6 from both sides. 2. Isolate B by itself on left by multiplying both sides by 3.

(continues)

CHAPTER ORGANIZER AND STUDY GUIDE
WITH CHECK FIGURES FOR EXTRA PRACTICE QUIZZES (continued)

Solving for unknowns from basic equations	Mechanical steps to solve unknowns	Key point(s)
Situation 6: Using parentheses in solving for unknown, p. 118	$6(A - 5) = 12$ $6A - 30 = 12$ $+30 \quad +30$ $\dfrac{6A}{6} = \dfrac{42}{6}$ $A = 7$	Parentheses indicate multiplication. Multiply 6 times A and 6 times -5. Result is $6A - 30$ on left side of the equation. Now add 30 to both sides to isolate $6A$ on left. To remove 6 in front of A, divide both sides by 6, to result in A equal to 7. Note that when deleting parentheses, we did not have to multiply the right side.
Situation 7: Combining like unknowns, p. 119	$6A + 2A = 64$ $\dfrac{8A}{8} = \dfrac{64}{8}$ $A = 8$	$6A + 2A$ combine to $8A$. To solve for A, we divide both sides by 8.

Solving for unknowns from word problems	Blueprint aid	Mechanical steps to solve unknown with check
Situation 1: Number problems, p. 121 U.S. Air reduced its airfare to California by $60. The sale price was $95. What was the original price?	<table><tr><td>Unknown(s)</td><td>Variable(s)</td><td>Relationship</td></tr><tr><td>Original price</td><td>P</td><td>$P - \$60 = $ Sale price Sale price $= \$95$</td></tr></table>	$P - \$60 = \$ \ 95$ $\underline{+60 \quad +60}$ $P = \$155$ **Check** $\$155 - \$60 = \$95$ $\$95 = \$95$
Situation 2: Finding the whole when part is known, p. 122 K. McCarthy spends ⅛ of her budget for school. What is the total budget if school costs $5,000?	<table><tr><td>Unknown(s)</td><td>Variable(s)</td><td>Relationship</td></tr><tr><td>Total budget</td><td>B</td><td>⅛B School $= \$5,000$</td></tr></table>	$\dfrac{1}{8}B = \$5,000$ $8\left(\dfrac{B}{8}\right) = \$5,000(8)$ $B = \$40,000$ **Check** $\dfrac{1}{8}(\$40,000) = \$5,000$ $\$5,000 = \$5,000$
Situation 3: Difference problems, p. 122 Moe sold 8 times as many suitcases as Bill. The difference in their sales is 280 suitcases. How many suitcases did each sell?	<table><tr><td>Unknown(s)</td><td>Variable(s)</td><td>Relationship</td></tr><tr><td>Suitcases sold: Moe Bill</td><td> $8S$ S</td><td> $8S$ $\underline{-S}$ 280 suitcases</td></tr></table>	$8S - S = 280$ (Bill) $\dfrac{7S}{7} = \dfrac{280}{7}$ $S = 40$ (Bill) $8(40) = 320$ (Moe) **Check** $320 - 40 = 280$ $280 = 280$
Situation 4: Calculating unit sales, p. 122 Moe sold 8 times as many suitcases as Bill. Together they sold a total of 360. How many did each sell?	<table><tr><td>Unknown(s)</td><td>Variable(s)</td><td>Relationship</td></tr><tr><td>Suitcases sold: Moe Bill</td><td> $8S$ S</td><td> $8S$ $\underline{+S}$ 360 suitcases</td></tr></table>	$8S + S = 280$ $\dfrac{9S}{9} = \dfrac{360}{9}$ $S = 40$ (Bill) $8(40) = 320$ (Moe) **Check** $320 + 40 = 360$ $360 = 360$

(continues)

CHAPTER ORGANIZER AND STUDY GUIDE
WITH CHECK FIGURES FOR EXTRA PRACTICE QUIZZES (concluded)

Solving for unknowns from word problems	Blueprint aid	Mechanical steps to solve unknown with check
Situation 5: Calculating unit and dollar sales (cost per unit) when *total units not given*, p. 123 Blue Furniture Company ordered sleepers ($300) and nonsleepers ($200) that cost $8,000. Blue expects sleepers to outsell nonsleepers 2 to 1. How many units of each were ordered? What were dollar costs of each?	(see table below)	$600N + 200N = 8,000$ $\dfrac{800N}{800} = \dfrac{8,000}{800}$ $N = \boxed{10}$ (nonsleepers) $2N = \boxed{20}$ (sleepers) **Check** $10 \times \$200 = \$2,000$ $20 \times \$300 = \underline{\ 6,000}$ $= \$8,000$
Situation 6: Calculating unit and dollar sales (cost per unit) when *total units given*, p. 123 Blue Furniture Company ordered 30 sofas (sleepers and nonsleepers) that cost $8,000. The wholesale unit cost was $300 for the sleepers and $200 for the nonsleepers. How many units of each were ordered? What were dollar costs of each?	(see table below) *Note:* When the total units are given, the higher-priced item (sleepers) is assigned to the variable first. This makes the mechanical steps easier to complete.	$\begin{aligned}300S + 200(30 - S) &= 8,000\\ 300S + 6,000 - 200S &= 8,000\\ 100S + 6,000 &= 8,000\\ -\,6,000 &\quad -6,000\\ \dfrac{100S}{100} &= \dfrac{2,000}{100}\\ S &= \boxed{20}\\ \text{Nonsleepers} = 30 - 20 &= \boxed{10}\end{aligned}$ **Check** $20(\$300) + 10(\$200) = \$8,000$ $\$6,000 + \ \ \$2,000 = \$8,000$ $\$8,000 = \$8,000$

Blueprint aid — Situation 5:

Unknown(s)	Variable(s)	Price	Relationship
Sleepers	2N	$300	600N
Nonsleepers	N	200	+200N
			$8,000 total cost

Blueprint aid — Situation 6:

Unknown(s)	Variable(s)	Price	Relationship
Unit costs			
Sleepers	S	$300	300S
Nonsleepers	30 − S	200	+200(30 − S)
			$ 8,000 total cost

KEY TERMS	Constants, *p. 116* Equation, *p. 116* Expression, *p. 116*	Formula, *p. 116* Knowns, *p. 116* Unknown, *p. 116*	Variables, *p. 116*

CHECK FIGURES FOR EXTRA PRACTICE QUIZZES WITH PAGE REFERENCES	LU 5–1a (p. 120)
	1. A. $Q/2 - 8 = 16$ B. $12(Q + 41) = 1,200$
	   C. $7 - 2Q = 1$ D. $4Q - 2 = 24$
	   E. $3Q + 3 = 19$ F. $2Q - 6 = 5$
	2. A. 56 B. 50 C. 11
	   D. 720 E. 28 F. 12
		LU 5–2a (p. 125)
		1. $P = \$190$
		2. $S = \$49,000$
		3. Morse 7; Micro 56
		4. Cara 120; Susie 240
		5. Meatball 72; cheese 216; Meatball = $504; cheese = $1,296
		6. Meatball $504; cheese $1,296

Critical Thinking Discussion Questions

1. Explain the difference between a variable and a constant. What would you consider your monthly car payment—a variable or a constant?

2. How does the opposite process rule help solve for the variable in an equation? If a Mercedes costs 3 times as much as a Saab, how could the opposite process rule be used? The selling price of the Mercedes is $60,000.

3. What is the difference between Word Problem Situations 5 and 6 in Learning Unit 5–2? Show why the more expensive item in Word Problem Situation 6 is assigned to the variable first.

Classroom Notes

Name __Anaisa Camacho__ Date __6__

DRILL PROBLEMS (First of Three Sets)

Solve the unknown from the following equations:

5–1. $D + 19 = 100$ **5–2.** $E + 90 = 200$ **5–3.** $Q + 100 = 400$ **5–4.** $Q - 60 = 850$

5–5. $5Y = 75$ **5–6.** $\dfrac{P}{6} = 92$ **5–7.** $8Y = 96$ **5–8.** $\dfrac{N}{16} = 5$

5–9. $4(P - 9) = 64$ **5–10.** $3(P - 3) = 27$

WORD PROBLEMS (First of Three Sets)

5–11. On February 14, 2007, *The Fresno Bee* reported Yosemite Fitness Center recently opened its second indoor climbing gym. The new gym, which is 6,975 square feet, is 3 times larger than the former gym. What was the size of the old gym?

5–12. In 1955 only 435 Kaiser-Darrins were built, because Kaiser-Frazer bailed out of the car business. Only 435 of these fantastic cars were ever built, they sold for $3,668 according to an article in the *Chicago Sun-Times* March 5, 2007 edition. The Kaiser-Darrin ended up being the most prized of Henry J. Kaiser's cars. It's valued today at $62,125 if in excellent condition, which is $1\frac{3}{4}$ times as much as a car in very nice condition—if you can find an owner willing to part with one for any price. What would be the value of the car in very nice condition?

5–13. Joe Sullivan and Hugh Kee sell cars for a Ford dealer. Over the past year, they sold 300 cars. Joe sells 5 times as many cars as Hugh. How many cars did each sell?

5–14. Nanda Yueh and Lane Zuriff sell homes for ERA Realty. Over the past 6 months they sold 120 homes. Nanda sold 3 times as many homes as Lane. How many homes did each sell?

5–15. Dots sells T-shirts ($2) and shorts ($4). In April, total sales were $600. People bought 4 times as many T-shirts as shorts. How many T-shirts and shorts did Dots sell? Check your answer.

5–16. Dots sells 250 T-shirts ($2) and shorts ($4). In April, total sales were $600. How many T-shirts and shorts did Dots sell? Check your answer. *Hint:* Let S = Shorts.

DRILL PROBLEMS (Second of Three Sets)

5–17. $8D = 640$

5–18. $7(A - 5) = 63$

5–19. $\dfrac{N}{9} = 7$

5–20. $18(C - 3) = 162$

5–21. $9Y - 10 = 53$

5–22. $7B + 5 = 26$

WORD PROBLEMS (Second of Three Sets)

5–23. On a flight from New York to Portland, Delta reduced its Internet price by $170.00. The sale price was $315.99. What was the original price?

5–24. Jill, an employee at Old Navy, budgets $\frac{1}{5}$ of her yearly salary for clothing. Jill's total clothing bill for the year is $8,000. What is her yearly salary?

5–25. Bill's Roast Beef sells 5 times as many sandwiches as Pete's Deli. The difference between their sales is 360 sandwiches. How many sandwiches did each sell?

5–26. Some job seekers who have difficulty finding new employment are described as discouraged workers. The September 6, 2003, issue of *The New York Times* reported that job losses were mounting. In August 2003, the count of discouraged workers rose to 503,000, $2\frac{1}{2}$ times as many as in August 2002. How many discouraged workers were there in August 2002?

5–27. Computer City sells batteries ($3) and small boxes of pens ($5). In August, total sales were $960. Customers bought 5 times as many batteries as boxes of pens. How many of each did Computer City sell? Check your answer.

5–28. Staples sells cartons of pens ($10) and rubber bands ($4). Leona ordered a total of 24 cartons for $210. How many cartons of each did Leona order? Check your answer. *Hint:* Let P = Pens.

DRILL PROBLEMS (Third of Three Sets)

5–29. $A + 90 - 15 = 210$

5–30. $5Y + 15(Y + 1) = 35$

5–31. $3M + 20 = 2M + 80$

5–32. $20(C - 50) = 19{,}000$

WORD PROBLEMS (Third of Three Sets)

5–33. The *St. Louis Post-Dispatch,* on October 25, 2006 reported on ticket scalpers. Cardinals World Series tickets were selling at 15 times more than the highest ticket at face value—others were about 8 times the lowest face value. Pete Moran paid $400 for the lowest ticket at face value. Dennis Spivey paid $9\frac{3}{8}$ times the amount paid by Pete.
How much did Dennis pay for his ticket?

5–34. At General Electric, shift 1 produced 4 times as much as shift 2. General Electric's total production for July was 5,500 jet engines. What was the output for each shift?

5–35. Ivy Corporation gave 84 people a bonus. If Ivy had given 2 more people bonuses, Ivy would have rewarded $\frac{2}{3}$ of the workforce. How large is Ivy's workforce?

5–36. Jim Murray and Phyllis Lowe received a total of $50,000 from a deceased relative's estate. They decided to put $10,000 in a trust for their nephew and divide the remainder. Phyllis received $\frac{3}{4}$ of the remainder; Jim received $\frac{1}{4}$. How much did Jim and Phyllis receive?

5–37. The first shift of GME Corporation produced $1\frac{1}{2}$ times as many lanterns as the second shift. GME produced 5,600 lanterns in November. How many lanterns did GME produce on each shift?

5–38. Wal-Mart sells thermometers ($2) and hot-water bottles ($6). In December, Wal-Mart's total sales were $1,200. Customers bought 7 times as many thermometers as hot-water bottles. How many of each did Wal-Mart sell? Check your answer.

5–39. Ace Hardware sells cartons of wrenches ($100) and hammers ($300). Howard ordered 40 cartons of wrenches and hammers for $8,400. How many cartons of each are in the order? Check your answer.

5–40. The *Omaha World-Herald* reported the number of homeless people counted during an August census. In homeless shelters, 572 men were counted. This number was $2\frac{3}{4}$ times the number of children and $2\frac{1}{2}$ times the number of women. **(a)** How many children were homeless? **(b)** How many women were homeless? **(c)** What was the total number of homeless? Round answers to the nearest whole number.

5–41. Bessy has 6 times as much money as Bob, but when each earns $6, Bessy will have 3 times as much money as Bob. How much does each have before and after earning the $6?

SUMMARY PRACTICE TEST

1. Delta reduced its round-trip ticket price from Portland to Boston by $140. The sale price was $401.90. What was the original price? *(p. 121)*

2. David Role is an employee of Google. He budgets $\frac{1}{7}$ of his salary for clothing. If Dave's total clothing for the year is $12,000, what is his yearly salary? *(p. 122)*

3. A local Best Buy sells 8 times as many iPods as Sears. The difference between their sales is 490 iPods. How many iPods did each sell? *(p. 122)*

4. Working at Staples, Jill Reese and Abby Lee sold a total of 1,200 calculators. Jill sold 5 times as many calculators as Abby. How many did each sell? *(p. 122)*

5. Target sells sets of pots ($30) and dishes ($20) at the local store. On the July 4 weekend, Target's total sales were $2,600. People bought 6 times as many pots as dishes. How many of each did Target sell? Check your answer. *(p. 123)*

6. A local Dominos sold a total of 1,600 small pizzas ($9) and pasta dinners ($13) during the Super Bowl. How many of each did Dominos sell if total sales were $15,600? Check your answer. *(p. 123)*

Personal Finance

RETIRE A MILLIONAIRE Time is on your side (and so is Uncle Sam)

The road to $1 million starts early, but if you're a late bloomer, help is at hand. The table below shows how much you need to save each month to accumulate $1 million by age 65, along with strategies for achieving that goal. At age 25, you're starting from scratch. At ages 35, 45 and 55, we assume you already have money in savings, on which you're earning 8% annually. If you're setting your goal lower or higher than $1 million, go to **kiplinger.com/ links/whatyouneed** to see how much you need to save if you're aiming to stockpile $500,000 or $2 million.

IF YOU'RE 25	IF YOU'RE 35	IF YOU'RE 45	IF YOU'RE 55

YOU'VE SAVED **$0**	YOU'VE SAVED **$0**	YOU'VE SAVED **$0**	YOU'VE SAVED **$0**
WHAT YOU NEED TO SAVE PER MONTH **$286**	WHAT YOU NEED TO SAVE PER MONTH **$671**	WHAT YOU NEED TO SAVE PER MONTH **$1,698**	WHAT YOU NEED TO SAVE PER MONTH **$5,466**

GET HELP FROM UNCLE SAM You may qualify for a retirement-savings tax credit of 10% to 50% of the amount you contribute to an IRA, 401(k) or other retirement account. The credit can reduce your tax bill by up to $1,000. To qualify, your income must be $25,000 or less if you're single, $37,500 or less if you're a head of household or $50,000 or less if you're married.

YOU'VE SAVED **$50,000**
WHAT YOU NEED TO SAVE PER MONTH **$304**

GET HELP FROM YOUR BOSS If your employer offers a matching contribution, contribute at least enough to your 401(k) to capture the full match. Otherwise, you're walking away from free money. Try to save 15% of your gross income for retirement, including your employer match.

YOU'VE SAVED **$50,000**
WHAT YOU NEED TO SAVE PER MONTH **$1,298**

YOU'VE SAVED **$100,000**
WHAT YOU NEED TO SAVE PER MONTH **$861**

PLAY CATCH-UP Aim to contribute the maximum $15,500 to your 401(k) this year or $4,000 to your traditional or Roth IRA. Once you turn 50, you can contribute an additional $5,000 in catch-up contributions to your 401(k) and an extra $1,000 to your IRA.

YOU'VE SAVED **$50,000**
WHAT YOU NEED TO SAVE PER MONTH **$4,859**

YOU'VE SAVED **$100,000**
WHAT YOU NEED TO SAVE PER MONTH **$4,253**

YOU'VE SAVED **$200,000**
WHAT YOU NEED TO SAVE PER MONTH **$3,040**

STAY ON THE JOB Working a few years longer can boost your savings.

SOURCE: Nuveen Investments

IS YOUR RETIREMENT SAVING ON COURSE? | Go to kiplinger.com/tools

BUSINESS MATH ISSUE

Saving at a young age is not realistic.

1. List the key points of the article and information to support your position.
2. Write a group defense of your position using math calculations to support your view.

PROJECT A
Calculate the total price tag for each item (do not include maintenance fee).

Owning Part of a Yacht or a Bentley

Silverton Marine

Sharing a Fancy Car or Boat
Several companies offer fractional ownership in recreational vehicles, fancy cars and large boats. A sampling:

COMPANY	THE GOODS	PRICE TAG	DETAILS
A. American QuarterCoach 800-789-4885 (ext. 712)	2005 Prevost, 45 feet, sleeps up to four people, location to be determined	$184,500 for a one-eighth share; $7,020 per year in maintenance	Owner gets five weeks of use per year; coach is sold after three years and owners split the proceeds.
B. Exotic Car Share 847-358-7522	2004 Bentley Continental GT, garaged in Palatine, Ill., outside of Chicago	$30,000 for a one-fifth share; $10,000 per year for maintenance	Exotic guarantees at least $18,500 back when it sells the Bentley after three years.
C. Great Lakes BoatShare 586-419-6798	2003 Silverton Motor Yacht 453, 48 feet, sleeps six to eight, will likely be docked in St. Clair Shores, Mich.	$102,363 for a one-sixth share; $7,243 for maintenance	Owner gets four weekends, and 15 weekdays between early May and the end of October. Boat is sold after three years.
D. YachtSmart of North America 866-869-2248	2004 Azimut, 85 feet, sleeps eight (not including crew), owners determine where yacht travels	$500,000 for a one-eighth share; $49,500 per year for maintenance	Four weeks of use per year (maintenance and transit eat up 20 weeks). Boat is sold after five years.

Wall Street Journal © 2005

Internet Projects: See text Web site (www.mhhe.com/slater9e) and The Business Math Internet Resource Guide.

136

CHAPTER 6

Percents and Their Applications

LEARNING UNIT OBJECTIVES

LU 6–1: Conversions

- Convert decimals to percents (including rounding percents), percents to decimals, and fractions to percents *(pp. 139–141)*.
- Convert percents to fractions *(p. 142)*.

LU 6–2: Application of Percents—Portion Formula

- List and define the key elements of the portion formula *(pp. 144–145)*.
- Solve for one unknown of the portion formula when the other two key elements are given *(pp. 145–148)*.
- Calculate the rate of percent decreases and increases *(pp. 148–151)*.

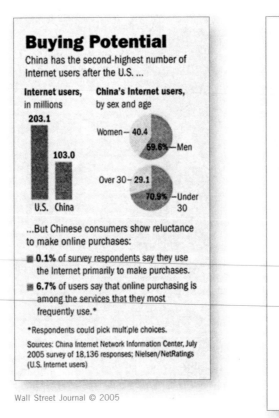

Did you know that 60% of Internet users in China are men and that Ford plans to cut 10% of its workforce of salaried jobs? These facts are from the two *Wall Street Journal* clippings "Buying Potential" and "Ford to Cut 4,000 U.S. Salaried Jobs in Retooling Effort." Note in these *Wall Street Journal* clippings how companies frequently use percents to express various decreases and increases between two or more numbers, or to determine a decrease or increase.

To understand percents, you should first understand the conversion relationship between decimals, percents, and fractions as explained in Learning Unit 6–1. Then, in Learning Unit 6–2, you will be ready to apply percents to personal and business events.

Learning Unit 6–1: Conversions

When we described parts of a whole in previous chapters, we used fractions and decimals. Percents also describe parts of a whole. The word *percent* means per 100. The percent symbol (%) indicates hundredths (division by 100). **Percents** are the result of expressing numbers as part of 100. Thus, Ford's 10% cut in its workforce of salaried jobs represents 10 out of 100.

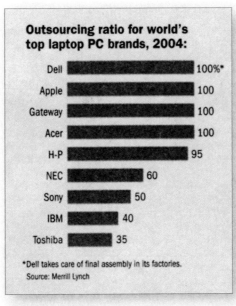

Percents can provide some revealing information. The *Wall Street Journal* clipping "Outsourcing Ratio for World's Top Laptop PC Brands, 2004" shows that Dell, Apple, Gateway, and Acer outsource 100% of their top laptop PC brands.

TABLE	6.1

Analyzing a bag of M&M's®

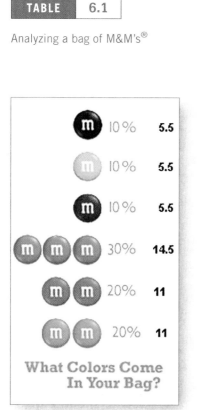

	10%	5.5
	10%	5.5
	10%	5.5
	30%	14.5
	20%	11
	20%	11

What Colors Come In Your Bag?

Information adapted from http://us.mms.com/us/about/products/milkchocolate/

Color	Fraction	Decimal (hundredth)	Percent (hundredth)
Yellow	$\frac{18}{55}$	.33	32.73%
Red	$\frac{10}{55}$	.18	18.18
Blue	$\frac{9}{55}$	.16	16.36
Orange	$\frac{7}{55}$	.13	12.73
Brown	$\frac{6}{55}$	.11	10.91
Green	$\frac{5}{55}$	.09	9.09
Total	$\frac{55}{55} = 1$	1.00	100.00%

Let's return to the M&M's® example from earlier chapters. In Table 6.1, we use our bag of 55 M&M's® to show how fractions, decimals, and percents can refer to the same parts of a whole. For example, the bag of 55 M&M's® contains 18 yellow M&M's®. As you can see in Table 6.1, the 18 candies in the bag of 55 can be expressed as a fraction ($\frac{18}{55}$), decimal (.33), and percent (32.73%). If you visit the M&M's® website, you will see that the standard is 11 yellow M&M's®. The clipping "What Colors Come in Your Bag?" shows an M&M's® Milk Chocolate Candies Color Chart.

In this unit we discuss converting decimals to percents (including rounding percents), percents to decimals, fractions to percents, and percents to fractions. You will see when you study converting fractions to percents why you should first learn how to convert decimals to percents.

Converting Decimals to Percents

The following Wall Street Journal clipping "Getting in the Door: More Online" shows that 2% or 2 out of 100 vendors are able to get a foot in the door of Wal-Mart. If the clipping had stated the 2% as a decimal (.02), could you give its equivalent in percent? The decimal .02 in decimal fraction is $\frac{2}{100}$. As you know, percents are the result of expressing numbers as part of 100, so $2\% = \frac{2}{100}$. You can now conclude that $.02 = \frac{2}{100} = 2\%$.

GETTING IN THE DOOR: *More Online*

Of the 10,000 suppliers who applied to become Wal-Mart vendors last year, only about 2% were accepted. For small businesses looking to get a foot in the door of the world's largest retailer, there are some ways to improve your chances.

Readers who would like to learn more can go to the Online Journal, at **WSJ.com/Free**, to hear an interview with the Journal's Gwendolyn Bounds as she offers tips gleaned from her reporting for this article. In the interview, Ms. Bounds discusses the importance of thinking locally and getting the price right, among other topics.

Wall Street Journal © 2005

The steps for converting decimals to percents are as follows:

CONVERTING DECIMALS TO PERCENTS
Step 1. Move the decimal point two places to the right. You are multiplying by 100. If necessary, add zeros. This rule is also used for whole numbers and mixed decimals.
Step 2. Add a percent symbol at the end of the number.

EXAMPLES

$$.66 = .66. = \boxed{66\%} \qquad .8 = .80. = \boxed{80\%} \qquad 8 = 8.00. = \boxed{800\%}$$

Add 1 zero to   Add 2 zeros to
make two places.   make two places.

$$.425 = .42.5 = \boxed{42.5\%} \qquad .007 = .00.7 = \boxed{.7\%} \qquad 2.51 = 2.51. = \boxed{251\%}$$

Caution: One percent means 1 out of every 100. Since .7% is less than 1%, it means $\frac{7}{10}$ of 1%—a very small amount. Less than 1% is less than .01. To show a number less than 1%, you must use more than two decimal places and add 2 zeros. Example: .7% = .007.

Rounding Percents

When necessary, percents should be rounded. Rounding percents is similar to rounding whole numbers. Use the following steps to round percents:

ROUNDING PERCENTS
Step 1. When you convert from a fraction or decimal, be sure your answer is in percent before rounding.
Step 2. Identify the specific digit. If the digit to the right of the identified digit is 5 or greater, round up the identified digit.
Step 3. Delete digits to right of the identified digit.

For example, Table 6.1 (p. 139) shows that the 18 yellow M&M's® rounded to the nearest hundredth percent is 32.73% of the bag of 55 M&M's®. Let's look at how we arrived at this figure.

When using a calculator, you press 18 ÷ 55 %. This allows you to go right to percent, avoiding the decimal step.

Step 1. $\dfrac{18}{55} = .3272727 = 32.72727\%$ Note that the number is in percent! Identify the hundredth percent digit.

Step 2.   32.73727%   Digit to the right of the identified digit is greater than 5, so the identified digit is increased by 1.

Step 3.   32.73%   Delete digits to the right of the identified digit.

Converting Percents to Decimals

Note that in the following Barron's clipping "Kellogg by the Numbers," 54.5% of Kellogg's revenue came from cereal sales.

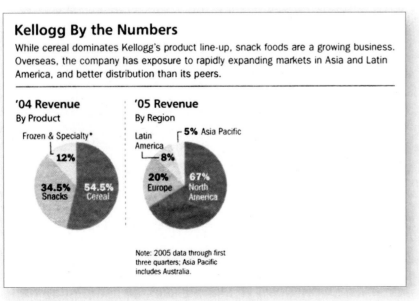

Kellogg By the Numbers

While cereal dominates Kellogg's product line-up, snack foods are a growing business. Overseas, the company has exposure to rapidly expanding markets in Asia and Latin America, and better distribution than its peers.

'04 Revenue
By Product

Frozen & Specialty*
12%
34.5% Snacks
54.5% Cereal

'05 Revenue
By Region

Latin America
5% Asia Pacific
8%
20% Europe
67% North America

Note: 2005 data through first three quarters; Asia Pacific includes Australia.

Barron's © 2006

Battle Creek Enquirer/Scott Erskine/ AP Wide World

In the paragraph and steps that follow, you will learn how to convert percents to decimals. The example below the steps using 2% comes from the clipping "Getting in the Door" (p. 139). As previously indicated, the example using 54.5% comes from the clipping "Kellogg by the Numbers."

To convert percents to decimals, you reverse the process used to convert decimals to percents. In our earlier discussion on converting decimals to percents (p. 139), we asked if the 2% in the "Getting in the Door" clipping had been in decimals and not percent, could you convert the decimals to the 2%? Once again, the definition of percent states that 2% = 2/100. The fraction 2/100 can be written in decimal form as .02. You can conclude that 2% = 2/100 = .02. Now you can see this procedure in the following conversion steps:

CONVERTING PERCENTS TO DECIMALS

Step 1. Drop the percent symbol.

Step 2. Move the decimal point two places to the left. You are dividing by 100. If necessary, add zeros.

EXAMPLES

Note that when a percent is less than 1%, the decimal conversion has at least two leading zeros before the number .0095.

$$.95\% = .00.95 = \boxed{.0095}$$ $$2\% = .02. = \boxed{.02}$$ $$66\% = .66. = \boxed{.66}$$

Add 2 zeros to make two places. Add 1 zero to make two places.

$$54.5\% = .54.5 = \boxed{.545}$$ $$824.4\% = 8.24.4 = \boxed{8.244}$$

Now we must explain how to change fractional percents such as $\frac{1}{5}\%$ to a decimal. Remember that fractional percents are values less than 1%. For example, $\frac{1}{5}\%$ is $\frac{1}{5}$ of 1%. Fractional percents can appear singly or in combination with whole numbers. To convert them to decimals, use the following steps:

CONVERTING FRACTIONAL PERCENTS TO DECIMALS

Step 1. Convert a single fractional percent to its decimal equivalent by dividing the numerator by the denominator. If necessary, round the answer.

Step 2. If a fractional percent is combined with a whole number (mixed fractional percent), convert the fractional percent first. Then combine the whole number and the fractional percent.

Step 3. Drop the percent symbol; move the decimal point two places to the left (this divides the number by 100).

EXAMPLES

$$\frac{1}{5}\% = .20\% = .00.20 = \boxed{.0020}$$ Think of $7\frac{3}{4}\%$ as

$$\frac{1}{4}\% = .25\% = .00.25 = \boxed{.0025}$$ $$7\% = .07$$

$$7\frac{3}{4}\% = 7.75\% = .07.75 = \boxed{.0775}$$ $$+\frac{3}{4}\% = +.0075$$

$$6\frac{1}{2}\% = 6.5\% = .06.5 = \boxed{.065}$$ $$7\frac{3}{4}\% = .0775$$

Converting Fractions to Percents

When fractions have denominators of 100, the numerator becomes the percent. Other fractions must be first converted to decimals; then the decimals are converted to percents.

CONVERTING FRACTIONS TO PERCENTS
Step 1. Divide the numerator by the denominator to convert the fraction to a decimal.
Step 2. Move the decimal point two places to the right; add the percent symbol.

EXAMPLES

$$\frac{3}{4} = .75 = .75. = \boxed{75\%} \qquad \frac{1}{5} = .20 = .20. = \boxed{20\%} \qquad \frac{1}{20} = .05 = .05. = \boxed{5\%}$$

Converting Percents to Fractions

Using the definition of percent, you can write any percent as a fraction whose denominator is 100. Thus, when we convert a percent to a fraction, we drop the percent symbol and write the number over 100, which is the same as multiplying the number by $\frac{1}{100}$. This method of multiplying by $\frac{1}{100}$ is also used for fractional percents.

CONVERTING A WHOLE PERCENT (OR A FRACTIONAL PERCENT) TO A FRACTION
Step 1. Drop the percent symbol.
Step 2. Multiply the number by $\frac{1}{100}$.
Step 3. Reduce to lowest terms.

EXAMPLES

$$76\% = 76 \times \frac{1}{100} = \frac{76}{100} = \frac{19}{25} \qquad \frac{1}{8}\% = \frac{1}{8} \times \frac{1}{100} = \frac{1}{800}$$

$$156\% = 156 \times \frac{1}{100} = \frac{156}{100} = 1\frac{56}{100} = 1\frac{14}{25}$$

Sometimes a percent contains a whole number and a fraction such as $12\frac{1}{2}\%$ or 22.5%. Extra steps are needed to write a mixed or decimal percent as a simplified fraction.

CONVERTING A MIXED OR DECIMAL PERCENT TO A FRACTION
Step 1. Drop the percent symbol.
Step 2. Change the mixed percent to an improper fraction.
Step 3. Multiply the number by $\frac{1}{100}$.
Step 4. Reduce to lowest terms.
Note: If you have a mixed or decimal percent, change the decimal portion to fractional equivalent and continue with Steps 1 to 4.

EXAMPLES
$$12\frac{1}{2}\% = \frac{25}{2} \times \frac{1}{100} = \frac{25}{200} = \frac{1}{8}$$

$$12.5\% = 12\frac{1}{2}\% = \frac{25}{2} \times \frac{1}{100} = \frac{25}{200} = \frac{1}{8}$$

$$22.5\% = 22\frac{1}{2}\% = \frac{45}{2} \times \frac{1}{100} = \frac{45}{200} = \frac{9}{40}$$

It's time to check your understanding of Learning Unit 6–1.

LU 6–1	PRACTICE QUIZ

Complete this **Practice Quiz** to see how you are doing

Convert to percents (round to the nearest tenth percent as needed):

1. .6666 _____   **2.** .832 _____

3. .004 _____   **4.** 8.94444 _____

Convert to decimals (remember, decimals representing less than 1% will have at least 2 leading zeros before the number):

5. $\frac{1}{4}\%$ _____   **6.** $6\frac{3}{4}\%$ _____

7. 87% _____   **8.** 810.9% _____

Convert to percents (round to the nearest hundredth percent):

9. $\frac{1}{7}$ _____   **10.** $\frac{2}{9}$ _____

Convert to fractions (remember, if it is a mixed number, first convert to an improper fraction):

11. 19% _____   **12.** $71\frac{1}{2}\%$ _____   **13.** 130% _____

14. $\frac{1}{2}\%$ _____   **15.** 19.9% _____

✓ **Solutions**

1. .66.66 = $\boxed{66.7\%}$ **2.** .83.2 = $\boxed{83.2\%}$

3. .00.4 = $\boxed{.4\%}$ **4.** 8.94.444 = $\boxed{894.4\%}$

5. $\frac{1}{4}\% = .25\% = \boxed{.0025}$ **6.** $6\frac{3}{4}\% = 6.75\% = \boxed{.0675}$

7. 87% = .87. = $\boxed{.87}$ **8.** 810.9% = 8.10.9 = $\boxed{8.109}$

9. $\frac{1}{7} = .14.285 = \boxed{14.29\%}$ **10.** $\frac{2}{9} = .22.2\bar{2} = \boxed{22.22\%}$

11. $19\% = 19 \times \frac{1}{100} = \boxed{\frac{19}{100}}$ **12.** $71\frac{1}{2}\% = \frac{143}{2} \times \frac{1}{100} = \boxed{\frac{143}{200}}$

13. $130\% = 130 \times \frac{1}{100} = \frac{130}{100} = 1\frac{30}{100} = 1\boxed{\frac{3}{10}}$ **14.** $\frac{1}{2}\% = \frac{1}{2} \times \frac{1}{100} = \boxed{\frac{1}{200}}$

15. $19\frac{9}{10}\% = \frac{199}{10} \times \frac{1}{100} = \boxed{\frac{199}{1,000}}$

LU 6–1a	EXTRA PRACTICE QUIZ

Need more practice? Try this **Extra Practice Quiz** (check figures in Chapter Organizer, p. 156)

Convert to percents (round to the nearest tenth percent as needed):

1. .4444   **2.** .782

3. .006   **4.** 7.93333

Convert to decimals (remember, decimals representing less than 1% will have at least 2 leading zeros before the number):

5. $\frac{1}{5}\%$ **6.** $7\frac{4}{5}\%$

7. 92%   **8.** 765.8%

Convert to percents (round to the nearest hundredth percent):

9. $\frac{1}{3}$ **10.** $\frac{3}{7}$

Convert to fractions (remember, if it is a mixed number, first convert to an improper fraction):

11. 17%   **12.** $82\frac{1}{4}\%$ **13.** 150%

14. $\frac{1}{4}\%$ **15.** 17.8%

Learning Unit 6–2: Application of Percents—Portion Formula

The bag of M&M's® we have been studying contains Milk Chocolate M&M's®. M&M/Mars also makes Peanut M&M's® and some other types of M&M's®. To study the application of percents to problems involving M&M's®, we make two key assumptions:

1. Total sales of Milk Chocolate M&M's®, Peanut M&M's®, and other M&M's® chocolate candies are $400,000.

2. Eighty percent of M&M's® sales are Milk Chocolate M&M's®. This leaves the Peanut and other M&M's® chocolate candies with 20% of sales (100% − 80%).

80% M&M's®	20% M&M's®	100%
Milk Chocolate +	Peanut and other =	Total sales
M&M's®	chocolate candies	($400,000)

Before we begin, you must understand the meaning of three terms—*base, rate,* and *portion.* These terms are the key elements in solving percent problems.

- **Base (B).** The **base** is the beginning whole quantity or value (100%) with which you will compare some other quantity or value. Often the problems give the base after the word *of.* For example, the whole (total) sales of M&M's®—Milk Chocolate M&M's, Peanut, and other M&M's® chocolate candies—are $400,000.

- **Rate (R).** The **rate** is a percent, decimal, or fraction that indicates the part of the base that you must calculate. The percent symbol often helps you identify the rate. For example, Milk Chocolate M&M's® currently account for 80% of sales. So the rate is 80%. Remember that 80% is also $\frac{4}{5}$, or .80.

- **Portion (P).** The **portion** is the amount or part that results from the base multiplied by the rate. For example, total sales of M&M's® are $400,000 (base); $400,000 times .80 (rate) equals $320,000 (portion), or the sales of Milk Chocolate M&M's®. *A key point to remember is that portion is a number and not a percent. In fact, the portion can be larger than the base if the rate is greater than 100%.*

Solving Percents with the Portion Formula

In problems involving portion, base, and rate, we give two of these elements. You must find the third element. Remember the following key formula:

Portion (*P*) = Base (*B*) × Rate (*R*)

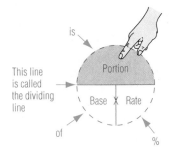

To help you solve for the portion, base, and rate, this unit shows pie charts. The shaded area in each pie chart indicates the element that you must solve for. For example, since we shaded *portion* in the pie chart at the left, you must solve for portion. To use the pie charts, put your finger on the shaded area (in this case portion). The formula that remains tells you what to do. So in the pie chart at the left, you solve the problem by multiplying base by the rate. Note the circle around the pie chart is broken since we want to emphasize that portion can be larger than base if rate is greater than 100%. The horizontal line in the pie chart is called the dividing line, and we will use it when we solve for base or rate.

The following example summarizes the concept of base, rate, and portion. Assume that you received a small bonus check of $100. This is a gross amount—your company did not withhold any taxes. You will have to pay 20% in taxes.

Base: 100%—whole. Usually given after the word *of*—but not always.	**Rate:** Usually expressed as a percent but could also be a decimal or fraction.	**Portion:** A number—not a percent and not the whole.
$100 bonus check	20% taxes	$20 taxes

First decide what you are looking for. You want to know how much you must pay in taxes—the portion. How do you get the portion? From the portion formula Portion (P) = Base (B) × Rate (R), you know that you must multiply the base ($100) by the rate (20%). When you do this, you get $100 × .20 = $20. So you must pay $20 in taxes.

Let's try our first word problem by taking a closer look at the M&M's® example to see how we arrived at the $320,000 sales of Milk Chocolate M&M's® given earlier. We will be using blueprint aids to help dissect and solve each word problem.

Solving for Portion

The Word Problem Sales of Milk Chocolate M&M's® are 80% of the total M&M's® sales. Total M&M's® sales are $400,000. What are the sales of Milk Chocolate M&M's®?

The facts	Solving for?	Steps to take	Key points
Milk Chocolate M&M's® sales: 80%. *Total M&M's® sales:* $400,000.	Sales of Milk Chocolate M&M's®.	Identify key elements. *Base:* $400,000. *Rate:* .80. *Portion:* ? Portion = Base × Rate.	Amount or part of beginning Portion (?) Base × Rate ($400,000) (.80) Beginning whole quantity (often after "of") Percent symbol or word (here we put into decimal) Portion and rate must relate to same piece of base.

Steps to solving problem

1. Set up the formula.   Portion = Base × Rate

2. Calculate portion (sales of Milk Chocolate M&M's®). $P = \$400,000 \times .80$
$P = \$320,000$

In the first column of the blueprint aid, we gather the facts. In the second column, we state that we are looking for sales of Milk Chocolate M&M's®. In the third column, we identify each key element and the formula needed to solve the problem. Review the pie chart in the fourth column. Note that the portion and rate must relate to the same piece of the base. In this word problem, we can see from the solution below the blueprint aid that sales of Milk Chocolate M&M's® are $320,000. The $320,000 does indeed represent 80% of the base. Note here that the portion ($320,000) is less than the base of $400,000 since the rate is less than 100%.

Now let's work another word problem that solves for the portion.

The Word Problem Sales of Milk Chocolate M&M's® are 80% of the total M&M's® sales. Total M&M's® sales are $400,000. What are the sales of Peanut and other M&M's® chocolate candies?

The facts	Solving for?	Steps to take	Key points
Milk Chocolate M&M's® sales: 80%. *Total M&M's® sales:* $400,000.	Sales of Peanut and other M&M's® chocolate candies.	Identify key elements. *Base:* $400,000. *Rate:* .20 (100% − 80%). *Portion:* ? Portion = Base × Rate.	If 80% of sales are Milk Chocolate M&M's, then 20% are Peanut and other M&M's® chocolate candies. Portion (?) Base × Rate ($400,000) (.20) Portion and rate must relate to same piece of base.

Steps to solving problem

1. Set up the formula.   Portion = Base × Rate

2. Calculate portion (sale of Peanut and other $P = \$400,000 \times .20$
   M&M's® chocolate candies). $P = \$80,000$

In the previous blueprint aid, note that we must use a rate that agrees with the portion so the portion and rate refer to the same piece of the base. Thus, if 80% of sales are Milk Chocolate M&M's®, 20% must be Peanut and other M&M's® chocolate candies (100% − 80% = 20%). So we use a rate of .20.

In Step 2, we multiplied $400,000 × .20 to get a portion of $80,000. This portion represents the part of the sales that were *not* Milk Chocolate M&M's®. Note that the rate of .20 and the portion of $80,000 relate to the same piece of the base—$80,000 is 20% of $400,000. Also note that the portion ($80,000) is less than the base ($400,000) since the rate is less than 100%.

Take a moment to review the two blueprint aids in this section. Be sure you understand why the rate in the first blueprint aid was 80% and the rate in the second blueprint aid was 20%.

Solving for Rate

The Word Problem Sales of Milk Chocolate M&M's® are $320,000. Total M&M's® sales are $400,000. What is the percent of Milk Chocolate M&M's® sales compared to total M&M's® sales?

The facts	Solving for?	Steps to take	Key points
Milk Chocolate M&M's® sales: $320,000. *Total M&M's® sales:* $400,000.	Percent of Milk Chocolate M&M's® sales to total M&M's® sales.	Identify key elements. *Base:* $400,000. *Rate:* ? *Portion:* $320,000 $\text{Rate} = \dfrac{\text{Portion}}{\text{Base}}$	Since portion is less than base, the rate must be less than 100% Portion ($320,000) Base × Rate ($400,000) (?) Portion and rate must relate to the same piece of base.

Steps to solving problem

1. Set up the formula. $\text{Rate} = \dfrac{\text{Portion}}{\text{Base}}$

2. Calculate rate (percent of Milk $R = \dfrac{\$320,000}{\$400,000}$
   Chocolate M&M's® sales).
                                                                                             $R = 80\%$

Note that in this word problem, the rate of 80% and the portion of $320,000 refer to the same piece of the base.

The Word Problem Sales of Milk Chocolate M&M's® are $320,000. Total sales of Milk Chocolate M&M's, Peanut, and other M&M's® chocolate candies are $400,000. What percent of Peanut and other M&M's® chocolate candies are sold compared to total M&M's® sales?

The facts	Solving for?	Steps to take	Key points
Milk Chocolate M&M's® sales: $320,000. *Total M&M's® sales:* $400,000.	Percent of Peanut and other M&M's® chocolate candies sales compared to total M&M's® sales.	Identify key elements. *Base:* $400,000. *Rate:* ? *Portion:* $80,000 ($400,000 − $320,000). $Rate = \dfrac{Portion}{Base}$	Represents sales of Peanut and other M&M's® chocolate candies Portion ($80,000) Base × Rate ($400,000) (?) When portion becomes $80,000, the portion and rate now relate to same piece of base.

Steps to solving problem

1. Set up the formula.

2. Calculate rate.

$$Rate = \frac{Portion}{Base}$$

$$R = \frac{\$80,000}{\$400,000} \quad (\$400,000 - \$320,000)$$

$$R = \boxed{20\%}$$

The word problem asks for the rate of candy sales that are *not* Milk Chocolate M&M's. Thus, $400,000 of total candy sales less sales of Milk Chocolate M&M's® ($320,000) allows us to arrive at sales of Peanut and other M&M's® chocolate candies ($80,000). The $80,000 portion represents 20% of total candy sales. The $80,000 portion and 20% rate refer to the same piece of the $400,000 base. Compare this blueprint aid with the blueprint aid for the previous word problem. Ask yourself why in the previous word problem the rate was 80% and in this word problem the rate is 20%. In both word problems, the portion was less than the base since the rate was less than 100%.

Now we go on to calculate the base. Remember to read the word problem carefully so that you match the rate and portion to the same piece of the base.

Solving for Base

The Word Problem Sales of Peanut and other M&M's® chocolate candies are 20% of total M&M's® sales. Sales of Milk Chocolate M&M's® are $320,000. What are the total sales of all M&M's®?

The facts	Solving for?	Steps to take	Key points
Peanut and other M&M's® chocolate candies sales: 20%. *Milk Chocolate M&M's® sales:* $320,000.	Total M&M's® sales.	Identify key elements. *Base:* ? *Rate:* .80 (100% − 20%) *Portion:* $320,000 $Base = \dfrac{Portion}{Rate}$	Portion ($320,000) Base × Rate (?) (.80) (100% − 20%) Portion ($320,000) and rate (.80) do relate to the same piece of base.

Steps to solving problem

1. Set up the formula.

$$\text{Base} = \frac{\text{Portion}}{\text{Rate}}$$

2. Calculate the base.

$$B = \frac{\$320,000}{.80} \longleftarrow \$320,000 \text{ is } 80\% \text{ of base}$$

$$B = \boxed{\$400,000}$$

Note that we could not use 20% for the rate. The $320,000 of Milk Chocolate M&M's® represents 80% (100% − 20%) of the total sales of M&M's®. We use 80% so that the portion and rate refer to same piece of the base. Remember that the portion ($320,000) is less than the base ($400,000) since the rate is less than 100%.

Calculating Percent Decreases and Increases

In the following *Wall Street Journal* clipping "Wal-Mart's Entry Likely to Reshape Warranty Game," we see a product's warranty as a percentage of the price of a 42-inch plasma TV. If you buy a 42-inch plasma TV, would you buy an extended warranty? Did you realize how much extended warranties can cost? Using this clipping, let's look at how to calculate percent decreases and increases.

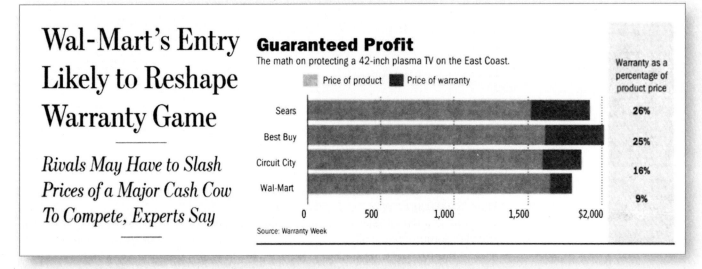

Wall Street Journal © 2005

Rate of Percent Decrease Using Sears

Assume: Sears drops its 42-inch plasma TV price to $900 from $1,500.

$$\text{Rate} = \frac{\text{Portion}}{\text{Base}} \quad \begin{array}{l} \longleftarrow \text{ Difference between old and new TV price} \\ \longleftarrow \text{ Old TV amount} \end{array}$$

$$R = \frac{\$600\,(\$1,500 - \$900)}{\$1,500}$$

$$R = \boxed{40\%}$$

Let's prove the 40% with a pie chart.

Decrease in TV price

Portion
($600)

Base × Rate
($1,500)   (?)

Original TV price

The formula for calculating Sears' **percent decrease** is as follows:

Percent decrease

$$\text{Percent of decrease } (R) \atop (40\%) = \frac{\text{Amount of decrease } (P) \atop (\$600)}{\text{Original TV price } (B) \atop (\$1,500)}$$

Now let's look at how to calculate Best Buy's *percent increase* in plasma TVs using the portion formula for solving the rate.

Rate of Percent Increase Using Best Buy

Assume: Best Buy increases its 42-inch plasma TV price to $1,200 from $1,000.

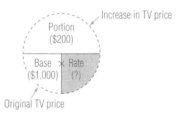

$$\text{Rate} = \frac{\text{Portion}}{\text{Base}} \overset{\text{Difference between old and new TV price}}{\underset{\text{Old TV amount}}{}}$$

$$R = \frac{\$200\,(\$1,200 - \$1,000)}{\$1,000}$$

$$R = \boxed{20\%}$$

Let's prove the 20% with a pie chart.

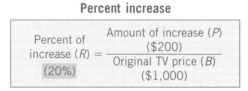

The formula for calculating Best Buy's **percent increase** is as follows:

Percent increase

$$\text{Percent of increase } (R) \atop (20\%) = \frac{\text{Amount of increase } (P) \atop (\$200)}{\text{Original TV price } (B) \atop (\$1,000)}$$

In conclusion, the following steps can be used to calculate percent decreases and increases:

CALCULATING PERCENT DECREASES AND INCREASES
Step 1. Find the difference between amounts (such as advertising costs).
Step 2. Divide Step 1 by the original amount (the base): $R = P \div B$. Be sure to express your answer in percent.

Before concluding this chapter, we will show how to calculate a percent increase and decrease using M&M's® (Figure 6.1).

FIGURE | **6.1**

Bag of 18.40-ounce M&M's®

Additional Examples Using M&M's

The Word Problem Sheila Leary went to her local supermarket and bought the bag of M&M's® shown in Figure 6.1 (p. 149). The bag gave its weight as 18.40 ounces, which was 15% more than a regular 1-pound bag of M&M's®. Sheila, who is a careful shopper, wanted to check and see if she was actually getting a 15% increase. Let's help Sheila dissect and solve this problem.

The facts	Solving for?	Steps to take	Key points
New bag of M&M's®: 18.40 oz. 15% increase in weight. *Original bag of M&M's®:* 16 oz. (1 lb.)	Checking percent increase of 15%.	Identify key elements. *Base:* 16 oz. *Rate:* ? *Portion:* 2.40 oz. $\begin{pmatrix} 18.40 \text{ oz.} \\ - 16.00 \\ \hline 2.40 \text{ oz.} \end{pmatrix}$ Rate $= \dfrac{\text{Portion}}{\text{Base}}$	Difference between base and new weight. Portion (2.40 oz.) Base × Rate (16 oz.) (?) Original amount sold

Steps to solving problem

1. Set up the formula.   Rate $= \dfrac{\text{Portion}}{\text{Base}}$

2. Calculate the rate. $R = \dfrac{2.40 \text{ oz.}}{16.00 \text{ oz.}}$ ← Difference between base and new weight. ← Old weight equals 100%.

   $R = 15\%$ increase

The new weight of the bag of M&M's® is really 115% of the old weight:

$$
\begin{array}{rcl}
16.00 \text{ oz.} & = & 100\% \\
+ \ 2.40 & = & + \ 15 \\
\hline
18.40 \text{ oz.} & = & 115\% = 1.15
\end{array}
$$

We can check this by looking at the following pie chart:

Portion = Base × Rate

18.40 oz. = 16 oz. × 1.15

Portion (18.40 oz.) Base × Rate (16 oz.) (1.15) 100%

Why is the portion greater than the base? Remember that the portion can be larger than the base only if the rate is greater than 100%. Note how the portion and rate relate to the same piece of the base—18.40 oz. is 115% of the base (16 oz.).

Let's see what could happen if M&M/Mars has an increase in its price of sugar. This is an additional example to reinforce the concept of percent decrease.

The Word Problem The increase in the price of sugar caused the M&M/Mars company to decrease the weight of each 1-pound bag of M&M's® to 12 ounces. What is the rate of percent decrease?

The facts	Solving for?	Steps to take	Key points
16-oz. bag of M&M's®: reduced to 12 oz.	Rate of percent decrease.	Identify key elements. *Base:* 16 oz. *Rate:* ? *Portion:* 4 oz. (16 oz. − 12 oz.) Rate $= \dfrac{\text{Portion}}{\text{Base}}$	Amount of decrease Portion (4 oz.) Base × Rate (16 oz.) (?) Old base 100%

Steps to solving problem

1. Set up the formula.

$$\text{Rate} = \frac{\text{Portion}}{\text{Base}}$$

2. Calculate the rate.

$$R = \frac{4 \text{ oz.}}{16.00 \text{ oz.}}$$

$R = 25\%$ decrease

The new weight of the bag of M&M's® is 75% of the old weight:

$$
\begin{array}{ll}
16 \text{ oz.} = & 100\% \\
\underline{-\ 4} & \underline{-\ 25} \\
12 \text{ oz.} = & 75\%
\end{array}
$$

We can check this by looking at the following pie chart:

Portion = Base × Rate

12 oz. = 16 oz. × .75

Portion
(12 oz.)

Base × Rate
(16 oz.) (.75)

100%

Note that the portion is smaller than the base because the rate is less than 100%. Also note how the portion and rate relate to the same piece of the base—12 ounces is 75% of the base (16 oz.).

After your study of Learning Unit 6–2, you should be ready for the Practice Quiz.

LU 6–2 **PRACTICE QUIZ**

Complete this **Practice Quiz** to see how you are doing

Solve for portion:

1. 38% of 900. **2.** 60% of $9,000.

Solve for rate (round to nearest tenth percent as needed):

3. 430 is _____ % of 5,000. **4.** 200 is _____ % of 700.

Solve for base (round to the nearest tenth as needed):

5. 55 is 40% of _____. **6.** 900 is $4\frac{1}{2}$% of _____.

Solve the following (blueprint aids are shown in the solution; you might want to try some on scrap paper):

7. Five out of 25 students in Professor Ford's class received an A grade. What percent of the class *did not* receive the A grade?

8. Abby Biernet has yet to receive 60% of her lobster order. Abby received 80 lobsters to date. What was her original order?

9. In 2006, Dunkin' Donuts Company had $300,000 in doughnut sales. In 2007, sales were up 40%. What are Dunkin' Donuts sales for 2007?

10. The price of an Apple computer dropped from $1,600 to $1,200. What was the percent decrease?

11. In 1982, a ticket to the Boston Celtics cost $14. In 2007, a ticket cost $50. What is the percent increase to the nearest hundredth percent?

✓ **Solutions**

1. $342 = 900 \times .38$
$(P) = (B) \times (R)$

2. $\$5,400 = \$9,000 \times .60$
$(P) = (B) \times (R)$

3. $\dfrac{(P)430}{(B)5,000} = .086 = 8.6\% \ (R)$

4. $\dfrac{(P)200}{(B)700} = .2857 = 28.6\% \ (R)$

5. $\dfrac{(P)55}{(R).40} = 137.5 \ (B)$

6. $\dfrac{(P)900}{(R).045} = 20,000 \ (B)$

7. Percent of Professor Ford's class that did not receive an A grade:

The facts	Solving for?	Steps to take	Key points
5 As. 25 in class.	Percent that did not receive A.	Identify key elements. *Base:* 25 *Rate:* ? *Portion:* 20 (25 − 5). Rate = $\dfrac{\text{Portion}}{\text{Base}}$	Portion (20) Base × Rate (25) (?) The whole Portion and rate must relate to same piece of base.

Steps to solving problem

1. Set up the formula.	Rate = $\dfrac{\text{Portion}}{\text{Base}}$	
2. Calculate the rate.	$R = \dfrac{20}{25}$	
	$R = 80\%$	

8. Abby Biernet's original order:

The facts	Solving for?	Steps to take	Key points
60% of the order not in. 80 lobsters received.	Total order of lobsters.	Identify key elements. *Base:* ? *Rate:* .40 (100% − 60%) *Portion:* 80. Base = $\dfrac{\text{Portion}}{\text{Rate}}$	Portion (80) Base × Rate (?) (.40) 80 lobsters represent 40% of the order Portion and rate must relate to same piece of base.

Steps to solving problem

1. Set up the formula.	Base = $\dfrac{\text{Portion}}{\text{Rate}}$	
2. Calculate the rate.	$B = \dfrac{80}{.40}$ ← 80 lobsters is 40% of base.	
	$B = 200$ lobsters	

9. Dunkin' Donuts Company sales for 2007:

The facts	Solving for?	Steps to take	Key points
2006: $300,000 sales. *2007:* Sales up 40% from 2006.	Sales for 2007.	Identify key elements. *Base:* $300,000. *Rate:* 1.40. Old year 100% New year $\underline{+\ 40}$ 140% *Portion:* ? Portion = Base × Rate.	2007 sales Portion (?) Base × Rate ($300,000) (1.40) 2006 sales When rate is greater than 100%, portion will be larger than base.

Steps to solving problem

1. Set up the formula.   Portion = Base × Rate

2. Calculate the portion. $P = \$300{,}000 \times 1.40$

$$P = \$420{,}000$$

10. Percent decrease in Apple computer price:

The facts	Solving for?	Steps to take	Key points
Apple computer was $1,600; now, $1,200.	Percent decrease in price.	Identify key elements. *Base:* $1,600. *Rate:* ? *Portion:* $400 ($1,600 − $1,200). $Rate = \dfrac{Portion}{Base}$	Difference in price — Portion ($400) / Base × Rate ($1,600) (?) — Original price

Steps to solving problem

1. Set up the formula. $Rate = \dfrac{Portion}{Base}$

2. Calculate the rate. $R = \dfrac{\$400}{\$1{,}600}$

$$R = 25\%$$

11. Percent increase in Boston Celtics ticket:

The facts	Solving for?	Steps to take	Key points
$14 ticket (old). $50 ticket (new).	Percent increase in price.	Identify key elements. *Base:* $14 *Rate:* ? *Portion:* $36 ($50 − $14) $Rate = \dfrac{Portion}{Base}$	Difference in price — Portion ($36) / Base × Rate ($14) (?) — Original price When portion is greater than base, rate will be greater than 100%.

Steps to solving problem

1. Set up the formula. $Rate = \dfrac{Portion}{Base}$

2. Calculate the rate. $R = \dfrac{\$36}{\$14}$

$$R = 2.5714 = 257.14\%$$

Need more practice? Try this **Extra Practice Quiz** (check figures in Chapter Organizer, p. 156)

Solve for portion:

1. 42% of 1,200

2. 7% of $8,000

Solve for rate (round to nearest tenth percent as needed):

3. 510 is _____ % of 6,000.

4. 400 is _____% of 900.

Solve for base (round to the nearest tenth as needed):

5. 30 is 60% of _____.

6. 1,200 is $3\frac{1}{2}$% of _____.

7. Ten out of 25 students in Professor Ford's class received an A grade. What percent of the class did not receive the A grade?

8. Abby Biernet has yet to receive 70% of her lobster order. Abby received 90 lobsters to date. What was her original order?

9. In 2006, Dunkin' Donuts Company had $400,000 in doughnut sales. In 2007, sales were up 35%. What are Dunkin' Donuts sales for 2007?

10. The price of an Apple computer dropped from $1,800 to $1,000. What was the percent decrease? (Round to the nearest hundredth percent.)

11. In 1982, a ticket to the Boston Celtics cost $14. In 2009, a ticket cost $75. What is the percent increase to the nearest hundredth percent?

CHAPTER ORGANIZER AND STUDY GUIDE
WITH CHECK FIGURES FOR EXTRA PRACTICE QUIZZES

Topic	Key point, procedure, formula	Example(s) to illustrate situation
Converting decimals to percents, p. 139	1. Move decimal point two places to right. If necessary, add zeros. This rule is also used for whole numbers and mixed decimals. 2. Add a percent symbol at end of number.	.81 = .81. = 81% .008 = .00.8 = .8% 4.15 = 4.15. = 415%
Rounding percents, p. 140	1. Answer must be in percent before rounding. 2. Identify specific digit. If digit to right is 5 or greater, round up. 3. Delete digits to right of identified digit.	Round to the nearest hundredth percent. $\frac{3}{7}$ = .4285714 = 42.85714% = 42.86%
Converting percents to decimals, p. 141	1. Drop percent symbol. 2. Move decimal point two places to left. If necessary, add zeros. For fractional percents: 1. Convert to decimal by dividing numerator by denominator. If necessary, round answer. 2. If a mixed fractional percent, convert fractional percent first. Then combine whole number and fractional percent. 3. Drop percent symbol, move decimal point two places to left.	.89% = .0089 95% = .95 195% = 1.95 $8\frac{3}{4}$% = 8.75% = .0875 $\frac{1}{4}$% = .25% = .0025 $\frac{1}{5}$% = .20% = .0020
Converting fractions to percents, p. 142	1. Divide numerator by denominator. 2. Move decimal point two places to right; add percent symbol.	$\frac{4}{5}$ = .80 = 80%

(continues)

CHAPTER ORGANIZER AND STUDY GUIDE
WITH CHECK FIGURES FOR EXTRA PRACTICE QUIZZES (continued)

Topic	Key point, procedure, formula	Example(s) to illustrate situation
Converting percents to fractions, p. 142	Whole percent (or fractional percent) to a fraction: 1. Drop percent symbol. 2. Multiply number by 3. Reduce to lowest terms. Mixed or decimal percent to a fraction: 1. Drop percent symbol. 2. Change mixed percent to an improper fraction. 3. Multiply number by 4. Reduce to lowest terms. If you have a mixed or decimal percent, change decimal portion to fractional equivalent and continue with Steps 1 to 4.	$64\% \longrightarrow 64 \times \dfrac{1}{100} = \dfrac{64}{100} = \boxed{\dfrac{16}{25}}$ $\dfrac{1}{4}\% \longrightarrow \dfrac{1}{4} \times \dfrac{1}{100} = \boxed{\dfrac{1}{400}}$ $119\% \longrightarrow 119 \times \dfrac{1}{100} = \dfrac{119}{100} = \boxed{1\dfrac{19}{100}}$ $16\dfrac{1}{4}\% \longrightarrow \dfrac{65}{4} \times \dfrac{1}{100} = \dfrac{65}{400} = \boxed{\dfrac{13}{80}}$ $16.25\% \longrightarrow 16\dfrac{1}{4}\% = \dfrac{65}{4} \times \dfrac{1}{100}$ $\qquad = \dfrac{65}{100} = \boxed{\dfrac{13}{80}}$
Solving for portion, p. 145		10% of Mel's paycheck of $1,000 goes for food. What portion is deducted for food? $\boxed{\$100} = \$1{,}000 \times .10$ *Note:* If question was what amount does not go for food, the portion would have been: $\boxed{\$900} = \$1{,}000 \times .90$ $(100\% - 10\% = 90\%$
Solving for rate, p. 146		Assume Mel spends $100 for food from his $1,000 paycheck. What percent of his paycheck is spent on food? $\dfrac{\$100}{\$1{,}000} = .10 = \boxed{10\%}$ *Note:* Portion is less than base since rate is less than 100%.
Solving for base, p. 147		Assume Mel spends $100 for food, which is 10% of his paycheck. What is Mel's total paycheck? $\dfrac{\$100}{.10} = \boxed{\$1{,}000}$
Calculating percent decreases and increases, p. 148		Stereo, $2,000 original price. Stereo, $2,500 new price. $\dfrac{\$500}{\$2{,}000} = .25 = \boxed{25\%}$ increase **Check** $\$2{,}000 \times 1.25 = \$2{,}500$ *Note:* Portion is greater than base since rate is greater than 100%.

KEY TERMS	Base, *p. 144* Percent decrease, *p. 149*	Percent increase, *p. 149* Percents, *p. 138*	Portion, *p. 144* Rate, *p. 144*

(continues)

CHAPTER ORGANIZER AND STUDY GUIDE
WITH CHECK FIGURES FOR EXTRA PRACTICE QUIZZES (concluded)

Topic	Key point, procedure, formula	Example(s) to illustrate situation
CHECK FIGURES FOR EXTRA PRACTICE QUIZZES WITH PAGE REFERENCES	LU 6–1a (p. 143) 1. 44.4% 8. 7.658 2. 78.2% 9. 33.33% 3. .6% 10. 42.86% 4. 793.3% 11. $\frac{17}{100}$ 5. .0020 12. $\frac{329}{400}$ 6. .0780 13. $1\frac{1}{2}$ 7. .92 14. $\frac{1}{400}$ 15. $\frac{89}{500}$	LU 6–2a (p. 154) 1. 504 7. 60% 2. 560 8. 300 3. 8.5% 9. $540,000 4. 44.4% 10. 44.44% 5. 50 11. 435.71% 6. 34,285.7

Note: For how to dissect and solve a word problem, see page 145.

Critical Thinking Discussion Questions

1. In converting from a percent to a decimal, when will you have at least 2 leading zeros before the whole number? Explain this concept, assuming you have 100 bills of $1.

2. Explain the steps in rounding percents. Count the number of students who are sitting in the back half of the room as a percent of the total class. Round your answer to the nearest hundredth percent. Could you have rounded to the nearest whole percent without changing the accuracy of the answer?

3. Define portion, rate, and base. Create an example using Walt Disney World to show when the portion could be larger than the base. Why must the rate be greater than 100% for this to happen?

4. How do we solve for portion, rate, and base? Create an example using IBM computer sales to show that the portion and rate do relate to the same piece of the base.

5. Explain how to calculate percent decreases or increases. Many years ago, comic books cost 10 cents a copy. Visit a bookshop or newsstand. Select a new comic book and explain the price increase in percent compared to the 10-cent comic. How important is the rounding process in your final answer?

6–69. Staples pays George Nagovsky an annual salary of $36,000. Today, George's boss informs him that he will receive a $4,600 raise. What percent of George's old salary is the $4,600 raise? Round to the nearest tenth percent.

6–70. In 2009, Dairy Queen had $550,000 in sales. In 2010, Dairy Queen's sales were up 35%. What were Dairy Queen's sales in 2010?

6–71. Blue Valley College has 600 female students. This is 60% of the total student body. How many students attend Blue Valley College?

6–72. Dr. Grossman was reviewing his total accounts receivable. This month, credit customers paid $44,000, which represented 20% of all receivables (what customers owe) due. What was Dr. Grossman's total accounts receivable?

6–73. Massachusetts has a 5% sales tax. Timothy bought a Toro lawn mower and paid $20 sales tax. What was the cost of the lawn mower before the tax?

6–74. The price of an antique doll increased from $600 to $800. What was the percent of increase? Round to the nearest tenth percent.

6–75. Borders bookstore ordered 80 marketing books but received 60 books. What percent of the order was missing?

6–76. At a Christie's auction, the auctioneer estimated that 40% of the audience was from within the state. Eight hundred people attended the auction. How many out-of-state people attended?

6–77. Due to increased mailing costs, the new rate will cost publishers $50 million; this is 12.5% more than they paid the previous year. How much did it cost publishers last year? Round to the nearest hundreds.

6–78. In 2010, Jim Goodman, an employee at Walgreens, earned $45,900, an increase of 17.5% over the previous year. What were Jim's earnings in 2009? Round to the nearest cent.

6–79. If the number of mortgage applications declined by 7% to 1,625,415, what had been the previous year's number of applications?

6–80. In 2010, the price of a business math text rose to $100. This is 6% more than the 2009 price. What was the old selling price? Round to the nearest cent.

6–81. Web Consultants, Inc., pays Alice Rose an annual salary of $48,000. Today, Alice's boss informs her that she will receive a $6,400 raise. What percent of Alice's old salary is the $6,400 raise? Round to nearest tenth percent.

6–82. Earl Miller, a lawyer, charges Lee's Plumbing, his client, 25% of what he can collect for Lee from customers whose accounts are past due. The attorney also charges, in addition to the 25%, a flat fee of $50 per customer. This month, Earl collected $7,000 from 3 of Lee's past-due customers. What is the total fee due to Earl?

6–83. Petco ordered 100 dog calendars but received 60. What percent of the order was missing?

6–84. Blockbuster Video uses MasterCard. MasterCard charges $2\frac{1}{2}\%$ on net deposits (credit slips less returns). Blockbuster made a net deposit of \$4,100 for charge sales. How much did MasterCard charge Blockbuster?

6–85. In 2009, Internet Access had \$800,000 in sales. In 2010, Internet Access sales were up 45%. What are the sales for 2010?

WORD PROBLEMS (Fourth of Four Sets)

6–86. Saab Corporation raised the base price of its popular 900 series by \$1,200 to \$33,500. What was the percent increase? Round to the nearest tenth percent.

6–87. The sales tax rate is 8%. If Jim bought a new Buick and paid a sales tax of \$1,920, what was the cost of the Buick before the tax?

6–88. Puthina Unge bought a new Compaq computer system on sale for \$1,800. It was advertised as 30% off the regular price. What was the original price of the computer? Round to the nearest dollar.

6–89. John O'Sullivan has just completed his first year in business. His records show that he spent the following in advertising:

Newspaper   \$600   Radio   \$650   Yellow Pages   \$700   Local flyers   \$400

What percent of John's advertising was spent on the Yellow Pages? Round to the nearest hundredth percent.

6–90. The *Cincinnati Post* reported holiday spending predictions. Columbus-based Big Research LLC surveyed nearly 7,700 consumers. The survey found 22% of consumers planned to begin shopping in either September or October, and another 17% had started in August or earlier. **(a)** How many consumers planned to begin shopping in September or October? **(b)** How many consumers planned to begin in August or earlier?

6–91. Abby Kaminsky sold her ski house at Attitash Mountain in New Hampshire for $35,000. This sale represented a loss of 15% off the original price. What was the original price Abby paid for the ski house? Round your answer to the nearest dollar.

6–92. Out of 4,000 colleges surveyed, 60% reported that SAT scores were not used as a high consideration in viewing their applications. How many schools view the SAT as important in screening applicants?

6–93. If refinishing your basement at a cost of $45,404 would add $18,270 to the resale value of your home, what percent of your cost is recouped? Round to the nearest percent.

6–94. A major airline laid off 4,000 pilots and flight attendants. If this was a 12.5% reduction in the workforce, what was the size of the workforce after the layoffs?

6–95. Assume 450,000 people line up on the streets to see the Macy's Thanksgiving Parade in 2008. If attendance is expected to increase 30%, what will be the number of people lined up on the street to see the 2009 parade?

6–96. Continental Airlines stock climbed 4% from $18.04. Shares of AMR Corporation, American Airlines' parent company, closed up 7% at $12.55. AirTran Airways went from $17.27 to $17.96. Round answers to the nearest hundredth. **(a)** What is the new price of Continental Airlines stock? **(b)** What had been the price of AMR Corporation stock? **(c)** What percent did AirTran Airways increase? Round to the nearest percent.

6–97. A local Dunkin' Donuts shop reported that its sales have increased exactly 22% per year for the last 2 years. This year's sales were $82,500. What were Dunkin' Donuts sales 2 years ago? Round each year's sales to the nearest dollar.

SUMMARY PRACTICE TEST

Convert the following decimals to percents. *(p. 139)*

1. .921   **2.** .4   **3.** 15.88   **4.** 8.00

Convert the following percents to decimals. *(p. 141)*

5. 42%   **6.** 7.98%   **7.** 400%   **8.** $\frac{1}{4}$%

Convert the following fractions to percents. Round to the nearest tenth percent. *(p. 142)*

9. $\frac{1}{6}$ **10.** $\frac{1}{3}$

Convert the following percents to fractions and reduce to the lowest terms as needed. *(p. 142)*

11. $19\frac{3}{8}$%   **12.** 6.2%

Solve the following problems for portion, base, or rate:

13. An Arby's franchise has a net income before taxes of $900,000. The company's treasurer estimates that 40% of the company's net income will go to federal and state taxes. How much will the Arby's franchise have left? *(p. 145)*

14. Domino's projects a year-end net income of $699,000. The net income represents 30% of its annual sales. What are Domino's projected annual sales? *(p. 147)*

15. Target ordered 400 iPods. When Target received the order, 100 iPods were missing. What percent of the order did Target receive? *(p. 146)*

16. Matthew Song, an employee at Putnam Investments, receives an annual salary of $120,000. Today his boss informed him that he would receive a $3,200 raise. What percent of his old salary is the $3,200 raise? Round to the nearest hundredth percent. *(p. 146)*

17. The price of a Delta airline ticket from Los Angeles to Boston increased to $440. This is a 15% increase. What was the old fare? Round to the nearest cent. *(p. 147)*

18. Scupper Grace earns a gross pay of $900 per week at Office Depot. Scupper's payroll deductions are 29%. What is Scupper's take-home pay? *(p. 145)*

19. Mia Wong is reviewing the total accounts receivable of Wong's department store. Credit customers paid $90,000 this month. This represents 60% of all receivables due. What is Mia's total accounts receivable? *(p. 147)*

A KIPLINGER APPROACH

HOME | Will remodeling pay off when you move? *By Patricia Mertz Esswein*

Live better and SELL HIGHER

REMODELING projects are enticing investments. You get to play the Iron Chef in a new, modern kitchen or pamper yourself in a spa-style bathroom, then recoup your money when you sell your house. In fact, anticipating that payback is often a driving force in convincing yourself—or your spouse—that a project is worth the money. But how much return can you count on? The latest report from *Remodeling* magazine says it's not uncommon to recover 80% or more.

Despite unrelenting new construction, the average U.S. home is 32 years old and in need of lifts, tucks and add-ons. So, home remodeling has become a national obsession. In 2004, Americans spent $186 billion on remodeling, according to Harvard University's Joint Center for Housing Studies.

The accompanying table shows the average price tag for a dozen popular projects, based on figures provided by HomeTech Information Systems, a company that develops software for estimating remodeling costs. The percentage of cost recouped at resale is based on estimates by members of the National Association of Realtors.

The numbers are national averages; the full report (which can be ordered for $37.50 at www.remodelingmaga zine.com) includes estimates by region and for 60 cities. The payback can vary dramatically by region.

Sal Alfano, editorial director of *Remodeling* magazine, notes that in extremely hot markets and those with a lot of new construction, resale values may slip below national averages. That's because buyers would just as soon purchase a new house with all the amenities than a remodeled house.

—Research: **KATY MARQUARDT**

PAYBACK The dollars and sense of a dozen popular projects

Check out the national average costs for 12 remodeling projects and estimates of how much that cost will be recouped. Payback can vary dramatically by region. The recovery for new siding, for example, ranges from 80% in the West to 105% in the East.

THE PROJECT	THE PRICE	% COST RECOUPED
Minor kitchen remodel	$15,273	93%
Major kitchen remodel, mid-range	$42,660	79%
Major kitchen remodel, upscale	$75,206	80%
Bathroom remodel, mid-range	$9,861	90%
Bathroom remodel, upscale	$25,273	86%
Bathroom addition, mid-range	$21,087	86%
Bathroom addition, upscale	$41,587	81%
Master suite, mid-range	$70,245	80%
Master suite, upscale	$134,364	78%
Window replacement, mid-range	$9,273	85%
Window replacement, upscale	$15,383	84%
Siding replacement	$6,946	93%

Source: Hanley Wood, LLC

FROM TOP: SUB-ZERO/WOLF; AMERICAN STANDARD; RICHARD LEO JOHNSON/GETTY IMAGES; ANDERSEN WINDOWS

BUSINESS MATH ISSUE

Kiplinger's © 2005

In today's real estate market these % recouped numbers are unrealistic.

1. List the key points of the article and information to support your position.
2. Write a group defense of your position using math calculations to support your view.

Slater's Business Math Scrapbook

with Internet Application

Putting Your Skills to Work

PROJECT A

What was the original circulation figure of the *New York Daily News*? Round to nearest hundredth. Check your answer.

Newspapers

Issues

Average weekday circulation for the six months ended March 31 and change from the year-earlier period

NEWSPAPER	CIRCULATION*	% CHANGE
USA Today	2,272,815	0.1%
The Wall Street Journal	2,049,786	-1.0
New York Times	1,142,464	0.5
Los Angeles Times	851,832	-5.4
Washington Post	724,242	-3.7
New York Daily News	708,477	-3.7
New York Post	673,379	-0.7
Chicago Tribune	579,079	0.9
Houston Chronicle	513,387	-3.6
Arizona Republic	438,722	-2.1

*Preliminary figures, subject to audit; includes bulk sales
Source: Audit Bureau of Circulations

Wall Street Journal © 2006

UPS to Raise Rates by Nearly 5%

ATLANTA—**United Parcel Service Inc.** will raise its 2007 list rates for ground shipments, air express and international shipments originating in the U.S. by nearly 5% on average.

The increases, which take effect Jan. 1, exceed those UPS announced a year ago for 2006 and come on the heels of air-shipment rate rises announced earlier this month by rival **FedEx Corp.**, underscoring confidence that demand for delivery services will remain strong.

UPS said list rates for ground shipments will go up 4.9% on average. The increase for air express and international shipments is based on a 6.9% rise in the base rate, minus two percentage points in the current fuel surcharge because of the declining price of oil. Last year the company, the world's largest package carrier in terms of deliveries, raised ground-shipment rates by 3.9% and air and international service rates

by 3.5%, excluding two percentage points related to fuel surcharges.

FedEx, the leader in air shipments, said on Nov. 3 that it would increase its net average shipping rate for FedEx Express, including U.S. domestic and U.S. export express package and freight shipments, by 3.5% as of Jan. 1, matching increases made for this year. FedEx is expected to match the ground rates at UPS.

Wall Street Journal © 2006

PROJECT B

Assume a package cost $42 to deliver by UPS in 2006. What would it cost assuming a new list rate increase of 4.9%?

Internet Projects: See text Web site (www.mhhe.com/slater9e) and The Business Math Internet Resource Guide.

Video Case

American President Lines (APL) has automated its terminal so the average turnaround time for a trucker picking up a 40-foot container is only 17 minutes.

APL uses an automated wireless system to track containers parked across its recently remodeled 160-acre facility in Seattle.

The fast turnaround time gives customers who operate under the just-in-time mode the opportunity to make more trips. Independent truck drivers also benefit.

The international freight industry is plagued by red tape and inefficiency. APL has used its website to help clients like Excel Corporation, the country's second-largest beef packer and processor, speed up its billing time. Excel now wants to ask online for a place on a ship and for a call from APL when room will be available.

The shipping market is enormous, estimated anywhere from $100 billion to $1 trillion. Imports in the United States alone totaled 10 million containers, while exports totaled 6.5 million containers, together carrying $375 billion worth of goods. One of the most difficult transactions is to source goods from overseas and have them delivered with minimal paperwork all the way through to the end customer. Shipping lines must provide real-time information on the location of ships and goods.

Most significant are attempts to automate shipping transactions online. The industry's administrative inefficiencies, which account for 4% to 10% of international trade costs, are targeted. Industry insiders peg error rates on documents even higher, at 25% to 30%. It's no secret that start-ups must overcome the reluctance of hidebound shipping lines, which have deep-seated emotional fears of dot-coms coming between them and their customers.

In conclusion, American President Lines needs to get on board by staying online, or it might go down with the ship.

PROBLEM 1

The $170 billion in international trade volume per year given in the video is expected to increase by 50% in 5 years and expected to double over the next 25 years. **(a)** What is the expected total dollar amount in 5 years? **(b)** What is the expected total dollar amount in 25 years?

PROBLEM 2

The video stated that thousands of containers arrive each day. Each 40-foot container will hold, for example, 16,500 boxes of running shoes, 132,000 videotapes, or 25,000 blouses. At an average retail price of $49.50 for a pair of running shoes, $14.95 for a videotape, and $26.40 for a blouse, what would be the total retail value of the goods in these three containers (assume different goods in each container)?

PROBLEM 3

APL spent $600 million to build a 230-acre shipping terminal in California. The terminal can handle 4 wide-body container ships. Each ship can hold 4,800 20-foot containers, or 2,400 40-foot containers. **(a)** What was the cost per acre to build the facility? **(b)** How many 20-foot containers can the terminal handle at one time? **(c)** How many 40-foot containers can the terminal handle at one time?

PROBLEM 4

According to *Shanghai Daily,* the recent decline in China's export container prices (which fell by 1.4%) has not taken its toll on the general interest in this sector. China's foreign trade grew by 35%, reaching $387.1 billion. APL reported that it would increase its services from Asia to Europe to take advantage of China's growth in exports. What was the dollar amount of China's foreign trade last year?

PROBLEM 5

APL has expanded its domestic fleet to 5,100 53-foot containers; it is expanding its global fleet to 253,000 containers. The 5,100 containers represent what percent of APL's total fleet? Round to the nearest hundredth percent.

PROBLEM 6

The cost of owning a shipping vessel is very high. Operating costs for large vessels can run between $75,000 and $80,000 per day. Using an average cost per day, what would be the operating costs for one week?

PROBLEM 7

The Port of Los Angeles financed new terminal construction through operating revenues and bonds. They will collect about $30 million a year in rent from APL, who signed a 30-year lease on the property. What is APL's monthly payment?

PROBLEM 8

According to port officials, APL expanded cargo-handling capabilities at the Los Angeles facility that are expected to generate 10,500 jobs, with $335 million in wages and annual industry sales of $1 billion. What would be the average wage received? Round to the nearest dollar.

PROBLEM 9

APL has disclosed that it ordered over 34,000 containers from a Chinese container manufacturer. With 253,000 containers in its possession, what will be the percent increase in containers owned by APL? Round to the nearest hundredth percent.

CHAPTER 7

Discounts: Trade and Cash

LEARNING UNIT OBJECTIVES

LU 7–1: Trade Discounts—Single and Chain (Includes Discussion of Freight)

- Calculate single trade discounts with formulas and complements *(pp. 171–172)*.
- Explain the freight terms *FOB shipping point* and *FOB destination (pp. 172–174)*.
- Find list price when net price and trade discount rate are known *(p. 174)*.
- Calculate chain discounts with the net price equivalent rate and single equivalent discount rate *(pp. 175–177)*.

LU 7–2: Cash Discounts, Credit Terms, and Partial Payments

- List and explain typical discount periods and credit periods that a business may offer *(pp. 179–185)*.
- Calculate outstanding balance for partial payments *(p. 186)*.

Online Retailers Are Watching You

Sites Take Shopper-Tracking To New Level to Customize Deals in Holiday Season

By JESSICA E. VASCELLARO

THIS HOLIDAY SHOPPING season, the price you pay online may depend on your gender and where you live. It may also hinge on what time of day you shop, the speed of your Internet connection, if you are an AOL user, or perhaps even your Google browsing habits.

It means a woman with a high-speed Internet connection in the South may get a flat-rate shipping offer from a retailer like Overstock.com, while a male counterpart in the West may see a promotion for live customer service instead. Some who logged on to Ice.com through AOL may be teased with a first-time buyer discount while someone who accessed the site directly would be left perkless. And someone using the word "cheap" while searching for gift baskets using Google may be surprised with a free shipping deal at a gourmet-food retailer like DelightfulDeliveries.com.

Browser beware: While they are loath to reveal which attributes affect which promotions—both in response to concerns about privacy and intense competition among online retailers—Internet merchants are picking up on a shopper's digital trail and mining the wealth of information they collect about shoppers to tailor their promotional offers with ever-greater precision.

Wall Street Journal © 2006

A Deal Seeker's Cheat Sheet

Veteran online bargain hunters employ a variety of strategies to secure the best prices. A look at some of them:

STRATEGY	WHERE TO GO	COMMENTS
Look for promotional coupon codes	CouponMountain.com, WOW-Coupons.com, CouponCraze.com, slickdeals.net	These and similar coupon Web sites list promotional codes and offer print-out coupons for discounts at many online retailers and stores. A Google search for a retailer's name and "coupons" can often lead to savings.
"Stack" mail-in rebates	fatwallet.com, GottaDeal.com	Learn of multiple mail-in rebates—a shopping strategy known as "stacking"—by monitoring the forums of these two sites. Occasionally, the value of the rebates can exceed the cost of the product, earning money for the buyer.
Shop via sites that share their commissions	fatwallet.com, Ebates.com, mrrebates.com	These Web sites earn commissions from referring customers to hundreds of online retailers and split some of the money with their members. Membership is free, but you must click on the participating retailers through the sites to qualify. One downside: As with mail-in rebates, it can take months to receive the cash.
Sign up for email alerts	fatwallet.com, FareAlert.net	Fatwallet sends out an early-morning, daily email alert filled with new and expiring online bargains, plus "hot deals" discovered by its members. FareAlert.net sends out occasional email alerts for "extraordinary" travel deals, including airline price mistakes.

Wall Street Journal © 2005

Are you a good online bargain hunter? The *Wall Street Journal* clipping "A Deal Seeker's Cheat Sheet" shows a variety of strategies customers can use to get the best price online.

This chapter discusses two types of discounts taken by retailers—trade and cash. A **trade discount** is a reduction off the original selling price (list price) of an item and is not related to early payment. A **cash discount** is the result of an early payment based on the terms of the sale.

Learning Unit 7–1: Trade Discounts—Single and Chain (Includes Discussion of Freight)

New Deals

Some of the non-car "employee discount" offerings:

- About 30% off on some bicycles at **Randall Scott Cycle Co.**, in Pompano Beach, Fla. (Sells online.)

- Discounts of 10% to 30% on golf gear at **Condor Golf** in Phoenix. (Sells online.)

- Price cuts on lamps (a $100 piece selling for between $30 and $35) at **Lighting Galleries** of Sarasota, Fla.

Wall Street Journal © 2005

Today we see "employee discounts" offered to non-employees. The *Wall Street Journal* clipping "New Deals" shows three examples of these nonemployee discounts offered by companies.

Where do companies like Randall Scott Cycle Co. get their merchandise? The merchandise sold by retailers is bought from manufacturers and wholesalers who sell only to retailers and not to customers. These manufacturers and wholesalers offer retailer discounts so retailers can resell the merchandise at a profit. The discounts are off the manufacturers' and wholesalers' **list price** (suggested retail price), and the amount of discount that retailers receive off the list price is the **trade discount amount.**

When you make a purchase, the retailer (seller) gives you a purchase **invoice.** Invoices are important business documents that help sellers keep track of sales transactions and buyers keep track of purchase transactions. North Shore Community College Bookstore is a retail seller of textbooks to students. The bookstore usually purchases its textbooks directly from publishers. Figure 7.1 (p. 172) shows a textbook invoice from McGraw-Hill/Irwin Publishing Company to the North Shore Community College Bookstore. Note that the trade discount amount is given in percent. This is the **trade discount rate,** which is a percent off the list price that retailers can deduct. The following formula

	Invoice No.: 5582

McGraw-Hill/Irwin Publishing Co.
1333 Burr Ridge Parkway
Burr Ridge, Illinois 60527

Date:　July 8, 2008
Ship:　Two-day UPS
Terms: 2/10, n/30

Sold to: North Shore Community College Bookstore
　　　　　1 Ferncroft Road
　　　　　Danvers, MA 01923

Description	Unit list price	Total amount
50　Financial Management—Block/Hirt	$95.66	$4,783.00
10　Introduction to Business—Nichols	89.50	895.00
	Total List Price	$5,678.00
	Less: Trade Discount 25%	−1,419.50
	Net Price	$4,258.50
	Plus: Prepaid Shipping Charge	125.00
	Total Invoice Amount	$4,383.50

for calculating a trade discount amount gives the numbers from the Figure 7.1 invoice in parentheses:

TRADE DISCOUNT AMOUNT FORMULA
Trade discount amount = List price × Trade discount rate
($1,419.50)　　　　($5,678.00)　　　　(25%)

The price that the retailer (bookstore) pays the manufacturer (publisher) or wholesaler is the **net price.** The following formula for calculating the net price gives the numbers from the Figure 7.1 invoice in parentheses:

NET PRICE FORMULA
Net price　　=　　List price　　−　　Trade discount amount
($4,258.50)　　　　($5,678.00)　　　　($1,419.50)

Frequently, manufacturers and wholesalers issue catalogs to retailers containing list prices of the seller's merchandise and the available trade discounts. To reduce printing costs when prices change, these sellers usually update the catalogs with new *discount sheets.* The discount sheet also gives the seller the flexibility of offering different trade discounts to different classes of retailers. For example, some retailers buy in quantity and service the products. They may receive a larger discount than the retailer who wants the manufacturer to service the products. Sellers may also give discounts to meet a competitor's price, to attract new retailers, and to reward the retailers who buy product-line products. Sometimes the ability of the retailer to negotiate with the seller determines the trade discount amount.

Retailers cannot take trade discounts on freight, returned goods, sales tax, and so on. Trade discounts may be single discounts or a chain of discounts. Before we discuss single trade discounts, let's study freight terms.

Freight Terms

Do you know how successful the shipping businesses of DHL, UPS, and FedEx are in China? The *Wall Street Journal* clipping "Faster, Faster . . ." shows that the shipping businesses of these three companies can be quite profitable.

Faster, Faster...

Helping manufacturers in China save time and money by managing increasingly complex supply chains.

■ **DHL's** business in China increased by more than 50% in the first half of this year. It started express deliveries there in 1981 and operates through a joint-venture with China's biggest delivery company Sinotrans. DHL ranks first among the foreign-express companies in China with an estimated third of the market.

■ **UPS** first flew to China in 1988 and posted a 125% increase in volume of packages handled during the July-September period of this year. It has a joint-venture with Sinotrans in Beijing but pays the company a fee to deliver its packages everywhere else. UPS has an estimated market share of 15%.

■ **FedEx** reported a 52% rise in exports from China for the three months ended in August. It began deliveries in 1984 and runs a joint-venture with DTW, a smaller Chinese concern. FedEx has a market share that investment bank CSFB estimates at 20%.

Sources: the companies; Credit Suisse First Boston

Wall Street Journal © 2004

The most common **freight terms** are *FOB shipping point* and *FOB destination*. These terms determine how the freight will be paid. The key words in the terms are *shipping point* and *destination*.

FOB shipping point means free on board at shipping point; that is, the buyer pays the freight cost of getting the goods to the place of business.

For example, assume that IBM in San Diego bought goods from Argo Suppliers in Boston. Argo ships the goods FOB Boston by plane. IBM takes title to the goods when the aircraft in Boston receives the goods, so IBM pays the freight from Boston to San Diego. Frequently, the seller (Argo) prepays the freight and adds the amount to the buyer's (IBM) invoice. When paying the invoice, the buyer takes the cash discount off the net price and adds the freight cost. FOB shipping point can be illustrated as follows:

FOB shipping point (Boston)

Boston — Argo Suppliers (IBM takes title here) → Buyer pays the freight → San Diego — IBM (Buyer pays the freight costs)

FOB destination means the seller pays the freight cost until it reaches the buyer's place of business. If Argo ships its goods to IBM FOB destination or FOB San Diego, the title to the goods remains with Argo. Then it is Argo's responsibility to pay the freight from Boston to IBM's place of business in San Diego. FOB destination can be illustrated as follows:

FOB destination (San Diego)

Boston — Argo Suppliers (Has title) → Seller pays the freight → IBM (Get title on arrival of goods)

The following *Wall Street Journal* clipping (p. 174) shows the results of a performance test of four companies: Federal Express, DHL, United Parcel Service, and the United States Postal Service. Note the costs and conveniences of these four online delivery services relating to pickup fees, fuel surcharge/own packaging, and website discounts. From the comments on the clipping, which of the four companies was most impressive?

SITE/TOTAL PRICE	PICK-UP FEE	FUEL SURCHARGE/OWN PACKAGING?	WEB SITE DISCOUNT	COMMENTS
dhl-usa.com $48.24	$0	$8.70/Yes	No	The most consistent site in several browsers, and the fewest printing headaches for shipping label and postage. Could have used more guidance on taxes and duties.
fedex.com $49.36	$4	$7.56/Yes	Yes, 10% savings on freight charges only when you register online.	The postage confirmation email we first received was not a firm commitment. We rescheduled online and got a real confirmation. An agent arrived that evening.
ups.com $49.22	No fee for international parcels	$5.47/Yes	Yes, retail site would have charged $54.56	Despite difficulties using PDF files to print invoices and download instructions, phone and email support was fast and efficient.
usps.com $23.51	$12.50 for pickup on demand service	No/No, needed clear envelope from post office	Yes, $1 cheaper than going to a post office.	Having to use USPS packaging makes a trip to the post office inevitable. Email customer support was good.

Wall Street Journal © 2005

Now you are ready for the discussion on single trade discounts.

Single Trade Discount

In the introduction to this unit, we showed how to use the trade discount amount formula and the net price formula to calculate the McGraw-Hill/Irwin Publishing Company textbook sale to the North Shore Community College Bookstore. Since McGraw-Hill/Irwin gave the bookstore only one trade discount, it is a **single trade discount.** In the following word problem, we use the formulas to solve another example of a single trade discount. Again, we will use a blueprint aid to help dissect and solve the word problem.

The Word Problem The list price of a Macintosh computer is $2,700. The manufacturer offers dealers a 40% trade discount. What are the trade discount amount and the net price?

The facts	Solving for?	Steps to take	Key points
List price: $2,700. *Trade discount rate:* 40%.	Trade discount amount. Net price.	Trade discount amount = List price × Trade discount rate. Net price = List price − Trade discount amount.	Trade discount amount — Portion (?) — Base ($2,700) × Rate (.40) — List price — Trade discount rate

Steps to solving problem

1. Calculate the trade discount amount. $2,700 × .40 = $1,080

2. Calculate the net price. $2,700 − $1,080 = $1,620

Now let's learn how to check the dealers' net price of $1,620 with an alternate procedure using a complement.

How to Calculate the Net Price Using Complement of Trade Discount Rate

The **complement** of a trade discount rate is the difference between the discount rate and 100%. The following steps show you how to use the complement of a trade discount rate:

CALCULATING NET PRICE USING COMPLEMENT OF TRADE DISCOUNT RATE
Step 1. To find the complement, subtract the single discount rate from 100%.
Step 2. Multiply the list price times the complement (from Step 1).

Think of a complement of any given percent (decimal) as the result of subtracting the percent from 100%.

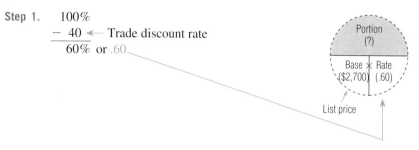

Step 1.   100%
            − 40 ← Trade discount rate
            60% or .60

The complement means that we are spending 60 cents per dollar because we save 40 cents per dollar. Since we planned to spend $2,700, we multiply .60 by $2,700 to get a net price of $1,620.

Step 2. $1,620 = $2,700 × .60

Note how the portion ($1,620) and rate (.60) relate to the same piece of the base ($2,700). The portion ($1,620) is smaller than the base, since the rate is less than 100%.

Be aware that some people prefer to use the trade discount amount formula and the net price formula to find the net price. Other people prefer to use the complement of the trade discount rate to find the net price. The result is always the same.

Finding List Price When You Know Net Price and Trade Discount Rate

The following formula has many useful applications:

CALCULATING LIST PRICE WHEN NET PRICE AND TRADE DISCOUNT RATE ARE KNOWN
List price = $\dfrac{\text{Net price}}{\text{Complement of trade discount rate}}$

Next, let's see how to dissect and solve a word problem calculating list price.

The Word Problem A Macintosh computer has a $1,620 net price and a 40% trade discount. What is its list price?

The facts	Solving for?	Steps to take	Key points
Net price: $1,620. *Trade discount rate:* 40%.	List price.	List price = $\dfrac{\text{Net price}}{\text{Complement of trade discount rate}}$	(diagram)

Steps to solving problem

1. Calculate the complement of the trade discount.

    100%
    − 40
    60% = .60

2. Calculate the list price.

    $\dfrac{\$1,620}{.60}$ = $2,700

Note that the portion ($1,620) and rate (.60) relate to the same piece of the base.

Let's return to the McGraw-Hill/Irwin invoice in Figure 7.1 (p. 172) and calculate the list price using the formula for finding list price when net price and trade discount rate are known. The net price of the textbooks is $4,258.50. The complement of the trade discount rate is 100% − 25% = 75% = .75. Dividing the net price $4,258.50 by the complement .75

equals $5,678.00, the list price shown in the McGraw-Hill/Irwin invoice. We can show this as follows:

$$\frac{\$4,258.50}{.75} = \$5,678.00, \text{ the list price}$$

Chain Discounts

Frequently, manufacturers want greater flexibility in setting trade discounts for different classes of customers, seasonal trends, promotional activities, and so on. To gain this flexibility, some sellers give **chain** or **series discounts**—trade discounts in a series of two or more successive discounts.

Sellers list chain discounts as a group, for example, 20/15/10. Let's look at how Mick Company arrives at the net price of office equipment with a 20/15/10 chain discount.

EXAMPLE   The list price of the office equipment is $15,000. The chain discount is 20/15/10. The long way to calculate the net price is as follows:

Step 1	Step 2	Step 3	Step 4
$15,000	$15,000	$12,000	$10,200
× .20	− 3,000	− 1,800	− 1,020
$ 3,000	$12,000	$10,200	$ 9,180 net price
	× .15	× .10	
	$ 1,800	$ 1,020	

Never add the 20/15/10 together.

Note how we multiply the percent (in decimal) times the new balance after we subtract the previous trade discount amount. For example, in Step 3, we change the last discount, 10%, to decimal form and multiply times $10,200. Remember that each percent is multiplied by a successively *smaller* base. You could write the 20/15/10 discount rate in any order and still arrive at the same net price. Thus, you would get the $9,180 net price if the discount were 10/15/20 or 15/20/10. However, sellers usually give the larger discounts first. *Never try to shorten this step process by adding the discounts.* Your net price will be incorrect because, when done properly, each percent is calculated on a different base.

Net Price Equivalent Rate

In the example above, you could also find the $9,180 net price with the **net price equivalent rate**—a shortcut method. Let's see how to use this rate to calculate net price.

CALCULATING NET PRICE USING NET PRICE EQUIVALENT RATE
Step 1. Subtract each chain discount rate from 100% (find the complement) and convert each percent to a decimal.
Step 2. Multiply the decimals. Do not round off decimals, since this number is the net price equivalent rate.
Step 3. Multiply the list price times the net price equivalent rate (Step 2).

The following word problem with its blueprint aid illustrates how to use the net price equivalent rate method.

The Word Problem   The list price of office equipment is $15,000. The chain discount is 20/15/10. What is the net price?

The facts	Solving for?	Steps to take	Key points
List price: $15,000. *Chain discount:* 20/15/10	Net price.	Net price equivalent rate. Net price = List price × Net price equivalent rate.	Do not round net price equivalent rate.

Steps to solving problem

1. Calculate the complement of each rate and convert each percent to a decimal.	$\begin{array}{r} 100\% \\ -\ 20 \\ \hline 80\% \end{array}$	$\begin{array}{r} 100\% \\ -\ 15 \\ \hline 85\% \end{array}$	$\begin{array}{r} 100\% \\ -\ 10 \\ \hline 90\% \end{array}$	
	↓	↓	↓	
	.8	.85	.9	

2. Calculate the net price equivalent rate. (Do not round.) $.8 \times .85 \times .9 = .612$ Net price equivalent rate For each $1, you are spending about 61 cents.

3. Calculate the net price (actual cost to buyer). $\$15,000 \times .612 = \boxed{\$9,180}$

Next we see how to calculate the trade discount amount with a simpler method.

In the previous word problem, we could calculate the trade discount amount as follows:

$\begin{array}{ll} \$15,000 & \leftarrow \text{List price} \\ -\ 9,180 & \leftarrow \text{Net price} \\ \hline \boxed{\$\ 5,820} & \leftarrow \text{Trade discount amount} \end{array}$

Single Equivalent Discount Rate

You can use another method to find the trade discount by using the **single equivalent discount rate.**

CALCULATING TRADE DISCOUNT AMOUNT USING SINGLE EQUIVALENT DISCOUNT RATE

Step 1. Subtract the net price equivalent rate from 1. This is the single equivalent discount rate.

Step 2. Multiply the list price times the single equivalent discount rate. This is the trade discount amount.

Let's now do the calculations.

Step 1. $\begin{array}{l} 1.000 \leftarrow \text{If you are using a calculator, just press 1.} \\ -\ .612 \\ \hline .388 \leftarrow \text{This is the single equivalent discount rate.} \end{array}$

Step 2. $\$15,000 \times .388 = \boxed{\$5,820} \rightarrow$ This is the trade discount amount.

Remember that when we use the net price equivalent rate, the buyer of the office equipment pays $.612 on each $1 of list price. Now with the single equivalent discount rate, we can say that the buyer saves $.388 on each $1 of list price. The .388 is the single equivalent discount rate for the 20/15/10 chain discount. Note how we use the .388 single equivalent discount rate as if it were the only discount.

It's time to try the Practice Quiz.

LU 7-1 PRACTICE QUIZ

Complete this **Practice Quiz** to see how you are doing[1]

1. The list price of a dining room set with a 40% trade discount is $12,000. What are the trade discount amount and net price (use complement method for net price)?
2. The net price of a video system with a 30% trade discount is $1,400. What is the list price?
3. Lamps Outlet bought a shipment of lamps from a wholesaler. The total list price was $12,000 with a 5/10/25 chain discount. Calculate the net price and trade discount amount. (Use the net price equivalent rate and single equivalent discount rate in your calculation.)

[1]For all three problems we will show blueprint aids. You might want to draw them on scrap paper.

✓ Solutions

1. Dining room set trade discount amount and net price:

The facts	Solving for?	Steps to take	Key points
List price: $12,000. *Trade discount rate:* 40%.	Trade discount amount. Net price.	Trade discount amount = List price × Trade discount rate. Net price = List price × Complement of trade discount rate.	Trade discount amount Portion (?) Base ($12,000) × Rate (.40) List price Trade discount rate

Steps to solving problem

1. Calculate the trade discount. $12,000 × .40 = **$4,800** Trade discount amount
2. Calculate the net price. $12,000 × .60 = **$7,200** (100% − 40% = 60%)

2. Video system list price:

The facts	Solving for?	Steps to take	Key points
Net price: $1,400. *Trade discount rate:* 30%.	List price.	List price = $\dfrac{\text{Net price}}{\text{Complement of trade discount}}$	Net price Portion ($1,400) Base (?) × Rate (.70) List price 100% −30%

Steps to solving problem

1. Calculate the complement of trade discount.

$$\begin{array}{r} 100\% \\ -\ 30 \\ \hline 70\% = .70 \end{array}$$

2. Calculate the list price.

$$\dfrac{\$1,400}{.70} = \boxed{\$2,000}$$

3. Lamps Outlet's net price and trade discount amount:

The facts	Solving for?	Steps to take	Key points
List price: $12,000. *Chain discount:* 5/10/25.	Net price. Trade discount amount.	Net price = List price × Net price equivalent rate. Trade discount amount = List price × Single equivalent discount rate.	Do not round off net price equivalent rate or single equivalent discount rate.

Steps to solving problem

1. Calculate the complement of each chain discount.

$$\begin{array}{ccc} 100\% & 100\% & 100\% \\ -\ 5 & -\ 10 & -\ 25 \\ \hline 95\% & 90\% & 75\% \end{array}$$

2. Calculate the net price equivalent rate.   .95 × .90 × .75 = .64125

3. Calculate the net price. $12,000 × .64125 = $7,695

4. Calculate the single equivalent discount rate.   1.00000
                                                        − .64125
                                                        ‾‾‾‾‾‾‾
                                                        .35875

5. Calculate the trade discount amount. $12,000 × .35875 = $4,305

LU 7–1a   EXTRA PRACTICE QUIZ

Need more practice? Try this **Extra Practice Quiz** (check figures in Chapter Organizer, p. 190)

1. The list price of a dining room set with a 30% trade discount is $16,000. What are the trade discount amount and net price (use complement method for net price)?

2. The net price of a video system with a 20% trade discount is $400. What is the list price?

3. Lamps Outlet bought a shipment of lamps from a wholesaler. The total list price was $14,000 with a 4/8/20 chain discount. Calculate the net price and trade discount amount. (Use the net price equivalent rate and single equivalent discount rate in your calculation.)

Learning Unit 7–2: Cash Discounts, Credit Terms, and Partial Payments

Sean Clayton/The Image Works

To introduce this learning unit, we will use the New Hampshire Propane Company invoice that follows. The invoice shows that if you pay your bill early, you will receive a 19-cent discount. Every penny counts.

New Hampshire Propane Company				
Date	Description	Qty.	Price	Total
	Previous Balance			**$0.00**
06/24/08	PROPANE	3.60	$3.40	$12.24
	Invoice No. 004433L		Totals this invoice:	$12.24
			AMOUNT DUE:	$12.24
	Invoice Date 6/26/08		Prompt Pay Discount: $0.19	
			Net Amount Due if RECEIVED by 07/10/08:	$12.05
		Due Date	7/26/08	

Now let's study cash discounts.

Cash Discounts

In the New Hampshire Propane Company invoice, we receive a cash discount of 19 cents. This amount is determined by the **terms of the sale,** which can include the credit period, cash discount, discount period, and freight terms.

Buyers can often benefit from buying on credit. The time period that sellers give buyers to pay their invoices is the **credit period.** Frequently, buyers can sell the goods bought during this credit period. Then, at the end of the credit period, buyers can pay sellers with the funds from the sales of the goods. When buyers can do this, they can use the consumer's money to pay the invoice instead of their money.

Sellers can also offer a cash discount, or reduction from the invoice price, if buyers pay the invoice within a specified time. This time period is the **discount period,** which is

A cash discount is for prompt payment. A trade discount is not.

part of the total credit period. Sellers offer this cash discount because they can use the dollars to better advantage sooner than later. Buyers who are not short of cash like cash discounts because the goods will cost them less and, as a result, provide an opportunity for larger profits.

Remember that buyers do not take cash discounts on freight, returned goods, sales tax, and trade discounts. Buyers take cash discounts on the *net price* of the invoice. Before we discuss how to calculate cash discounts, let's look at some aids that will help you calculate credit **due dates** and **end of credit periods.**

Trade discounts should be taken before cash discounts.

Aids in Calculating Credit Due Dates

Sellers usually give credit for 30, 60, or 90 days. Not all months of the year have 30 days. So you must count the credit days from the date of the invoice. The trick is to remember the number of days in each month. You can choose one of the following three options to help you do this.

Years divisible by 4 are leap years. Leap years occur in 2008 and 2012.

Option 1: Days-in-a-Month Rule You may already know this rule. Remember that every 4 years is a leap year.

> Thirty days has September, April, June, and November; all the rest have 31 except February has 28, and 29 in leap years.

Option 2: Knuckle Months Some people like to use the knuckles on their hands to remember which months have 30 or 31 days. Note in the following diagram that each knuckle represents a month with 31 days. The short months are in between the knuckles.

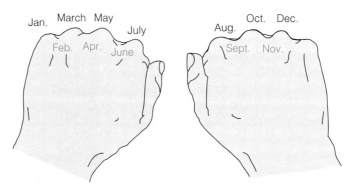

31 days: Jan., March, May, July, Aug., Oct., Dec.

Option 3: Days-in-a-Year Calendar The days-in-a-year calendar (excluding leap year) is another tool to help you calculate dates for discount and credit periods (Table 7.1). For example, let's use Table 7.1 to calculate 90 days from August 12.

EXAMPLE   By Table 7.1: August 12 =   224 days
                                    + 90
                                  ─────────
                                    314 days

Search for day 314 in Table 7.1. You will find that day 314 is November 10. In this example, we stayed within the same year. Now let's try an example in which we overlap from year to year.

EXAMPLE   What date is 80 days after December 5?

Table 7.1 shows that December 5 is 339 days from the beginning of the year. Subtracting 339 from 365 (the end of the year) tells us that we have used up 26 days by the end of the year. This leaves 54 days in the new year. Go back in the table and

| TABLE | 7.1 | Exact days-in-a-year calendar (excluding leap year)* |

Day of month	31 Jan.	28 Feb.	31 Mar.	30 Apr.	31 May	30 June	31 July	31 Aug.	30 Sept.	31 Oct.	30 Nov.	31 Dec.
1	1	32	60	91	121	152	182	213	244	274	305	335
2	2	33	61	92	122	153	183	214	245	275	306	336
3	3	34	62	93	123	154	184	215	246	276	307	337
4	4	35	63	94	124	155	185	216	247	277	308	338
5	5	36	64	95	125	156	186	217	248	278	309	339
6	6	37	65	96	126	157	187	218	249	279	310	340
7	7	38	66	97	127	158	188	219	250	280	311	341
8	8	39	67	98	128	159	189	220	251	281	312	342
9	9	40	68	99	129	160	190	221	252	282	313	343
10	10	41	69	100	130	161	191	222	253	283	314	344
11	11	42	70	101	131	162	192	223	254	284	315	345
12	12	43	71	102	132	163	193	224	255	285	316	346
13	13	44	72	103	133	164	194	225	256	286	317	347
14	14	45	73	104	134	165	195	226	257	287	318	348
15	15	46	74	105	135	166	196	227	258	288	319	349
16	16	47	75	106	136	167	197	228	259	289	320	350
17	17	48	76	107	137	168	198	229	260	290	321	351
18	18	49	77	108	138	169	199	230	261	291	322	352
19	19	50	78	109	139	170	200	231	262	292	323	353
20	20	51	79	110	140	171	201	232	263	293	324	354
21	21	52	80	111	141	172	202	233	264	294	325	355
22	22	53	81	112	142	173	203	234	265	295	326	356
23	23	54	82	113	143	174	204	235	266	296	327	357
24	24	55	83	114	144	175	205	236	267	297	328	358
25	25	56	84	115	145	176	206	237	268	298	329	359
26	26	57	85	116	146	177	207	238	269	299	330	360
27	27	58	86	117	147	178	208	239	270	300	331	361
28	28	59	87	118	148	179	209	240	271	301	332	362
29	29	—	88	119	149	180	210	241	272	302	333	363
30	30	—	89	120	150	181	211	242	273	303	334	364
31	31	—	90	—	151	—	212	243	—	304	—	365

*Often referred to as a Julian calendar.

start with the beginning of the year and search for 54 (80 − 26) days. The 54th day is February 23.

By table

365 days in year
− 339 days until December 5
26 days used in year

80 days from December 5
− 26 days used in year
54 days in new year or February 23

Without use of table

December 31
− December 5
26
+ 31 days in January
57
+ 23 due date (February 23)
80 total days

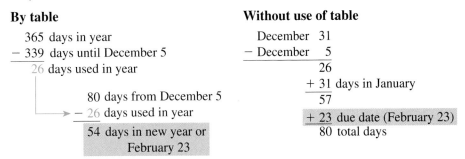

When you know how to calculate credit due dates, you can understand the common business terms sellers offer buyers involving discounts and credit periods. Remember that discount and credit terms vary from one seller to another.

Common Credit Terms Offered by Sellers

The common credit terms sellers offer buyers include *ordinary dating, receipt of goods (ROG),* and *end of month (EOM).* In this section we examine these credit terms. To determine the due dates, we used the exact days-in-a-year calendar (Table 7.1, p. 181).

Ordinary Dating

Today, businesses frequently use the **ordinary dating** method. It gives the buyer a cash discount period that begins with the invoice date. The credit terms of two common ordinary dating methods are 2/10, n/30 and 2/10, 1/15, n/30.

2/10, n/30 Ordinary Dating Method The 2/10, n/30 is read as "two ten, net thirty." Buyers can take a 2% cash discount off the gross amount of the invoice if they pay the bill within 10 days from the invoice date. If buyers miss the discount period, the net amount—without a discount—is due between day 11 and day 30. *Freight, returned goods, sales tax, and trade discounts must be subtracted from the gross before calculating a cash discount.*

EXAMPLE $400 invoice dated July 5; terms 2/10, n/30; no freight; paid on July 11.

Step 1. Calculate end of 2% discount period:

> July 5 date of invoice
> + 10 days
> July 15 end of 2% discount period

Step 2. Calculate end of credit period:

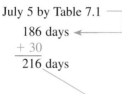

> July 5 by Table 7.1
> 186 days
> + 30
> 216 days

> Search in Table 7.1 for 216 → August 4 → end of credit period

Step 3. Calculate payment on July 11:

> .02 × $400 = $8 cash discount
> $400 − $8 = $392 paid

> *Note:* A 2% cash discount means that you save 2 cents on the dollar and pay 98 cents on the dollar. Thus, $.98 × $400 = $392.

The following time line illustrates the 2/10, n/30 ordinary dating method beginning and ending dates of the above example:

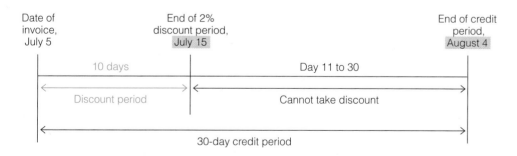

2/10, 1/15, n/30 Ordinary Dating Method The 2/10, 1/15, n/30 is read "two ten, one fifteen, net thirty." The seller will give buyers a 2% (2 cents on the dollar) cash discount if they pay within 10 days of the invoice date. If buyers pay between day 11 and day 15 from the date of the invoice, they can save 1 cent on the dollar. If buyers do not pay on day 15, the net or full amount is due 30 days from the invoice date.

EXAMPLE $600 invoice dated May 8; $100 of freight included in invoice price; paid on May 22. Terms 2/10, 1/15, n/30.

Step 1. Calculate the end of the 2% discount period:

May   8 date of invoice
  + 10 days
May 18 end of 2% discount period

Step 2. Calculate end of 1% discount period:

May 18 end of 2% discount period
  +   5 days
May 23 end of 1% discount period

Step 3. Calculate end of credit period:

May 8 by Table 7.1
    128 days
  + 30
    158 days

Search in Table 7.1 for 158 → June 7 → end of credit period

Step 4. Calculate payment on May 22 (14 days after date of invoice):

$600 invoice
− 100 freight
  $500
× .01
  $5.00

$500 − $5.00 + $100 freight = $595

> A 1% discount means we pay $.99 on the dollar or
> $500 × $.99 = $495 + $100 freight = $595.
>
> *Note:* Freight is added back since no cash discount is taken on freight.

The following time line illustrates the 2/10, 1/15, n/30 ordinary dating method beginning and ending dates of the above example:

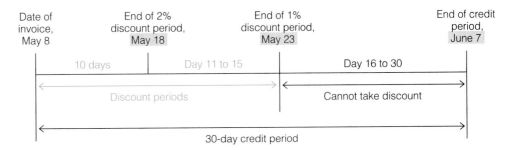

Date of invoice, May 8	End of 2% discount period, May 18	End of 1% discount period, May 23	End of credit period, June 7
	10 days	Day 11 to 15	Day 16 to 30
	Discount periods		Cannot take discount
	30-day credit period		

Receipt of Goods (ROG)

3/10, n/30 ROG With the **receipt of goods (ROG),** the cash discount period begins when buyer receives goods, *not* the invoice date. Industry often uses the ROG terms when buyers cannot expect delivery until a long time after they place the order. Buyers can take a 3% discount within 10 days *after* receipt of goods. Full amount is due between day 11 and day 30 if cash discount period is missed.

EXAMPLE $900 invoice dated May 9; no freight or returned goods; the goods were received on July 8; terms 3/10, n/30 ROG; payment made on July 20.

Step 1. Calculate the end of the 3% discount period:

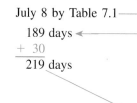

July   8 date goods arrive
+ 10 days
July 18 end of 3% discount period

Step 2. Calculate the end of the credit period:

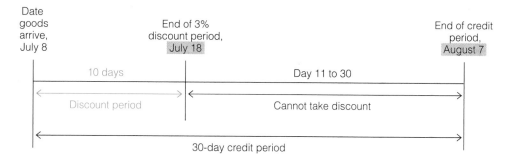

July 8 by Table 7.1
189 days
+ 30
219 days

Search in Table 7.1 for 219 → August 7 → end of credit period

Step 3. Calculate payment on July 20:

Missed discount period and paid net or full amount of $900.

The following time line illustrates 3/10, n/30 ROG beginning and ending dates of the above example:

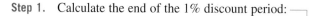

Date goods arrive, July 8 | End of 3% discount period, July 18 | End of credit period, August 7

10 days | Day 11 to 30
Discount period | Cannot take discount
30-day credit period

End of Month (EOM)[2]

In this section we look at terms involving **end of the month (EOM).** If an invoice is dated the *25th or earlier* of a month, we follow one set of rules. If an invoice is dated after the 25th of the month, a new set of rules is followed. Let's look at each situation.

Invoice Dated 25th or Earlier in Month, 1/10 EOM If sellers date an invoice on the 25th or earlier in the month, buyers can take the cash discount if they pay the invoice by the first 10 days of the month following the sale (next month). If buyers miss the discount period, the full amount is due within 20 days after the end of the discount period.

EXAMPLE $600 invoice dated July 6; no freight or returns; terms 1/10 EOM; paid on August 8.

Step 1. Calculate the end of the 1% discount period:

August 10 ← First 10 days of month following sale.

Step 2. Calculate the end of the credit period:

August 10
+ 20 days
August 30 → Credit period is 20 days after discount period.

Step 3. Calculate payment on August 8:

.99 × $600 = $594

---

[2]Sometimes the Latin term *proximo* is used. Other variations of EOM exist, but the key point is that the seller guarantees the buyer 15 days' credit. We assume a 30-day month.

The following timeline illustrates the beginning and ending dates of the EOM invoice of the above example:

*Even though the discount period begins with the next month following the sale, if buyers wish, they can pay before the discount period (date of invoice until the discount period).

Invoice Dated after 25th of Month, 2/10 EOM When sellers sell goods *after* the 25th of the month, buyers gain an additional month. The cash discount period ends on the 10th day of the second month that follows the sale. Why? This occurs because the seller guarantees the 15 days' credit of the buyer. If a buyer bought goods on August 29, September 10 would be only 12 days. So the buyer gets the extra month.

EXAMPLE $800 invoice dated April 29; no freight or returned goods; terms 2/10 EOM; payment made on June 18.

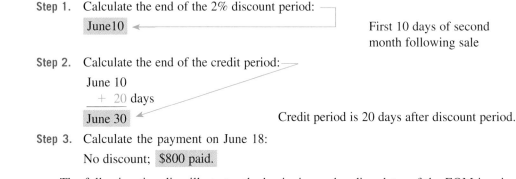

Step 1. Calculate the end of the 2% discount period:
> June 10 ←   First 10 days of second month following sale

Step 2. Calculate the end of the credit period:
> June 10
> + 20 days
> June 30 ←   Credit period is 20 days after discount period.

Step 3. Calculate the payment on June 18:
> No discount; $800 paid.

The following time line illustrates the beginning and ending dates of the EOM invoice of the above example:

*Even though the discount period begins with the second month following the sale, if buyers wish, they can pay before the discount date (date of invoice until the discount period)

Solving a Word Problem with Trade and Cash Discount

Now that we have studied trade and cash discounts, let's look at a combination that involves both a trade and a cash discount.

The Word Problem Hardy Company sent Regan Corporation an invoice for office equipment with a $10,000 list price. Hardy dated the invoice July 29 with terms of 2/10 EOM (end of month). Regan receives a 30% trade discount and paid the invoice on September 6. Since terms were FOB destination, Regan paid no freight charge. What was the cost of office equipment for Regan?

The facts	Solving for?	Steps to take	Key points
List price: $10,000. *Trade discount rate:* 30%. *Terms:* 2/10 EOM. *Invoice date:* 7/29. *Date paid:* 9/6.	Cost of office equipment.	Net price = List price × Complement of trade discount rate. After 25th of month for EOM. Discount period is 1st 10 days of second month that follows sale.	Trade discounts are deducted before cash discounts are taken. Cash discounts are not taken on freight or returns.

Steps to solving problem

1. Calculate the net price. $10,000 × .70 = $7,000   ⎡ 100%
                                                              ⎣ − 30% (trade discount)

2. Calculate the discount period.   Sale: 7/29 Month 1: Aug. Month 2: Sept 10 → Paid on Sept. 6—is entitled to 2% off.

3. Calculate the cost of office equipment. $7,000 × .98 = $6,860   If you save 2 cents on a dollar, you are spending 98 cents.
                                                100%
                                                − 2%

Partial Payments

Often buyers cannot pay the entire invoice before the end of the discount period. To calculate partial payments and outstanding balance, use the following steps:

CALCULATING PARTIAL PAYMENTS AND OUTSTANDING BALANCE
Step 1. Calculate the complement of a discount rate.
Step 2. Divide partial payments by the complement of a discount rate (Step 1). This gives the amount credited.
Step 3. Subtract Step 2 from the total owed. This is the outstanding balance.

EXAMPLE   Molly McGrady owed $400. Molly's terms were 2/10, n/30. Within 10 days, Molly sent a check for $80. The actual credit the buyer gave Molly is as follows:

Step 1. $100\% - 2\% = 98\% \rightarrow .98$

Step 2. $\dfrac{\$80}{.98} = \$81.63$ $\dfrac{\$80}{1 - .02} \leftarrow$ Discount rate

Step 3. $400.00
              $\underline{- \ 81.63}$ partial payment—although sent in $80
              318.37 outstanding balance

Note: We do not multiply .02 × $80 because the seller did not base the original discount on $80. When Molly makes a payment within the 10-day discount period, 98 cents pays each $1 she owes. Before buyers take discounts on partial payments, they must have permission from the seller. Not all states allow partial payments.

You have completed another unit. Let's check your progress.

LU 7-2 PRACTICE QUIZ

Complete this **Practice Quiz** to see how you are doing

Complete the following table:

	Date of invoice	Date goods received	Terms	Last day* of discount period	End of credit period
1.	July 6		2/10, n/30		
2.	February 19	June 9	3/10, n/30 ROG		
3.	May 9		4/10, 1/30, n/60		
4.	May 12		2/10 EOM		
5.	May 29		2/10 EOM		

*If more than one discount, assume date of last discount.

6. Metro Corporation sent Vasko Corporation an invoice for equipment with an $8,000 list price. Metro dated the invoice May 26. Terms were 2/10 EOM. Vasko receives a 20% trade discount and paid the invoice on July 3. What was the cost of equipment for Vasko? (A blueprint aid will be in the solution to help dissect this problem.)

7. Complete amount to be credited and balance outstanding:

Amount of invoice: $600

Terms: 2/10, 1/15, n/30

Date of invoice: September 30

Paid October 3: $400

✓ **Solutions**

1. End of discount period: July 6 + 10 days = July 16

End of credit period: By Table 7.1, July 6 = 187 days
+ 30 days
217 → search → Aug. 5

2. End of discount period: June 9 + 10 days = June 19

End of credit period: By Table 7.1, June 9 = 160 days
+ 30 days
190 → search → July 9

3. End of discount period: By Table 7.1, May 9 = 129 days
+ 30 days
159 → search → June 8

End of credit period: By Table 7.1, May 9 = 129 days
+ 60 days
189 → search → July 8

4. End of discount period: June 10

End of credit period: June 10 + 20 = June 30

5. End of discount period: July 10

End of credit period: July 10 + 20 = July 30

6. Vasko Corporation's cost of equipment:

The facts	Solving for?	Steps to take	Key points
List price: $8,000. *Trade discount rate:* 20%. *Terms:* 2/10 EOM. *Invoice date:* 5/26. *Date paid:* 7/3.	Cost of equipment.	Net price = List price × Complement of trade discount rate. *EOM before 25th:* Discount period is 1st 10 days of month that follows sale.	Trade discounts are deducted before cash discounts are taken. Cash discounts are not taken on freight or returns.

Steps to solving problem

1. Calculate the net price. $8,000 × .80 = $6,400   [100% − 20%]

2. Calculate the discount period.   Until July 10

3. Calculate the cost of office equipment. $6,400 × .98 = **$6,272**   (100% − 2%)

7. $\dfrac{\$400}{.98} = \$408.16$, amount credited.

$\$600 - \$408.16 = \boxed{\$191.84}$, balance outstanding.

LU 7–2a: EXTRA PRACTICE QUIZ

Need more practice? Try this **Extra Practice Quiz** (check figures in Chapter Organizer, p. 190)

Complete the following table:

	Date of invoice	Date goods received	Terms	Last day of discount period*	End of credit period
1.	July 8		2/10, n/30		
2.	February 24	June 12	3/10, n/30 ROG		
3.	May 12		4/10, 1/30, n/60		
4.	April 14		2/10 EOM		
5.	April 27		2/10 EOM		

*If more than one discount, assume date of last discount.

6. Metro Corporation sent Vasko Corporation an invoice for equipment with a $9,000 list price. Metro dated the invoice June 29. Terms were 2/10 EOM. Vasko receives a 30% trade discount and paid the discount on August 9. What was the cost of equipment for Vasko?

7. Complete amount to be credited and balance outstanding:

Amount of invoice: $700
Terms: 2/10, 1/15, n/30
Date of invoice: September 28
Paid October 3: $600

CHAPTER ORGANIZER AND STUDY GUIDE
WITH CHECK FIGURES FOR EXTRA PRACTICE QUIZZES

Topic	Key point, procedure, formula	Example(s) to illustrate situation
Trade discount amount, p. 171	$\dfrac{\text{Trade discount}}{\text{amount}} = \dfrac{\text{List}}{\text{price}} \times \dfrac{\text{Trade discount}}{\text{rate}}$	$600 list price 30% trade discount rate Trade discount amount = $600 × .30 = $180
Calculating net price, p. 172	$\text{Net price} = \dfrac{\text{List}}{\text{price}} - \dfrac{\text{Trade discount}}{\text{amount}}$ or $\dfrac{\text{List}}{\text{price}} \times \dfrac{\text{Complement of trade}}{\text{discount price}}$	$600 list price 30% trade discount rate Net price = $600 × .70 = $420 $\begin{array}{r} 1.00 \\ -\ .30 \\ \hline .70 \end{array}$
Freight, p. 173	FOB shipping point—buyer pays freight. FOB destination—seller pays freight.	Moose Company of New York sells equipment to Agee Company of Oregon. Terms of shipping are FOB New York. Agee pays cost of freight since terms are FOB shipping point.
Calculating list price when net price and trade discount rate are known, p. 175	$\text{List price} = \dfrac{\text{Net price}}{\dfrac{\text{Complement of}}{\text{trade discount rate}}}$	40% trade discount rate Net price, $120 $\dfrac{\$120}{.60} = \$200$ list price (1.00 − .40)

(continues)

CHAPTER ORGANIZER AND STUDY GUIDE
WITH CHECK FIGURES FOR EXTRA PRACTICE QUIZZES (continued)

Topic	Key point, procedure, formula	Example(s) to illustrate situation
Chain discounts, p. 176	Successively lower base.	5/10 on a $100 list item $\begin{array}{cc} \$\ 100 & \$\ \ 95 \\ \times\ .05 & \times\ .10 \\ \hline \$5.00 & \$9.50 \end{array}$ (running balance) $\begin{array}{l} \$95.00 \\ -\ 9.50 \\ \hline \boxed{\$85.50}\ \text{net price} \end{array}$
Net price equivalent rate, p. 176	$\begin{array}{l}\text{Actual cost}\\ \text{to buyer}\end{array} = \begin{array}{l}\text{List}\\ \text{price}\end{array} \times \begin{array}{l}\text{Net price}\\ \text{equivalent rate}\end{array}$ Take complement of each chain discount and multiply—do not round. $\begin{array}{l}\text{Trade discount}\\ \text{amount}\end{array} = \begin{array}{l}\text{List}\\ \text{price}\end{array} - \begin{array}{l}\text{Actual cost}\\ \text{to buyer}\end{array}$	Given: 5/10 on $1,000 list price Take complement: .95 × .90 = .855 $\qquad\qquad$ (net price equivalent) $1,000 × .855 = \boxed{\$855}$ $\qquad\qquad$ (actual cost or net price) $\begin{array}{l} \$1,000 \\ -\ \ \ 855 \\ \hline \boxed{\$\ \ 145}\ \text{trade discount amount} \end{array}$
Single equivalent discount rate, p. 177	$\begin{array}{l}\text{Trade discount}\\ \text{amount}\end{array} = \begin{array}{l}\text{List}\\ \text{price}\end{array} \times \begin{array}{l}1 - \text{Net price}\\ \text{equivalent rate}\end{array}$	See preceding example for facts: 1 − .855 = .145 .145 × $1,000 = \boxed{\$145}$
Cash discounts, p. 179	Cash discounts, due to prompt payment, are not taken on freight, returns, etc.	Gross $\quad$ $1,000 (includes freight) Freight $\quad$ $25 $\qquad$ Terms, 2/10, n/30 Returns $\quad$ $25 $\qquad$ Purchased: Sept. 9; $\qquad\qquad\qquad\qquad$ paid Sept. 15 Cash discount = $950 × .02 = \boxed{\$19}$
Calculating due dates, p. 180	*Option 1:* Thirty days has September, April, June, and November; all the rest have 31 except February has 28, and 29 in leap years. *Option 2:* Knuckles—31-day month; in between knuckles are short months. *Option 3:* Days-in-a-year table.	Invoice $500 on March 5; terms 2/10, n/30 $\qquad$ March $\ \ $ 5 *End of discount* $\qquad\qquad\quad$ + 10 *period:* $\longrightarrow$ $\boxed{\text{March 15}}$ *End of credit* $\quad$ March 5 = 64 days *period by* $\qquad\qquad\qquad$ + 30 *Table 7.1:* $\longrightarrow$ 94 days Search in Table 7.1 $\boxed{\text{April 4}}$
Common terms of sale **a. Ordinary dating, p. 182**	Discount period begins from date of invoice. Credit period ends 20 days from the end of the discount period unless otherwise stipulated; example, 2/10, n/60—the credit period ends 50 days from end of discount period.	Invoice $600 (freight of $100 included in price) dated March 8; payment on March 16; 3/10, n/30. $\quad$ March $\ \ $ 8 *End of discount* $\qquad\qquad\quad$ + 10 *period:* $\longrightarrow$ $\boxed{\text{March 18}}$ *End of credit* $\quad$ March 8 = $\ $ 67 days *period by* $\qquad\qquad\qquad$ + 30 *Table 7.1:* $\longrightarrow$ 97 days Search in Table 7.1 $\boxed{\text{April 7}}$ *If paid on March 16:* .97 × $500 = $485 $\qquad\qquad$ + $\ $ 100 freight $\qquad\qquad$ $\boxed{\$585}$

(continues)

CHAPTER ORGANIZER AND STUDY GUIDE
WITH CHECK FIGURES FOR EXTRA PRACTICE QUIZZES (concluded)

Topic	Key point, procedure, formula	Example(s) to illustrate situation
b. Receipt of goods (ROG), p. 183	Discount period begins when goods are received. Credit period ends 20 days from end of discount period.	4/10, n/30, ROG. $600 invoice; no freight; dated August 5; goods received October 2, payment made October 20. October 2 *End of discount* + 10 *period:* → October 12 *End of* October 2 = 275 *credit period* + 30 *by Table 7.1:* → 305 ↓ Search in Table 7.1 November 1 *Payment on October 20:* No discount, pay $600
c. End of month (EOM), p. 184	On or before 25th of the month, discount period is 10 days after month following sale. After 25th of the month, an additional month is gained.	$1,000 invoice dated May 12; no freight or returns; terms 2/10 EOM. *End of discount period* → June 10 *End of credit period* → June 30
Partial payments, p. 186	Amount credited = $\dfrac{\text{Partial payment}}{1 - \text{Discount rate}}$	$200 invoice, terms 2/10, n/30, dated March 2, paid $100 on March 5. $\dfrac{\$100}{1 - .02} = \dfrac{\$100}{.98} = \$102.04$
KEY TERMS	Cash discount, *p. 179* Chain discounts, *p. 176* Complement, *p. 174* Credit period, *p. 179* Discount period, *p. 179* Due dates, *p. 180* End of credit period, *p. 180* End of month (EOM), *p. 184* FOB destination, *p. 173*	FOB shipping point, *p. 173* Freight terms, *p. 173* Invoice, *p. 171* List price, *p. 171* Net price, *p. 172* Net price equivalent rate, *p. 176* Ordinary dating, *p. 182* Receipt of goods (ROG), *p. 183* · Series discounts, *p. 176* Single equivalent discount rate, *p. 177* Single trade discount, *p. 174* Terms of the sale, *p. 179* Trade discount, *p. 171* Trade discount amount, *p. 171* Trade discount rate, *p. 171*
CHECK FIGURES FOR EXTRA PRACTICE QUIZZES WITH PAGE REFERENCES	LU 7–1a (p. 179) 1. $4,800 TD; $11,200 NP 2. $500 3. $9,891.84 NP; TD $4,108.16	LU 7–2a (p. 188) 1. July 18; Aug. 7 2. June 22; July 12 3. June 11; July 11 4. May 10; May 30 5. June 10; June 30 6. $6,174 7. a) $612.24 b) $87.76

Critical Thinking Discussion Questions

1. What is the net price? June Long bought a jacket from a catalog company. She took her trade discount off the original price plus freight. What is wrong with June's approach? Who would benefit from June's approach—the buyer or the seller?

2. How do you calculate the list price when the net price and trade discount rate are known? A publisher tells the bookstore its net price of a book along with a suggested trade discount of 20%. The bookstore uses a 25% discount rate. Is this ethical when textbook prices are rising?

3. Explain FOB shipping point and FOB destination. Think back to your last major purchase. Was it FOB shipping point or FOB destination? Did you get a trade or a cash discount?

4. What are the steps to calculate the net price equivalent rate? Why is the net price equivalent rate *not* rounded?

5. What are the steps to calculate the single equivalent discount rate? Is this rate off the list or net price? Explain why this calculation of a single equivalent discount rate may not always be needed.

6. What is the difference between a discount and credit period? Are all cash discounts taken before trade discounts? Agree or disagree? Why?

7. Explain the following credit terms of sale:
   a.   2/10, n/30.
   b.   3/10, n/30 ROG.
   c.   1/10 EOM (on or before 25th of month).
   d.   1/10 EOM (after 25th of month).

8. Explain how to calculate a partial payment. Whom does a partial payment favor—the buyer or the seller?

Classroom Notes

Name _____ Date _____

DRILL PROBLEMS

For all problems, round your final answer to the nearest cent. Do not round net price equivalent rates or single equivalent discount rates.

Complete the following:

	Item	List price	Chain discount	Net price equivalent rate (in decimals)	Single equivalent discount rate (in decimals)	Trade discount	Net price
7–1.	Apple iPod	$300	5/2				
7–2.	Panasonic DVD player	$199	8/4/3				
7–3.	IBM scanner	$269	7/3/1				

Complete the following:

	Item	List price	Chain discount	Net price	Trade discount
7–4.	Trotter treadmill	$3,000	9/4		
7–5.	Maytag dishwasher	$450	8/5/6		
7–6.	Hewlett-Packard scanner	$320	3/5/9		
7–7.	Land Rover roofrack	$1,850	12/9/6		

7–8. Which of the following companies, A or B, gives a higher discount? Use the single equivalent discount rate to make your choice (convert your equivalent rate to the nearest hundredth percent).

Company A
8/10/15/3

Company B
10/6/16/5

Complete the following:

	Invoice	Dates when goods received	Terms	Last day* of discount period	Final day bill is due (end of credit period)
7–9.	June 18		1/10, n/30		
7–10.	Nov. 27		2/10 EOM		
7–11.	May 15	June 5	3/10, n/30, ROG		
7–12.	April 10		2/10, 1/30, n/60		
7–13.	June 12		3/10 EOM		
7–14.	Jan. 10	Feb. 3 (no leap year)	4/10, n/30, ROG		

*If more than one discount, assume date of last discount.

Complete the following by calculating the cash discount and net amount paid:

	Gross amount of invoice (freight charge already included)	Freight charge	Date of invoice	Terms of invoice	Date of payment	Cash discount	Net amount paid
7–15.	$7,000	$100	4/8	2/10, n/60	4/15		
7–16.	$600	None	8/1	3/10, 2/15, n/30	8/13		
7–17.	$200	None	11/13	1/10 EOM	12/3		
7–18.	$500	$100	11/29	1/10 EOM	1/4		

Complete the following:

	Amount of invoice	Terms	Invoice date	Actual partial payment made	Date of partial payment	Amount of payment to be credited	Balance outstanding
7–19.	$700	2/10, n/60	5/6	$400	5/15		

194

7–20. $600   4/10, n/60   7/5 $400   7/14

7–21. The list price of a Luminox watch is $475. Barry Katz receives a trade discount of 40%. Find the trade discount amount and the net price.

7–22. A model NASCAR race car lists for $79.99 with a trade discount of 40%. What is the net price of the car?

7–23. An article in *The* (Biloxi, MS) *Sun Herald* on August 4, 2006, discussed quantity discounts for schools and businesses. Publisher, Andrews McMeel's books are available at quantity discounts with bulk purchases for educational or business use. School district 510 purchased 50 books at $26.95 each with a quantity discount of 5%. **(a)** What was total list price for the books? **(b)** What was the total discount amount? **(c)** What was the total net price for the books? Round to the nearest cent.

7–24. Levin Furniture buys a living room set with a $4,000 list price and a 55% trade discount. Freight (FOB shipping point) of $50 is not part of the list price. What is the delivered price (including freight) of the living room set, assuming a cash discount of 2/10, n/30, ROG? The invoice had an April 8 date. Levin received the goods on April 19 and paid the invoice on April 25.

7–25. A manufacturer of skateboards offered a 5/2/1 chain discount to many customers. Bob's Sporting Goods ordered 20 skateboards for a total $625 list price. What was the net price of the skateboards? What was the trade discount amount?

7–26. Home Depot wants to buy a new line of shortwave radios. Manufacturer A offers a 21/13 chain discount. Manufacturer B offers a 26/8 chain discount. Both manufacturers have the same list price. What manufacturer should Home Depot buy from?

7–27. Maplewood Supply received a $5,250 invoice dated 4/15/06. The $5,250 included $250 freight. Terms were 4/10, 3/30, n/60. **(a)** If Maplewood pays the invoice on April 27, what will it pay? **(b)** If Maplewood pays the invoice on May 21, what will it pay?

7–28. Sport Authority ordered 50 pairs of tennis shoes from Nike Corporation. The shoes were priced at $85 for each pair with the following terms: 4/10, 2/30, n/60. The invoice was dated October 15. Sports Authority sent in a payment on October 28. What should have been the amount of the check?

7–29. Macy of New York sold Marriott of Chicago office equipment with a $6,000 list price. Sale terms were 3/10, n/30 FOB New York. Macy agreed to prepay the $30 freight. Marriott pays the invoice within the discount period. What does Marriott pay Macy?

7–30. Royal Furniture bought a sofa for $800. The sofa had a $1,400 list price. What was the trade discount rate Royal received? Round to the nearest hundredth percent.

7–31. Amazon.com paid a $6,000 net price for textbooks. The publisher offered a 30% trade discount. What was the publisher's list price? Round to the nearest cent.

7–32. Bally Manufacturing sent Intel Corporation an invoice for machinery with a $14,000 list price. Bally dated the invoice July 23 with 2/10 EOM terms. Intel receives a 40% trade discount. Intel pays the invoice on August 5. What does Intel pay Bally?

7–33. On August 1, Intel Corporation (Problem 7–32) returns $100 of the machinery due to defects. What does Intel pay Bally on August 5? Round to nearest cent.

7–34. Stacy's Dress Shop received a $1,050 invoice dated July 8 with 2/10, 1/15, n/60 terms. On July 22, Stacy's sent a $242 partial payment. What credit should Stacy's receive? What is Stacy's outstanding balance?

7–35. On March 11, Jangles Corporation received a $20,000 invoice dated March 8. Cash discount terms were 4/10, n/30. On March 15, Jangles sent an $8,000 partial payment. What credit should Jangles receive? What is Jangles' outstanding balance?

ADDITIONAL SET OF WORD PROBLEMS

7–36. In the February 2007 issue of *The Tax Adviser*, it was reported that trade discounts are not income. Westpac Pacific Food agreed to buy a minimum quantity of merchandise and receive a volume discount. Westpac Pacific Food received a 4 percent quantity discount. Total amount of an order placed by Westpac amounted to $20,500. What was the net price paid by Westpac?

7–37. Borders.com paid a $79.99 net price for each calculus textbook. The publisher offered a 20% trade discount. What was the publisher's list price?

7–38. Home Office.com buys a computer from Compaq Corporation. The computers have a $1,200 list price with a 30% trade discount. What is the trade discount amount? What is the net price of the computer? Freight charges are FOB destination.

7–39. Vail Ski Shop received a $1,201 invoice dated July 8 with 2/10, 1/15, n/60 terms. On July 22, Vail sent a $485 partial payment. What credit should Vail receive? What is Vail's outstanding balance?

7–40. True Value received an invoice dated 4/15/02. The invoice had a $5,500 balance that included $300 freight. Terms were 4/10, 3/30, n/60. True Value pays the invoice on April 29. What amount does True Value pay?

7–41. Staples purchased seven new computers for $850 each. It received a 15% discount because it purchased more than five and an additional 6% discount because it took immediate delivery. Terms of payment were 2/10, n/30. Staples pays the bill within the cash discount period. How much should the check be? Round to the nearest cent.

7–42. On May 14, Talbots of Boston sold Forrest of Los Angeles $7,000 of fine clothes. Terms were 2/10 EOM FOB Boston. Talbots agreed to prepay the $80 freight. If Forrest pays the invoice on June 8, what will Forrest pay? If Forrest pays on June 20, what will Forrest pay?

7–43. Sam's Ski Boards.com offers 5/4/1 chain discounts to many of its customers. The Ski Hut ordered 20 ski boards with a total list price of $1,200. What is the net price of the ski boards? What was the trade discount amount? Round to the nearest cent.

7–44. Majestic Manufacturing sold Jordans Furniture a living room set for an $8,500 list price with 35% trade discount. The $100 freight (FOB shipping point) was not part of the list price. Terms were 3/10, n/30 ROG. The invoice date was May 30. Jordans received the goods on July 18 and paid the invoice on July 20. What was the final price (include cost of freight) of the living room set?

7–45. Boeing Truck Company received an invoice showing 8 tires at $110 each, 12 tires at $160 each, and 15 tires at $180 each. Shipping terms are FOB shipping point. Freight is $400; trade discount is 10/5; and a cash discount of 2/10, n/30 is offered. Assuming Boeing paid within the discount period, what did Boeing pay?

7–46. The *Greeley Tribune* (Greeley, CO) on February 24, 2007 reported on discounts. Republican Representative Kevin Lundberg, of Berthoud, Colorado, said the law defined "cost" as the wholesale price of goods plus any overhead costs, but stores sell things below cost all the time. Jim Riesberg purchased slacks for $25.00, with an original price of $125. What was the percent discount Jim received?

7–47. Verizon offers to sell cellular phones listing for $99.99 with a chain discount of 15/10/5. Cellular Company offers to sell its cellular phones that list at $102.99 with a chain discount of 25/5. If Irene is to buy 6 phones, how much could she save if she buys from the lower-priced company?

7–48. Bryant Manufacture sells its furniture to wholesalers and retailers. It offers to wholesalers a chain discount of 15/10/5 and to retailers a chain discount of 15/10. If a sofa lists for $500, how much would the wholesaler and retailer pay?

CHALLENGE PROBLEMS

7–49. The original price of a 2003 Honda Insight to the dealer is $17,995, but the dealer will pay only $16,495. If the dealer pays Honda within 15 days, there is a 1% cash discount. **(a)** How much is the rebate? **(b)** What percent is the rebate? Round to nearest hundredth percent. **(c)** What is the amount of the cash discount if the dealer pays within 15 days? **(d)** What is the dealer's final price? **(e)** What is the dealer's total savings? Round answer to the nearest hundredth.

7–50. On March 30, Century Television received an invoice dated March 28 from ACME Manufacturing for 50 televisions at a cost of $125 each. Century received a 10/4/2 chain discount. Shipping terms were FOB shipping point. ACME prepaid the $70 freight. Terms were 2/10 EOM. When Century received the goods, 3 sets were defective. Century returned these sets to ACME. On April 8, Century sent a $150 partial payment. Century will pay the balance on May 6. What is Century's final payment on May 6? Assume no taxes.

 SUMMARY PRACTICE TEST (Round to the Nearest Cent as Needed)

Complete the following: *(p. 172)*

Item	List price	Single trade discount	Net price
1. Apple iPod	$350	5%	
2. Palm Pilot		10%	$190

Calculate the net price and trade discount (use net price equivalent rate and single equivalent discount rate) for the following: *(p. 176)*

Item	List price	Chain discount	Net price	Trade discount
3. Sony HD flat-screen TV	$899	5/4		

4. From the following, what is the last date for each discount period and credit period? *(p. 187)*

	Date of invoice	Terms	End of discount period	End of credit period
a.	Nov. 4	2/10, n/30		
b.	Oct. 3, 2009	3/10, n/30 ROG (Goods received March 10, 2010)		
c.	May 2	2/10 EOM		
d.	Nov. 28	2/10 EOM		

5. Best Buy buys an iPod from a wholesaler with a $300 list price and a 5% trade discount. What is the trade discount amount? What is the net price of the iPod? *(p. 182)*

6. Jordan's of Boston sold Lee Company of New York computer equipment with a $7,000 list price. Sale terms were 4/10, n/30 FOB Boston. Jordan's agreed to prepay the $400 freight. Lee pays the invoice within the discount period. What does Lee pay Jordan's? *(p. 174)*

7. Julie Ring wants to buy a new line of Tonka trucks for her shop. Manufacturer A offers a 14/8 chain discount. Manufacturer B offers a 15/7 chain discount. Both manufacturers have the same list price. Which manufacturer should Julie buy from? *(p. 177)*

8. Office.com received a $8,000 invoice dated April 10. Terms were 2/10, 1/15, n/60. On April 14, Office.com sent an $1,900 partial payment. What credit should Office.com receive? What is Office.com's outstanding balance? Round to the nearest cent. *(p. 186)*

9. Logan Company received from Furniture.com an invoice dated September 29. Terms were 1/10 EOM. List price on the invoice was $8,000 (freight not included). Logan receives a 8/7 chain discount. Freight charges are Logan's responsibility, but Furniture.com agreed to prepay the $300 freight. Logan pays the invoice on November 7. What does Logan Company pay Furniture.com? *(p. 177)*

Personal Finance

TECH | Cable, phone and Internet packages dangle attractive prices. *By Jeff Bertolucci*

Save a **BUNDLE** on telecom services

TYING UP your telecom services in a single package is the lure many local telephone and cable companies are casting in selected areas around the U.S. For about $100 a month, you can get cable or satellite TV, local and long-distance telephone service, plus high-speed Internet service. In addition to paying just one bill, you have just one company to call if you have a technical or billing issue. Then again, this one-stop-shop approach can backfire if your vendor's customer service stinks.

Many bundled deals (often marketed as "triple plays" or "triple packs") are limited-time offers ranging from three to 12 months. The Comcast Triple Play, for instance, includes Internet, phone and cable service for $99 per month for one year. After the year is up, will the hammer fall—and the price skyrocket? Not necessarily. You can expect Comcast's package to cost "about $130 per month," says company spokeswoman Jenni Moyer.

Patrick Matters, who lives in Indianapolis, signed up for Comcast's Triple Play about a year ago. He pays $100 to $110 per month ("a little more if my daughters buy a movie"), a savings of more than $50 over his previous a la carte plans. At $130 per month, he'd still be ahead.

The Triple Play is for new customers only. But current Comcast subscribers can also get discounts if they add new services. For example, a Comcast cable-TV customer can sign up for the company's phone service for $33 per month for one year. If you're already a sub-

● About $100 a month will buy you TV, phone and Internet service.

scriber, check your vendor's Web site for bundled discounts.

Some vendors are offering quadruple plays that add wireless phone service. AT&T's Quad Pack, for instance, bundles Internet, telephone, Dish Network satellite TV and Cingular Wireless service for $123 per month. Its Triple Pack—Internet, telephone and wireless—costs $95 per month.

Regional offers. Bundles vary depending on where you live. For example, in Qwest's 14-state region, the starting price for a package including Internet, phone and DirecTV is about $90 per

month. In southern California, bundles from Time Warner Cable with Internet, phone and cable start at about $100. And in areas of Massachusetts and other states where Verizon has wired homes with its FiOS high-speed fiber-optic service, subscribers can get Internet, telephone and nearly 200 digital cable TV and music channels for $105 per month. Verizon offers bundles with satellite TV in other markets.

Although price is a big draw, a bundle isn't worth it if it excludes services you want. The AT&T Quad Pack, for instance, allows only 100 minutes per month of direct-dial calls from your home. More long-distance minutes cost 9 cents each.

And there may be other drawbacks. If a single high-speed line brings all communications to your home, you could lose your phone, cable and Internet service at the same time if the line goes down. Some digital phone services that use the Internet for voice calls don't support faxing—a significant shortcoming for home-based businesses.

And bundles make it more difficult to change providers for a specific service—for instance, switching from cable to satellite TV. Of course, from a telecom company's perspective, that's the whole idea.

Still, the convenience and relatively low prices make bundled services appealing. And there should be plenty of competition as telephone and cable companies duke it out.

BUSINESS MATH ISSUE

If you get a bundled package you will always save.

1. List the key points of the article and information to support your position.
2. Write a group defense of your position using math calculations to support your view.

Slater's Business Math Scrapbook

with Internet Application
Putting Your Skills to Work

PROJECT A
Pick a product and how this article will change your buying habits.

Green Thumb / *Growing Your Money* ◈ *By Sarah McBride*

How Do You Get a Break in the Price Of Practically Anything? Easy, Just Ask

MOST PEOPLE don't think twice about bargaining when it comes to something big, like a new car or home. But getting a price cut on smaller things—cable bills, doctors' fees, electronics goods—can be surprisingly easy: Just ask.

That goes against the grain for millions of Americans. Maybe our ancestors haggled at the dry-goods store. But today's big-box supermarkets, laser price scanners and uniformed checkout personnel present a barrier.

The good news is, in many situations, it's getting easier to ask for, and get, a price break. Increasingly, retailers and others are empowering rank-and-file employees to give discounts. At hotels, for example, most desk clerks can give 10% to 25% off the advertised rate, whereas a few years ago that might have required a discussion with the manager, says Rick Doble, a discount-advice writer and accomplished haggler.

Don't just think retail. Doctors and hospitals have a surprising amount of leeway to bargain. Some patients have taken to negotiating fees in advance with doctors, but even after the bill comes in, it's not too late to ask for cuts. Sympathetic billing offices will often reduce the portion insurance didn't pay, or even waive it altogether. Another common approach: Interest-free installment plans, which are basically a free loan.

Mr. Doble himself goes to considerable lengths to save a buck, such as tracking down the manager of the grocery-store dairy aisle to get a break on about-to-expire milk and cheese. But getting a deal doesn't have to take a lot of time, or even require an appetite for dubious cheddar. Some guidance:

Pick your store, and your moment. Try small boutiques and family-owned businesses. Look for somebody who seems knowledgeable and comfortable in their job, not the high-school student who started last week. Go in when the store isn't busy—a harried staffer has less time or inclination to negotiate.

Ease into it. Chat with the salesperson, and ask a lot about prices, so they can see that is a concern. Ask if they take an American Automobile Association discount, or a local discount card, even if you know they don't. After a few leading questions, it's possible a shopkeeper will simply volunteer 10% off.

Offer to pay in cash. Credit-card companies take 2% to 3% of the price in fees out of the merchant's pocket. At some stores, nicely asking whether you get a break for paying in cash can quickly get you 5% or 10% off—more than the credit-card fees.

Make it easy for them to pull it off: Ask if it's possible for you to ride on the coattails of a "friends and family" discount, or employee discount.

Call your phone company, ISP and cable providers and say you're thinking about switching. Often, you'll immediately get transferred to the company's "retention" desk, where the staff is prepped with special offers designed to retain wavering customers.

Finally, assume there is a promotion going on. Mr. Doble, author of the book "Savvy Discounts," says he never checks into a hotel before asking, "Don't you have a special at this time of year?" Much of the time, the answer is "yes," he says. And after he has finished cutting a deal, he asks for an upgrade. And free breakfast.

Send comments to sarah.mcbride@wsj.com.

Discount Haggling

- Offer to pay cash; it saves shopkeepers on credit-card fees.

- Tell your phone or cable company you might switch; it can shake loose special deals.

- Doctors often have leeway to negotiate—it can't hurt to ask.

Internet Projects: See text Web site (www.mhhe.com/slater9e) and The Business Math Internet Resource Guide.

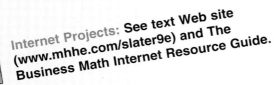

Video Case

HILLERICH & BRADSBY COMPANY "LOUISVILLE SLUGGER"

According to Bob Hill, author of *Crack of the Bat: The Louisville Slugger Story,* in 1884 the star outfielder Pete "The Gladiator" Browning of the Louisville Eclipses was in a batting slump. Bud Hillerich, son of J.F. Hillerich, made Browning a bat. After Browning got three hits with his new bat, his teammates began clamoring for the Hillerich bat.

In 1910, during the rebuilding process following a factory fire, Hillerich hired Frank Bradsby to oversee the company's sales policy. In 1916, Bradsby's salesman skills won him a partnership and the company's name was changed to Hillerich & Bradsby (H & B) Company. After 118 years, H & B remains the leading manufacturer of baseball bats. H & B makes customized bats for players according to their specifications for bat weight, length, and wood preference (white ash or maple). Players rarely use bats over 34.5 inches long and 33 ounces in weight. Maple bats are denser and heavier than ash. About 20% of the 200,000 big league bats produced by H & B are made of maple. Big league teams pay $41 for a white ash bat and $51 for a maple bat.

In the early 1970s, aluminum bats became very popular with amateur players. Aluminum bats are considered safer and more durable than wood bats. Aluminum bats are also more economical. Since batters can swing the aluminum bats faster, the ball travels farther. The decline in white ash availability led to the increased cost of wood bats and increased use of aluminum bats. While aluminum bats rarely break, a college team would go through more than 350 wood bats per season. Basic models of aluminum bats sell for around $100; high-tech metal bats sell for as much as $500.

Interest in bats was renewed after Sammy Sosa's bat broke, spraying cork in the infield. Players and fans wanted to know how bats differ and how batters benefited from different types of bats.

In 1971, aluminum bats were approved for Little League play; in 1975 they were approved for college play. As early as 1970, H & B contracted an outside aluminum company to manufacture H & B aluminum bats; however, H & B remained focused on Louisville Slugger wood bats. H & B felt aluminum bats would detract from the game of baseball.

After aluminum bats were introduced, the *Dayton Daily News* reported that Louisville Slugger wood bat sales shrank from seven million to 800,000. Now new sales are back up to one million. After being in a slump, it looks like H & B hit a "home run."

PROBLEM 1

The video stated that in 1974, when the NCAA legalized aluminum bats in college, production of wood bats dropped from 7,000,000 to 800,000. The average retail price of a wood bat is $46. **(a)** What was the percent decrease in production? Round to the nearest hundredth percent. **(b)** How much did revenue decrease?

PROBLEM 2

The video states that the Ontario, California, plant produces over 300 different models of aluminum baseball bats. The plant produces 5,500 bats each day. Assume the average price is $175 per bat. **(a)** What would be the revenue generated for a week's production (5-day week)? **(b)** How many bats would be produced annually? **(c)** What would be the total annual sales?

PROBLEM 3

The April 11, 2003, issue of the *Dayton Daily News* reported that the Massachusetts Interscholastic Athletic Association created a stir by switching from aluminum bats to wood, citing safety concerns. Of the state's 40 leagues, 62.5% have decided to use wood during the regular season. How many have decided to stay with aluminum bats?

PROBLEM 4

On April 14, 2003, *Forbes* reported that H & B receives nearly $\frac{3}{4}$ of its $110 million in annual revenue from baseball and softball bats. **(a)** What is the total amount received for baseball and softball bats? **(b)** How much revenue is received from other items?

PROBLEM 5

The average number of bats used by a Major Leaguer in a season is 90. There are 30 teams with a roster of 25 players. The cost of a bat is $41 to $51. **(a)** What is the percent increase? Round to the nearest tenth. **(b)** Using an average price, what is the total amount of dollars spent on baseball bats by Major Leaguers?

PROBLEM 6

On April 13, 2003, the *Chicago Sun-Times* reported aluminum bats typically cost $100 to $250 and have one-year warranties. Wood bats typically cost $35 to $90. Aluminum bats are cheaper in the long run because they don't break. A high school hitter can go through four wood bats in one season. **(a)** What is the most a high school hitter would pay for wood bats during the season? **(b)** What is the least amount paid for wood bats during the season? **(c)** What is the average percent savings using aluminum as compared to wood?

PROBLEM 7

On September 30, 2003, the *Chicago Sun-Times* reported that a 34-inch, 38-ounce Louisville Slugger commemorative bat honoring the Chicago Cubs 2003 National League Central Division Champions hit the market. The bats retail at $129.95 plus shipping. Personalized (recipient's name engraved) bats are sold by H & B for $54.00. **(a)** What is the percent change for the commemorative bat? Round to the nearest tenth. **(b)** If shipping costs for the commemorative bats are an additional 11.54%, what is the amount charged for shipping? Round to the nearest dollar. **(c)** What would be the total cost for the commemorative bat?

CHAPTER 8

Markups and Markdowns

Disney Signs Direct Shoe Deal With Payless

By MERISSA MARR

Walt Disney Co. has forged an agreement for exclusive Disney-branded children's footwear to be made and sold by **Payless ShoeSource** Inc., the latest move by Disney to cut out licensees in favor of working directly with retailers.

Under Consumer Products Chairman Andy Mooney, Disney has been moving toward direct-to-retail deals, in which it collaborates closely with a retailer, which then gets an exclusive product. That is different from the traditional retail model in which the company signs deals with licensees, which in turn take the products to retailers.

The multiyear deal, set to be announced today, gives Disney more con-

trol over the design and sale of its shoes. The agreement, which will feature characters including Disney Princesses, Winnie the Pooh and the cast from Power Rangers, is both companies' first direct-to-retail program for character footwear.

Ranging between $12 and $22, the shoes will be available exclusively in Payless's almost 4,600 stores and on Payless.com. The footwear will start hitting Payless stores in the spring, with the full lines filling shelves over the summer.

"Traditional layers between the customers and brands have inflated pricing," says Matt Rubel, chief executive of Payless, who previously worked with Mr. Mooney at Nike Inc. Mr. Mooney

adds: "By going directly to the retailer, both the quality and price improves."

Payless, a leading retailer of kids shoes, has been shifting its strategy to sell more high-end footwear at moderate prices. Retailers in general are pushing for more exclusivity on branded and character products. "Our deal with Disney is the direction of the future," says Mr. Rubel.

As part of its direct-to-retail strategy, Disney has been opening offices in cities where major retailers have their headquarters, including Bentonville, Ark., where **Wal-Mart Stores** Inc. is located, and Paris, where **Carrefour** SA is based. Disney says it plans to bulk up those offices in the next few years.

Wall Street Journal © 2006

LEARNING UNIT OBJECTIVES

LU 8–1: Markups[1] Based on Cost (100%)

LU 8–2: Markups Based on Selling Price (100%)

LU 8–3: Markdowns

[1]Some texts use the term *markon* (selling price minus cost).

Levi Strauss Sells Low-Cost Jeans To Target in Bid to Increase Sales

By SALLY BEATTY

Levi Strauss & Co. has begun selling its new low-cost line of jeans to Target stores, in a gamble that the struggling jeansmaker can boost sales without alienating its core department-store customers.

The launch of the new Levi Strauss Signature brand in **Target** Corp.'s Target division stores should bolster revenue at a time when Levi sales have been sagging. But it also risks damaging the cachet of the Levi brand. The Signature line originally sold for about $23, while the company's main "red tab" label, sold at department stores, normally costs about $35. The company is betting that Signature, which debuted at **Wal-Mart Stores** Inc. in July, won't cut into sales of its "red tab" line, which continues to account for the bulk of Levi sales.

The McGraw-Hill Companies, Ken Cavanagh photographer

Are you one of the many shoppers who shop at Target? If you wear jeans, you may be interested in the *Wall Street Journal* clipping "Levi Strauss Sells Low-Cost Jeans to Target in Bid to Increase Sales." The clipping states that Levi Strauss & Co. has begun selling its Levi Strauss Signature™ brand jeans to Target. If you are familiar with products from Levi Strauss & Co. and shop at the mass-channel retail stores that carry Levi Strauss Signature™ brand jeans, such as Target and Wal-Mart, you will probably look at these lower-cost jeans. Levi Strauss & Co. wants to boost sales with their Levi Strauss Signature™ brand products by appealing to a new group of value-conscious consumers who don't buy their other branded products.

Before we study the two pricing methods available to Target (percent markup on cost and percent markup on selling price), we must know the following terms:

- **Selling price.** The price retailers charge consumers. The total selling price of all the goods sold by a retailer (like Target) represents the retailer's total sales.
- **Cost.** The price retailers pay to a manufacturer or supplier to bring the goods into the store.
- **Markup, margin, or gross profit.** These three terms refer to the difference between the cost of bringing the goods into the store and the selling price of the goods. As an example of high-margin sales, Sharper Image customers are buying more high-margin gadgets. This helps the company fuel a 15% rise in same-store sales.
- **Operating expenses or overhead.** The regular expenses of doing business such as wages, rent, utilities, insurance, and advertising.
- **Net profit or net incomes.** The profit remaining after subtracting the cost of bringing the goods into the store and the operating expenses from the sale of the goods (including any returns or adjustments).

From these definitions, we can conclude that **markup** represents the amount that retailers must add to the cost of the goods to cover their operating expenses and make a profit.[2]

Let's assume Target pays Levi Strauss & Co. $18 for a pair for jeans and sells them for $23.[3]

---

[2]In this chapter, we concentrate on the markup of retailers. Manufacturers and suppliers also use markup to determine selling price.

[3]Amounts used are hypothetical; prices and markups may vary.

Basic selling price formula

Selling price (S)	=	Cost (C)	+	Markup (M)
↑		↑		↑
$23	=	$18	+	$5
		(price paid to bring jeans into store)		(amount in dollars to cover operating expenses and make a profit)

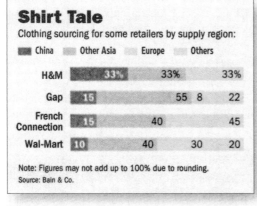

Shirt Tale

Clothing sourcing for some retailers by supply region:

■ China   ▨ Other Asia   ▨ Europe   □ Others

	China	Other Asia	Europe	Others
H&M	33%	33%		33%
Gap	15	55	8	22
French Connection	15	40		45
Wal-Mart	10	40	30	20

Note: Figures may not add up to 100% due to rounding.
Source: Bain & Co.

Wall Street Journal © 2005

In the Levi Strauss example, the markup is a dollar amount, or a **dollar markup.** Markup is also expressed in percent. When expressing markup in percent, retailers can choose a percent based on *cost* (Learning Unit 8–1) or a percent based on *selling price* (Learning Unit 8–2).

When you study the *Wall Street Journal* clipping "Shirt Tale," you will see how the clothing sourcing for some retailers is divided by supply regions. These retailers include H&M, Gap, French Connection, and Wal-Mart. Do you shop at any of these retailers?

Learning Unit 8–1: Markups Based on Cost (100%)

In Chapter 6 you were introduced to the portion formula, which we used to solve percent problems. We also used the portion formula in Chapter 7 to solve problems involving trade and cash discounts. In this unit you will see how we use the basic selling price formula and the portion formula to solve percent markup situations based on cost. We will be using blueprint aids to show how to dissect and solve all word problems in this chapter.

Many manufacturers mark up goods on cost because manufacturers can get cost information more easily than sales information. Since retailers have the choice of using percent markup on cost or selling price, in this unit we assume Target has chosen percent markup on cost. In Learning Unit 8–2 we show how Target would determine markup if it decided to use percent markup on selling price.

Businesses that use **percent markup on cost** recognize that cost is 100%. This 100% represents the base of the portion formula. All situations in this unit use cost as 100%.

To calculate percent markup on cost, we will use the Levi Strauss Signature™ brand jeans sold at Target and begin with the basic selling price formula given in the chapter introduction. When we know the dollar markup, we can use the portion formula to find the percent markup on cost.

Markup expressed in dollars:

Selling price ($23) = Cost ($18) + Markup ($5)

Markup expressed as a percent markup on cost:

Cost	100.00%
+ Markup	+ 27.78
= Selling price	127.78%

> Cost is 100%—the base. Dollar markup is the portion, and percent markup on cost is the rate.

In Situation 1 (p. 206) we show why Target has a 27.78% markup based on cost by presenting the Levi Strauss Signature™ brand jeans as a word problem. We solve the problem with the blueprint aid used in earlier chapters. In the second column, however, you will see footnotes after two numbers. These refer to the steps we use below the blueprint aid to solve the problem. Throughout the chapter, the numbers that we are solving for are in red. Remember that cost is the base for this unit.

Situation 1: Calculating Dollar Markup and Percent Markup on Cost

Dollar markup is calculated with the basic selling price formula $S = C + M$. When you know the cost and selling price of goods, reverse the formula to $M = S - C$. Subtract the cost from the selling price, and you have the dollar markup.

The percent markup on cost is calculated with the portion formula. For Situation 1 the *portion* (P) is the dollar markup, which you know from the selling price formula. In this unit the *rate* (R) is always the percent markup on cost and the *base* (B) is always the cost (100%). To find the percent markup on cost (R), use the portion formula $R = \frac{P}{B}$ and divide the dollar markup (P) by the cost (B). Convert your answer to a percent and round if necessary.

Now we will look at the Target example to see how to calculate the 27.78% markup on cost.

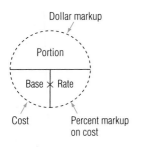

The Word Problem Target buys Levi Strauss Signature™ brand jeans for $18 and plans to sell them for $23. What is Target's dollar markup? What is the percent markup on cost (round to the nearest hundredth percent)?

The facts	Solving for?	Steps to take	Key points
Signature™ jeans cost: $18. *Signature™ jeans selling price:* $23.	$\begin{array}{lccc} & \% & \$ \\ C & 100.00\% & \$18 \\ + M & 27.78^2 & 5^1 \\ = S & 127.78\% & \$23 \end{array}$ ¹Dollar markup. ²Percent markup on cost.	$\dfrac{\text{Dollar}}{\text{markup}} = \dfrac{\text{Selling}}{\text{price}} - \text{Cost.}$ $\dfrac{\text{Percent}}{\text{markup on cost}} = \dfrac{\text{Dollar markup}}{\text{Cost}}$	

Steps to solving problem

1. Calculate the dollar markup.

$$\text{Dollar markup} = \text{Selling price} - \text{Cost}$$
$$\$5 = \$23 - \$18$$

2. Calculate the percent markup on cost.

$$\text{Percent markup on cost} = \dfrac{\text{Dollar markup}}{\text{Cost}}$$
$$= \dfrac{\$5}{\$18} = 27.78\%$$

Check

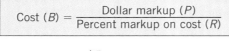

$$\text{Cost } (B) = \dfrac{\text{Dollar markup } (P)}{\text{Percent markup on cost } (R)}$$

$$= \dfrac{\$5}{.2778} = \$18$$

In the check note how we calculate the cost when we know the dollar markup and percent markup on cost.

Situation 2: Calculating Selling Price When You Know Cost and Percent Markup on Cost

Now let's look at Mel's Furniture where we calculate Mel's dollar markup and selling price.

The Word Problem Mel's Furniture bought a lamp that cost $100. To make Mel's desired profit, he needs a 65% markup on cost. What is Mel's selling price? What is his dollar markup?

The facts	Solving for?	Steps to take	Key points
Lamp cost: $100. *Markup on cost:* 65%.	$\begin{array}{lll} & \% & \$ \\ C & 100\% & \$100 \\ + M & 65 & 65^2 \\ \hline = S & 165\% & \$165^1 \end{array}$ ¹Dollar markup. ²Selling price.	$S = \text{Cost} \times \left(1 + \begin{array}{c}\text{Percent} \\ \text{markup} \\ \text{on cost}\end{array}\right)$ $M = S - C.$	Selling price Portion (?) Base × Rate ($100) (1.65) Cost 100% +65%

Steps to solving problem

1. Calculate the selling price.

$$\underset{(P)}{\text{Selling price}} = \underset{(B)}{\text{Cost}} \times \underset{(R)}{(1 + \text{Percent markup on cost})} = \$100 \times 1.65 = \boxed{\$165}$$

2. Calculate the dollar markup. $M = S - C$

$$\$65 = \$165 - \$100$$

Situation 3: Calculating Cost When You Know Selling Price and Percent Markup on Cost

The Word Problem Jill Sport, owner of Sports, Inc., sells tennis rackets for $50. To make her desired profit, Jill needs a 40% markup on cost. What do the tennis rackets cost Jill? What is the dollar markup?

The facts	Solving for?	Steps to take	Key points
Selling price: $50. *Markup on cost:* 40%.	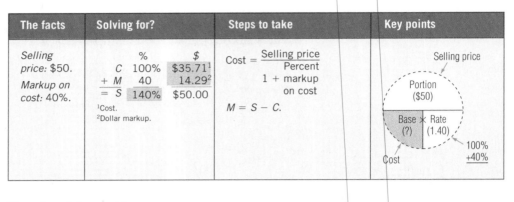	$\text{Cost} = \dfrac{\text{Selling price}}{\text{Percent}}$ $\dfrac{}{1 + \text{markup on cost}}$ $M = S - C.$	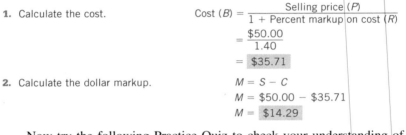

Steps to solving problem

1. Calculate the cost.

$$\text{Cost } (B) = \frac{\text{Selling price } (P)}{1 + \text{Percent markup on cost } (R)}$$

$$= \frac{\$50.00}{1.40}$$

$$= \$35.71$$

2. Calculate the dollar markup.

$$M = S - C$$
$$M = \$50.00 - \$35.71$$
$$M = \$14.29$$

Now try the following Practice Quiz to check your understanding of this unit.

LU 8–1	PRACTICE QUIZ

Solve the following situations (markups based on cost):

1. Irene Westing bought a desk for $400 from an office supply house. She plans to sell the desk for $600. What is Irene's dollar markup? What is her percent markup on cost? Check your answer.

2. Suki Komar bought dolls for her toy store that cost $12 each. To make her desired profit, Suki must mark up each doll 35% on cost. What is the selling price? What is the dollar markup of each doll? Check your answer.

3. Jay Lyman sells calculators. His competitor sells a new calculator line for $14 each. Jay needs a 40% markup on cost to make his desired profit, and he must meet price competition. At what cost can Jay afford to bring these calculators into the store? What is the dollar markup? Check your answer.

✓ **Solutions**

1. Irene's dollar markup and percent markup on cost:

The facts	Solving for?	Steps to take	Key points
Desk cost: $400. *Desk selling price:* $600.	$$\begin{array}{ccc} & \% & \$ \\ C & 100\% & \$400 \\ +\,M & 50^2 & 200^1 \\ \hline =\,S & 150\% & \$600 \end{array}$$ ¹Dollar markup. ²Percent markup on cost.	$\dfrac{\text{Dollar}}{\text{markup}} = \dfrac{\text{Selling}}{\text{price}} - \text{Cost.}$ $\dfrac{\text{Percent}}{\text{markup}} = \dfrac{\text{Dollar markup}}{\text{Cost}}$ on cost	Dollar markup — Portion ($200) — Base ($400) × Rate (?) — Cost

Steps to solving problem

1. Calculate the dollar markup.

$$\text{Dollar markup} = \text{Selling price} - \text{Cost}$$
$$\boxed{\$200} = \$600 - \$400$$

2. Calculate the percent markup on cost.

$$\text{Percent markup on cost} = \dfrac{\text{Dollar markup}}{\text{Cost}}$$
$$= \dfrac{\$200}{\$400} = \boxed{50\%}$$

$$\text{Cost } (B) = \dfrac{\text{Dollar markup } (P)}{\text{Percent markup on cost } (R)}$$

$$= \dfrac{\$200}{.50} = \$400$$

2. Dollar markup and selling price of doll:

The facts	Solving for?	Steps to take	Key points
Doll cost: $12 each. Markup on cost: 35%.	% $ C 100% $12.00 + M 35 4.20[2] = S 135% $16.20[1] [1]Dollar markup. [2]Selling price.	$S = \text{Cost} \times \left(1 + \dfrac{\text{Percent}}{\substack{\text{markup} \\ \text{on cost}}} \right)$ $M = S - C.$	

Steps to solving problem

1. Calculate the dollar markup. $S =$ $16.20

$$\underset{(P)}{\text{Selling price}} = \underset{(B)}{\text{Cost}} \times (1 + \underset{(R)}{\text{Percent markup on cost}}) = \$12.00 \times 1.35 = \$16.20$$

2. Calculate the selling price. $M = S - C$

$$M = \$16.20 - \$12.00$$

$$M = \$4.20$$

3. Cost and dollar markup:

The facts	Solving for?	Steps to take	Key points
Selling price: $14. Markup on cost: 40%.	% $ C 100% $10[1] + M 40 4[2] = S 140% $14 [1]Cost. [2]Dollar markup.	$\text{Cost} = \dfrac{\text{Selling price}}{\substack{\text{Percent} \\ 1 + \text{markup} \\ \text{on cost}}}$ $M = S - C.$	

Steps to solving problem

1. Calculate the cost.

$$\text{Cost } (B) = \frac{\text{Selling price } (P)}{1 + \text{Percent markup on cost } (R)} = \frac{\$14}{1.40} = \$10$$

2. Calculate the dollar markup. $M = S - C$

$$M = \$14 - \$10$$

$$M = \$4$$

LU 8–1a	EXTRA PRACTICE QUIZ

Need more practice? Try this **Extra Practice Quiz** (check figures in Chapter Organizer, p. 222)

Solve the following situations (markups based on cost):

1. Irene Westing bought a desk for $800 from an office supply house. She plans to sell the desk for $1,200. What is Irene's dollar markup? What is her percent markup on cost? Check your answer.

2. Suki Komar bought dolls for her toy store that cost $14 each. To make her desired profit, Suki must mark up each doll 38% on cost. What is the selling price? What is the dollar of each doll? Check your answer.

3. Jay Lyman sells calculators. His competitor sells a new calculator line for $16 each. Jay needs a 42% markup on cost to make his desired profit, and he must meet price competition. At what cost can Jay afford to bring these calculators into the store? What is the dollar markup? Check your answer.

Learning Unit 8–2: Markups Based on Selling Price (100%)

Many retailers mark up their goods on the selling price since sales information is easier to get than cost information. These retailers use retail prices in their inventory and report their expenses as a percent of sales.

Businesses that mark up their goods on selling price recognize that selling price is 100%. We begin this unit by assuming Target has decided to use percent markup based on selling price. We repeat Target's selling price formula expressed in dollars.

Markup expressed in dollars:

Selling price ($23) = Cost ($18) + Markup ($5)

Markup expressed as **percent markup on selling price:**

Cost	78.26%	
+ Markup	+21.74	Selling price is 100%—the base. Dollar markup is the portion, and percent markup on selling price is the rate.
= Selling price	100.00%	

In Situation 1 (below) we show why Target has a 21.74% markup based on selling price. In the last unit, markups were on *cost*. In this unit, markups are on *selling price*.

Situation 1: Calculating Dollar Markup and Percent Markup on Selling Price

The dollar markup is calculated with the selling price formula used in Situation 1, Learning Unit 8–1: $M = S - C$. To find the percent markup on selling price, use the portion formula $R = \frac{P}{B}$, where rate (the percent markup on selling price) is found by dividing the portion (dollar markup) by the base (selling price). Note that when solving for percent markup on cost in Situation 1, Learning Unit 8–1, you divided the dollar markup by the cost.

The Word Problem Target buys Levi Strauss Signature™ brand jeans for $18 and plans to sell them for $23. What is Target's dollar markup? What is its percent markup on selling price? (Round to nearest hundredth percent.)

The facts	Solving for?			Steps to take		Key points
Signature™ jeans cost: $18. Signature™ jeans selling price: $23.		%	$	$\dfrac{\text{Dollar}}{\text{markup}} = \dfrac{\text{Selling}}{\text{price}} - \text{Cost}.$		Dollar markup
	C	78.26%	$18			
	$+\ M$	21.74%[2]	5[1]	$\dfrac{\text{Percent}}{\text{markup on}} = \dfrac{\text{Dollar markup}}{\text{Selling}}$		Portion ($5)
	$=\ S$	100.00%	$23	selling price	price	
	[1]Dollar markup. [2]Percent markup on selling price.					Base × Rate ($23) (?)
						Selling price

Steps to solving problem

1. Calculate the dollar markup.

$$\text{Dollar markup} = \text{Selling price} - \text{Cost}$$
$$\boxed{\$5} = \$23 - \$18$$

2. Calculate the percent markup on selling price.

$$\dfrac{\text{Percent markup}}{\text{on selling price}} = \dfrac{\text{Dollar markup}}{\text{Selling price}}$$
$$= \dfrac{\$5}{\$23} = \boxed{21.74\%}$$

You can check the percent markup on selling price with the portion formula by dividing the dollar markup (P) by the percent markup on selling price (R).

Check

$$\text{Selling price } (B) = \dfrac{\text{Dollar markup } (P)}{\text{Percent markup on selling price } (R)}$$

$$= \dfrac{\$5}{.2174} = \$23$$

Situation 2: Calculating Selling Price When You Know Cost and Percent Markup on Selling Price

The Word Problem Mel's Furniture bought a lamp that cost $100. To make Mel's desired profit, he needs a 65% markup on selling price. What are Mel's selling price and his dollar markup?

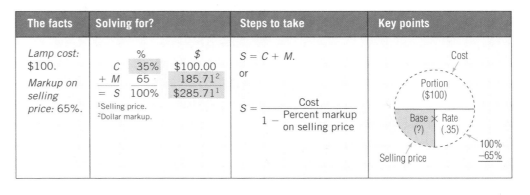

The facts	Solving for?	Steps to take	Key points

Lamp cost: $100.

Markup on selling price: 65%.

	%	$
C	35%	$100.00
$+ M$	65	185.71[2]
$= S$	100%	$285.71[1]

[1]Selling price.
[2]Dollar markup.

$S = C + M.$
or

$$S = \dfrac{\text{Cost}}{1 - \text{Percent markup on selling price}}$$

Steps to solving problem

1. Calculate the selling price.

$$\text{Selling price } (B) = \dfrac{\text{Cost } (P)}{1 - \text{Percent markup on selling price } (R)}$$

$$= \dfrac{\$100.00}{1 - .65} = \dfrac{\$100.00}{.35} = \$285.71$$

2. Calculate the dollar markup.

M	$=$	S	$-$	C
$185.71	$=$	$285.71	$-$	$100.00

Situation 3: Calculating Cost When You Know Selling Price and Percent Markup on Selling Price

The Word Problem Jill Sport, owner of Sports, Inc., sells tennis rackets for $50. To make her desired profit, Jill needs a 40% markup on the selling price. What do the tennis rackets cost Jill? What is the dollar markup?

The facts	Solving for?	Steps to take	Key points
Selling price: $50.	$\begin{array}{lcc} & \% & \$ \\ C & 60\% & \$30^1 \\ + M & 40 & 20^2 \\ = S & 100\% & \$50 \end{array}$	Cost = Selling price $\times$ $\left(1 - \dfrac{\text{Percent markup}}{\text{on selling price}}\right)$	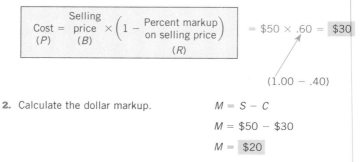
Markup on selling price: 40%.	¹Dollar markup. ²Cost.		

Steps to solving problem

1. Calculate the cost.

$$\underset{(P)}{\text{Cost}} = \underset{(B)}{\underset{\text{price}}{\text{Selling}}} \times \left(1 - \underset{(R)}{\underset{\text{on selling price}}{\text{Percent markup}}}\right) = \$50 \times .60 = \boxed{\$30}$$

$$(1.00 - .40)$$

2. Calculate the dollar markup.

$$M = S - C$$
$$M = \$50 - \$30$$
$$M = \boxed{\$20}$$

To check your cost, use the portion formula Cost (P) = Selling price $(B) \times (100\%$ selling price $-$ Percent markup on selling price) (R).

In Table 8.1, we compare percent markup on cost with percent markup on retail (selling price). This table is a summary of the answers we calculated from the word problems in Learning Units 8–1 and 8–2. The word problems in the units were the same except in Learning Unit 8–1, we assumed markups were on cost, while in Learning Unit 8–2, markups were on selling price. Note that in Situation 1, the dollar markup is the same $5, but the percent markup is different.

Let's now look at how to convert from percent markup on cost to percent markup on selling price and vice versa. We will use Situation 1 from Table 8.1.

TABLE	8.1	Markup based on cost— Learning Unit 8–1	Markup based on selling price— Learning Unit 8–2
		Situation 1: Calculating dollar amount of markup and percent markup on cost.	*Situation 1: Calculating dollar amount of markup and percent markup on selling price.*
		Signature™ jeans cost, $18.	Signature™ jeans cost, $18.
		Signature™ jeans selling price, $23.	Signature™ jeans selling price, $23.
		$M = S - C$	$M = S - C$
		$M = \$23 - \$18 = $ $5 markup (p. 206)	$M = \$23 - \$18 = $ $5 markup (p. 212)
		$M \div C = \$5 \div \$18 = 27.78\%$	$M \div S = \$5 \div \$23 = 21.74\%$
		Situation 2: Calculating selling price on cost.	*Situation 2: Calculating selling price on selling price.*
		Lamp cost, $100. 65% markup on cost	Lamp cost, $100. 65% markup on selling price
		$S = C \times (1 + \text{Percent markup on cost})$	$S = C \div (1 - \text{Percent markup on selling price})$
		$S = \$100 \times 1.65 = $ $165 (p. 207)	$S = \$100.00 \div .35$
			$(100\% - 65\% = 35\% = .35)$
		$(100\% + 65\% = 165\% = 1.65)$	$S = $ $285.71 (p. 213)
		Situation 3: Calculating cost on cost.	*Situation 3: Calculating cost on selling price.*
		Tennis racket selling price, $50. 40% markup on cost	Tennis racket selling price, $50. 40% markup on selling price
		$C = S \div (1 + \text{Percent markup on cost})$	$C = S \times (1 - \text{Percent markup on selling price})$
		$C = \$50.00 \div 1.40$	$C = \$50 \times .60 = $ $30 (p. 214)
		$(100\% + 40\% = 140\% = 1.40)$	
		$C = $ $35.71 (p. 208)	$(100\% - 40\% = 60\% = .60)$

Comparison of markup on cost versus markup on selling price

Formula for Converting Percent Markup on Cost to Percent Markup on Selling Price

To convert percent markup on cost to percent markup on selling price:

$$\frac{\text{Percent markup on cost}}{1 + \text{Percent markup on cost}}$$

$$\frac{.2778}{1 + .2778} = \boxed{21.74\%}$$

Formula for Converting Percent Markup on Selling Price to Percent Markup on Cost

To convert percent markup on selling price to percent markup on cost:

$$\frac{\text{Percent markup on selling price}}{1 - \text{Percent markup on selling price}}$$

$$\frac{.2174}{1 - .2174} = \boxed{27.78\%}$$

Key point: A 21.74% markup on selling price or a 27.78% markup on cost results in same dollar markup of $5.

Now let's test your knowledge of Learning Unit 8–2.

LU 8–2 **PRACTICE QUIZ**

Complete this **Practice Quiz** to see how you are doing

Solve the following situations (markups based on selling price). Note numbers 1, 2, and 3 are parallel problems to those in Practice Quiz 8–1.

1. Irene Westing bought a desk for $400 from an office supply house. She plans to sell the desk for $600. What is Irene's dollar markup? What is her percent markup on selling price (round to the nearest tenth percent)? Check your answer. Selling price will be slightly off due to rounding.

2. Suki Komar bought dolls for her toy store that cost $12 each. To make her desired profit, Suki must mark up each doll 35% on the selling price. What is the selling price of each doll? What is the dollar markup? Check your answer.

3. Jay Lyman sells calculators. His competitor sells a new calculator line for $14 each. Jay needs a 40% markup on the selling price to make his desired profit, and he must meet price competition. At what cost can Jay afford to bring these calculators into the store? What is Jay's dollar markup? Check your answer.

4. Dan Flow sells wrenches for $10 that cost $6. What is Dan's percent markup at cost? Round to the nearest tenth percent. What is Dan's percent markup on selling price? Check your answer.

✓ Solutions

1. Irene's dollar markup and percent markup on selling price:

The facts	Solving for?	Steps to take	Key points
Desk cost: $400. Desk selling price: $600.	$$\begin{array}{lcc} & \% & \$ \\ C & 66.7\% & \$400 \\ + M & 33.3^2 & 200^1 \\ = S & 100\% & \$600 \end{array}$$ ¹Dollar markup. ²Percent markup on selling price.	$$\frac{\text{Dollar}}{\text{markup}} = \frac{\text{Selling}}{\text{price}} - \text{Cost}$$ $$\frac{\text{Percent}}{\text{markup on}} = \frac{\text{Dollar}}{\text{markup}}$$ selling price Selling price	(diagram) Markup, Portion ($200), Base × Rate ($600) (?), Selling price

Steps to solving problem

1. Calculate the dollar markup.

$$\text{Dollar markup} = \text{Selling price} - \text{Cost}$$
$$\$200 = \$600 - \$400$$

2. Calculate the percent markup on selling price.

$$\frac{\text{Percent markup}}{\text{on selling price}} = \frac{\text{Dollar markup}}{\text{Selling price}}$$
$$= \frac{\$200}{\$600} = 33.3\%$$

Check

$$\frac{\text{Selling}}{\text{price } (B)} = \frac{\text{Dollar markup } (P)}{\text{Percent markup on selling price } (R)}$$

$$= \frac{\$200}{.333} = \$600.60*$$

(not exactly $600 due to rounding)

*Off due to rounding.

2. Selling price of doll and dollar markup:

The facts	Solving for?	Steps to take	Key points
Doll cost: $12 each. Markup on selling price: 35%.	$$\begin{array}{lcc} & \% & \$ \\ C & 65\% & \$12.00 \\ + M & 35 & 6.46^2 \\ = S & 100\% & \$18.46^1 \end{array}$$ ¹Selling price. ²Dollar markup.	$$S = \frac{\text{Cost}}{1 - \begin{array}{l}\text{Percent markup}\\\text{on selling price}\end{array}}$$	(diagram) Cost, Portion ($12), Base × Rate (?) (.65), Selling price, 100% −35%

Steps to solving problem

1. Calculate the selling price.

$$\text{Selling price } (B) = \frac{\text{Cost } (P)}{1 - \text{Percent markup on selling price } (R)} = \frac{\$12.00}{.65} = \boxed{\$18.46}$$

2. Calculate the dollar markup.

	M	=	S	–	C
	$\boxed{\$6.46}$	=	$\$18.46$	–	$\$12.00$

3. Dollar markup and cost:

The facts	Solving for?	Steps to take	Key points
Selling price: $14. *Markup on selling price:* 40%.	$\begin{array}{lcc} & \% & \$ \\ C & 60\% & \$\ 8.40^1 \\ +\ M & 40 & 5.60^2 \\ \hline =\ S & 100\% & \$14.00 \end{array}$ ^{1}Dollar markup. ^{2}Cost.	$\text{Cost} = \text{Selling price} \times$ $\left(1 - \dfrac{\text{Percent markup}}{\text{on selling price}}\right)$	Cost Portion (?) Base × Rate ($14) (.60) Selling price 100% −40%

Steps to solving problem

1. Calculate the cost.

$$\underset{(P)}{\text{Cost}} = \underset{(B)}{\text{Selling price}} \times (1 - \underset{(R)}{\text{Percent markup on selling price}}) = \$14.00 \times .60 = \boxed{\$8.40}$$

$$(1.00 - .40)$$

2. Calculate the dollar markup.

$$M = S - C$$
$$M = \$14 - \$8.40$$
$$M = \boxed{\$5.60}$$

4. $\text{Cost} = \dfrac{\$4}{\$6} = \boxed{66.7\%}$ $\qquad\qquad \dfrac{.40}{1-.40} = \dfrac{.40}{.60} = \dfrac{2}{3} = 66.7\%$

   $\text{Selling price} = \dfrac{\$4}{\$10} = \boxed{40\%}$ $\qquad \dfrac{.667}{1+.667} = \dfrac{.667}{1.667} = 40\%$ (due to rounding)

LU 8–2a EXTRA PRACTICE QUIZ

Need more practice? Try this **Extra Practice Quiz** (check figures in Chapter Organizer, p. 222)

Solve the following situations (markups based on selling price).

1. Irene Westing bought a desk for $800 from an office supply house. She plans to sell the desk for $1,200. What is Irene's dollar markup? What is her percent markup on selling price (round to the nearest tenth percent)? Check your answer. Selling price will be slightly off due to rounding.

2. Suki Komar bought dolls for her toy store that cost $14 each. To make her desired profit, Suki must mark up each doll 38% on selling price. What is the selling price of each doll? What is the dollar markup? Check your answer.

3. Jay Lyman sells calculators. His competitor sells a new calculator line for $16 each. Jay needs a 42% markup on the selling price to make his desired profit, and he must meet price competition. At what cost can Jay afford to bring these calculators into the store? What is Jay's dollar markup? Check your answer.

4. Dan Flow sells wrenches for $12 that cost $7. What is Dan's percent markup at cost? Round to the nearest tenth percent. What is Dan's percent markup on selling price? Check your answer.

Learning Unit 8–3: Markdowns

"Would you like to see the markup?"

Barron's © 2005

Christopher Weyant for Barron's

Have you ever wondered how your local retail store determines a typical markdown on clothing? The following *Wall Street Journal* clipping "Sale Rack Shuffle" explains the typical markdown money arrangement between a clothing vendor and a retailer. Evidently, the retailer does not always take the entire financial loss when a piece of clothing is marked down until it sells.

Sale Rack Shuffle

How a typical markdown-money arrangement between a clothing vendor and a retailer works:

1. Vendor makes dress at cost of **$50**
2. Sells to retailer at wholesale price of **$80**
3. Retailer marks up dress to **$200**
4. Dress gets marked down after 8 to 12 weeks (starting at 25% off) **$150**
5. The dress gets marked down again until it sells; the retailer and the vendor negotiate how to share the cost of the markdown.

Wall Street Journal © 2005

This learning unit focuses your attention on how to calculate markdowns.

Markdowns

Markdowns are reductions from the original selling price caused by seasonal changes, special promotions, style changes, and so on. We calculate the markdown percent as follows:

$$\text{Markdown percent} = \frac{\text{Dollar markdown}}{\text{Selling price (original)}}$$

Let's look at the following Kmart example:

EXAMPLE Kmart marked down an $18 video to $10.80. Calculate the **dollar markdown** and the markdown percent.

Dollar markdown

Portion ($7.20)

Base ($18) × Rate (?)

Original selling price

$18.00 Original selling price
− 10.80 Sale price
$ 7.20 Markdown

$$\frac{\text{Dollar markdown, } \$7.20}{\text{Selling price (original), } \$18.00} = 40\%$$

Calculating a Series of Markdowns and Markups

Often the final selling price is the result of a series of markdowns (and possibly a markup in between markdowns). We calculate additional markdowns on the previous selling price. Note in the following example how we calculate markdown on selling price after we add a markup.

EXAMPLE Jones Department Store paid its supplier $400 for a TV. On January 10, Jones marked the TV up 60% on selling price. As a special promotion, Jones marked the TV down 30% on February 8 and another 20% on February 28. No one purchased the TV, so Jones marked it up 10% on March 11. What was the selling price of the TV on March 11?

January 10: Selling price = Cost   + Markup

$$S = \$400 + .60S$$

$$- .60S \qquad\qquad - .60S$$

$$\frac{.40S}{.40} = \frac{\$400}{.40}$$

$$S = \$1,000$$

Check
$$S = \frac{\text{Cost}}{1 - \text{Percent markup on selling price}}$$

$$S = \frac{\$400}{1 - .60} = \frac{\$400}{.40} = \$1,000$$

February 8
markdown:
$$\begin{array}{r} 100\% \\ -\ 30 \\ \hline 70\% \end{array}$$ → .70 × \$1,000 = \$700 selling price

February 28
additional markdown:
$$\begin{array}{r} 100\% \\ -\ 20 \\ \hline 80\% \end{array}$$ → .80 × \$700 = \$560

March 11 additional
markup:
$$\begin{array}{r} 100\% \\ +\ 10 \\ \hline 110\% \end{array}$$ → 1.10 × \$560 = $\boxed{\$616}$

It's time to try the Practice Quiz on p. 220.

LU 8–3   PRACTICE QUIZ

Complete this **Practice Quiz** to see how you are doing

1. Sunshine Music Shop bought a stereo for $600 and marked it up 40% on selling price. To promote customer interest, Sunshine marked the stereo down 10% for one week. Since business was slow, Sunshine marked the stereo down an additional 5%. After a week, Sunshine marked the stereo up 2%. What is the new selling price of the stereo to the nearest cent? What is the markdown percent based on the original selling price to the nearest hundredth percent?

✓ **Solution**

1. $S = \dfrac{\text{Cost}}{1 - \text{Percent markup on selling price}}$

$S = \dfrac{\$600}{1 - .40} = \dfrac{\$600}{.60} = \$1,000$

First markdown: $.90 \times \$1,000 = \$900$ selling price

Second markdown: $.95 \times \$900 = \$855$ selling price

Markup: $1.02 \times \$855 = \boxed{\$872.10}$ final selling price

$\$1,000 - \$872.10 = \dfrac{\$127.90}{\$1,000} = \boxed{12.79\%}$

LU 8–3a   EXTRA PRACTICE QUIZ

Need more practice? Try this **Extra Practice Quiz** (check figures in Chapter Organizer, p. 222)

1. Sunshine Music Shop bought a stereo for $800 and marked it up 30% on selling price. To promote customer interest, Sunshine marked the stereo down 10% for one week. Since business was slow, Sunshine marked the stereo down an additional 5%. After a week, Sunshine marked the stereo up 2%. What is the new selling price of the stereo to the nearest cent? What is the markdown percent based on the original selling price to the nearest hundredth percent?

CHAPTER ORGANIZER AND STUDY GUIDE
WITH CHECK FIGURES FOR EXTRA PRACTICE QUIZZES

Topic	Key point, procedure, formula	Example(s) to illustrate situation
Markups based on cost: Cost is 100% (base), p. 205	Selling price (S) = Cost (C) + Markup (M)	$\begin{array}{ccc} \$400 = & \$300 + & \$100 \\ S \ = & C \ + & M \end{array}$
Percent markup on cost, p. 206	$\dfrac{\text{Dollar markup (portion)}}{\text{Cost (base)}} = \dfrac{\text{Percent markup}}{\text{on cost (rate)}}$	$\dfrac{\$100}{\$300} = \dfrac{1}{3} = 33\frac{1}{3}\%$
Cost, p. 206	$C = \dfrac{\text{Dollar markup}}{\text{Percent markup on cost}}$	$\dfrac{\$100}{.33} = \$303$ Off slightly due to rounding
Calculating selling price, p. 207	$S = \text{Cost} \times (1 + \text{Percent markup on cost})$	Cost, $6; percent markup on cost, 20% $S = \$6 + .20(\$6)$ **Check** $S = \$6 + \$1.20$ ↓ $S = \boxed{\$7.20}$ $\boxed{\$6 \times 1.20 = \$7.20}$

(continues)

CHAPTER ORGANIZER AND STUDY GUIDE
WITH CHECK FIGURES FOR EXTRA PRACTICE QUIZZES (continued)

Topic	Key point, procedure, formula	Example(s) to illustrate situation
Calculating cost, p. 208	$$\text{Cost} = \frac{\text{Selling price}}{1 + \text{Percent markup on cost}}$$	$S = \$100$; $M = 70\%$ of cost $S = C + M$ $\$100 = C + .70C$ $\quad$ $\left(\begin{array}{c}Remember,\\ C = 1.00C\end{array}\right)$ $\$100 = 1.7C$ $\dfrac{\$100}{1.7} = C$ $\quad$ **Check** $\boxed{\$58.82} = C$ $\quad$ $\dfrac{\$100}{1 + .70} = \$58.82$
Markups based on selling price: selling price is 100% (Base), p. 211	Dollar markup = Selling price − Cost	$M = S - C$ $\boxed{\$600} = \$1,000 - \$400$
Percent markup on selling price, p. 212	$$\frac{\text{Dollar markup (portion)}}{\text{Selling price (base)}} = \frac{\text{Percent markup}}{\text{selling price (rate)}}$$	$\dfrac{\$600}{\$1,000} = \boxed{60\%}$
Selling price, p. 212	$$S = \frac{\text{Dollar markup}}{\text{Percent markup on selling price}}$$	$\dfrac{\$600}{.60} = \boxed{\$1,000}$
Calculating selling price, p. 213	$$\text{Selling price} = \frac{\text{Cost}}{1 - \begin{array}{c}\text{Percent markup}\\ \text{on selling price}\end{array}}$$	Cost, $\$400$; percent markup on S, 60% $S = C + M$ $S = \$400 + .60S$ $S - .60S = \$400 + .60S - .60S$ $\dfrac{.40S}{.40} = \dfrac{\$400}{.40}$ $\quad \boxed{S = \$1,000}$ **Check** → $\boxed{\dfrac{\$400}{1 - .60} = \dfrac{\$400}{.40} = \$1,000}$
Calculating cost, p. 214	$$\text{Cost} = \begin{array}{c}\text{Selling}\\ \text{price}\end{array} \times \left(1 - \begin{array}{c}\text{Percent markup}\\ \text{on selling price}\end{array}\right)$$	$\$1,000 = C + 60\%(\$1,000)$ $\$1,000 = C + \$600$ $\boxed{\$400} = C$ **Check** $\longrightarrow$ $\boxed{\begin{array}{l}\$1,000 \times (1 - .60)\\ \$1,000 \times .40 = \$400\end{array}}$
Conversion of markup percent, p. 215	Percent markup $\quad$ Percent markup on cost $\quad$ to $\quad$ on selling price $\boxed{\dfrac{\text{Percent markup on cost}}{1 + \text{Percent markup on cost}}}$ Percent markup $\quad$ Percent markup on selling price $\quad$ to $\quad$ on cost $\boxed{\dfrac{\text{Percent markup on selling price}}{1 - \text{Percent markup on selling price}}}$	*Round to nearest percent:* 54% markup on cost → $\boxed{35\%}$ markup $\quad\quad\quad\quad\quad\quad\quad\quad\quad\quad$ on selling price $\boxed{\dfrac{.54}{1 + .54} = \dfrac{.54}{1.54} = 35\%}$ 35% markup on $\longrightarrow$ $\boxed{54\%}$ markup selling price $\quad\quad\quad\quad\quad\quad$ on cost $\boxed{\dfrac{.35}{1 - .35} = \dfrac{.35}{.65} = 54\%}$
Markdowns, p. 218	$$\text{Markdown percent} = \frac{\text{Dollar markdown}}{\text{Selling price (original)}}$$	$\$40$ selling price 10% markdown $\$40 \times .10 = \$4$ markdown $\dfrac{\$4}{\$40} = \boxed{10\%}$

(continues)

CHAPTER ORGANIZER AND STUDY GUIDE
WITH CHECK FIGURES FOR EXTRA PRACTICE QUIZZES (concluded)

Topic	Key point, procedure, formula		Example(s) to illustrate situation
KEY TERMS	Cost, *p. 204* Dollar markdown, *p. 218* Dollar markup, *p. 205* Gross profit, *p. 204* Margin, *p. 204*	Markdowns, *p. 218* Markup, *p. 204* Net profit (net income), *p. 204* Operating expenses (overhead), *p. 204*	Percent markup on cost, *p. 205* Percent markup on selling price, *p. 211* Selling price, *p. 204*
CHECK FIGURES FOR EXTRA PRACTICE QUIZZES WITH PAGE REFERENCES	LU 8–1a (p. 211) 1. $400; 50% 2. $5.32; $19.32 3. $11.27; $4.73	LU 8–2a (p. 217) 1. $400; 33.3% 2. $22.58; $8.58 3. $6.72; $9.28 4. 71.4%; 41.7%	LU 8–3a (p. 220) 1. $996.68; 12.79%

Critical Thinking Discussion Questions

1. Assuming markups are based on cost, explain how the portion formula could be used to calculate cost, selling price, dollar markup, and percent markup on cost. Pick a company and explain why it would mark goods up on cost rather than on selling price.

2. Assuming markups are based on selling price, explain how the portion formula could be used to calculate cost, selling price, dollar markup, and percent markup on selling price. Pick a company and explain why it would mark up goods on selling price rather than on cost.

3. What is the formula to convert percent markup on selling price to percent markup on cost? How could you explain that a 40% markup on selling price, which is a 66.7% markup on cost, would result in the same dollar markup?

4. Explain how to calculate markdowns. Do you think stores should run one-day-only markdown sales? Would it be better to offer the best price "all the time"?

Name _____ Date _____

DRILL PROBLEMS

Assume markups in Problems 8–1 to 8–6 are based on cost. Find the dollar markup and selling price for the following problems. Round answers to the nearest cent.

Item	Cost	Markup percent	Dollar markup	Selling price
8–1. Apple iPod	$300	40%		
8–2. Luminox Navy Seal watch	$300	30%		

Solve for cost (round to the nearest cent):

8–3. Selling price of office furniture at Staples, $6,000

Percent markup on cost, 40%

Actual cost?

8–4. Selling price of lumber at Home Depot, $4,000

Percent markup on cost, 30%

Actual cost?

Complete the following:

	Cost	Selling price	Dollar markup	Percent markup on cost*
8–5.	$15.10	$22.00	?	?
8–6.	?	?	$4.70	102.17%

*Round to the nearest hundredth percent.

Assume markups in Problems 8–7 to 8–12 are based on selling price.
Find the dollar markup and cost (round answers to the nearest cent):

Item	Selling price	Markup percent	Dollar markup	Cost
8–7. Panasonic plasma TV	$450	40%		
8–8. IBM scanner	$80	30%		

Solve for the selling price (round to the nearest cent):

8–9. Selling price of a complete set of pots and pans at Wal-Mart?

40% markup on selling price

Cost, actual, $66.50

8–10. Selling price of a dining room set at Macy's?

55% markup on selling price

Cost, actual, $800

Complete the following:

	Cost	Selling price	Dollar markup	Percent markup on selling price (round to nearest tenth percent)
8–11.	$14.80	$49.00	?	?
8–12.	?	?	$4	20%

By conversion of the markup formula, solve the following (round to the nearest whole percent as needed):

	Percent markup on cost	Percent markup on selling price
8–13.	12.4%	?
8–14.	?	13%

Complete the following:

8–15. Calculate the final selling price to the nearest cent and markdown percent to the nearest hundredth percent:

Original selling price	First markdown	Second markdown	Markup	Final markdown
$5,000	20%	10%	12%	5%

8–16. Matthew Kaminsky bought an old Walter Lantz Woody Woodpecker oil painting for $10,000. He plans to resell it on eBay for $15,000. What are the dollar markup and percent markup on cost? Check the cost figure.

8–17. Chin Yov, store manager for Best Buy, does not know how to price a GE freezer that cost the store $600. Chin knows his boss wants a 45% markup on cost. Help Chin price the freezer.

8–18. Cecil Green sells golf hats. He knows that most people will not pay more than $20 for a golf hat. Cecil needs a 40% markup on cost. What should Cecil pay for his golf hats? Round to the nearest cent.

8–19. Macy's was selling Calvin Klein jean shirts that were originally priced at $58.00 for $8.70. **(a)** What was the amount of the markdown? **(b)** Based on the selling price, what is the percent markdown?

8–20. The *Miami Herald*, on January 31, 2007, ran a story on Super Bowl ticket prices. Ticket reseller Stubhub.com reported the average Super Bowl seat was selling for $4,445 with a face value of $700. **(a)** What is the percent markup based on cost? **(b)** What is the percent markup based on selling price? Round to the nearest hundredth percent.

8–21. The February 3, 2007 issue of *Billboard* reported on hefty markups by leading music merchants. Canadian Indies say they generally sell all products to independent distributors at between $8.00 and $9.50 per unit, which is then supplied to retailers at between $13.50 and $14.50. **(a)** What is the percent markup on cost for the lower price? **(b)** What is the percent markup on cost for the higher price? Round to the nearest hundredth percent.

8–22. Misu Sheet, owner of the Bedspread Shop, knows his customers will pay no more than $120 for a comforter. Misu wants a 30% markup on selling price. What is the most that Misu can pay for a comforter?

8–23. Assume Misu Sheet (Problem 8–22) wants a 30% markup on cost instead of on selling price. What is Misu's cost? Round to the nearest cent.

8–24. Misu Sheet (Problem 8–22) wants to advertise the comforter as "percent markup on cost." What is the equivalent rate of percent markup on cost compared to the 30% markup on selling price? Check your answer. Is this a wise marketing decision? Round to the nearest hundredth percent.

8–25. DeWitt Company sells a kitchen set for $475. To promote July 4, DeWitt ran the following advertisement:

Beginning each hour up to 4 hours, we will mark down the kitchen set 10%. At the end of each hour, we will mark up the set 1%.

Assume Ingrid Swenson buys the set 1 hour 50 minutes into the sale. What will Ingrid pay? Round each calculation to the nearest cent. What is the markdown percent? Round to the nearest hundredth percent.

8–26. PFS Fitness bought a treadmill for $700. PFS has a 70% markup on selling price. What is the selling price of the treadmill (to the nearest dollar)?

8–27. Sachi Wong, store manager for Hawk Appliance, does not know how to price a GE dishwasher that cost the store $399. Sachi knows her boss wants a 40% markup on cost. Can you help Sachi price the dishwasher?

8–28. Working off an 18% margin, with markups based on cost, the Food Co-op Club boasts that they have 5,000 members and a 200% increase in sales. The markup is 36% based on cost. What would be their percent markup if selling price were the base? Round to the nearest hundredth percent.

8–29. At a local Bed and Bath Superstore, the manager, Jill Roe, knows her customers will pay no more than $300 for a bedspread. Jill wants a 35% markup on selling price. What is the most that Jill can pay for a bedspread?

(Cont. on p. 228)

8–30. *U.S. News & World Report* October 9, 2006, reported RV dealer markups can top 40 percent. Jim Abbott purchased a $60,000 RV with a 40 percent markup on selling price. **(a)** What was the amount of the dealer's markup? **(b)** What was the dealers original cost?

8–31. Circuit City sells a hand-held personal planner for $199.99. Circuit City marked up the personal planner 35% on the selling price. What is the cost of the hand-held personal planner?

8–32. An Apple Computer Center sells computers for $1,258.60. Assuming the computers cost $10,788 per dozen, find for each computer the **(a)** dollar markup, **(b)** percent markup on cost, and **(c)** percent markup on selling price (nearest hundredth percent).

Prove **(b)** and **(c)** of the above problem using the equivalent formulas.

(Cont. on p. 229)

8–33. Virtual dealer, Dirt Cheap, says it marks up its jewelry a mere 8%. That is why Peter Bertling could buy a two-carat pair of diamond earrings for $5,000—49% of what he would pay at a conventional retailer. **(a)** Based on selling price, what is Dirt Cheap's cost? **(b)** What is Dirt Cheap's markup amount? **(c)** What was the selling price of the conventional retailer? **(d)** How much did Peter save? Round to the nearest hundredth.

8–34. On July 8, 2009, Leon's Kitchen Hut bought a set of pots with a $120 list price from Lambert Manufacturing. Leon's receives a 25% trade discount. Terms of the sale were 2/10, n/30. On July 14, Leon's sent a check to Lambert for the pots. Leon's expenses are 20% of the selling price. Leon's must also make a profit of 15% of the selling price. A competitor marked down the same set of pots 30%. Assume Leon's reduces its selling price by 30%.

   a.   What is the sale price at Kitchen Hut?

   b.   What was the operating profit or loss?

 SUMMARY PRACTICE TEST

1. Sunset Co. marks up merchandise 40% on cost. A DVD player costs Sunset $90. What is Sunset's selling price? Round to the nearest cent. *(p. 206)*

2. JCPenney sells jeans for $49.50 that cost $38.00. What is the percent markup on cost? Round to the nearest hundredth percent. Check the cost. *(p. 207)*

3. Best Buy sells a flat-screen high-definition TV for $700. Best Buy marks up the TV 45% on cost. What is the cost and dollar markup of the TV? *(p. 208)*

4. Sports Authority marks up New Balance sneakers $30 and sells them for $109. Markup is on cost. What are the cost and percent markup to the nearest hundredth percent? *(p. 207)*

5. The Shoe Outlet bought boots for $60 and marks up the boots 55% on the selling price. What is the selling price of the boots? Round to the nearest cent. *(p. 212)*

6. Office Max sells a desk for $450 and marks up the desk 35% on the selling price. What did the desk cost Office Max? Round to the nearest cent. *(p. 214)*

7. Zales sells diamonds for $1,100 that cost $800. What is Zales's percent markup on selling price? Round to the nearest hundredth percent. Check the selling price. *(p. 212)*

8. Earl Miller, a customer of J. Crew, will pay $400 for a new jacket. J. Crew has a 60% markup on selling price. What is the most that J. Crew can pay for this jacket? *(p. 214)*

9. Home Liquidators mark up its merchandise 35% on cost. What is the company's equivalent markup on selling price? Round to the nearest tenth percent. *(p. 215)*

Personal Finance

INSURANCE | Yes, you can afford coverage that pays nursing-home costs. *By Kimberly Lankford*

A fresh look at **LONG TERM** care

COULD YOU afford to withdraw $250,000 from your retirement savings to pay for one year in a nursing home? Based on current charges, that's the projected cost in 25 years, when today's 55-year-old is likely to need care. And with nursing-home stays averaging about 2.5 years, your total bill could top $600,000—which could quickly drain your retirement accounts, leaving you and your spouse with little savings and your heirs without an inheritance.

Buying long-term-care insurance is the best way to protect your retirement savings from astronomical bills. And a new law, which makes it more difficult to qualify for medicaid coverage of nursing-home costs, gives long-term-care policies a boost (see "Medicaid Gets Tough," on page 86).

Long-term-care coverage doesn't come cheap. Prices for new policies have jumped by 20% to 40% over the past few years. It can now cost a 55-year-old nearly $5,000 per year for a lifetime policy with a $200 daily benefit (the average nursing-home cost nationwide), 5% compound inflation protection and a 60-day waiting period before benefits begin. That's nearly $7,000 for a married couple, even with a spousal discount. But with some smart planning, you can buy all the coverage you need for a fraction of that amount.

A shorter benefit period. For starters, you probably don't need a policy that pays lifetime benefits. Milliman, an actuarial consulting firm, recently stud-

Glen and Joan Berwick stretched their premium dollars by buying six-year shared-care policies.

ied more than 1.6 million long-term-care policies and found that only about 8% of 70-year-old claimants are likely to need care for longer than five years—leaving 92% with claims of five years or fewer. Dawn Helwig, the study's co-author, points out that the average claim period is even shorter, because most people don't activate their policies until they are in their eighties.

Shortening the benefit period can

cut your premiums significantly. A John Hancock policy with a $200 daily benefit and a five-year benefit period would cost a 55-year-old $2,900 per year—about $2,000 less than lifetime coverage, or $3,000 less per couple annually. For example, Glen and Joan Berwick of South Glastonbury, Conn., each bought a six-year policy with a $150 daily benefit from John Hancock four years ago, when Glen was 63 and Joan was 59, saving them thousands of dollars.

One caveat: Of the 8% of nursing-home residents likely to need extended care, many will have chronic conditions, such as Alzheimer's. If you have a family history of a chronic disease, you're better off with a policy with a ten-year benefit period, which would still cost a 55-year-old $1,000 less a year than a lifetime-benefits policy.

Shared care. The best deal of all may be a shared-care policy, which gives you and your spouse a pool of benefits. If you each buy, say, a five-year shared-care policy, you actually get ten years to split between you. Most long-term-care insurers offer such policies, which generally cost about 10% more than separate policies with the same benefit period.

BUSINESS MATH ISSUE

There is little markup on long-term care and thus it is a bargain at any age.

1. List the key points of the article and information to support your position.
2. Write a group defense of your position using math calculations to support your view.

PROJECT A

Using an example, explain the following: product cost; other direct costs; net profit margin.

For Dining Chains, Lucrative Drinks Could Make for Very Happy Hours

By Joseph T. Hallinan

CASH-STRAPPED CONSUMERS are eating out less often, leading Bennigan's, Applebee's and other so-called casual-dining chains to lean harder on some of their most profitable menu items: alcoholic drinks.

Beer, wine and liquor-based concoctions often have profit margins more than double those of food—making them just the ticket for a restaurant's sagging bottom line. And the timing is right: Americans' alcohol consumption, after dropping for nearly two decades, is on the rise again—due in large measure to recent effective marketing campaigns by wine and spirits makers.

In an effort to attract sales clerks, hotel workers and other late-shift service-industry workers looking for a place to go after work, **Applebee's International** Inc., of Overland Park, Kan., the nation's leading casual-dining chain, has knocked $1 off the price of a 16-ounce glass of draft beer after 9 p.m., and some Applebee's restaurants have begun offering half-price appetizers at that time. The chain also has introduced a new line of smoothies and fruit drinks, as well as specialty drinks like the "Dos 'Rita Rocks," a Margarita made with two premium tequilas, Red Apple Sangria and the Mucho Mary, a Bloody Mary drink.

Metromedia Restaurant Group's Bennigan's Grill & Tavern unit last month rolled out a menu of inexpensive "bar bites," in an effort to target 25- to 45-year-old working professionals and singles. Bennigan's goal is to boost alcohol sales to 25% of its total sales, up from the current 20%.

"It works for me," said Jeff Rykal, a 41-year-old telecommunications director, just after 5:30 p.m. on a recent Monday at a Chicago Bennigan's.

He was munching on a $4 basket of small cheeseburgers—"Burger Bites"—and fries, and washing it down with a $2.50 Budweiser.

With him, Mark Linman, 41, was working on his own Burger Bites and a bottle of Miller Genuine Draft. The men said it was their first trip to Bennigan's.

Bennigan's new bar menu, supported by TV and print ads, is part of a larger makeover of the chain's bar operations. Earlier this year, the company foresaw a softening in the economy, says Clay Dover, Bennigan's vice president of marketing, "and we wanted to react accordingly."

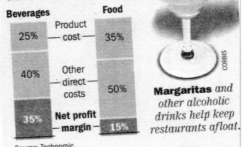

Profit Punch

Alcoholic beverages, including beer, wine and spirits, bring in more money for restaurants than food. Revenue breakdown:

Beverages		Food	
25%	Product cost	35%	
40%	Other direct costs	50%	
35%	Net profit margin	15%	

Source: Technomic

Margaritas and other alcoholic drinks help keep restaurants afloat.

Across the casual-dining sector—where dinner tabs typically run between $10 and $30 per dinner—servings of alcoholic drinks for the first six months of 2006 were up 3% over a year ago, according to NPD Group, a Port Washington, N.Y., market research firm.

"Even though traffic may be down or moderating slightly, at these casual-dining restaurants their alcoholic beverage sales are up," says Tex McCarthy, president of national accounts and sales development in North America for **Diageo** PLC, the world's largest spirits maker by volume. He said this trend is true not only for spirits, but for beer and wine as well. Diageo sells all three.

Restaurants love to sell alcohol for good reason: It takes less time and fewer people to prepare a drink than it does to prepare a meal. That leads to tasty profit margins of about 35% for alcoholic beverages, compared with 15% for food, according to Technomic, a Chicago restaurant-consulting firm.

Internet Projects: See text Web site (www.mhhe.com/slater9e) and The Business Math Internet Resource Guide.

Video Case

You may not have heard of the Kimpton Group, but you have probably heard the name of at least one of their 40 stylish boutique hotels that combine affordability with personality. The company believes it is cheaper to renovate old downtown buildings into charming hotels featuring popular restaurants than build new chain hotels. Developing a classy boutique property costs $150,000 per room compared to $350,000 a room for a new chain hotel. Investors also see a more rapid return.

The late Bill Kimpton, a former Lehman Bros. investment banker, created the boutique hotel concept and founded the Kimpton Hotel & Restaurant Group, a San Francisco–based chain, in 1981. Today the Kimpton Group runs 40 luxury hotels and 36 restaurants in the United States and Canada. Rates run from $100 to $200 per night, the average being $140, which is usually about 25% to 30% less than comparative nearby hotels. The average occupancy is 62%.

The Kimpton Group is known for its innovative ideas. All seven hotels offer the "Guppy Love" goldfish service. Steve Pinetti, senior vice president–sales and marketing, came up with the goldfish idea. He suggested providing complimentary goldfish to guests. Among the other concepts that Kimpton claims to have originated are pet-friendly hotels, custom-made "tall" beds, and complimentary wine hours for guests. U.S. hotel operators look to Kimpton for inspiration and credit it with inventing boutique hotels.

When a new hotel is planned, Kimpton invites people from theaters, galleries, and department stores in the area to offer ideas that might suit the particular location. Kimpton's philosophy is that travelers want something different and exciting in a hotel, and the element of excitement should not be underestimated no matter what the age group or location. Goldfish seem to be hooking customers for Kimpton.

PROBLEM 1

As shown in the video, Hotel Monaco's clients are 65% business travelers, of which 35% are with groups. Hotel Monaco has 192 rooms with the occupancy rate running about 62%. **(a)** On a given evening, how many guests would be business travelers? **(b)** How many would be group business travelers? Round to the nearest whole number.

PROBLEM 2

On May 16, 2003, the *Chicago Sun Times* reported Chicago downtown hotels were averaging occupancy of 50.5% for the first two months of 2003, with rates averaging $121. Regionwide, occupancy was 47.9%, up almost 4 percentage points from the same period a year ago, but average room rates inched down to $92 from $93 last year. Hotel Monaco has 192 rooms, averaging $199 per room. **(a)** What is the percent change in Hotel Monaco's average rate compared to the industry average rate? **(b)** What is the percent change in regionwide rates? Round to the nearest hundredths. **(c)** What would be the revenue generated by Hotel Monaco for one evening? Round to the nearest dollar.

PROBLEM 3

Hotel Monaco's occupancy rate topped 62% in 2001 and 70% in 2000. The average rate is $199 per evening. What would be the dollar change in total revenue for one week (7 days) based on 192 rooms? Round final answer to the nearest dollar.

PROBLEM 4

The average daily hotel room rate totaled $104.32 at year-end 2002, $113.12 at year-end 2001, and $116.42 at year-end 2000. **(a)** With 2000 as the base year, what were the percent changes each year? **(b)** Using 2002 as the base year, what were the percent changes each year? Round to the nearest hundredth.

PROBLEM 5

On April 9, 2002, *USA Today* reported total nationwide revenue for boutique hotels dropped 13% to $1.6 billion in 2001 from the previous year. Revenue per available room—another measure of the hotel industry's financial health—fell 16% in 2001 for boutique hotels, compared with 6% for all hotels. **(a)** What had been the total revenue in 2000? Round to the nearest tenth. **(b)** Based on an average room rate of $199, what was the dollar change for boutique hotels? **(c)** With the same average rate, what was the dollar change for hotels? Round to the nearest whole dollar.

PROBLEM 6

Thomas LaTour, CEO of the Kimpton Group, stated it is more profitable to develop boutique hotels than large chain hotels because it is cheaper to renovate an old downtown building than build new chain hotels. To develop a classy boutique property costs $150,000 per room compared to $350,000 per room for a new chain hotel. **(a)** What is the percent increase in the cost of a new chain hotel? Round to the nearest hundredth. **(b)** What would be the total cost of a 192-room boutique? **(c)** What would be the total cost of a 192-room new chain hotel?

PROBLEM 7

Revenue in 2001 for the private Kimpton Group fell 15% to $350 million. CEO Thomas LaTour predicted sales growth of 5% for 2002. Room occupancy rates, which sank to 45% after September 11, have risen to 66% during the month of April. **(a)** What had been the total revenue in 2002? Round to the nearest million. **(b)** What is the amount of sales growth projected for 2002? **(c)** With 192 rooms, what is the change in room occupancy? Round to the nearest whole number.

A Word Problem Approach—Chapters 6, 7, 8

1.   Assume Kellogg's produced 715,000 boxes of Corn Flakes this year. This was 110% of the annual production last year. What was last year's annual production? (p. 150)

2.   A new Sony camcorder has a list price of $420. The trade discount is 10/20 with terms of 2/10, n/30. If a retailer pays the invoice within the discount period, what is the amount the retailer must pay? (p. 175)

3.   JCPenney sells loafers with a markup of $40. If the markup is 30% on cost, what did the loafers cost J.C. Penney? Round to the nearest dollar. (p. 207)

4.   Aster Computers received from Ring Manufacturers an invoice dated August 28 with terms 2/10 EOM. The list price of the invoice is $3,000 (freight not included). Ring offers Aster a 9/8/2 trade chain discount. Terms of freight are FOB shipping point, but Ring prepays the $150 freight. Assume Aster pays the invoice on October 9. How much will Ring receive? (p. 175)

5.   Runners World marks up its Nike jogging shoes 25% on selling price. The Nike shoe sells for $65. How much did the store pay for them? (p. 214)

6.   Ivan Rone sells antique sleds. He knows that the most he can get for a sled is $350. Ivan needs a 35% markup on cost. Since Ivan is going to an antiques show, he wants to know the maximum he can offer a dealer for an antique sled. (p. 208)

Payroll

LEARNING UNIT OBJECTIVES

LU 9–1: Calculating Various Types of Employees' Gross Pay

- Define, compare, and contrast weekly, biweekly, semimonthly, and monthly pay periods (p. 236).
- Calculate gross pay with overtime on the basis of time (p. 237).
- Calculate gross pay for piecework, differential pay schedule, straight commission with draw, variable commission scale, and salary plus commission (pp. 238–240).

LU 9–2: Computing Payroll Deductions for Employees' Pay; Employers' Responsibilities

- Prepare and explain the parts of a payroll register (p. 241–244).
- Explain and calculate federal and state unemployment taxes (p. 244).

Delta, Pilots Agree on Interim Pay Cuts

By Evan Perez

Averting a potentially crippling impasse, **Delta Air Lines** Inc. and its pilots union reached an agreement on interim pay cuts and a timetable for the two sides to negotiate a long-term deal on concessions the company says are necessary to complete its bankruptcy restructuring.

The Air Line Pilots Association agreed to accept a 14% wage cut and other cost cuts that would be equal to an additional 1% wage cut, and said it would submit the tentative agreement to its members for ratification by Dec. 28. Delta had sought a 19% wage reduction as part of a package of cuts totaling $325 million annually.

The agreement, reached yesterday, avoids for now a showdown over Delta's threat to abrogate the collective bargaining agreement with its 6,100 pilots. Bankruptcy-court hearings on Delta's request

to impose terms on the union were set to continue today, and a deadline loomed Friday, when Delta had said it could reject the union's contract. The union had threatened a possible strike in retaliation. Both the company and union leaders believed the company couldn't survive a labor shutdown.

Based on Delta's valuation of its earlier demand, the agreement on a 14% wage cut should save the company $143 million annually. That is higher than the union's initial offer of a 9% pay cut. The union estimated that initial offer would save Delta $90 million, not including other work-rule changes. In court filings, Delta says its average pilot salary is just under $170,000, though the union says that figure is misleadingly high.

The Atlanta company began seeking union concessions well before it filed for Chapter 11 reorganization Sept. 14, but the two sides have been at a standoff

ever since. Bankruptcy Court Judge Prudence Carter Beatty has pushed the two sides to come to an agreement in recent weeks to make it unnecessary for her to rule on Delta's motion to cancel the pilot contract.

The union and the company said they would continue negotiating to reach a permanent agreement by March 1.

In a letter to union members, Lee Moak, a Delta captain who chairs its leadership committee, said the interim agreement "buys us time. We were facing possible rejection of the contract in a matter of days."

Under the tentative deal, the company agreed to end a program to rehire recently retired pilots on a contract basis to fly some of its routes. Active pilots disliked the program because the retired pilots held higher-paid slots that they otherwise could move into.

Wall Street Journal © 2005

Tom Uhlman/AP Wide World

The *Wall Street Journal* clipping "Delta, Pilots Agree on Interim Pay Cuts" shows how pilots have agreed to a 14% pay cut. Note that the average pilot salary is $170,000. A 14% pay cut means a loss of $23,800.

This chapter discusses (1) the type of pay people work for, (2) how employers calculate paychecks and deductions, and (3) what employers must report and pay in taxes.

Learning Unit 9–1: Calculating Various Types of Employees' Gross Pay

Logan Company manufactures dolls of all shapes and sizes. These dolls are sold worldwide. We study Logan Company in this unit because of the variety of methods Logan uses to pay its employees.

Companies usually pay employees **weekly, biweekly, semimonthly,** or **monthly.** How often employers pay employees can affect how employees manage their money. Some employees prefer a weekly paycheck that spreads the inflow of money. Employees who have monthly bills may find the twice-a-month or monthly paycheck more convenient. All employees would like more money to manage.

Let's assume you earn $50,000 per year. The following table shows what you would earn each pay period. Remember that 13 weeks equals one quarter. Four quarters or 52 weeks equals a year.

Salary paid	Period (based on a year)	Earnings for period (dollars)
Weekly	52 times (once a week)	$ 961.54 ($50,000 ÷ 52)
Biweekly	26 times (every two weeks)	$1,923.08 ($50,000 ÷ 26)
Semimonthly	24 times (twice a month)	$2,083.33 ($50,000 ÷ 24)
Monthly	12 times (once a month)	$4,166.67 ($50,000 ÷ 12)

Now let's look at some pay schedule situations and examples of how Logan Company calculates its payroll for employees of different pay status.

Situation 1: Hourly Rate of Pay; Calculation of Overtime

The **Fair Labor Standards Act** sets minimum wage standards and overtime regulations for employees of companies covered by this federal law. The law provides that employees working for an hourly rate receive time-and-a-half pay for hours worked in excess of their regular 40-hour week. The current hourly minimum wage is $5.85, rising to $6.55 in summer of 2008 and then $7.25 in summer of 2009. Many managerial people, however, are exempt from the time-and-a-half pay for all hours in excess of a 40-hour week.

Ryan McVay/Getty Images

As Tech Matures, Workers File A Spate of Salary Complaints

Fewer Dreams of Riches Mean More Suits for Overtime And Other Mundane Pay

Electronic Arts Rethinks Perks

**By PUI-WING TAM
And NICK WINGFIELD**

A hallmark of the boom years in high-tech was its work ethic: killer hours, often at modest salaries, without complaint. It was a small price for the excitement and the shot at a bonanza someday.

But as high-tech riches have faded, a different attitude toward employers is popping up: Pay me overtime, or I'll sue.

Wall Street Journal © 2005

In addition to many managerial people being exempt from time-and-a-half pay for more than 40 hours, other workers may also be exempt. Note in the *Wall Street Journal* clipping "As Tech Matures, Workers File a Spate of Salary Complaints" that many employees in the tech sector plan to sue if they do not get overtime pay.

Now we return to our Logan Company example. Logan Company is calculating the weekly pay of Ramon Valdez who works in its manufacturing division. For the first 40 hours Ramon works, Logan calculates his **gross pay** (earnings before **deductions**) as follows:

> Gross pay = Hours employee worked × Rate per hour

Ramon works more than 40 hours in a week. For every hour over his 40 hours, Ramon must be paid an **overtime** pay of at least 1.5 times his regular pay rate. The following formula is used to determine Ramon's overtime:

> Hourly overtime pay rate = Regular hourly pay rate × 1.5

Logan Company must include Ramon's overtime pay with his regular pay. To determine Ramon's gross pay, Logan uses the following formula:

> Gross pay = Earnings for 40 hours + Earnings at time-and-a-half rate (1.5)

We are now ready to calculate Ramon's gross pay from the following data:

EXAMPLE

Employee	M	T	W	Th	F	S	Total hours	Rate per hour
Ramon Valdez	13	$8\frac{1}{2}$	10	8	$11\frac{1}{4}$	$10\frac{3}{4}$	$61\frac{1}{2}$	$9

$$\begin{array}{r} 61\frac{1}{2} \text{ total hours} \\ -40 \text{ regular hours} \\ \hline 21\frac{1}{2} \text{ hours overtime}^1 \end{array}$$ Time-and-a-half pay: $9 × 1.5 = $13.50

Gross pay = (40 hours × $9) + ($21\frac{1}{2}$ hours × $13.50)

= $360   + $290.25

= $650.25

Note that the $13.50 overtime rate came out even. However, throughout the text, *if an overtime rate is greater than two decimal places, do not round it. Round only the final answer. This gives greater accuracy.*

Situation 2: Straight Piece Rate Pay

Some companies, especially manufacturers, pay workers according to how much they produce. Logan Company pays Ryan Foss for the number of dolls he produces in a week. This gives Ryan an incentive to make more money by producing more dolls. Ryan receives $.96 per doll, less any defective units. The following formula determines Ryan's gross pay:

> Gross pay = Number of units produced × Rate per unit

Companies may also pay a guaranteed hourly wage and use a piece rate as a bonus. However, Logan uses straight piece rate as wages for some of its employees.

EXAMPLE   During the last week of April, Ryan Foss produced 900 dolls. Using the above formula, Logan Company paid Ryan $864.

Gross pay = 900 dolls × $.96

= $864

Situation 3: Differential Pay Schedule

Some of Logan's employees can earn more than the $.96 straight piece rate for every doll they produce. Logan Company has set up a **differential pay schedule** for these employees. The company determines the rate these employees make by the amount of units the employees produce at different levels of production.

EXAMPLE   Logan Company pays Abby Rogers on the basis of the following schedule:

	Units produced	Amount per unit
First 50 →	1–50	$ .50
Next 100 →	51–150	.62
Next 50 →	151–200	.75
	Over 200	1.25

Last week Abby produced 300 dolls. What is Abby's gross pay?
Logan calculated Abby's gross pay as follows:

(50 × $.50) + (100 × $.62) + (50 × $.75) + (100 × $1.25)

$25   + $62   + $37.50   + $125   = $249.50

---

[1] Some companies pay overtime for time over 8 hours in one day; Logan Company pays overtime for time over 40 hours per week.

Now we will study some of the other types of employee commission payment plans.

Situation 4: Straight Commission with Draw

Companies frequently use **straight commission** to determine the pay of salespersons. This commission is usually a certain percentage of the amount the salesperson sells. An example of one group of companies ceasing to pay commissions is the rental-car companies.

Companies such as Logan Company allow some of its salespersons to draw against their commission at the beginning of each month. A **draw** is an advance on the salesperson's commission. Logan subtracts this advance later from the employee's commission earned based on sales. When the commission does not equal the draw, the salesperson owes Logan the difference between the draw and the commission.

EXAMPLE   Logan Company pays Jackie Okamoto a straight commission of 15% on her net sales (net sales are total sales less sales returns). In May, Jackie had net sales of $56,000. Logan gave Jackie a $600 draw in May. What is Jackie's gross pay?

Logan calculated Jackie's commission minus her draw as follows:

$$\$56,000 \times .15 = \quad \begin{array}{r} \$8,400 \\ - \quad 600 \\ \hline \$7,800 \end{array}$$

Logan Company pays some people in the sales department on a variable commission scale. Let's look at this, assuming the employee had no draw.

Situation 5: Variable Commission Scale

A company with a **variable commission scale** uses different commission rates for different levels of net sales.

EXAMPLE   Last month, Jane Ring's net sales were $160,000. What is Jane's gross pay based on the following schedule?

Up to $35,000	4%
Excess of $35,000 to $45,000	6%
Over $45,000	8%

$$\text{Gross pay} = (\$35,000 \times .04) + (\$10,000 \times .06) + (\$115,000 \times .08)$$

$$= \quad \$1,400 \quad + \quad \$600 \quad + \quad \$9,200$$

$$= \boxed{\$11,200}$$

Situation 6: Salary Plus Commission

Logan Company pays Joe Roy a $3,000 monthly salary plus a 4% commission for sales over $20,000. Last month Joe's net sales were $50,000. Logan calculated Joe's gross monthly pay as follows:

$$\text{Gross pay} = \text{Salary} + (\text{Commission} \times \text{Sales over } \$20,000)$$

$$= \$3,000 + \qquad (.04 \times \$30,000)$$

$$= \$3,000 + \qquad \$1,200$$

$$= \boxed{\$4,200}$$

Before you take the Practice Quiz, you should know that many managers today receive **overrides.** These managers receive a commission based on the net sales of the people they supervise.

LU 9–1   PRACTICE QUIZ

Complete this **Practice Quiz**
to see how you are doing

1. Jill Foster worked 52 hours in one week for Delta Airlines. Jill earns $10 per hour. What is Jill's gross pay, assuming overtime is at time-and-a-half?
2. Matt Long had $180,000 in sales for the month. Matt's commission rate is 9%, and he had a $3,500 draw. What was Matt's end-of-month commission?
3. Bob Meyers receives a $1,000 monthly salary. He also receives a variable commission on net sales based on the following schedule (commission doesn't begin until Bob earns $8,000 in net sales):

| $8,000–$12,000 | 1% | Excess of $20,000 to $40,000 | 5% |
| Excess of $12,000 to $20,000 | 3% | More than $40,000 | 8% |

Assume Bob earns $40,000 net sales for the month. What is his gross pay?

✓ Solutions

1. 40 hours × $10.00 = $400.00
   12 hours × $15.00 =   180.00 ($10.00 × 1.5 = $15.00)
                      $580.00

2. $180,000 × .09 = $16,200
                    −   3,500
                      $12,700

3. Gross pay = $1,000 + ($4,000 × .01) + ($8,000 × .03) + ($20,000 × .05)
             = $1,000 + $40   + $240   + $1,000
             = $2,280

LU 9–1a   EXTRA PRACTICE QUIZ

Need more practice? Try this
Extra Practice Quiz (check
figures in Chapter Organizer,
p. 247)

1. Jill Foster worked 54 hours in one week for Delta Airlines. Jill earns $12 per hour. What is Jill's gross pay, assuming overtime is at time-and-a-half?
2. Matt Long had $210,000 in sales for the month. Matt's commission rate is 8%, and he had a $4,000 draw. What was Matt's end-of-month commission?
3. Bob Myers receives a $1,200 monthly salary. He also receives a variable commission on net sales based on the following schedule (commission doesn't begin until Bob earns $9,000 in net sales).

| $9,000–$12,000 | 1% | Excess of $20,000 to $40,000 | 5% |
| Excess of $12,000 to $20,000 | 3% | More than $40,000 | 8% |

Assume Bob earns $60,000 net sales for the month. What is his gross pay?

Learning Unit 9–2: Computing Payroll Deductions for Employees' Pay; Employers' Responsibilities

Did you know that Wal-Mart is the largest employer in twenty-one states? Can you imagine the accounting involved to pay all these employees?

This unit begins by dissecting a paycheck. Then we give you an insight into the tax responsibilities of employers.

Computing Payroll Deductions for Employees

Companies often record employee payroll information in a multicolumn form called a **payroll register.** The increased use of computers in business has made computerized registers a timesaver for many companies.

Glo Company uses a multicolumn payroll register. On page 241 is Glo's partial payroll register showing the payroll information for Alice Rey during week 44. Let's check each column to see if Alice's take-home pay of $1,324.36 is correct. Note how the circled letters in the register correspond to the explanations that follow.

| | | | | | | | | | FICA Taxable Earnings | | Deductions | | | | | |
| Employee name | Allow. & marital status | Cum. earn. | Sal. per week | Earnings | | | Cum. earn. | | | FICA | | | | | Health ins. | Net pay |
				Reg.	Ovt.	Gross		S.S.	Med.	S.S.	Med.	FIT	SIT		
Rey, Alice	M-2	96,750	2,250	2,250	—	2,250	99,000	750	2,250	46.50	32.63	355.96	135	100	1,579.91
	Ⓐ	Ⓑ	Ⓒ		Ⓓ		Ⓔ	Ⓕ	Ⓖ	Ⓗ	Ⓘ	Ⓙ	Ⓚ	Ⓛ	Ⓜ

GLO COMPANY
Payroll Register
Week #44

Payroll Register Explanations
Ⓐ—Allowance and marital status
Ⓑ,Ⓒ,Ⓓ—Cumulative earnings before payroll, salaries, earnings
Ⓔ—Cumulative earnings after payroll

Ⓕ,Ⓖ—Taxable earnings for Social Security and Medicare

When Alice was hired, she completed the **W-4 (Employee's Withholding Allowance Certificate)** form shown in Figure 9.1 stating that she is married and claims an allowance (exemption) of 2. Glo Company will need this information to calculate the federal income tax Ⓙ.

Before this pay period, Alice has earned $96,750 (43 weeks × $2,250 salary per week). Since Alice receives no overtime, her $2,250 salary per week represents her gross pay (pay before any deductions).

After this pay period, Alice has earned $99,000 ($96,750 + $2,250).

The **Federal Insurance Contribution Act (FICA)** funds the **Social Security** program. The program includes Old Age and Disability, Medicare, Survivor Benefits, and so on. The FICA tax requires separate reporting for Social Security and **Medicare.** We will use the following rates for Glo Company:

	Rate	Base
Social Security	6.20%	$97,500
Medicare	1.45	No base

These rates mean that Alice Rey will pay Social Security taxes on the first $97,500 she earns this year. After earning $97,500, Alice's wages will be exempt from Social Security. Note that Alice will be paying Medicare taxes on all wages since Medicare has no base cutoff.

To help keep Glo's record straight, the *taxable earnings column only shows what wages will be taxed. This amount is not the tax.* For example, in week 44, only $750 of Alice's salary will be taxable for Social Security.

$97,500 Social Security base
− 96,750 Ⓑ
$ 750

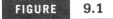

FIGURE 9.1

Employee's W-4 form

| Form **W-4** Department of the Treasury Internal Revenue Service | **Employee's Withholding Allowance Certificate** ► For Privacy Act and Paperwork Reduction Act Notice, see reverse. | OMB No. 1545-0010 **20XX** |

1 Type or print your first name and middle initial Alice | Last name Rey | **2** Your social security number 021 36 9494

Home address (number and street or rural route) 2 Roundy Road | **3** ☐ Single ☒ Married ☐ Married, but withhold at higher Single rate. Note: If married, but legally separated, or spouse is a nonresident alien, check the Single box.

City or town, state, and ZIP code Marblehead, MA 01945 | **4** If your last name differs from that on your social security card, check here and call 1-800-772-1213 for a new card . . . . . . ► ☐

5 Total number of allowances you are claiming (from line G above or from the worksheets on page 2 if they apply) . | **5** 2
6 Additional amount, if any, you want withheld from each paycheck . . . . | **6** $
7 I claim exemption from withholding for 1995 and I certify that I meet **BOTH** of the following conditions for exemption:
• Last year I had a right to a refund of **ALL** Federal income tax withheld because I had **NO** tax liability; **AND**
• This year I expect a refund of **ALL** Federal income tax withheld because I expect to have **NO** tax liability.
If you meet both conditions, enter "EXEMPT" here . . . . ► | **7**
Under penalties of perjury, I certify that I am entitled to the number of withholding allowances claimed on this certificate or entitled to claim exempt status.

Employee's signature ► *Alice Rey* | Date ► 1/1   , 20 XX
8 Employer's name and address (Employer: Complete 8 and 10 only if sending to the IRS) | **9** Office code (optional) | **10** Employer identification number

Cat. No. 10220Q

TABLE	9.1

Percentage method income tax withholding table

Payroll Period	One Withholding Allowance
Weekly	$ 65.38
Biweekly	130.77
Semimonthly	141.67
Monthly	283.33
Quarterly	850.00
Semiannually	1,700.00
Annually	3,400.00
Daily or miscellaneous (each day of the payroll period)	13.08

Dept. of the Treasury, Internal Revenue Service Publication 15, Jan. 2007.

Ⓗ—Social Security

To calculate Alice's Social Security tax, we multiply $750 Ⓕ by 6.2%:

$$\$750 \times .062 = \boxed{\$46.50}$$

Ⓘ—Medicare

Since Medicare has no base, Alice's entire weekly salary is taxed 1.45%, which is multiplied by $2,250.

$$\$2,250 \times .0145 = \boxed{\$32.63}$$

Ⓙ—FIT

Using the W-4 form Alice completed, Glo deducts **federal income tax withholding (FIT).** The more allowances an employee claims, the less money Glo deducts from the employee's paycheck. Glo uses the percentage method to calculate FIT.[2]

The Percentage Method[3]

Today, since many companies do not want to store the tax tables, they use computers for their payroll. These companies use the **percentage method.** For this method we use Table 9.1 and Table 9.2 from Circular E to calculate Alice's FIT.

Step 1. In Table 9.1, locate the weekly withholding for one allowance. Multiply this number by 2.

$$\$65.38 \times 2 = \$130.76$$

Step 2. Subtract $130.76 in Step 1 from Alice's total pay.

$$\begin{array}{r} \$2,250.00 \\ -\quad 130.76 \\ \hline \$2,119.24 \end{array}$$

Step 3. In Table 9.2, locate the married person's weekly pay table. The $2,119.24 falls between $1,360 and $2,573. The tax is $166.15 plus 25% of the excess over $1,360.00.

$$\begin{array}{r} \$2,119.24 \\ -\quad 1,360.00 \\ \hline \$\quad 759.24 \end{array}$$

Tax $166.15 + .25 ($759.24)

$$\$166.15 + \$189.81 = \boxed{\$355.96}$$

Ⓚ—SIT

We assume a 6% **state income tax (SIT).**

$$\$2,250 \times .06 = \$135.00$$

Ⓛ—Health insurance
Ⓜ—Net pay

Alice contributes $100 per week for health insurance. Alice's **net pay** is her gross pay less all deductions.

$$\begin{array}{rl} \$2,250.00 & \text{gross} \\ -\quad 46.50 & \text{Social Security} \\ -\quad 32.63 & \text{Medicare} \\ -\quad 355.96 & \text{FIT} \\ -\quad 135.00 & \text{SIT} \\ -\quad 100.00 & \text{health insurance} \\ \hline = \$1,579.91 & \text{net pay} \end{array}$$

[2]The *Business Math Handbook* has a sample of the wage bracket method.

[3]An alternative method is called the wage bracket method that is shown in the *Business Math Handbook.*

TABLE **9.2**   Percentage method income tax withholding taxes

TABLE 1—WEEKLY Payroll Period

(a) SINGLE person (including head of household)—

If the amount of wages (after subtracting withholding allowances) is: The amount of income tax to withhold is:

Not over $51 . . . . . $0

Over—	But not over—		of excess over—
$51	—$195	10%	—$51
$195	—$645	$14.40 plus 15%	—$195
$645	—$1,482	$81.90 plus 25%	—$645
$1,482	—$3,131	$291.15 plus 28%	—$1,482
$3,131	—$6,763	$752.87 plus 33%	—$3,131
$6,763	. . . . . .	$1,951.43 plus 35%	—$6,763

(b) MARRIED person—

If the amount of wages (after subtracting withholding allowances) is: The amount of income tax to withhold is:

Not over $154 . . . . . $0

Over—	But not over—		of excess over—
$154	—$449	10%	—$154
$449	—$1,360	$29.50 plus 15%	—$449
$1,360	—$2,573	$166.15 plus 25%	—$1,360
$2,573	—$3,907	$469.40 plus 28%	—$2,573
$3,907	—$6,865	$842.92 plus 33%	—$3,907
$6,865	. . . . . .	$1,819.06 plus 35%	—$6,865

TABLE 2—BIWEEKLY Payroll Period

(a) SINGLE person (including head of household)—

If the amount of wages (after subtracting withholding allowances) is: The amount of income tax to withhold is:

Not over $102 . . . . $0

Over—	But not over—		of excess over—
$102	—$389	10%	—$102
$389	—$1,289	$28.70 plus 15%	—$389
$1,289	—$2,964	$163.70 plus 25%	—$1,289
$2,964	—$6,262	$582.45 plus 28%	—$2,964
$6,262	—$13,525	$1,505.89 plus 33%	—$6,262
$13,525	. . . . .	$3,902.68 plus 35%	—$13,525

(b) MARRIED person—

If the amount of wages (after subtracting withholding allowances) is: The amount of income tax to withhold is:

Not over $308 . . . . $0

Over—	But not over—		of excess over—
$308	—$898	10%	—$308
$898	—$2,719	$59.00 plus 15%	—$898
$2,719	—$5,146	$332.15 plus 25%	—$2,719
$5,146	—$7,813	$938.90 plus 28%	—$5,146
$7,813	—$13,731	$1,685.66 plus 33%	—$7,813
$13,731	. . . . .	$3,638.60 plus 35%	—$13,731

TABLE 3—SEMIMONTHLY Payroll Period

(a) SINGLE person (including head of household)—

If the amount of wages (after subtracting withholding allowances) is: The amount of income tax to withhold is:

Not over $110 . . . . . $0

Over—	But not over—		of excess over—
$110	—$422	10%	—$110
$422	—$1,397	$31.20 plus 15%	—$422
$1,397	—$3,211	$177.45 plus 25%	—$1,397
$3,211	—$6,783	$630.95 plus 28%	—$3,211
$6,783	—$14,652	$1,631.11 plus 33%	—$6,783
$14,652	. . . . .	$4,227.88 plus 35%	—$14,652

(b) MARRIED person—

If the amount of wages (after subtracting withholding allowances) is: The amount of income tax to withhold is:

Not over $333 . . . . . $0

Over—	But not over—		of excess over—
$333	—$973	10%	—$333
$973	—$2,946	$64.00 plus 15%	—$973
$2,946	—$5,575	$359.95 plus 25%	—$2,946
$5,575	—$8,465	$1,017.20 plus 28%	—$5,575
$8,465	—$14,875	$1,826.40 plus 33%	—$8,465
$14,875	. . . . .	$3,941.70 plus 35%	—$14,875

TABLE 4—MONTHLY Payroll Period

(a) SINGLE person (including head of household)—

If the amount of wages (after subtracting withholding allowances) is: The amount of income tax to withhold is:

Not over $221 . . . . . $0

Over—	But not over—		of excess over—
$221	—$843	10%	—$221
$843	—$2,793	$62.20 plus 15%	—$843
$2,793	—$6,423	$354.70 plus 25%	—$2,793
$6,423	—$13,567	$1,262.20 plus 28%	—$6,423
$13,567	—$29,304	$3,262.52 plus 33%	—$13,567
$29,304	. . . . .	$8,455.73 plus 35%	—$29,304

(b) MARRIED person—

If the amount of wages (after subtracting withholding allowances) is: The amount of income tax to withhold is:

Not over $667 . . . . . $0

Over—	But not over—		of excess over—
$667	—$1,946	10%	—$667
$1,946	—$5,892	$127.90 plus 15%	—$1,946
$5,892	—$11,150	$719.80 plus 25%	—$5,892
$11,150	—$16,929	$2,034.30 plus 28%	—$11,150
$16,929	—$29,750	$3,652.42 plus 33%	—$16,929
$29,750	. . . . .	$7,883.35 plus 35%	—$29,750

Dept. of the Treasury, Internal Revenue Service Publication 15, Jan. 2007.

Employers' Responsibilities

Workers' Comp Costs Increase Nearly 10%

WASHINGTON—Employers' costs for workers' compensation have risen nearly 10%, even though the number of people covered under such programs has declined, largely as a result of higher insurance premiums, according to a new study.

Wall Street Journal © 2005

In the first section of this unit, we saw that Alice contributed to Social Security and Medicare. Glo Company has the legal responsibility to match her contributions. Besides matching Social Security and Medicare, Glo must pay two important taxes that employees do not have to pay—federal and state unemployment taxes. Note that the *Wall Street Journal* clipping "Workers' Comp Costs Increase Nearly 10%" states that employers now face an increase in their worker's compensation costs.

RF/Corbis

Federal Unemployment Tax Act (FUTA)

The federal government participates in a joint federal-state unemployment program to help unemployed workers. At this writing, employers pay the government a 6.2% **FUTA** tax on the first $7,000 paid to employees as wages during the calendar year. Any wages in excess of $7,000 per worker are exempt wages and are not taxed for FUTA. If the total cumulative amount the employer owes the government is less than $100, the employer can pay the liability yearly (end of January in the following calendar year). If the tax is greater than $100, the employer must pay it within a month after the quarter ends.

Companies involved in a state unemployment tax fund can usually take a 5.4% credit against their FUTA tax. *In reality, then, companies are paying .8% (.008) to the federal unemployment program.* In all our calculations, FUTA is .008.

EXAMPLE   Assume a company had total wages of $19,000 in a calendar year. No employee earned more than $7,000 during the calendar year. The FUTA tax is .8% (6.2% minus the company's 5.4% credit for state unemployment tax). How much does the company pay in FUTA tax?

The company calculates its FUTA tax as follows:

$$
\begin{array}{rl}
 & 6.2\% \text{ FUTA tax} \\
- & 5.4\% \text{ credit for SUTA tax} \\
\hline
= & .8\% \text{ tax for FUTA}
\end{array}
$$

.008 × $19,000 = $152 FUTA tax due to federal government

State Unemployment Tax Act (SUTA)

The current **SUTA** tax in many states is 5.4% on the first $7,000 the employer pays an employee. Some states offer a merit rating system that results in a lower SUTA rate for companies with a stable employment period. The federal government still allows 5.4% credit on FUTA tax to companies entitled to the lower SUTA rate. Usually states also charge companies with a poor employment record a higher SUTA rate. However, these companies cannot take any more than the 5.4% credit against the 6.2% federal unemployment rate.

EXAMPLE   Assume a company has total wages of $20,000 and $4,000 of the wages are exempt from SUTA. What are the company's SUTA and FUTA taxes if the company's SUTA rate is 5.8% due to a poor employment record?

The exempt wages (over $7,000 earnings per worker) are not taxed for SUTA or FUTA. So the company owes the following SUTA and FUTA taxes:

$$
\begin{array}{rl}
 & \$20,000 \\
- & 4,000 \text{ (exempt wages)} \\
\hline
 & \$16,000 \times .058 = \boxed{\$928} \text{ SUTA}
\end{array}
$$

Federal FUTA tax would then be:

$16,000 × .008 = $128

You can check your progress with the following Practice Quiz.

LU 9–2   PRACTICE QUIZ

1. Calculate Social Security taxes, Medicare taxes, and FIT for Joy Royce. Joy's company pays her a monthly salary of $9,500. She is single and claims 1 deduction. Before this payroll, Joy's cumulative earnings were $94,000. (Social Security maximum is 6.2% on $97,500, and Medicare is 1.45%.) Calculate FIT by the percentage method.

2. Jim Brewer, owner of Arrow Company, has three employees who earn $300, $700, and $900 a week. Assume a state SUTA rate of 5.1%. What will Jim pay for state and federal unemployment taxes for the first quarter?

✓ **Solutions**

1. **Social Security**

$$\begin{array}{r} \$97,500 \\ - 94,000 \\ \hline \$\ 3,500 \times .062 = \end{array}$$ $217.00

Medicare

$9,500 × .0145 = $137.75

FIT

Percentage method: $9,500.00

$283.33 × 1 =   − 283.33 (Table 9.1)

$9,216.67

$6,423 to $13,567 → $1,262.20 plus 28% of excess over $6,423
(Table 9.2)

$$\begin{array}{r} \$9,216.67 \\ - 6,423.00 \\ \hline \$2,793.67 \times .28 = \end{array}$$ $$\begin{array}{r} \$\ \ 782.23^* \\ + 1,262.20 \\ \hline \$2,044.43 \end{array}$$

*Due to rounding.

2. 13 weeks × $300 = $ 3,900
    13 weeks × $700 =   9,100 ($9,100 − $7,000) → $2,100 ⎫ Exempt wages
    13 weeks × $900 = 11,700 ($11,700 − $7,000) → 4,700 ⎬ (not taxed for
                       ─────   ───── ⎭ FUTA or SUTA)
                      $24,700 $6,800

    $24,700 − $6,800 = $17,900 taxable wages

    SUTA = .051 × $17,900 = $912.90

    FUTA = .008 × $17,900 = $143.20

    Note: FUTA remains at .008 whether SUTA rate is higher or lower than standard.

LU 9–2a   EXTRA PRACTICE QUIZ

1. Calculate Social Security taxes, Medicare taxes, and FIT for Joy Royce. Joy's company pays her a monthly salary of $10,000. She is single and claims 1 deduction. Before this payroll, Joy's cumulative earnings were $97,000. (Social Security maximum is 6.2% on $97,500, and Medicare is 1.45%.) Calculate FIT by the percentage method.

2. Jim Brewer, owner of Arrow Company, has three employees who earn $200, $800, and $950 a week. Assume a state SUTA rate of 5.1%. What will Jim pay for state and federal unemployment taxes for the first quarter?

CHAPTER ORGANIZER AND STUDY GUIDE
WITH CHECK FIGURES FOR EXTRA PRACTICE QUIZZES

Topic	Key point, procedure, formula	Example(s) to illustrate situation
Gross pay, p. 237	$\text{Hours employee worked} \times \text{Rate per hour}$	$6.50 per hour at 36 hours Gross pay $= 36 \times \$6.50 = \boxed{\$234}$
Overtime, p. 237	$\text{Gross earnings (pay)} = \text{Regular pay} + \text{Earnings at overtime rate } (1\frac{1}{2})$	$6 per hour; 42 hours Gross pay $= (40 \times \$6) + (2 \times \$9)$ $= \$240 + \$18 = \boxed{\$258}$
Straight piece rate, p. 238	$\text{Gross pay} = \text{Number of units produced} \times \text{Rate per unit}$	1,185 units; rate per unit, $.89 Gross pay $= 1,185 \times \$.89$ $= \boxed{\$1,054.65}$
Differential pay schedule, p. 238	Rate on each item is related to the number of items produced.	1–500 at $.84; 501–1,000 at $.96; 900 units produced. $\text{Gross pay} = (500 \times \$.84) + (400 \times \$.96)$ $= \$420 + \$384 = \boxed{\$804}$
Straight commission, p. 239	Total sales × Commission rate Any draw would be subtracted from earnings.	$155,000 sales; 6% commission $\$155,000 \times .06 = \boxed{\$9,300}$
Variable commission scale, p. 239	Sales at different levels pay different rates of commission.	Up to $5,000, 5%; $5,001 to $10,000, 8%; over $10,000, 10% Sold: $6,500 Solution: $(\$5,000 \times .05) + (\$1,500 \times .08)$ $= \$250 + \$120 = \boxed{\$370}$
Salary plus commission, p. 239	$\text{Regular wages (fixed)} + \text{Commissions earned}$	Base $400 per week + 2% on sales over $14,000 Actual sales: $16,000 $\$400 \text{ (base)} + (.02 \times \$2,000) = \boxed{\$440}$
Payroll register, p. 241	Multicolumn form to record payroll. Married and paid weekly. (Table 9.2) Claims 1 allowance. FICA rates from chapter.	(table below)
FICA, p. 241 **Social Security** **Medicare**	6.2% on $97,500 (S.S.) 1.45% (Med.)	If John earns $99,000, what did he contribute for the year to Social Security and Medicare? S.S.: $\$97,500 \times .062 = \boxed{\$6,045.00}$ Med.: $\$99,000 \times .0145 = \boxed{\$1,435.50}$
FIT calculation (percentage method), p. 242	*Facts:* Al Doe: Married Claims: 2 Paid weekly: $1,600	$1,600.00 $- 130.76$ ($65.38 × 2) Table 9.1 $1,469.24 By Table 9.2 $\quad \$1,469.24$ $\underline{- \ 1,360.00}$ $\quad \$ \ \ 109.24$ $166.15 + .25(\$109.24)$ $166.15 + \$27.31 = \boxed{\$193.46}$

Payroll register example:

Earnings	Deductions			Net pay
	FICA			
Gross	S.S.	Med.	FIT	
1,100	68.20	15.95	117.34	898.51

(continues)

CHAPTER ORGANIZER AND STUDY GUIDE
WITH CHECK FIGURES FOR EXTRA PRACTICE QUIZZES (concluded)

Topic	Key point, procedure, formula	Example(s) to illustrate situation
State and federal unemployment, p. 244	Employer pays these taxes. Rates are 6.2% on $7,000 for federal and 5.4% for state on $7,000. 6.2% − 5.4% = .8% federal rate after credit. If state unemployment rate is higher than 5.4%, no additional credit is taken. If state unemployment rate is less than 5.4%, the full 5.4% credit can be taken for federal unemployment.	Cumulative pay before payroll, $6,400; this week's pay, $800. What are state and federal unemployment taxes for employer, assuming a 5.2% state unemployment rate? State → .052 × $600 = $31.20 Federal → .008 × $600 = $4.80 ($6,400 + $600 = $7,000 maximum)

KEY TERMS

Biweekly, *p. 236*
Deductions, *p. 237*
Differential pay
  schedule, *p. 238*
Draw, *p. 239*
Employee's Withholding
  Allowance Certificate
  (W-4), *p. 241*
Fair Labor Standards
  Act, *p. 237*
Federal income tax
  withholding (FIT), *p. 242*

Federal Insurance
  Contribution Act
  (FICA), *p. 241*
Federal Unemployment
  Tax Act (FUTA), *p. 244*
Gross pay, *p. 237*
Medicare, *p. 241*
Monthly, *p. 236*
Net pay, *p. 242*
Overrides, *p. 239*
Overtime, *p. 237*
Payroll register, *p. 240*

Percentage method, *p. 242*
Semimonthly, *p. 236*
Social Security, *p. 241*
State income tax
  (SIT), *p. 242*
State Unemployment Tax
  Act (SUTA), *p. 244*
Straight commission, *p. 239*
Variable commission
  scale, *p. 239*
W-4, *p. 241*
Weekly, *p. 236*

CHECK FIGURES FOR EXTRA PRACTICE QUIZZES WITH PAGE REFERENCES

LU 9–1a (p. 240)
1. $732
2. $12,800
3. $4,070

LU 9–2a (p. 245)
1. $31; 145; $2,184.43
2. $846.60; $132.80

Critical Thinking Discussion Questions

1. Explain the difference between biweekly and semimonthly. Explain what problems may develop if a retail store hires someone on straight commission to sell cosmetics.

2. Explain what each column of a payroll register records (p. 241) and how each number is calculated. Social Security tax is based on a specific rate and base; Medicare tax is based on a rate but no base. Do you think this is fair to all taxpayers?

3. What taxes are the responsibility of the employer? How can an employer benefit from a merit-rating system for state unemployment?

Classroom Notes

Name _____ Date _____

DRILL PROBLEMS

Complete the following table:

	Employee	M	T	W	Th	F	Hours	Rate per hour	Gross pay
9–1.	Tom Bradey	11	7	8	7	6		$7.50	
9–2.	Kristina Shaw	5	9	10	8	8		$8.10	

Complete the following table (assume the overtime for each employee is a time-and-a-half rate after 40 hours):

	Employee	M	T	W	Th	F	Sa	Total regular hours	Total overtime hours	Regular rate	Overtime rate	Gross earnings
9–3.	Blue	12	9	9	9	9	3			$8.00		
9–4.	Tagney	14	8	9	9	5	1			$7.60		

Calculate gross earnings:

	Worker	Number of units produced	Rate per unit	Gross earnings
9–5.	Lang	510	$2.10	
9–6.	Swan	846	$ .58	

Calculate the gross earnings for each apple picker based on the following differential pay scale:

1–1,000: $.03 each   1,001–1,600: $.05 each   Over 1,600: $.07 each

	Apple picker	Number of apples picked	Gross earnings
9–7.	Ryan	1,600	
9–8.	Rice	1,925	

	Employee	Total sales	Commission rate	Draw	End-of-month commission received
9–9.	Reese	$300,000	7%	$8,000	

Ron Company has the following commission schedule:

Commission rate	Sales
2%	Up to $80,000
3.5%	Excess of $80,000 to $100,000
4%	More than $100,000

Calculate the gross earnings of Ron Company's two employees:

	Employee	Total sales	Gross earnings
9–10.	Bill Moore	$ 70,000	
9–11.	Ron Ear	$155,000	

Complete the following table, given that A Publishing Company pays its salespeople a weekly salary plus a 2% commission on all net sales over $5,000 (no commission on returned goods):

	Employee	Gross sales	Return	Net sales	Given quota	Commission sales	Commission rates	Total commission	Regular wage	Total wage
9–12.	Ring	$ 8,000	$ 25		$5,000		2%		$250	
9–13.	Porter	$12,000	$100		$5,000		2%		$250	

Calculate the Social Security and Medicare deductions for the following employees (assume a tax rate of 6.2% on $97,500 for Social Security and 1.45% for Medicare):

	Employee	Cumulative earnings before this pay period	Pay amount this period	Social Security	Medicare
9–14.	Lee	$96,500	$2,000		
9–15.	Chin	$90,000	$8,000		
9–16.	Davis	$500,000	$4,000		

Complete the following payroll register. Calculate FIT by the percentage method for this weekly period; Social Security and Medicare are the same rates as in the previous problems. No one will reach the maximum for FICA.

	Employee	Marital status	Allowances claimed	Gross pay	FIT	FICA S.S.	FICA Med.	Net pay
9–17.	Jim Day	M	2	$1,400				
9–18.	Ursula Lang	M	4	$1,900				

9–19. Given the following, calculate the state (assume 5.3%) and federal unemployment taxes that the employer must pay for each of the first two quarters. The federal unemployment tax is .8% on the first $7,000.

PAYROLL SUMMARY		
	Quarter 1	Quarter 2
Bill Adams	$4,000	$ 8,000
Rich Haines	8,000	14,000
Alice Smooth	3,200	3,800

WORD PROBLEMS

9–20. On February 7, 2007 the *San Jose Mercury News* reported on Bay Area workers average pay. Bay Area workers pocketed 23 percent more pay last year than workers in Los Angeles with $26.10 compared to $21.21 an hour. Jim Moody, a Bay Area worker, worked $10\frac{1}{4}$, $8\frac{1}{2}$, $9\frac{3}{4}$, $8\frac{3}{4}$ and $9\frac{1}{4}$ hours last week. Jim is paid an overtime pay of 1.5 times his regular pay. What is Jim's total gross pay for the week? Round to the nearest cent.

9–21. *The Telegraph* (Nashau, NH) on December 6, 2006, described the living wage needed in New Hampshire. Jessica Bullard is a single parent with one child and claims 2. She needs to make $17.71 an hour to get by in Hillsborough County. However Jessica Bullard only earns $13.00 an hour. Jessica works 40 hours a week. Social Security tax is 6.2 percent and Medicare is 1.45 percent (a) What is her gross pay per week? (b) How much is deducted for Social Security Tax? (c) How much is deducted for Medicare? (d) How much is withheld for FIT, assuming she claims 2? (e) What is her net pay? Round to the nearest cent.

9–22. The Social Security Administration increased the taxable wage base from $94,200 to $97,500. The 6.2% tax rate is unchanged. Joe Burns earned over $100,000 each of the past two years. **(a)** What is the percent increase in the base? Round to the nearest hundredth percent. **(b)** What is Joe's increase in Social Security tax for the new year?

9–23. Dennis Toby is a salesclerk at Northwest Department Store. Dennis receives $8 per hour plus a commission of 3% on all sales. Assume Dennis works 30 hours and has sales of $1,900. What is his gross pay?

9–24. Owing to a bill signed by Governor Arnold Schwarzenegger that increased the minimum wage from $6.75 to $8.00 an hour, by 2008, *The Business Press* (San Bernardino, CA) on September 18, 2006 reports firms are weighing leaving the state. Donna Carter, single, works 37 hours per week with one withholding exemption. Using the same percentage withholding for wages paid in 2007, (a) what is the amount of FIT withheld for 2007? (b) What would be the amount of FIT withheld for 2008? Round to the nearest cent.

9–25. Robin Hartman earns $600 per week plus 3% of sales over $6,500. Robin's sales are $14,000. How much does Robin earn?

9–26. Pat Maninen earns a gross salary of $2,100 each week. What are Pat's first week's deductions for Social Security and Medicare? Will any of Pat's wages be exempt from Social Security and Medicare for the calendar year? Assume a rate of 6.2% on $97,500 for Social Security and 1.45% for Medicare.

9–27. Richard Gaziano is a manager for Health Care, Inc. Health Care deducts Social Security, Medicare, and FIT (by percentage method) from his earnings. Assume the same Social Security and Medicare rates as in Problem 9–26. Before this payroll, Richard is $1,000 below the maximum level for Social Security earnings. Richard is married, is paid weekly, and claims 2 exemptions. What is Richard's net pay for the week if he earns $1,300?

9–28. Len Mast earned $2,200 for the last two weeks. He is married, is paid biweekly, and claims 3 exemptions. What is Len's income tax? Use the percentage method.

9–29. Westway Company pays Suzie Chan $2,200 per week. By the end of week 50, how much did Westway deduct for Suzie's Social Security and Medicare for the year? Assume Social Security is 6.2% on $97,500 and 1.45% for Medicare. What state and federal unemployment taxes does Westway pay on Suzie's yearly salary? The state unemployment rate is 5.1%. FUTA is .8%.

9–30. Morris Leste, owner of Carlson Company, has three employees who earn $400, $500, and $700 per week. What are the total state and federal unemployment taxes that Morris owes for the first 11 weeks of the year and for week 30? Assume a state rate of 5.6% and a federal rate of .8%.

CHALLENGE PROBLEMS

9–31. The Victorville, California, *Daily Press* stated that the San Bernardino County Fair hires about 150 people during fair time. Their wages range from $6.75 to $8.00. California has a state income tax of 9%. Sandy Denny earns $8.00 per hour; George Barney earns $6.75 per hour. They both worked 35 hours this week. Both are married; however, Sandy claims 2 exemptions and George claims 1 exemption. Assume a rate of 6.2% on $97,500 for Social Security and 1.45% for Medicare. **(a)** What is Sandy's net pay after FIT, Social Security tax, state income tax, and Medicare have been taken out? **(b)** What is George's net pay after the same deductions? **(c)** How much more is Sandy's net pay versus George's net pay? Round to the nearest cent.

9–32. Bill Rose is a salesperson for Boxes, Inc. He believes his $1,460.47 monthly paycheck is in error. Bill earns a $1,400 salary per month plus a 9.5% commission on sales over $1,500. Last month, Bill had $8,250 in sales. Bill believes his traveling expenses are 16% of his weekly gross earnings before commissions. Monthly deductions include Social Security, $126.56; Medicare, $29.60; FIT, $239.29; union dues, $25.00; and health insurance, $16.99. Calculate the following: **(a)** Bill's monthly take-home pay, and indicate the amount his check was under- or overstated, and **(b)** Bill's weekly traveling expenses. Round your final answer to the nearest dollar.

1. Calculate Sam's gross pay (he is entitled to time-and-a-half). *(p. 237)*

M	T	W	Th	F	Total hours	Rate per hour	Gross pay
$9\frac{1}{4}$	$9\frac{1}{4}$	$10\frac{1}{2}$	$8\frac{1}{2}$	$11\frac{1}{2}$		$8.00	

2. Mia Kaminsky sells shoes for Macy's. Macy's pays Mia $12 per hour plus a 5% commission on all sales. Assume Mia works 37 hours for the week and has $7,000 in sales. What is Mia's gross pay? *(p. 237)*

3. Lee Company pays its employees on a graduated commission scale: 6% on the first $40,000 sales, 7% on sales from $40,001 to $80,000, and 13% on sales of more than $80,000. May West, an employee of Lee, has $230,000 in sales. What commission did May earn? *(p. 239)*

4. Matty Kim, an accountant for Vernitron, earned $90,000 from January to June. In July, Matty earned $20,000. Assume a tax rate of 6.2% for Social Security on $97,500 and 1.45% on Medicare. How much are the July taxes for Social Security and Medicare? *(p. 241)*

5. Grace Kelley earns $2,000 per week. She is married and claims 2 exemptions. What is Grace's income tax? Use the percentage method. *(p. 242)*

6. Jean Michaud pays his two employees $900 and $1,200 per week. Assume a state unemployment tax rate of 5.7% and a federal unemployment tax rate of .8%. What state and federal unemployment taxes will Jean pay at the end of quarter 1 and quarter 2? *(p. 244)*

● Short-term policies can pay the bills if a young adult needs medical care.

CORBIS

INSURANCE | Earning a diploma often means losing medical coverage.

HEALTHY choices

Although finding a job may be the top priority for most new college graduates, parents are often more concerned about continuing their children's health coverage. Insurers typically drop kids from their parents' health plan once they grab that diploma (or by the time they turn 25).

Sandy D'Annunzio, a nurse in Sterling Heights, Mich., bought short-term health-insurance policies from Golden Rule (www .goldenrule.com) for her two daughters, Jennifer and Kelly. D'Annunzio pays about $57 a month for each policy, both of which have a $1,000 deductible and 20% co-insurance (meaning the insurer picks up 80% of a claim after the deductible is met). "If one of them broke a leg, it could cost 70 times as much," says D'Annunzio.

Most short-term policies last six months to a year, after which you may reapply, as long as you remain healthy. But they don't typically cover preventive care or preexisting conditions, so they're really just a temporary fix.

For longer coverage, consider an individual policy with a high deductible. For a policy with a $1,500 deductible and 20% co-insurance, a young female nonsmoker would pay $124 per month in Chicago. That's more expensive than short-term insurance, but it covers many of the medical expenses that short-term policies exclude.

If graduation is still a few months away, buying student health insurance may be a cheaper way to go. But don't delay. Assurant Health, a major provider of such plans, requires that coverage begin at least 31 days *before* a student graduates.

Like short-term health insurance, student health coverage has a long list of exclusions. But in most cases, it is less expensive than a short-term policy and is renewable. For example, a 22-year-old female non-smoker in Chicago would pay $66 a month for a student health policy with a $1,000 deductible and 20% co-insurance through eHealthInsurance.com. A similar short-term policy would cost $104 a month.

If your child has a medical condition, such as asthma or depression, buying individual health insurance can be tough. In that case, take advantage of COBRA; the law allows your adult child to remain on your policy for up to 36 months. COBRA coverage isn't cheap because you have to pay both the employer share and the employee share of your group premium, but it can serve as a safety net while you look into other options. A number of states are taking steps to extend coverage for young adults.
——**THOMAS M. ANDERSON**

BUSINESS MATH ISSUE

If you're young you really don't need health insurance.

1. List the key points of the article and information to support your position.
2. Write a group defense of your position using math calculations to support your view.

Slater's Business Math Scrapbook

with Internet Application

Putting Your Skills to Work

PROJECT A

Do you think FedEx employees should be independent contractors?

FedEx Introduces Concessions To Drivers Amid Labor Discord

By Corey Dade

FedEx Corp., facing mounting regulatory and labor challenges to the use of independent contractors to drive delivery trucks in its FedEx Ground unit, is quietly rolling out concessions to more than 15,000 drivers.

The move comes as the Memphis, Tenn., company was dealt the latest in a series of setbacks on the issue Friday. The National Labor Relations Board announced that 32 drivers at two ground terminals in Wilmington, Mass., voted to join the International Brotherhood of Teamsters.

In part to quell complaints and head off further union efforts, FedEx, which is challenging the vote, recently began stationing 18 contractor "advocates," some pulled from the ranks of contract drivers, across North America. The company says they are responsible for helping drivers increase their shipment volumes, solve problems they might have with management, and other duties. The company also is creating an executive position in charge of contractor relations, reporting directly to the head of the ground unit. FedEx also has increased fuel subsidies to drivers who operate multiple trucks and is eliminating some fines on drivers resulting from customer claims of failed deliveries.

The Teamsters have targeted FedEx Ground, which specializes in lower-cost deliveries using a ground-based truck network, as one of its top priorities in a push to build membership. The union already represents nearly 250,000 drivers and others at **United Parcel Service Inc.** Sean O'Brien, president of the Teamsters Local 25 in Boston, said the FedEx vote was "historical and should also be inspirational to labor across the country."

The only major employee group represented by a union at FedEx is its pilots, and the company has argued strongly that its employees don't need or want union representation. Drivers in the company's FedEx Ground unit are classified not as employees but independent contractors who own and manage their own vehicles, routes and schedules. As contractors, they are also unable to organize themselves as a union and engage in collective bargaining with the company.

But several drivers, some with the backing of the Teamsters, recently have challenged their classification as independent contractors, saying FedEx doesn't actually allow them to set their own schedules or manage their business affairs. A California court determined that a group of drivers in that state were employees and ordered FedEx to pay the workers $5.3 million as part of an $18 million award. FedEx is appealing and oral arguments are scheduled to begin on Tuesday.

PROJECT B

Why do you think Indian law forbids overtime?

A Stitch in Time

Orient Craft could boost capacity by 25% at its New Delhi factories, such as the one above, if workers did two extra hours of overtime a day, something not allowed under Indian law, says the company's chairman. At right, combined U.S. and EU clothing imports from India and China, from January through July, in billions

China	2004	$14.1
	2005	$22.0
India		$3.8
		$4.9

Sources: International Labor Organization; Global Trade Atlas

Internet Projects: See text Web site (www.mhhe.com/slater9e) and The Business Math Internet Resource Guide.

Video Case

Washburn International, founded in 1883, makes 80 models of instruments, both custom and for the mass market. Washburn is a privately held company with over 100 employees and annual sales of $48 million. This compares to its annual sales of $300,000 when Rudy Schlacher took over in 1976. When he acquired the company, about 250 guitars were produced per month; now 15,000 are produced each month.

The Washburn tradition of craftsmanship and innovation has withstood the tests of economics, brand competition, and fashion. Since its birth in Chicago, the name Washburn has been branded into the world's finest stringed instruments. To maintain quality, Washburn must have an excellent pool of qualified employees who are passionate about craftsmanship.

Washburn consolidated its four divisions in an expansive new 130,000 square foot plant in Mundelein, Illinois. The catalyst for consolidating operations in Mundelein was a chronic labor shortage in Elkhart and Chicago. The Mundelein plant was the ideal home for all Washburn operations because it had the necessary space, was cost effective, and gave Washburn access to a labor pool.

To grow profitably, Washburn must also sell its other products. To keep Washburn's 16 domestic salespeople tuned in to the full line, the company offers an override incentive. It is essential that to produce quality guitars, Washburn must keep recruiting dedicated, well-qualified, and team-oriented employees and provide them with profitable incentives.

PROBLEM 1

$120,000 was paid to 16 of Washburn's salespeople in override commissions. **(a)** What was the average amount paid to each salesperson? **(b)** What amount of the average sales commission will go toward the salesperson's Social Security tax? **(c)** What amount will go toward Medicare?

PROBLEM 2

Washburn is seeking a Sales and Marketing Coordinator with a bachelor's degree or equivalent experience, knowledgeable in Microsoft Office. This position pays $25,000 to $35,000, depending on experience. Assume a person is paid weekly and earns $32,500. Using the percentage method, what would be the taxes withheld for a married person who claims 3 exemptions?

PROBLEM 3

Guitarists hoping for a little country music magic in their playing can now buy an instrument carved out of oak pews from the former home of the Grand Ole Opry. Only 243 of the Ryman Limited Edition Acoustic Guitars are being made, each costing $6,250. Among the first customers were singers Vince Gill, Amy Grant, and Loretta Lynn, Ms. Lynn purchased two guitars. What would be the total revenue received by Washburn if all the guitars are sold?

PROBLEM 4

Under Washburn's old pay system, phone reps received a commission of 1.5% only on instruments they sold. Now the phone reps are paid an extra .75% commission on field sales made in their territory; the outside salespeople still get a commission up to 8%, freeing them to focus on introducing new products and holding in-store clinics. Assume sales were $65,500: **(a)** How much would phone reps receive? **(b)** How much would the outside salespeople receive?

PROBLEM 5

Washburn introduced the Limited Edition EA27 Gregg Allman Signature Series Festival guitar—only 500 guitars were produced with a selling price of $1,449.90. If Washburn's markup is 35% on selling price, what was Washburn's total cost for the 500 guitars?

PROBLEM 6

Retailers purchased $511 million worth of guitars from manufacturers—some 861,300 guitars—according to a study done by the National Association of Music Merchants. **(a)** What would be the average selling price of a guitar? **(b)** Based on the average selling price, if manufacturer's markup on cost is 40%, what would be the average cost?

PROBLEM 7

A Model NV 300 acoustic-electric guitar is being sold for a list price of $1,899.90, with a cash discount of 3/10, n/30. Sales tax is 7% and shipping is $30.40. How much is the final price if the cash discount period was met?

PROBLEM 8

A Model M3SWE mandolin has a list price of $1,299.90, with a chain discount of 5/3/2. **(a)** What would be the trade discount amount? **(b)** What would be the net price?

PROBLEM 9

A purchase was made of 2 Model J282DL six-string acoustic guitars at $799.90 each, with cases priced at $159.90, and 3 Model EA10 festival series acoustic-electric guitars at $729.90, with cases listed at $149.90. If sales tax is 6%, what is the total cost?

PROBLEM 10

Production of guitars has increased by what percent since Rudy Schlacher took over Washburn?

CHAPTER 10

Simple Interest

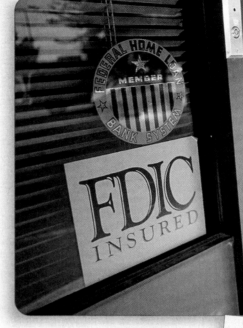

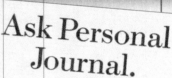

LEARNING UNIT OBJECTIVES

LU 10–1: Calculation of Simple Interest and Maturity Value

- Calculate simple interest and maturity value for months and years *(p. 259)*.
- Calculate simple interest and maturity value by **(a)** exact interest and **(b)** ordinary interest *(pp. 260–261)*.

LU 10–2: Finding Unknown in Simple Interest Formula

- Using the interest formula, calculate the unknown when the other two (principal, rate, or time) are given *(pp. 262–263)*.

LU 10–3: U.S. Rule—Making Partial Note Payments before Due Date

- List the steps to complete the U.S. Rule *(pp. 264–265)*.
- Complete the proper interest credits under the U.S. Rule *(pp. 264–265)*.

Ask Personal Journal.

Q: *Is a bank's insolvency all that the FDIC insures for and only up to $100,000? Do banks cover situations like fraud or identity theft?*
—LAUREL GONSALVES, NEW YORK

A: The Federal Deposit Insurance Corp. insures deposits only when banks fail and only up to $100,000. Customers tend to get about 72 to 73 cents for each dollar above that, the FDIC says. As for unauthorized transactions, your bank will generally refund the full amount if you notify it in a timely manner, says Nessa Feddis, senior federal counsel for the American Bankers Association. How soon you have to notify your bank and your liability (typically $50 to $500) depends on the transaction, since electronic and paper transactions fall under different laws. Your bank will typically investigate to make sure you didn't give authorization. If a relative or friend was responsible for a fraud, you may have trouble getting your money.
—*Jennifer Saranow*

Wall Street Journal © 2005

Digital Vision/Getty Images

Major Issuers Boost Costs For Late Payments Past 30% Amid Rising Interest Rates

By JANE J. KIM

Being late on your credit-card payments has never been more expensive, as penalty rates among major credit-card issuers hit new highs.

Some major issuers, including **J.P. Morgan Chase** & Co., **Citigroup** Inc.'s Citibank and **Bank of America** Corp., are now charging maximum penalty rates that have edged past 30%. Although some banks charge a fixed penalty rate, other rates are typically tied to the prime rate—

the rate banks charge their best customers—plus a fixed percentage that varies by bank. Now, many of those variable rates are expected to climb even higher given the Federal Reserve's increase in the short-term interest rate to 3.5% this week, which pushes the prime rate to 6.5%.

Penalty rates, which become the new rate paid on any outstanding balances, typically kick in when cardholders are late on a payment or two, exceed their credit limit or bounce a check. Bank of America's penalty rate, for example, could apply if cardholders miss two consecutive payments or are past due two times within a six-month period, according to a company spokeswoman.

Wall Street Journal © 2005

Are you careless about making your credit payments on time? Do you realize that some penalty rates can increase when the Federal Reserve increases its short-term interest rate? The *Wall Street Journal* clipping "Major Issuers Boost Costs for Late Payment Past 30% Amid Rising Interest Rates" shows how expensive it can be if you do not pay your credit bills on time, if you bounce checks, or if you exceed your credit limit.

In this chapter, you will study simple interest. The principles discussed apply whether you are paying interest or receiving interest. Let's begin by learning how to calculate simple interest.

Learning Unit 10–1: Calculation of Simple Interest and Maturity Value

Jan Carley, a young attorney, rented an office in a professional building. Since Jan recently graduated from law school, she was short of cash. To purchase office furniture for her new office, Jan went to her bank and borrowed $30,000 for 6 months at an 8% annual interest rate.

The original amount Jan borrowed ($30,000) is the **principal** (face value) of the loan. Jan's price for using the $30,000 is the interest rate (8%) the bank charges on a yearly basis. Since Jan is borrowing the $30,000 for 6 months, Jan's loan will have a **maturity value** of $31,200—the principal plus the interest on the loan. Thus, Jan's price for using the furniture before she can pay for it is $1,200 interest, which is a percent of the principal for a specific time period. To make this calculation, we use the following formula:

$$\text{Maturity value } (MV) = \text{Principal } (P) + \text{Interest } (I)$$

$$\$31{,}200 \quad = \quad \$30{,}000 \quad + \quad \$1{,}200$$

Jan's furniture purchase introduces **simple interest**—the cost of a loan, usually for 1 year or less. Simple interest is only on the original principal or amount borrowed. Let's examine how the bank calculated Jan's $1,200 interest.

Simple Interest Formula

To calculate simple interest, we use the following **simple interest formula:**

$$\text{Simple interest } (I) = \text{Principal } (P) \times \text{Rate } (R) \times \text{Time } (T)$$

In this formula, rate is expressed as a decimal, fraction, or percent; and time is expressed in years or a fraction of a year.

EXAMPLE Jan Carley borrowed $30,000 for office furniture. The loan was for 6 months at an annual interest rate of 8%. What are Jan's interest and maturity value?

Using the simple interest formula, the bank determined Jan's interest as follows:

In your calculator, multiply $30,000 times .08 times 6. Divide your answer by 12. You could also use the % key—multiply $30,000 times 8% times 6 and then divide your answer by 12.

Step 1. Calculate the interest.

$$I = \$30,000 \times .08 \times \frac{6}{12}$$
$$\quad (P) \qquad (R) \quad (T)$$
$$= \$1,200$$

Step 2. Calculate the maturity value.

$$MV = \$30,000 + \$1,200$$
$$\qquad (P) \qquad (I)$$
$$= \$31,200$$

Now let's use the same example and assume Jan borrowed $30,000 for 1 year. The bank would calculate Jan's interest and maturity value as follows:

Step 1. Calculate the interest.

$$I = \$30,000 \times .08 \times 1 \text{ year}$$
$$\quad (P) \qquad (R) \qquad (T)$$
$$= \$2,400$$

Step 2. Calculate the maturity value.

$$MV = \$30,000 + \$2,400$$
$$\qquad (P) \qquad (I)$$
$$= \$32,400$$

Let's use the same example again and assume Jan borrowed $30,000 for 18 months. Then Jan's interest and maturity value would be calculated as follows:

Step 1. Calculate the interest.

$$I = \$30,000 \times .08 \times \frac{18^{1}}{12}$$
$$\quad (P) \qquad (R) \quad (T)$$
$$= \$3,600$$

Step 2. Calculate the maturity value.

$$MV = \$30,000 + \$3,600$$
$$\qquad (P) \qquad (I)$$
$$= \$33,600$$

Next we'll turn our attention to two common methods we can use to calculate simple interest when a loan specifies its beginning and ending dates.

Two Methods for Calculating Simple Interest and Maturity Value

Method 1: Exact Interest (365 Days) The Federal Reserve banks and the federal government use the **exact interest** method. The *exact interest* is calculated by using a 365-day year. For **time,** we count the exact number of days in the month that the borrower has the loan. The day the loan is made is not counted, but the day the money is returned is counted as a full day. This method calculates interest by using the following fraction to represent time in the formula:

$$\text{Time} = \frac{\text{Exact number of days}}{365} \longleftarrow \text{Exact interest}$$

For this calculation, we use the exact days-in-a-year calendar from the *Business Math Handbook*. You learned how to use this calendar in Chapter 7, p. 181.

EXAMPLE On March 4, Peg Carry borrowed $40,000 at 8% interest. Interest and principal are due on July 6. What is the interest cost and the maturity value?

Step 1. Calculate the interest.

$$I = P \times R \times T$$
$$= \$40,000 \times .08 \times \frac{124}{365}$$
$$= \$1,087.12 \text{ (rounded to nearest cent)}$$

From the *Business Math Handbook*

July 6	187th day
March 4	− 63rd day
	124 days (exact time of loan)
March	31
	− 4
	27
April	30
May	31
June	30
July	+ 6
	124 days

[1]This is the same as 1.5 years.

Step 2.   Calculate the maturity value.

$$MV = P + I$$
$$= \$40,000 + \$1,087.12$$
$$= \boxed{\$41,087.12}$$

Method 2: Ordinary Interest (360 Days) In the **ordinary interest** method, time in the formula $I = P \times R \times T$ is equal to the following:

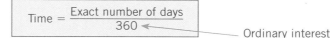

$$\text{Time} = \frac{\text{Exact number of days}}{360} \longleftarrow \text{Ordinary interest}$$

Since banks commonly use the ordinary interest method, it is known as the **Banker's Rule.** Banks charge a slightly higher rate of interest because they use 360 days instead of 365 in the denominator. By using 360 instead of 365, the calculation is supposedly simplified. Consumer groups, however, are questioning why banks can use 360 days, since this benefits the bank and not the customer. The use of computers and calculators no longer makes the simplified calculation necessary. For example, after a court case in Oregon, banks began calculating interest on 365 days except in mortgages.

Now let's replay the Peg Carry example we used to illustrate Method 1 to see the difference in bank interest when we use Method 2.

EXAMPLE   On March 4, Peg Carry borrowed $40,000 at 8% interest. Interest and principal are due on July 6. What are the interest cost and the maturity value?

Step 1.   Calculate the interest.

$$I = \$40,000 \times .08 \times \frac{124}{360}$$
$$= \$1,102.22$$

Step 2.   Calculate the maturity value.

$$MV = P + I$$
$$= \$40,000 + \$1,102.22$$
$$= \boxed{\$41,102.22}$$

Note: By using Method 2, the bank increases its interest by $15.10.

$$
\begin{array}{r}
\$1,102.22 \leftarrow \text{Method 2} \\
- \ 1,087.12 \\
\hline
\$ \quad 15.10 \leftarrow \text{Method 1}
\end{array}
$$

Now you should be ready for your first Practice Quiz in this chapter.

LU 10–1   PRACTICE QUIZ

Complete this **Practice Quiz** to see how you are doing

Calculate simple interest (round to the nearest cent):

1. $14,000 at 4% for 9 months   **2.** $25,000 at 7% for 5 years
3. $40,000 at $10\frac{1}{2}$% for 19 months
4.   On May 4, Dawn Kristal borrowed $15,000 at 8%. Dawn must pay the principal and interest on August 10. What are Dawn's simple interest and maturity value if you use the exact interest method?
5.   What are Dawn Kristal's (Problem 4) simple interest and maturity value if you use the ordinary interest method?

✓ **Solutions**

1. $\$14,000 \times .04 \times \dfrac{9}{12} = \boxed{\$420}$

2. $\$25,000 \times .07 \times 5 = \boxed{\$8,750}$

3. $\$40,000 \times .105 \times \dfrac{19}{12} = \boxed{\$6,650}$

4. August 10 → 222 $15,000 \times .08 \times \dfrac{98}{365} = $ 322.19

May 4 → -124

98 $MV = \$15,000 + \$322.19 = \$15,322.19$

5. $15,000 \times .08 \times \dfrac{98}{360} = $ 326.67 $MV = \$15,000 + \$326.67 = \$15,326.67$

LU 10–1a EXTRA PRACTICE QUIZ

Need more practice? Try this **Extra Practice Quiz** (check figures in Chapter Organizer, p. 267)

Calculate simple interest (round to the nearest cent):

1. $16,000 at 3% for 8 months
2. $15,000 at 6% for 6 years
3. $50,000 at 7% for 18 months
4. On May 6, Dawn Kristal borrowed $20,000 at 7%. Dawn must pay the principal and interest on August 14. What are Dawn's simple interest and maturity value if you use the exact interest method?
5. What are Dawn Kristal's (Problem 4) simple interest and maturity value if you use the ordinary interest method?

Learning Unit 10–2: Finding Unknown in Simple Interest Formula

This unit begins with the formula used to calculate the principal of a loan. Then it explains how to find the *principal*, *rate*, and *time* of a simple interest loan. In all the calculations, we use 360 days and round only final answers.

Finding the Principal

EXAMPLE Tim Jarvis paid the bank $19.48 interest at 9.5% for 90 days. How much did Tim borrow using ordinary interest method?

The following formula is used to calculate the principal of a loan:

$$\text{Principal} = \frac{\text{Interest}}{\text{Rate} \times \text{Time}}$$

Note how we illustrated this in the margin. The shaded area is what we are solving for. When solving for principal, rate, or time, you are dividing. Interest will be in the numerator, and the denominator will be the other two elements multiplied by each other.

Step 1. Set up the formula.

$$P = \frac{\$19.48}{.095 \times \dfrac{90}{360}}$$

Step 2. When using a calculator, press

.095 × 90 ÷ 360 M+ .

Step 2. Multiply the denominator.

.095 times 90 divided by 360 (do not round)

$$P = \frac{\$19.48}{.02375}$$

Step 3. When using a calculator, press

19.48 ÷ MR = .

Step 3. Divide the numerator by the result of Step 2.

$P = 820.21

Step 4. Check your answer.

$$\$19.48 = \$820.21 \times .095 \times \frac{90}{360}$$

(I) (P) (R) (T)

Finding the Rate

EXAMPLE Tim Jarvis borrowed $820.21 from a bank. Tim's interest is $19.48 for 90 days. What rate of interest did Tim pay using ordinary interest method?

The following formula is used to calculate the rate of interest:

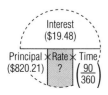

$$\text{Rate} = \frac{\text{Interest}}{\text{Principal} \times \text{Time}}$$

Step 1.	Set up the formula.	$R = \dfrac{\$19.48}{\$820.21 \times \dfrac{90}{360}}$

Step 2.	Multiply the denominator. Do not round the answer.	$R = \dfrac{\$19.48}{\$205.0525}$

Step 3.	Divide the numerator by the result of Step 2.	$R = 9.5\%$

Step 4.	Check your answer.	$\$19.48 = \$820.21 \times .095 \times \dfrac{90}{360}$

$$(I) \qquad (P) \qquad (R) \quad (T)$$

Finding the Time

EXAMPLE   Tim Jarvis borrowed $820.21 from a bank. Tim's interest is $19.48 at 9.5%. How much time does Tim have to repay the loan using ordinary interest method?
The following formula is used to calculate time:

$$\text{Time (in years)} = \frac{\text{Interest}}{\text{Principal} \times \text{Rate}}$$

Interest
($19.48)

Principal × Rate × Time
($820.21) | (.095) | ?

Step 2. When using a calculator, press

820.21 × .095 M+ .

Step 3. When using a calculator, press

19.48 ÷ MR = .

Step 1.	Set up the formula.	$T = \dfrac{\$19.48}{\$820.21 \times .095}$

Step 2.	Multiply the denominator. Do not round the answer.	$T = \dfrac{\$19.48}{\$77.91995}$

Step 3.	Divide the numerator by the result of Step 2.	$T = .25$ years

Step 4.	Convert years to days (assume 360 days).	$.25 \times 360 = $ **90 days**

Step 5.	Check your answer.	$\$19.48 = \$820.21 \times .095 \times \dfrac{90}{360}$

$$(I) \qquad (P) \qquad (R) \qquad (T)$$

Before we go on to Learning Unit 10–3, let's check your understanding of this unit.

LU 10–2	PRACTICE QUIZ

Complete this **Practice Quiz** to see how you are doing

Complete the following (assume 360 days):

	Principal	Interest rate	Time (days)	Simple interest
1.	?	5%	90 days	$8,000
2.	$7,000	?	220 days	350
3.	$1,000	8%	?	300

✓ **Solutions**

1. $\dfrac{\$8,000}{.05 \times \dfrac{90}{360}} = \dfrac{\$8,000}{.0125} = $ **$640,000** $\qquad P = \dfrac{I}{R \times T}$

2. $\dfrac{\$350}{\$7,000 \times \dfrac{220}{360}} = \dfrac{\$350}{\$4,277.7777} = $ **8.18%** $\qquad R = \dfrac{I}{P \times T}$

(do not round)

3. $\dfrac{\$300}{\$1,000 \times .08} = \dfrac{\$300}{\$80} = 3.75 \times 360 = $ **1,350 days** $\qquad T = \dfrac{I}{P \times R}$

LU 10–2a EXTRA PRACTICE QUIZ

Complete the following (assume 360 days):

	Principal	Interest rate	Time (days)	Simple interest
1.	?	4%	90 days	$9,000
2.	$6,000	?	180 days	280
3.	$900	6%	?	190

Learning Unit 10–3: U.S. Rule—Making Partial Note Payments before Due Date

Often a person may want to pay off a debt in more than one payment before the maturity date. The **U.S. Rule** allows the borrower to receive proper interest credits. This rule states that any partial loan payment first covers any interest that has built up. The remainder of the partial payment reduces the loan principal. Courts or legal proceedings generally use the U.S. Rule. The Supreme Court originated the U.S. Rule in the case of *Story* v. *Livingston*.

EXAMPLE   Joe Mill owes $5,000 on an 11%, 90-day note. On day 50, Joe pays $600 on the note. On day 80, Joe makes an $800 additional payment. Assume a 360-day year. What is Joe's adjusted balance after day 50 and after day 80? What is the ending balance due?

To calculate $600 payment on day 50:

Step 1. Calculate interest on principal from date of loan to date of first principal payment. Round to nearest cent.

$I = P \times R \times T$

$I = \$5,000 \times .11 \times \dfrac{50}{360}$

$I = \$76.39$

Step 2. Apply partial payment to interest due. Subtract remainder of payment from principal. This is the **adjusted balance** (principal).

$\$600.00$ payment
$- \quad 76.39$ interest
$\$523.61$

$\$5,000.00$ principal
$- \quad 523.61$
$\$4,476.39$ adjusted balance— principal

To calculate $800 payment on day 80:

Step 3. Calculate interest on adjusted balance that starts from previous payment date and goes to new payment date. Then apply Step 2.

Compute interest on $4,476.39 for 30 days (80 − 50)

$I = \$4,476.39 \times .11 \times \dfrac{30}{360}$

$I = \$41.03$

$\$800.00$ payment
$- \quad 41.03$ interest
$\$758.97$

$\$4,476.39$
$- \quad 758.97$
$\$3,717.42$ adjusted balance

Step 4. At maturity, calculate interest from last partial payment. *Add* this interest to adjusted balance.

Ten days are left on note since last payment.

$I = \$3,717.42 \times .11 \times \dfrac{10}{360}$

$I = \$11.36$

Balance owed = $\$3,728.78$ $\left(\begin{array}{r} \$3,717.42 \\ + \quad 11.36 \end{array} \right)$

Note that when Joe makes two partial payments, Joe's total interest is $128.78 ($76.39 + $41.03 + $11.36). If Joe had repaid the entire loan after 90 days, his interest payment would have been $137.50—a total savings of $8.72.

Let's check your understanding of the last unit in this chapter.

LU 10–3 | PRACTICE QUIZ

Complete this **Practice Quiz** to see how you are doing

Polly Flin borrowed $5,000 for 60 days at 8%. On day 10, Polly made a $600 partial payment. On day 40, Polly made a $1,900 partial payment. What is Polly's ending balance due under the U.S. Rule (assume a 360-day year)?

✓ **Solutions**

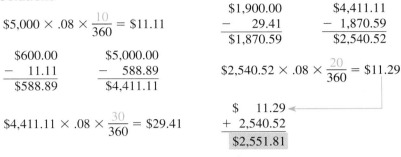

$$\$5,000 \times .08 \times \frac{10}{360} = \$11.11$$

$$
\begin{array}{r}
\$1,900.00 \\
- \quad 29.41 \\
\hline
\$1,870.59
\end{array}
\qquad
\begin{array}{r}
\$4,411.11 \\
- \ 1,870.59 \\
\hline
\$2,540.52
\end{array}
$$

$$
\begin{array}{r}
\$600.00 \\
- \quad 11.11 \\
\hline
\$588.89
\end{array}
\qquad
\begin{array}{r}
\$5,000.00 \\
- \quad 588.89 \\
\hline
\$4,411.11
\end{array}
$$

$$\$2,540.52 \times .08 \times \frac{20}{360} = \$11.29$$

$$\$4,411.11 \times .08 \times \frac{30}{360} = \$29.41$$

$$
\begin{array}{r}
\$ \quad 11.29 \\
+ \ 2,540.52 \\
\hline
\boxed{\$2,551.81}
\end{array}
$$

LU 10–3a | EXTRA PRACTICE QUIZ

Need more practice? Try this **Extra Practice Quiz** (check figures in Chapter Organizer, p. 267)

Polly Flin borrowed $4,000 for 60 days at 4%. On day 15, Polly made a $700 partial payment. On day 40, Polly made a $2,000 partial payment. What is Polly's ending balance due under the U.S. Rule (assume a 360-day year)?

CHAPTER ORGANIZER AND STUDY GUIDE
WITH CHECK FIGURES FOR EXTRA PRACTICE QUIZZES

Topic	Key point, procedure, formula	Example(s) to illustrate situation
Simple interest for months, p. 259	Interest = Principal × Rate × Time 　(*I*)　　(*P*)　　(*R*)　(*T*)	$2,000 at 9% for 17 months $I = \$2,000 \times .09 \times \frac{17}{12}$ $I = \boxed{\$255}$
Exact interest, p. 260	$T = \dfrac{\text{Exact number of days}}{365}$ $I = P \times R \times T$	$1,000 at 10% from January 5 to February 20 $I = \$1,000 \times .10 \times \frac{46}{365}$ Feb. 20:　51 days Jan. 5:　− 5 　　　　46 days $I = \boxed{\$12.60}$
Ordinary interest (Bankers Rule), p. 261	$T = \dfrac{\text{Exact number of days}}{360}$ $I = P \times R \times T$　 Higher interest costs	$I = \$1,000 \times .10 \times \frac{46}{360}$ (51 − 5) $I = \boxed{\$12.78}$
Finding unknown in simple interest formula (use 360 days), p. 262	$I = P \times R \times T$	Use this example for illustrations of simple interest formula parts: $1,000 loan at 9%, 60 days $I = \$1,000 \times .09 \times \frac{60}{360} = \boxed{\$15}$

(continues)

CHAPTER ORGANIZER AND STUDY GUIDE
WITH CHECK FIGURES FOR EXTRA PRACTICE QUIZZES (continued)

Topic	Key point, procedure, formula	Example(s) to illustrate situation
Finding the principal, p. 262	$P = \dfrac{I}{R \times T}$	$P = \dfrac{\$15}{.09 \times \dfrac{60}{360}} = \dfrac{\$15}{.015} = \boxed{\$1,000}$
Finding the rate, p. 262	$R = \dfrac{I}{P \times T}$	$R = \dfrac{\$15}{\$1,000 \times \dfrac{60}{360}} = \dfrac{\$15}{166.66666} = .09$ $= \boxed{9\%}$ *Note:* We did not round the denominator.
Finding the time, p. 263	$T = \dfrac{I}{P \times R}$ (in years) Multiply answer by 360 days to convert answer to days for ordinary interest.	$T = \dfrac{\$15}{\$1,000 \times .09} = \dfrac{\$15}{\$90} = .1666666$ $.1666666 \times 360 = 59.99 = \boxed{60 \text{ days}}$
U.S. Rule (use 360 days), p. 264	Calculate interest on principal from date of loan to date of first partial payment. Calculate adjusted balance by subtracting from principal the partial payment less interest cost. The process continues for future partial payments with the adjusted balance used to calculate cost of interest from last payment to present payment. Balance owed equals last adjusted balance plus interest cost from last partial payment to final due date.	12%, 120 days, $2,000 *Partial payments:* On day 40; $250 On day 60; $200 *First payment:* $I = \$2,000 \times .12 \times \dfrac{40}{360}$ $I = \$26.67$ $\begin{array}{r} \$250.00 \text{ payment} \\ -\ 26.67 \text{ interest} \\ \hline \$223.33 \end{array}$ $\begin{array}{r} \$2,000.00 \text{ principal} \\ -\ 223.33 \\ \hline \$1,776.67 \text{ adjusted balance} \end{array}$ *Second payment:* $I = \$1,776.67 \times .12 \times \dfrac{20}{360}$ $I = \$11.84$ $\begin{array}{r} \$200.00 \text{ payment} \\ -\ 11.84 \text{ interest} \\ \hline \$188.16 \end{array}$ $\begin{array}{r} \$1,776.67 \\ -\ 188.16 \\ \hline \$1,588.51 \text{ adjusted balance} \end{array}$ *60 days left:* $\$1,588.51 \times .12 \times \dfrac{60}{360} = \$31.77$ $\$1,588.51 + \$31.77 = \boxed{\$1,620.28 \text{ balance due}}$ $\begin{array}{r} \text{Total interest} = \ \ \$26.67 \\ 11.84 \\ +\ 31.77 \\ \hline \$70.28 \end{array}$

(continues)

CHAPTER ORGANIZER AND STUDY GUIDE
WITH CHECK FIGURES FOR EXTRA PRACTICE QUIZZES (concluded)

Topic	Key point, procedure, formula		Example(s) to illustrate situation
KEY TERMS	Adjusted balance, *p. 264* Banker's Rule, *p. 261* Exact interest, *p. 260* Interest, *p. 259*	Maturity value, *p. 259* Ordinary interest, *p. 261* Principal, *p. 259* Simple interest, *p. 259*	Simple interest formula, *p. 259* Time, *p. 263* U.S. Rule, *p. 267*

CHECK FIGURES FOR EXTRA PRACTICE QUIZZES WITH PAGE REFERENCES	LU 10–1a (p. 262)
	1. $320
	2. $5,400
	3. $5,250
	4. $20,383.56;
	    Interest = $383.56
	5. $20,388.89;
	    Interest = $388.89
		LU 10–2a (p. 264)
		1. $900,000
		2. 9.33%
		3. 1,267 days
			LU 10–3a (p. 265)
			$1,318.78

Critical Thinking Discussion Questions

1. What is the difference between exact interest and ordinary interest? With the increase of computers in banking, do you think that the ordinary interest method is a dinosaur in business today?

2. Explain how to use the portion formula to solve the unknowns in the simple interest formula. Why would rounding the answer of the denominator result in an inaccurate final answer?

3. Explain the U.S. Rule. Why in the last step of the U.S. Rule is the interest added, not subtracted?

Classroom Notes

10–26. On September 14, Jennifer Rick went to Park Bank to borrow $2,500 at $11\frac{3}{4}$% interest. Jennifer plans to repay the loan on January 27. Assume the loan is on ordinary interest. What interest will Jennifer owe on January 27? What is the total amount Jennifer must repay at maturity?

10–27. Steven Linden met Jennifer Rick (Problem 10–26) at Park Bank and suggested she consider the loan on exact interest. Recalculate the loan for Jennifer under this assumption.

10–28. Lance Lopes went to his bank to find out how long it will take for $1,000 to amount to $1,700 at 12% simple interest. Can you solve Lance's problem? Round time in years to the nearest tenth.

10–29. Margie Pagano is buying a car. Her June monthly interest at $12\frac{1}{2}$% was $195. What was Margie's principal balance at the beginning of June? Use 360 days. Do not round the denominator before dividing.

10–30. Shawn Bixby borrowed $17,000 on a 120-day, 12% note. After 65 days, Shawn paid $2,000 on the note. On day 89, Shawn paid an additional $4,000. What is the final balance due? Determine total interest and ending balance due by the U.S. Rule. Use ordinary interest.

10–31. Carol Miller went to Europe and forgot to pay her $740 mortgage payment on her New Hampshire ski house. For her 59 days overdue on her payment, the bank charged her a penalty of $15. What was the rate of interest charged by the bank? Round to the nearest hundredth percent (assume 360 days).

10–32. Abe Wolf bought a new kitchen set at Sears. Abe paid off the loan after 60 days with an interest charge of $9. If Sears charges 10% interest, what did Abe pay for the kitchen set (assume 360 days)?

10–33. Joy Kirby made a $300 loan to Robinson Landscaping at 11%. Robinson paid back the loan with interest of $6.60. How long in days was the loan outstanding (assume 360 days)? Check your answer.

10–34. Molly Ellen, bookkeeper for Keystone Company, forgot to send in the payroll taxes due on April 15. She sent the payment November 8. The IRS sent her a penalty charge of 8% simple interest on the unpaid taxes of $4,100. Calculate the penalty. (Remember that the government uses exact interest.)

10–35. Oakwood Plowing Company purchased two new plows for the upcoming winter. In 200 days, Oakwood must make a single payment of $23,200 to pay for the plows. As of today, Oakwood has $22,500. If Oakwood puts the money in a bank today, what rate of interest will it need to pay off the plows in 200 days (assume 360 days)?

CHALLENGE PROBLEMS

10–36. The *Downers Grove Reporter* ran an ad for a used 1998 Harley-Davidson Sportster 883 for $6,750. Patrick Schmidt is interested in the motorcycle but does not have the money right now. Patrick contacted the owner on October 19, and he agreed to give Patrick a loan plus 5.5% exact interest. The loan must be paid back by December 22 of the same year. The First National Bank will lend the $6,750 at 5%. Patrick would have 3 months to pay off the loan. **(a)** What is the total amount Patrick will have to pay the owner of the motorcycle assuming exact interest? **(b)** What is the total amount Patrick will have to pay the bank? **(c)** Which option offers the most savings to Patrick? **(d)** How much will Patrick save?

10–37. Janet Foster bought a computer and printer at Computerland. The printer had a $600 list price with a $100 trade discount and 2/10, n/30 terms. The computer had a $1,600 list price with a 25% trade discount but no cash discount. On the computer, Computerland offered Janet the choice of (1) paying $50 per month for 17 months with the 18th payment paying the remainder of the balance or (2) paying 8% interest for 18 months in equal payments.

    a. Assume Janet could borrow the money for the printer at 8% to take advantage of the cash discount. How much would Janet save (assume 360 days)?

    b. On the computer, what is the difference in the final payment between choices 1 and 2?

SUMMARY PRACTICE TEST

1. Lorna Hall's real estate tax of $2,010.88 was due on December 14, 2009. Lorna lost her job and could not pay her tax bill until February 27, 2010. The penalty for late payment is $6\frac{1}{2}\%$ ordinary interest. *(p. 261)*

   a. What is the penalty Lorna must pay?

   b. What is the total amount Lorna must pay on February 27?

2. Ann Hopkins borrowed $60,000 for her child's education. She must repay the loan at the end of 8 years in one payment with $5\frac{1}{2}\%$ interest. What is the maturity value Ann must repay? *(p. 260)*

3. On May 6, Jim Ryan borrowed $14,000 from Lane Bank at $7\frac{1}{2}\%$ interest. Jim plans to repay the loan on March 11. Assume the loan is on ordinary interest. How much will Jim repay on March 11? *(p. 261)*

4. Gail Ross met Jim Ryan (Problem 3) at Lane Bank. After talking with Jim, Gail decided she would like to consider the same loan on exact interest. Can you recalculate the loan for Gail under this assumption? *(p. 260)*

5. Claire Russell is buying a car. Her November monthly interest was $210 at $7\frac{3}{4}\%$ interest. What is Claire's principal balance (to the nearest dollar) at the beginning of November? Use 360 days. Do not round the denominator in your calculation. *(p. 262)*

6. Comet Lee borrowed $16,000 on a 6%, 90-day note. After 20 days, Comet paid $2,000 on the note. On day 50, Comet paid $4,000 on the note. What are the total interest and ending balance due by the U.S. Rule? Use ordinary interest. *(p. 264)*

Christina Pridgen, with Sara, 11, and Alex, 9.

SOLVED | Sometimes it doesn't make much sense to pay the money you owe.

My unpaid **DEBT** still haunts me

CHRISTINA Pridgen struggled with debt as she went through a divorce and began a new life for herself and her two kids. She admits she never paid $14,000 in joint credit-card debt incurred while she was married. Collectors have pretty much stopped bugging her, but she wonders: If she could find the resources to pay off the debt, would her credit rating be resurrected? "I had an excellent credit history," says Pridgen, 34, a nursing student who lives near Charlotte, N.C. "I'd like to start over."

Believe it or not, paying back the $14,000 would do little to repair Pridgen's credit history. And the black marks on her credit report will disappear in 18 months, anyway. Under federal law, a report of a bad debt must be removed seven and a half years after the first missed payment. If the creditors had sued and won a judgment against Pridgen, they'd have had at least ten years to collect. But that didn't happen—probably because of the relatively small amounts involved with each card issuer. The statute of limitations for such suits (three years in North Carolina, but as many as six elsewhere) has passed.

There's no limit on how long debt collectors can try to collect (see "Debt Police Who Go Too Far," Nov.). For now, Pridgen is best off using her limited resources to finish her education and care for her kids. She can always try to cut a deal to clear the debt—and her conscience—when she's out of school, working full-time.

Do you have a money problem we can solve? E-mail us at solved@kiplinger.com.

MIKE CARROLL

BUSINESS MATH ISSUE

Christina should never pay back the debt.

1. List the key points of the article and information to support your position.
2. Write a group defense of your position using math calculations to support your view.

Slater's Business Math Scrapbook

with Internet Application

Putting Your Skills to Work

Green Thumb / By Ron Lieber

Where to Look for Cheaper Loans

Credit Unions Often Do Better Than Banks; the 'Flower' Trick

IT'S GETTING EASIER to join a credit union—and if you're not checking their rates, you may be costing yourself a lot of money by not doing so.

That may come as a surprise. Credit unions have their roots early in the 20th century, when they were created to serve the needs of people of modest means whom banks were ignoring. Over the years, however, they've expanded their reach. Today they claim 88 million members in the U.S., including plenty of people who could just as easily use any regular bank.

Why do they choose credit unions instead? In large part because the interest rates they pay depositors are often higher, and their loan rates are frequently lower, than those at regular banks. For instance, the average credit-union 48-month used-car loan is 6.08%; at banks it's 7.94%, according to Datatrac, a research firm that surveys thousands of financial institutions for the Credit Union National Association, or CUNA.

The credit unions can afford these deals partly because they don't have to pay most income taxes. This irks bankers to no end, given they have to compete with credit unions—and pay taxes. They're fighting back: In November, the American Bankers Association filed two federal lawsuits challenging the membership rules at two credit unions.

Traditionally, it was tougher for consumers to get these deals: You often had to work for a certain company or live in a certain place.

Not anymore. Today, many credit unions are basically clubs that anyone can join. That's thanks in part to a 1998 law that permitted federal credit unions to invite other groups in who don't have much in common with each other.

Do you like flowers? Then you can join the Tower Hill Botanic Garden in Boylston, Mass.—and one of the fringe benefits is eligibility for the Digital Federal Credit Union, which is still going strong even though the Digital Equipment Corp. brand no longer is. "Everyone Can Join DCU," its Web site says. (The credit union was originally founded to serve employees.)

The Pentagon Federal Credit Union, which lends nationwide, is open to anyone who joins the National Military Family Association, an advocacy group that anyone is eligible for. "It's kind of like an affinity partnership," says NMFA's Cynthia Fox, who says that a couple thousand people join each month just to get access to PenFed.

Looking for a credit union near you with equally liberal eligibility rules? Hunt by zip code at www.creditunion.coop/cu_locator, CUNA's Web site, then check its membership regulations. Inquire where you work too, since many companies that don't have their own affiliated credit unions arrange membership eligibility elsewhere as a perk.

Big credit unions may offer better rates than smaller ones. Online banking and other technology may not be state of the art at all institutions. And you'll often find better mortgage rates elsewhere. But credit unions generally do better than their normal bank competitors on car loans, personal loans, credit cards and home-equity lending.

If something feels slightly sneaky about benefiting from a credit union that wasn't really set up with you in mind, consider this: The tax breaks they enjoy ultimately come out of your pocket.

No bankers' hours at ron.lieber@wsj.com

Getting Credit

Credit unions can offer savings on everything from credit cards to auto loans. Here's how to find one:

- Use the zip-code search at cuna.org
- Ask at work if your employment makes you eligible for membership
- Look for membership groups that bestow eligibility

Wall Street Journal © 2006

CHAPTER 11

Promissory Notes, Simple Discount Notes, and the Discount Process

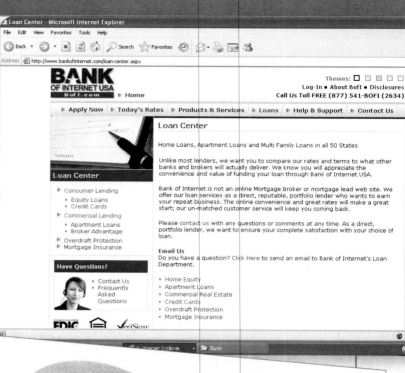

LEARNING UNIT OBJECTIVES

LU 11–1: Structure of Promissory Notes; the Simple Discount Note

- Differentiate between interest-bearing and noninterest-bearing notes (*pp. 279–280*).
- Calculate bank discount and proceeds for simple discount notes (*p. 280*).
- Calculate and compare the interest, maturity value, proceeds, and effective rate of a simple interest note with a simple discount note (*p. 281*).
- Explain and calculate the effective rate for a Treasury bill (*p. 281*).

LU 11–2: Discounting an Interest-Bearing Note before Maturity

- Calculate the maturity value, bank discount, and proceeds of discounting an interest-bearing note before maturity (*pp. 282–283*).
- Identify and complete the four steps of the discounting process (*p. 283*).

Borrowing Online

Financial-services firms are offering lower-cost alternatives to consumers who take out loans online. Here are a few new options:

COMPANY	LOAN
Bank of Internet USA (bankofinternet.com/LoanCenter)	Began offering home-equity loans online in seven states earlier this year, with a national rollout expected later this year. Annual percentage rates range from 7.1% to 7.7%. No closing costs.
Citibank (Citibank.com/lending)*	Citibank Direct plans to offer loans with lower online-only rates. The bank is promoting home-equity lines of credit with variable rates of 5.99% for six months or 7.24% for the life of the loans.
E-Loan (eloan.com)	Offers a range of online loans, including home and auto loans. The company is planning to launch personal lines of credit, with rates ranging from 7.99% to 19.99%.
Prosper.com	Offers person-to-person loans. Rates for borrowers have been averaging 8% for those with the best credit to 24% for those with the lowest or no credit. Offers 3-year loans ranging from $1,000 to $25,000.

*Web site should be active shortly.

Source: the companies

Wall Street Journal © 2006

Saks Inc.'s Debt Rating Is Cut After Default Notice on Notes

Wall Street Journal © 2005

This *Wall Street Journal* heading states that Saks is having financial problems. Unlike credit cardholders who fail to meet their financial obligations, Saks has the option of tapping a $650 million credit line to help its financial situation.

This chapter begins with a discussion of the structure of promissory notes and simple discount notes. We also look at the application of discounting with Treasury bills. The chapter concludes with an explanation of how to calculate the discounting of promissory notes.

Learning Unit 11–1: Structure of Promissory Notes; the Simple Discount Note

Although businesses frequently sign promissory notes, customers also sign promissory notes. For example, some student loans may require the signing of promissory notes. Appliance stores often ask customers to sign a promissory note when they buy large appliances on credit. In this unit, promissory notes usually involve interest payments.

Structure of Promissory Notes

To borrow money, you must find a lender (a bank or a company selling goods on credit). You must also be willing to pay for the use of the money. In Chapter 10 you learned that interest is the cost of borrowing money for periods of time.

Money lenders usually require that borrowers sign a **promissory note.** This note states that the borrower will repay a certain sum at a fixed time in the future. The note often includes the charge for the use of the money, or the rate of interest. Figure 11.1 shows a sample promissory note with its terms identified and defined. Take a moment to look at each term.

In this section you will learn the difference between interest-bearing notes and noninterest-bearing notes.

Interest-Bearing versus Noninterest-Bearing Notes

A promissory note can be interest bearing or noninterest bearing. To be **interest bearing,** the note must state the rate of interest. Since the promissory note in Figure 11.1 states that its interest is 9%, it is an interest-bearing note. When the note matures, Regal Corporation "will pay back the original amount (**face value**) borrowed plus interest. The simple interest formula (also known as the interest formula) and the maturity value formula from Chapter 10 are used for this transaction."

> Interest = Face value (principal) × Rate × Time
> Maturity value = Face value (principal) + Interest

FIGURE   11.1

Interest-bearing promissory note

$10,000 a.	LAWTON, OKLAHOMA *October 2, 2007* c.
_____ *Sixty days* b. _____ AFTER DATE we PROMISE TO PAY TO	
THE ORDER OF _____ *G.J. Equipment Company* d.	
Ten thousand and 00/100 --------------------DOLLARS.	
PAYABLE AT _____ *Able National Bank*	
VALUE RECEIVED WITH INTEREST AT _9%_ e. REGAL CORPORATION f.	
NO. _114_ DUE *December 1, 2007*	*J.M. Moore*
g.	TREASURER

a. **Face value:** Amount of money borrowed—$10,000. The face value is also the principal of the note.
b. **Term:** Length of time that the money is borrowed—60 days.
c. **Date:** The date that the note is issued—October 2, 2007.
d. **Payee:** The company extending the credit—G.J. Equipment Company.
e. **Rate:** The annual rate for the cost of borrowing the money—9%.
f. **Maker:** The company issuing the note and borrowing the money—Regal Corporation.
g. **Maturity date:** The date the principal and interest rate are due—December 1, 2007.

TABLE | **11.1**

Comparison of simple interest note and simple discount note (Calculations from the Pete Runnels example)

Simple interest note (Chapter 10)	Simple discount note (Chapter 11)
1. A promissory note for a loan with a term of usually less than 1 year. *Example:* 60 days.	1. A promissory note for a loan with a term of usually less than 1 year. *Example:* 60 days.
2. Paid back by one payment at maturity. Face value equals actual amount (or principal) of loan (this is not maturity value).	2. Paid back by one payment at maturity. Face value equals maturity value (what will be repaid).
3. Interest computed on face value or what is actually borrowed. *Example:* $186.67.	3. Interest computed on maturity value or what will be repaid and not on actual amount borrowed. *Example:* $186.67.
4. Maturity value = Face value + Interest. *Example:* $14,186.67.	4. Maturity value = Face value. *Example:* $14,000.
5. Borrower receives the face value. *Example:* $14,000.	5. Borrower receives proceeds = Face value − Bank discount. *Example:* $13,813.33.
6. Effective rate (true rate is same as rate stated on note). *Example:* 8%.	6. Effective rate is higher since interest was deducted in advance. *Example:* 8.11%.
7. Used frequently instead of the simple discount note. *Example:* 8%.	7. Not used as much now because in 1969 congressional legislation required that the true rate of interest be revealed. Still used where legislation does not apply, such as personal loans.

If you sign a **noninterest-bearing** promissory note for $10,000, you pay back $10,000 at maturity. The maturity value of a noninterest-bearing note is the same as its face value. Usually, noninterest-bearing notes occur for short time periods under special conditions. For example, money borrowed from a relative could be secured by a noninterest-bearing promissory note.

Simple Discount Note

The total amount due at the end of the loan, or the **maturity value (MV),** is the sum of the face value (principal) and interest. Some banks deduct the loan interest in advance. When banks do this, the note is a **simple discount note.**

In the simple discount note, the **bank discount** is the interest that banks deduct in advance and the **bank discount rate** is the percent of interest. The amount that the borrower receives after the bank deducts its discount from the loan's maturity value is the note's **proceeds.** Sometimes we refer to simple discount notes as noninterest-bearing notes. Remember, however, that borrowers *do* pay interest on these notes.

In the example that follows, Pete Runnels has the choice of a note with a simple interest rate (Chapter 10) or a note with a simple discount rate (Chapter 11). Table 11.1 provides a summary of the calculations made in the example and gives the key points that you should remember. Now let's study the example, and then you can review Table 11.1.

EXAMPLE   Pete Runnels has a choice of two different notes that both have a face value (principal) of $14,000 for 60 days. One note has a simple interest rate of 8%, while the other note has a simple discount rate of 8%. For each type of note, calculate **(a)** interest owed, **(b)** maturity value, **(c)** proceeds, and **(d)** effective rate.

Simple interest note—Chapter 10	Simple discount note—Chapter 11
Interest	**Interest**
a. I = Face value (principal) $\times R \times T$ $I = \$14,000 \times .08 \times \dfrac{60}{360}$ $I = \$186.67$	**a.** I = Face value (principal) $\times R \times T$ $I = \$14,000 \times .08 \times \dfrac{60}{360}$ $I = \$186.67$
Maturity value	**Maturity value**
b. MV = Face value + Interest $MV = \$14,000 + \$186.67$ $MV = \$14,186.67$	**b.** MV = Face value $MV = \$14,000$
Proceeds	**Proceeds**
c. Proceeds = Face value = $14,000	**c.** Proceeds = MV − Bank discount = $14,000 − $186.67 = $13,813.33

Simple interest note—Chapter 10	Simple discount note—Chapter 11
Effective rate	**Effective rate**
d. Rate = $\dfrac{\text{Interest}}{\text{Proceeds} \times \text{Time}}$	**d.** Rate = $\dfrac{\text{Interest}}{\text{Proceeds} \times \text{Time}}$
$= \dfrac{\$186.67}{\$14,000 \times \frac{60}{360}}$	$= \dfrac{\$186.67}{\$13,813.33 \times \frac{60}{360}}$
$= 8\%$	$= 8.11\%$

Note that the interest of $186.67 is the same for the simple interest note and the simple discount note. The maturity value of the simple discount note is the same as the face value. In the simple discount note, interest is deducted in advance, so the proceeds are less than the face value. Note that the effective rate for a simple discount note is higher than the stated rate, since the bank calculated the rate on the face of the note and not on what Pete received.

Application of Discounting—Treasury Bills

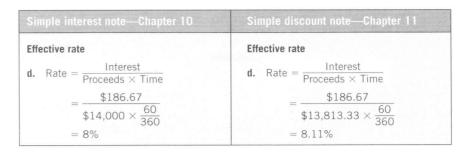

Treasury-Bill Sales Will Raise $6 Billion

WASHINGTON—The Treasury plans to raise about $6 billion of new cash next week with the sale of short-term bills.

Details of the offerings:

■ A sale on Monday to sell about $32 billion in three- and six-month bills is planned to raise about $997 million in new cash.

Maturing bills outstanding total $31 billion. The offering will be divided between $17 billion of 13-week bills and $15 billion of 26-week bills maturing on Feb. 15, 2007, and May 17, 2007, respectively.

The Cusip number for the three-month bills is 912795YT2. The Cusip number for the six-month bills is 912795ZG9.

Wall Street Journal © 2006

When the government needs money, it sells Treasury bills. A **Treasury bill** is a loan to the federal government for 28 days (4 weeks), 91 days (13 weeks), or 1 year. Note that the *Wall Street Journal* clipping Treasury—bill sales will raise $6 billion.

Treasury bills can be bought over the phone or on the government website. (See Business Math Scrapbook, page 293, for details.) The purchase price (or proceeds) of a Treasury bill is the value of the Treasury bill less the discount. For example, if you buy a $10,000, 13-week Treasury bill at 8%, you pay $9,800 since you have not yet earned your interest ($10,000 $\times$ .08 $\times \frac{13}{52}$ = $200). At maturity—13 weeks—the government pays you $10,000. You calculate your effective yield (8.16% rounded to the nearest hundredth percent) as follows:

($10,000 − $200) ⟶ $\dfrac{\$200}{\$9,800 \times \frac{13}{52}} = \boxed{8.16\%}$ effective rate

Now it's time to try the Practice Quiz and check your progress.

LU 11–1   PRACTICE QUIZ

1. Warren Ford borrowed $12,000 on a noninterest-bearing, simple discount, $9\frac{1}{2}\%$, 60-day note. Assume ordinary interest. What are **(a)** the maturity value, **(b)** the bank's discount, **(c)** Warren's proceeds, and **(d)** the effective rate to the nearest hundredth percent?

2. Jane Long buys a $10,000, 13-week Treasury bill at 6%. What is her effective rate? Round to the nearest hundredth percent.

✓ Solutions

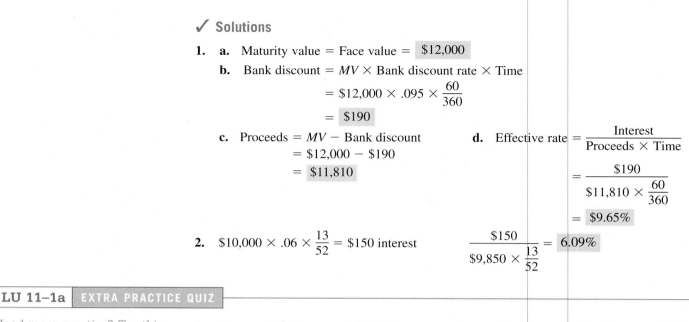

1. **a.** Maturity value = Face value = $12,000
   b. Bank discount = *MV* × Bank discount rate × Time
   $$= \$12{,}000 \times .095 \times \frac{60}{360}$$
   $$= \$190$$
   c. Proceeds = *MV* − Bank discount
   $$= \$12{,}000 - \$190$$
   $$= \$11{,}810$$
   d. Effective rate $= \dfrac{\text{Interest}}{\text{Proceeds} \times \text{Time}}$
   $$= \frac{\$190}{\$11{,}810 \times \frac{60}{360}}$$
   $$= \$9.65\%$$

2. $\$10{,}000 \times .06 \times \dfrac{13}{52} = \$150$ interest
   $$\frac{\$150}{\$9{,}850 \times \frac{13}{52}} = 6.09\%$$

LU 11–1a EXTRA PRACTICE QUIZ

Need more practice? Try this **Extra Practice Quiz** (check figures in Chapter Organizer, p. 286)

1. Warren Ford borrowed $14,000 on a noninterest-bearing, simple discount, 4½%, 60-day note. Assume ordinary interest. What are **(a)** the maturity value, **(b)** the bank's discount, **(c)** Warren's proceeds, and **(d)** the effective rate to the nearest hundredth percent?
2. Jane Long buys a $10,000 13-week Treasury bill at 4%. What is her effective rate? Round to the nearest hundredth percent.

Learning Unit 11–2: Discounting an Interest-Bearing Note before Maturity

Manufacturers frequently deliver merchandise to retail companies and do not request payment for several months. For example, Roger Company manufactures outdoor furniture that it delivers to Sears in March. Payment for the furniture is not due until September. Roger will have its money tied up in this furniture until September. So Roger requests that Sears sign promissory notes.

If Roger Company needs cash sooner than September, what can it do? Roger Company can take one of its promissory notes to the bank, assuming the company that signed the note is reliable. The bank will buy the note from Roger. Now Roger has discounted the note and has cash instead of waiting until September when Sears would have paid Roger.

Remember that when Roger Company discounts the promissory note to the bank, the company agrees to pay the note at maturity if the maker of the promissory note fails to pay the bank. The potential liability that may or may not result from discounting a note is called a **contingent liability.**

Think of **discounting a note** as a three-party arrangement. Roger Company realizes that the bank will charge for this service. The bank's charge is a **bank discount.** The actual amount Roger receives is the **proceeds** of the note. The four steps below and the formulas in the example that follows will help you understand this discounting process.

DISCOUNTING A NOTE	
Step 1.	Calculate the interest and maturity value.
Step 2.	Calculate the discount period (time the bank holds note).
Step 3.	Calculate the bank discount.
Step 4.	Calculate the proceeds.

EXAMPLE Roger Company sold the following promissory note to the bank:

Date of note	Face value of note	Length of note	Interest rate	Bank discount rate	Date of discount
March 8	$2,000	185 days	10%	9%	August 9

What are Roger's (1) interest and maturity value (*MV*)? What are the (2) discount period and (3) bank discount? (4) What are the proceeds?

1. *Calculate Roger's interest and maturity value (MV):*

> MV = Face value (principal) + Interest

$$\text{Interest} = \$2,000 \times .10 \times \frac{185}{360} \quad \text{Exact number of days over 360}$$

$$= \$102.78$$

$$MV = \$2,000 + \$102.78$$

$$= \$2,102.78$$

Calculating days without table:

March	31
	− 8
	23
April	30
May	31
June	30
July	31
August	9
	154

185 days—length of note
−154 days Roger held note
 31 days bank waits

2. *Calculate **discount period:***
Determine the number of days that the bank will have to wait for the note to come due (discount period).

August 9	221 days
March 8	− 67
	154 days passed before note is discounted
	185 days
	− 154
	31 days bank waits for note to come due

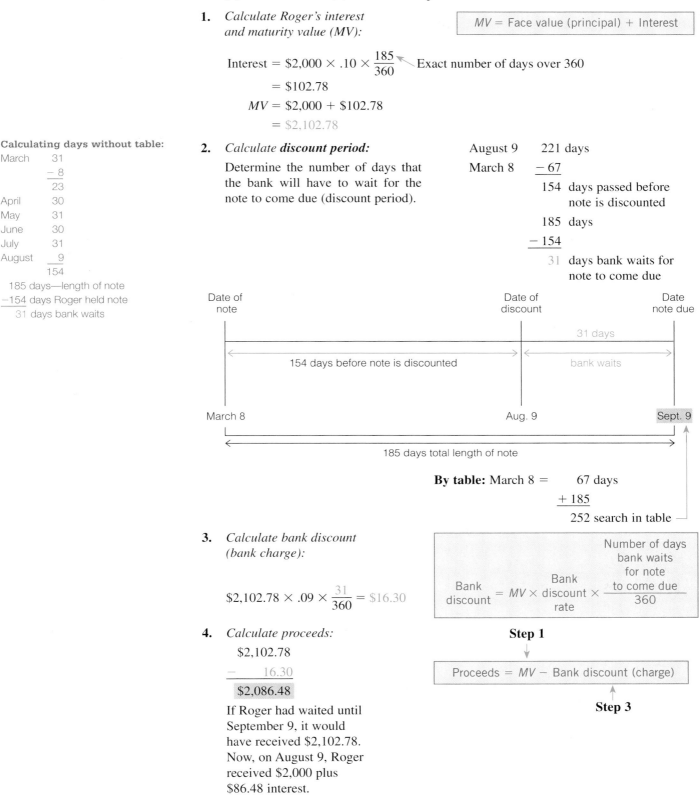

By table: March 8 =   67 days
                     + 185
                     252 search in table

3. *Calculate bank discount (bank charge):*

$$\$2,102.78 \times .09 \times \frac{31}{360} = \$16.30$$

> Bank discount = MV × Bank discount rate × $\dfrac{\text{Number of days bank waits for note to come due}}{360}$

Step 1

4. *Calculate proceeds:*

	$2,102.78
−	16.30
	$2,086.48

If Roger had waited until September 9, it would have received $2,102.78. Now, on August 9, Roger received $2,000 plus $86.48 interest.

> Proceeds = MV − Bank discount (charge)

Step 3

Now let's assume Roger Company received a noninterest-bearing note. Then we follow the four steps for discounting a note except the maturity value is the amount of the loan. No interest accumulates on a noninterest-bearing note. Today, many banks use simple interest instead of discounting. Also, instead of discounting notes, many companies set up *lines of credit* so that additional financing is immediately available.

Finding Funding
Breaking down the basics of small-business borrowing

Loan Lineup
Among small businesses using credit, the percentage that tap these types of funding to finance their operations
- Personal credit card . . . . **.46%**
- Business credit card **34**
- Line of credit **28**
- Vehicle loan **21**
- Owner loan* **14**
- Mortgage loan **13**
- Lease **11**
- Equipment loan **10**
- Other **10**

Getting Started
Here are selected resources where entrepreneurs can research small-business financing options

www.sba.gov/financing
The Small Business Administration's Web site provides a primer on the basics of financing, as well as calculators for estimating costs, lists of grant resources, a summary of loan requirements and information on the agency's own loan programs.

www.microenterpriseworks.org
The site of the Association for Enterprise Opportunity, a national member-based group dedicated to microenterprise development, provides a listing of microenterprise groups by state that can be tapped for financing guidance and funding itself.

www.smartonline.com
This for-profit company provides an array of financial calculators as well as Web-based services and templates on writing business and marketing plans, incorporating and applying for loans.

www.count-me-in.org
This site is aimed at helping women-run small businesses obtain business loans, consultation and education. An online microlender, Count Me In makes loans of $500 to $10,000 available to U.S. women who have difficulty finding funding elsewhere. The site also has a help resource center with checklists, educational videos, and an online library about credit and business planning.

*Loan from the owner to the business.   Sources: Small Business Administration, Office of Advocacy; WSJ research

Wall Street Journal © 2004

The *Wall Street Journal* clipping "Finding Funding" shows that 28% of small businesses surveyed use a line of credit to finance their operations.

The Practice Quiz that follows will test your understanding of this unit.

LU 11–2   PRACTICE QUIZ

Complete this **Practice Quiz** to see how you are doing

Date of note	Face value (principal) of note	Length of note	Interest rate	Bank discount rate	Date of discount
April 8	$35,000	160 days	11%	9%	June 8

From the above, calculate **(a)** interest and maturity value, **(b)** discount period, **(c)** bank discount, and **(d)** proceeds. Assume ordinary interest.

✓ Solutions

a. $I = \$35,000 \times .11 \times \dfrac{160}{360} =$ $\boxed{\$1,711.11}$

MV = $35,000 + $1,711.11 = $\boxed{\$36,711.11}$

b.   Discount period = 160 − 61 = $\boxed{99 \text{ days.}}$

April 30	**Or by table:**
− 8	June 8 159
22	April 8 − 98
May + 31	61
53	
June + 8	
61	

c. Bank discount = $36,711.11 × .09 × $\frac{99}{360}$ = $908.60

d. Proceeds = $36,711.11 − $908.60 = $35,802.51

LU 11–2a EXTRA PRACTICE QUIZ

Need more practice? Try this **Extra Practice Quiz** (check figures in Chapter Organizer, p. 286)

From the information below, calculate **(a)** interest and maturity value, **(b)** discount period, **(c)** bank discount, and **(d)** proceeds. Assume ordinary interest.

Date of note	Face value (principal) of note	Length of note	Interest rate	Bank discount rate	Date of discount
April 10	$40,000	170 days	5%	2%	June 10

CHAPTER ORGANIZER AND STUDY GUIDE
WITH CHECK FIGURES FOR EXTRA PRACTICE QUIZZES

Topic	Key point, procedure, formula	Example(s) to illustrate situation
Simple discount note, p. 280	Bank discount (interest) = MV × Bank discount rate × Time Interest based on amount paid back and not what received.	$6,000 × .09 × $\frac{60}{360}$ = $90 Borrower receives $5,910 (the proceeds) and pays back $6,000 at maturity after 60 days. A Treasury bill is a good example of a simple discount note.
Effective rate, p. 281	$\frac{\text{Interest}}{\text{Proceeds} \times \text{Time}}$ What borrower receives (Face value − Discount)	*Example:* $10,000 note, discount rate 12% for 60 days. $I = $10,000 × .12 × $\frac{60}{360}$ = $200 Effective rate: $\frac{\$200}{\$9,800 \times \frac{60}{360}} = \frac{\$200}{\$1,633.3333} = 12.24\%$ Amount borrower received

Discounting an interest-bearing note, p. 282	1. Calculate interest and maturity value.
	   I = Face value × Rate × Time
	   MV = Face value + Interest
	2. Calculate number of days bank will wait for note to come due (discount period).
	3. Calculate bank discount (bank charge).
	   $MV \times$ discount rate $\times \frac{\text{Number of days bank waits}}{360}$
	4. Calculate proceeds.
	   MV − Bank discount (charge)
		Example: $1,000 note, 6%, 60-day, dated November 1 and discounted on December 1 at 8%.
		
		1. $I = $1,000 × .06 × $\frac{60}{360}$ = $10
		   $MV = $1,000 + $10 = $1,010
		2. 30 days
		3. $1,010 × .08 × $\frac{30}{360}$ = $6.73
		4. $1,010 − $6.73 = $1,003.27

KEY TERMS	Bank discount, *pp. 280, 282* Bank discount rate, *p. 280* Contingent liability, *p. 282* Discounting a note, *p. 282* Discount period, *p. 283* Effective rate, *p. 281* Face value, *p. 279*	Interest-bearing note, *p. 279* Maker, *p. 279* Maturity date, *p. 279* Maturity value (*MV*), *p. 279* Noninterest-bearing note, *p. 280* Payee, *p. 279* Proceeds, *pp. 280, 283* Promissory note, *p. 279* Simple discount note, *p. 280* Treasury bill, *p. 281*

(continues)

CHAPTER ORGANIZER AND STUDY GUIDE
WITH CHECK FIGURES FOR EXTRA PRACTICE QUIZZES (concluded)

Topic	Key point, procedure, formula	Example(s) to illustrate situation
CHECK FIGURES FOR EXTRA PRACTICE QUIZZES WITH PAGE REFERENCES	LU 11–1a (p. 282) 1. A. $14,000 B. $105 C. $13,895 D. 4.53% 2. 4.04%	LU 11–2a (p. 285) 1. A. Int. = $944.44; $40,944.44 B. 109 days C. $247.94 D. $40,696.50

Critical Thinking Discussion Questions

1. What are the differences between a simple interest note and a simple discount note? Which type of note would have a higher effective rate of interest? Why?

2. What are the four steps of the discounting process? Could the proceeds of a discounted note be less than the face value of the note?

3. What is a line of credit? What could be a disadvantage of having a large credit line?

Name _____ Date _____

DRILL PROBLEMS

Complete the following table for these simple discount notes. Use the ordinary interest method.

	Amount due at maturity	Discount rate	Time	Bank discount	Proceeds
11–1.	$18,000	$4\frac{1}{4}\%$	300 days		
11–2.	$20,000	$6\frac{1}{4}\%$	180 days		

Calculate the discount period for the bank to wait to receive its money:

	Date of note	Length of note	Date note discounted	Discount period
11–3.	April 12	45 days	May 2	
11–4.	March 7	120 days	June 8	

Solve for maturity value, discount period, bank discount, and proceeds (assume for Problems 11–5 and 11–6 a bank discount rate of 9%).

	Face value (principal)	Rate of interest	Length of note	Maturity value	Date of note	Date note discounted	Discount period	Bank discount	Proceeds
11–5.	$50,000	11%	95 days		June 10	July 18			
11–6.	$25,000	9%	60 days		June 8	July 10			

11–7. Calculate the effective rate of interest (to the nearest hundredth percent) of the following Treasury bill.
Given: $10,000 Treasury bill, 4% for 13 weeks.

WORD PROBLEMS

Use ordinary interest as needed.

11–8. On March 19, 2006, *The Saint Paul Pioneer Press* reported on interest loans which include an additional, one time $20 fee. Wilbert McKee's bank deducts interest in advance and also deducts $20.00 fee in advance. Wilbert needs a loan for $500. The bank charges 5% interest. Wilbert will need the loan for 90 days. What is the effective rate for this loan? Round to the nearest hundredth percent. Do not round denominator in calculation.

11–9. Jack Tripper signed a $9,000 note at Fleet Bank. Fleet charges a $9\frac{1}{4}\%$ discount rate. If the loan is for 200 days, find **(a)** the proceeds and **(b)** the effective rate charged by the bank (to the nearest tenth percent).

11–10. On January 18, 2007, *BusinessWeek* reported yields on Treasury bills. Bruce Martin purchased a $10,000 13 week Treasury bill at $9,881.25. **(a)** What was the amount of interest? **(b)** What was the effective rate of interest? Round to the nearest hundredth percent.

11–11. On September 5, Sheffield Company discounted at Sunshine Bank a $9,000 (maturity value), 120-day note dated June 5. Sunshine's discount rate was 9%. What proceeds did Sheffield Company receive?

11–12. The Treasury Department auctioned $21 billion in three month bills in denominations of ten thousand dollars at a discount rate of 4.965%, according to the March 13, 2007 issue of the *Chicago Sun-Times*. What would be the effective rate of interest? Round your answer to the nearest hundredth percent.

11–13. Annika Scholten bought a $10,000, 13-week Treasury bill at 5%. What is her effective rate? Round to the nearest hundredth percent.

11–14. Ron Prentice bought goods from Shelly Katz. On May 8, Shelly gave Ron a time extension on his bill by accepting a $3,000, 8%, 180-day note. On August 16, Shelly discounted the note at Roseville Bank at 9%. What proceeds does Shelly Katz receive?

11–15. Rex Corporation accepted a $5,000, 8%, 120-day note dated August 8 from Regis Company in settlement of a past bill. On October 11, Rex discounted the note at Park Bank at 9%. What are the note's maturity value, discount period, and bank discount? What proceeds does Rex receive?

11–16. On May 12, Scott Rinse accepted an $8,000, 12%, 90-day note for a time extension of a bill for goods bought by Ron Prentice. On June 12, Scott discounted the note at Able Bank at 10%. What proceeds does Scott receive?

11–17. Hafers, an electrical supply company, sold $4,800 of equipment to Jim Coates Wiring, Inc. Coates signed a promissory note May 12 with 4.5% interest. The due date was August 10. Short of funds, Hafers contacted Charter One Bank on July 20; the bank agreed to take over the note at a 6.2% discount. What proceeds will Hafers receive?

11–18. *Market News Publishing* reported on the sale of a promissory note. ZTEST Electronics announced that it agreed to sell a promissory note (the "Note") in the principal amount of $318,019.95 owed to them by Parmatech Electronic Corporation. The note, negotiated on March 15, is a 360-day note with 8.5% interest per annum. Halfway through the life of the note, Alpha Bank offered to purchase the note at 8.75%. Baker Bank offered to purchase the note at 9.0%. **(a)** What proceeds will ZTEST receive from Alpha Bank? **(b)** What proceeds will ZTEST receive from Baker Bank? **(c)** How much more will ZTEST receive from Alpha Bank? Round to the nearest cent.

11–19. Tina Mier must pay a $2,000 furniture bill. A finance company will loan Tina $2,000 for 8 months at a 9% discount rate. The finance company told Tina that if she wants to receive exactly $2,000, she must borrow more than $2,000. The finance company gave Tina the following formula:

$$\text{What to ask for} = \frac{\text{Amount in cash to be received}}{1 - (\text{Discount} \times \text{Time of loan})}$$

Calculate Tina's loan request and the effective rate of interest to nearest hundredth percent.

 SUMMARY PRACTICE TEST

1. On December 12, Lowell Corporation accepted a $160,000, 120-day, noninterest-bearing note from Able.com. What is the maturity value of the note? *(p. 279)*

2. The face value of a simple discount note is $17,000. The discount is 4% for 160 days. Calculate the following. *(p. 280)*

   a. Amount of interest charged for each note.

   b. Amount borrower would receive.

   c. Amount payee would receive at maturity.

   d. Effective rate (to the nearest tenth percent).

3. On July 14, Gracie Paul accepted a $60,000, 6%, 160-day note from Mike Lang. On November 12, Gracie discounted the note at Lend Bank at 7%. What proceeds did Gracie receive? *(p. 282)*

4. Lee.com accepted a $70,000, $6\frac{3}{4}$%, 120-day note on July 26. Lee discounts the note on October 28 at LB Bank at 6%. What proceeds did Lee receive? *(p. 282)*

5. The owner of Lease.com signed a $60,000 note at Reese Bank. Reese charges a $7\frac{1}{4}$% discount rate. If the loan is for 210 days, find **(a)** the proceeds and **(b)** the effective rate charged by the bank (to the nearest tenth percent). *(p. 280)*

6. Sam Slater buys a $10,000, 13-week Treasury bill at $5\frac{1}{2}$%. What is the effective rate? Round to the nearest hundredth percent. *(p. 281)*

● Students who take out Stafford loans after July 1 will pay a fixed interest rate of 6.8%.

ML HARRIS/GETTY IMAGES

COLLEGE | To save on student-loan interest rates, consolidate your debt by July 1. *By Jane Bennett Clark*

Last chance to **LOCK** in

IT SEEMS LIKE only yesterday that student-loan rates were sinking faster than a December sun. Alas, the days of magically vanishing—or modestly rising—rates are about to end. Starting July 1, the Deficit Reduction Act of 2005 will set a fixed rate of 6.8% on new Stafford loans, about two percentage points above this past year's lowest rate. Similarly, PLUS loans for parent borrowers will be fixed at 8.5%, up from the current 6.1%.

But the fixed rates won't apply to outstanding Stafford and PLUS loans. On those loans, rates will continue to change each July 1 based on the 91-day Treasury-bill yield set the last Thursday in May. The T-bill rate is expected to rise, so it pays to consolidate your loans and lock in the lower rate.

Things get a little tricky if you con-solidated last spring to take advantage of bottom-cruising rates (as low as 2.87% for Stafford loans and 4.17% for PLUS loans) and have since taken out new loans. You can consolidate the new loans, but you'll want to keep the two consolidations separate, says Gary Carpenter, executive director of the National Institute of Certified College Planners (www.niccp.com). "If you roll an old consolidation into a new one, you get a blended rate—the lower rate is lost," says Carpenter. And you may have to shop for a lender; some balk at consolidating loans of less than $7,500.

Although financial-aid packages were calculated this spring, next fall's freshmen will pay the post-July, fixed rate on Staffords; likewise, PLUS loans for parents of incoming freshmen will carry the new fixed rate. However, parents of currently enrolled students can apply for a PLUS now and consoli-date to lock in this year's rate, says Mark Brenner, of College Loan Corp. (www.collegeloan.com), which makes such loans. Ask your school's financial-aid office for details.

Other options. After July 1, parents choosing between a PLUS loan with an 8.5% fixed rate and a variable-rate home-equity line of credit should take a closer look at the latter, says Carpen-ter. The average rate for equity lines was recently 7.67%, and interest is deductible.

With rates fixed on Stafford loans, private loans, which are issued at variable rates, could someday end up costing less than Staffords. Sallie Mae (www.salliemae.com), the largest of the student-loan companies, offers private loans at the prime rate—lately 7.5%—with no fees for borrowers who have a good credit history.

Even if rates head south, borrowers "should exhaust federal loans first," says Sallie Mae spokeswoman Martha Holler. Unlike private loans, payments on those loans can be extended, de-ferred or forgiven in certain cases.

A mixed bag. As for the other provi-sions of the Deficit Reduction Act, they represent "a mixed bag" for under-graduates, says Brenner. For Stafford loans, the law boosts the maximum amount you can borrow in each of the first two years of college (the total amount remains the same), phases out origination fees and expands Pell Grants for math and science students. Married couples will no longer be able to consolidate loans taken out separate-ly into a single loan. And, as of July 1, students can no longer consolidate Staffords while they're still in school.

But Brenner says the changes "should in no way discourage American families from applying for the college of their choice." There's plenty of mon-ey for students who need it, he says, and federally sponsored loans remain "a hell of a deal."

BUSINESS MATH ISSUE

The Deficit Reduction Act of 2005 is too complicated for students needing loans.

1. List the key points of the article and information to support your position.
2. Write a group defense of your position using math calculations to support your view.

PROJECT A

Go to www.treasurydirect.gov and find out the latest rates for Treasury bills.

Investors Can More Easily Buy Treasurys Online

By ERIN E. ARVEDLUND

The federal government is making it easier to buy Treasury bonds online.

Beginning Monday, the Treasury Department will allow individual investors to purchase, manage and redeem Treasury bonds, bills and notes electronically by opening up an online account through its TreasuryDirect Web site (www.treasurydirect.gov). Previously, investors could buy or redeem only savings bonds in their online accounts. If they wanted to buy Treasury bonds, they had to open a paper-based account and, for the most part, pay by check for any transaction.

U.S. Treasurys are considered the safest investments for individuals, as they are backed by the full faith and credit of the U.S. government. What's more, any interest earned on Treasurys is exempt from state and local income taxes.

Once you open a TreasuryDirect account online, you are eligible to purchase and hold so-called marketable Treasury securities—which include bills, notes and bonds. Bills are short-term Treasurys sold at a discount to face value; notes are interest-bearing Treasurys with maturities of up to 10 years; and bonds are interest-bearing Treasurys with maturities of more than 10 years. "Marketable" means they can be bought and sold on secondary markets, though TreasuryDirect offers them only when issued.

Investors also can purchase Treasury Inflation Protected Securities, or TIPS, whose principal value increases with the rate of inflation. Previously, only Series I and EE U.S. Savings Bonds were available to online TreasuryDirect account holders since the Web site's inception in October 2002.

Currently, the three-month T-bill is yielding 3.54% and the 10-year bond is yielding 4.33%. The five-year real TIPS yield is 1.45% and the 20-year is 1.93%.

TIPS usually are purchased by investors seeking to outpace inflation, while regular bonds often are favored by those looking for a safe haven and to generate income. Treasurys also can be purchased through a broker, but investors usually will be charged a commission.

TreasuryDirect accounts are accessible by going to the Web site and clicking on "Open an Account." You need to provide your phone number, bank account, the bank's routing number, your Social Security number and driver's license or state identification number. All debits and credits for your Treasury purchases and redemptions will go directly into or out of your bank account.

Investors also can purchase bonds as gifts online. The minimum purchase for a savings bond is $25, and the minimum for Treasurys is $1,000 or a multiple of that amount, for all maturities. The accounts are free of any purchase charges or maintenance fees, but there is a sales charge of $45 per security.

> **TIPS are usually purchased by investors seeking to outpace inflation.**

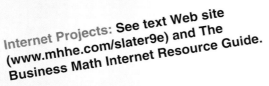

Internet Projects: See text Web site (www.mhhe.com/slater9e) and The Business Math Internet Resource Guide.

Video Case

Online banking is very cost effective for the banking industry. Many customers enjoy the convenience; others, however, have doubts. For these individuals, online banking is a different way of thinking.

Banks want customers flocking online because it costs less after initial startup fees. A teller transaction typically costs a bank on average $1 to $1.50, while Internet transactions cost less than 5 cents. Less cost means more profit.

The Gartner Group, a research firm, says that 27 million Americans—one in 10—now do at least some of their banking online, up from 9 million a year earlier. According to a new Gallup poll, online banking services soared by 60% in the year 2000. CyberDialogue, an Internet consulting firm, predicted online banking will rise to 50.9 million customers by 2005. Most sites allow customers to view account information, transfer money, and pay bills online; some sites offer investment account data and transactions. Other applications are coming, including the ability to view and print account statements and canceled checks.

Pundits wrote off most Web banking because of all the things customers couldn't do—close on a loan, sign for a mortgage, or withdraw cash. The startups are applying increasingly innovative strategies to clear these hurdles. Security was, and still is, an issue for many people. According to a recent study, 85% of information technology staffs at corporations and government agencies had detected a computer security breach in the past 12 months, and 64% acknowledged financial losses as a result. Measures are being taken to improve security.

In addition to the usual conveniences of online banking, online banks can pay higher rates on deposits than branch-based banks. However, problems do exist in online banking, such as you can rack up late fees for bill paying and not even know it.

When picking an online banking service, look for the following: (1) 128-bit encryption, the standard in the industry; (2) written guarantees to protect from losses in case of online fraud or bank error; (3) automatic lockout if you wrongly enter your password more than three or four times; and (4) evidence that the bank is FDIC insured.

PROBLEM 1

In 2000, the number of households accessing their accounts through a computer increased to 12.5 million, an 81.42% increase from a year earlier. These numbers support the push for online banking. What was the number of online users last year? Round to the nearest million.

PROBLEM 2

Jupiter Media Metrix, an online research firm, estimated that banking online will increase from 12.5 million to about 43.3 million in 2005. CyberDialogue, an Internet consulting firm, predicted that by the end of 2000, 24.6 million people would bank online and by 2005, the number would rise to 50.9 million. **(a)** What percent increase is Jupiter Media Metrix forecasting? **(b)** What percent increase is CyberDialogue forecasting? Round to the nearest hundredth percent.

PROBLEM 3

E*Trade Bank pays at least 3.1% on checking accounts with balances of $1,000 or more. The national average is 0.78% for interest-bearing checking. If you have $2,300 in your account and bank at E*Trade based on simple interest: **(a)** How much interest would you earn at the end of 30 days (ordinary interest)? **(b)** How much interest would you earn at a non-online bank?

PROBLEM 4

Online banking users—people who do basic banking tasks such as occasionally transferring money between accounts online—jumped to an estimated 20 million in December 2000 from 15.9 million in September 2000. What was the percent increase? Round to the nearest hundredth percent.

PROBLEM 5

On January 9, 2001, Bank of America Corporation announced that it had more than 3 million online banking customers. If 130,000 customers are added in a month, what is the percent increase? Round to the nearest hundredth percent.

PROBLEM 6

The E*Trade Bank is an Internet bank in Menlo Park, California, owned by Internet brokerage company E*Trade Group. On January 4, 2001, E*Trade Bank said it had added more than $1 billion in net new deposits in its fourth quarter of 2000, bringing its total deposits to more than $5.7 billion. E*Trade had a total of $1.1 billion in deposits at the end of 1998. What is the percent increase in net deposits in the year 2000 compared to 1998? Round to the nearest hundredth percent.

PROBLEM 7

The research firm The Gartner Group says that in 2001, 27 million Americans—one in 10—do at least some of their banking online, up from 9 million a year earlier. **(a)** How many were banking online last year? **(b)** What was the percent increase in online banking in 2001? Round to nearest hundredth percent.

PROBLEM 8

Industry experts expect that online banking and bill payment, like other forms of e-commerce, will continue to grow at a rapid pace. According to Killen & Associates, the number of bills paid online will rise to 11.7 billion by 2001, a 77% increase. What had been the amount of users in 2000? Round to the nearest tenth.

Compound Interest and Present Value

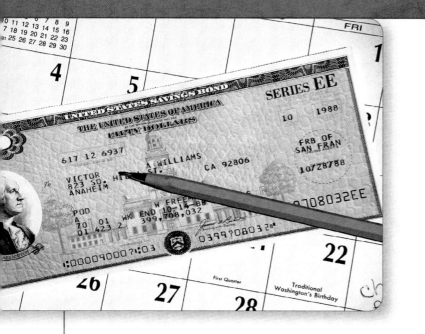

LEARNING UNIT OBJECTIVES

Note: A complete set of plastic overlays showing the concepts of compound interest and present value is found in Chapter 13.

LU 12–1: Compound Interest (Future Value)—The Big Picture

• Compare simple interest with compound interest (*pp. 296–298*).
• Calculate the compound amount and interest manually and by table lookup (*pp. 298–301*).
• Explain and compute the effective rate (APY) (*p. 301*).

LU 12–2: Present Value—The Big Picture

• Compare present value (PV) with compound interest (FV) (*p. 303*).
• Compute present value by table lookup (*pp. 304–306*).
• Check the present value answer by compounding (*p. 306*).

How Math Fattens Your Wallet

As the years roll by, this investment compounding can generate eye-popping performance. At a steady 8% annual return, you would earn a cumulative 47% after five years, 116% after 10 years, 585% after 25 years and 4,590% after 50 years. Impressed? It's amazing what you can amass with a little money and a lot of time.

Indeed, every so often, newspapers will carry stories about folks who die in their nineties and, to the shock of friends and neighbors, leave behind estates worth millions of dollars. The stories always have the same basic elements: These millionaires never earned a lot of money, they lived modestly, they drove used cars and they didn't have grand homes.

Often, the newspapers will speculate that these folks were brilliant investors. But the explanation is usually more prosaic.

Would you like to save a million dollars? We omitted the beginning of the *Wall Street Journal* clipping "How Math Fattens Your Wallet" because it explained the years involved in recouping losses when interest is only charged on the principal. The clipping contrasts this extended time by introducing compound interest, which means that interest is added to the principal and then additional interest is paid on both the old principal and its interest. This compounding can make it possible for you to save a million dollars.

In this chapter we look at the power of compounding—interest paid on earned interest. Let's begin by studying Learning Unit 12–1, which shows you how to calculate compound interest.

Wall Street Journal © 2005

Learning Unit 12–1: Compound Interest (Future Value)—The Big Picture

Check out the plastic overlays that appear within Chapter 13 to review these concepts.

So far we have discussed only simple interest, which is interest on the principal alone. Simple interest is either paid at the end of the loan period or deducted in advance. From the chapter introduction, you know that interest can also be compounded.

Compounding involves the calculation of interest periodically over the life of the loan (or investment). After each calculation, the interest is added to the principal. Future calculations are on the adjusted principal (old principal plus interest). **Compound interest,** then, is the interest on the principal plus the interest of prior periods. **Future value (FV),** or the **compound amount,** is the final amount of the loan or investment at the end of the last period. In the beginning of this unit, do not be concerned with how to calculate compounding but try to understand the meaning of compounding.

Figure 12.1 shows how $1 will grow if it is calculated for 4 years at 8% annually. This means that the interest is calculated on the balance once a year. In Figure 12.1, we start with $1, which is the **present value (PV).** After year 1, the dollar with interest is worth $1.08. At the end of year 2, the dollar is worth $1.17. By the end of year 4, the dollar is worth $1.36 . Note how we start with the present and look to see what the dollar will be worth in the future. *Compounding goes from present value to future value.*

FIGURE 12.1

Future value of $1 at 8% for four periods

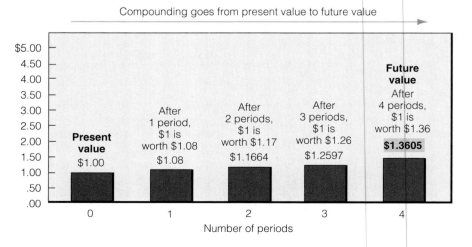

Before you learn how to calculate compound interest and compare it to simple interest, you must understand the terms that follow. These terms are also used in Chapter 13.

- **Compounded annually:** Interest calculated on the balance once a year.

- **Compounded semiannually:** Interest calculated on the balance every 6 months or every $\frac{1}{2}$ year.

- **Compounded quarterly:** Interest calculated on the balance every 3 months or every $\frac{1}{4}$ year.

- **Compounded monthly:** Interest calculated on the balance each month.

- **Compounded daily:** Interest calculated on the balance each day.

- **Number of periods:**[1] Number of years multiplied by the number of times the interest is compounded per year. For example, if you compound $1 for 4 years at 8% annually, semiannually, or quarterly, the following periods will result:

  Annually: 4 years $\times$ 1 = 4 periods

  Semiannually: 4 years $\times$ 2 = 8 periods

  Quarterly: 4 years $\times$ 4 = 16 periods

- **Rate for each period:**[2] Annual interest rate divided by the number of times the interest is compounded per year. Compounding changes the interest rate for annual, semiannual, and quarterly periods as follows:

  Annually: 8% $\div$ 1 = 8%

  Semiannually: 8% $\div$ 2 = 4%

  Quarterly: 8% $\div$ 4 = 2%

Note that both the number of periods (4) and the rate (8%) for the annual example did not change. You will see later that rate and periods (not years) will always change unless interest is compounded yearly.

Now you are ready to learn the difference between simple interest and compound interest.

Simple versus Compound Interest

Did you know that money invested at 6% will double in 12 years? The following *Wall Street Journal* clipping "Confused by Investing?" shows how to calculate the number of years it takes for your investment to double.

Confused by Investing?

If there's something about your investment portfolio that doesn't seem to add up, maybe you should check your math.

Lots of folks are perplexed by the mathematics of investing, so I thought a refresher course might help. Here's a look at some key concepts:

■ **10 Plus 10 is 21**

Imagine you invest $100, which earns 10% this year and 10% next. How much have you made? If you answered 21%, go to the head of the class.

Here's how the math works. This year's 10% gain turns your $100 into $110. Next year, you also earn 10%, but you start the year with $110. Result? You earn $11, boosting your wealth to $121.

Thus, your portfolio has earned a *cumulative* 21% return over two years, but the *annualized* return is just 10%. The fact that 21% is more than double 10% can be attributed to the effect of investment compounding, the way that you earn money each year not only on your original investment, but also on earnings from prior years that you've reinvested.

■ **The Rule of 72**

To get a feel for compounding, try the rule of 72. What's that? If you divide a particular annual return into 72, you'll find out how many years it will take to double your money. Thus, at 10% a year, an investment will double in value in a tad over seven years.

---

[1]Periods are often expressed with the letter N for number of periods.

[2]Rate is often expressed with the letter i for interest.

The following three situations of Bill Smith will clarify the difference between simple interest and compound interest.

Situation 1: Calculating Simple Interest and Maturity Value

EXAMPLE   Bill Smith deposited $80 in a savings account for 4 years at an annual interest rate of 8%. What is Bill's simple interest?

To calculate simple interest, we use the following simple interest formula:

$$\boxed{\text{Interest } (I) = \text{Principal } (P) \times \text{Rate } (R) \times \text{Time } (T)}$$

$$\boxed{\$25.60} \quad = \quad \$80 \quad \times \quad .08 \quad \times \quad 4$$

In 4 years Bill receives a total of $105.60 ($80.00 + $25.60)—principal plus simple interest.

Now let's look at the interest Bill would earn if the bank compounded Bill's interest on his savings.

Situation 2: Calculating Compound Amount and Interest without Tables[3]

You can use the following steps to calculate the compound amount and the interest manually:

CALCULATING COMPOUND AMOUNT AND INTEREST MANUALLY
Step 1. Calculate the simple interest and add it to the principal. Use this total to figure next year's interest.
Step 2. Repeat for the total number of periods.
Step 3. Compound amount − Principal = Compound interest.

EXAMPLE   Bill Smith deposited $80 in a savings account for 4 years at an annual compounded rate of 8%. What are Bill's compound amount and interest?

The following shows how the compounded rate affects Bill's interest:

	Year 1	Year 2	Year 3	Year 4
	$80.00	$86.40	$ 93.31	$100.77
	× .08	× .08	× .08	× .08
Interest	$ 6.40	$ 6.91	$ 7.46	$ 8.06
Beginning balance	+ 80.00	+ 86.40	+ 93.31	+ 100.77
Amount at year-end	$86.40	$93.31	$100.77	$108.83

Note that the beginning year 2 interest is the result of the interest of year 1 added to the principal. At the end of each interest period, we add on the period's interest. This interest becomes part of the principal we use for the calculation of the next period's interest. We can determine Bill's compound interest as follows:[4]

Compound amount	$108.83	
Principal	− 80.00	*Note:* In Situation 1 the interest was $25.60.
Compound interest	$ 28.83	

We could have used the following simplified process to calculate the compound amount and interest:

---

[3]For simplicity of presentation, round each calculation to nearest cent before continuing the compounding process. The compound amount will be off by 1 cent.

[4]The formula for compounding is $A = P(1 + i)^N$, where A equals compound amount, P equals the principal, i equals interest per period, and N equals number of periods. The calculator sequence would be as follows for Bill Smith: 1 $+$ .08 y^x 4 × 80 $=$ 108.84. A Financial Calculator Guide booklet is available that shows how to operate HP 10BII and TI BA II Plus.

Year 1	Year 2	Year 3	Year 4
$80.00	$86.40	$ 93.31	$100.77
× 1.08	× 1.08	× 1.08	× 1.08
$86.40	$93.31	$100.77	$108.83 [5] ← Future value

When using this simplification, you do not have to add the new interest to the previous balance. Remember that compounding results in higher interest than simple interest. Compounding is the *sum* of principal and interest multiplied by the interest rate we use to calculate interest for the next period. So, 1.08 above is 108%, with 100% as the base and 8% as the interest.

Situation 3: Calculating Compound Amount by Table Lookup

To calculate the compound amount with a future value table, use the following steps:

CALCULATING COMPOUND AMOUNT BY TABLE LOOKUP
Step 1. Find the periods: Years multiplied by number of times interest is compounded in 1 year.
Step 2. Find the rate: Annual rate divided by number of times interest is compounded in 1 year.
Step 3. Go down the Period column of the table to the number of periods desired; look across the row to find the rate. At the intersection of the two columns is the table factor for the compound amount of $1.
Step 4. Multiply the table factor by the amount of the loan. This gives the compound amount.

In Situation 2, Bill deposited $80 into a savings account for 4 years at an interest rate of 8% compounded annually. Bill heard that he could calculate the compound amount and interest by using tables. In Situation 3, Bill learns how to do this. Again, Bill wants to know the value of $80 in 4 years at 8%. He begins by using Table 12.1 (p. 300).

Looking at Table 12.1, Bill goes down the Period column to period 4, then across the row to the 8% column. At the intersection, Bill sees the number 1.3605. The marginal notes show how Bill arrived at the periods and rate. The 1.3605 table number means that $1 compounded at this rate will increase in value in 4 years to about $1.36. Do you recognize the $1.36? Figure 12.1 showed how $1 grew to $1.36. Since Bill wants to know the value of $80, he multiplies the dollar amount by the table factor as follows:

Four Periods

No. of times compounded × No. of years in 1 year

$\quad$ 1 $\quad$ × $\quad$ 4

$80.00 × 1.3605 = $108.84

Principal × Table factor = Compound amount (future value)

8% Rate

8% rate = $\frac{8\%}{1}$ → Annual rate → No. of times compounded in 1 year

Figure 12.2 (p. 300) illustrates this compounding procedure. We can say that compounding is a future value (FV) since we are looking into the future. Thus,

$108.84 − $80.00 = $28.84 interest for 4 years at 8% compounded annually on $80.00

Now let's look at two examples that illustrate compounding more than once a year.

EXAMPLE Find the interest on $6,000 at 10% compounded semiannually for 5 years. We calculate the interest as follows:

Periods = 2 × 5 years = 10

Rate = 10% ÷ 2 = 5%

10 periods, 5%, in Table 12.1 = 1.6289 (table factor)

$6,000 × 1.6289 = $9,773.40
− 6,000.00
$3,773.40 interest

[5]Off 1 cent due to rounding.

| TABLE | 12.1 | Future value of $1 at compound interest |

Period	1%	1½%	2%	3%	4%	5%	6%	7%	8%	9%	10%
1	1.0100	1.0150	1.0200	1.0300	1.0400	1.0500	1.0600	1.0700	1.0800	1.0900	1.1000
2	1.0201	1.0302	1.0404	1.0609	1.0816	1.1025	1.1236	1.1449	1.1664	1.1881	1.2100
3	1.0303	1.0457	1.0612	1.0927	1.1249	1.1576	1.1910	1.2250	1.2597	1.2950	1.3310
4	1.0406	1.0614	1.0824	1.1255	1.1699	1.2155	1.2625	1.3108	1.3605	1.4116	1.4641
5	1.0510	1.0773	1.1041	1.1593	1.2167	1.2763	1.3382	1.4026	1.4693	1.5386	1.6105
6	1.0615	1.0934	1.1262	1.1941	1.2653	1.3401	1.4185	1.5007	1.5869	1.6771	1.7716
7	1.0721	1.1098	1.1487	1.2299	1.3159	1.4071	1.5036	1.6058	1.7138	1.8280	1.9487
8	1.0829	1.1265	1.1717	1.2668	1.3686	1.4775	1.5938	1.7182	1.8509	1.9926	2.1436
9	1.0937	1.1434	1.1951	1.3048	1.4233	1.5513	1.6895	1.8385	1.9990	2.1719	2.3579
10	1.1046	1.1605	1.2190	1.3439	1.4802	1.6289	1.7908	1.9672	2.1589	2.3674	2.5937
11	1.1157	1.1780	1.2434	1.3842	1.5395	1.7103	1.8983	2.1049	2.3316	2.5804	2.8531
12	1.1268	1.1960	1.2682	1.4258	1.6010	1.7959	2.0122	2.2522	2.5182	2.8127	3.1384
13	1.1381	1.2135	1.2936	1.4685	1.6651	1.8856	2.1329	2.4098	2.7196	3.0658	3.4523
14	1.1495	1.2318	1.3195	1.5126	1.7317	1.9799	2.2609	2.5785	2.9372	3.3417	3.7975
15	1.1610	1.2502	1.3459	1.5580	1.8009	2.0789	2.3966	2.7590	3.1722	3.6425	4.1772
16	1.1726	1.2690	1.3728	1.6047	1.8730	2.1829	2.5404	2.9522	3.4259	3.9703	4.5950
17	1.1843	1.2880	1.4002	1.6528	1.9479	2.2920	2.6928	3.1588	3.7000	4.3276	5.0545
18	1.1961	1.3073	1.4282	1.7024	2.0258	2.4066	2.8543	3.3799	3.9960	4.7171	5.5599
19	1.2081	1.3270	1.4568	1.7535	2.1068	2.5270	3.0256	3.6165	4.3157	5.1417	6.1159
20	1.2202	1.3469	1.4859	1.8061	2.1911	2.6533	3.2071	3.8697	4.6610	5.6044	6.7275
21	1.2324	1.3671	1.5157	1.8603	2.2788	2.7860	3.3996	4.1406	5.0338	6.1088	7.4002
22	1.2447	1.3876	1.5460	1.9161	2.3699	2.9253	3.6035	4.4304	5.4365	6.6586	8.1403
23	1.2572	1.4084	1.5769	1.9736	2.4647	3.0715	3.8197	4.7405	5.8715	7.2579	8.9543
24	1.2697	1.4295	1.6084	2.0328	2.5633	3.2251	4.0489	5.0724	6.3412	7.9111	9.8497
25	1.2824	1.4510	1.6406	2.0938	2.6658	3.3864	4.2919	5.4274	6.8485	8.6231	10.8347
26	1.2953	1.4727	1.6734	2.1566	2.7725	3.5557	4.5494	5.8074	7.3964	9.3992	11.9182
27	1.3082	1.4948	1.7069	2.2213	2.8834	3.7335	4.8223	6.2139	7.9881	10.2451	13.1100
28	1.3213	1.5172	1.7410	2.2879	2.9987	3.9201	5.1117	6.6488	8.6271	11.1672	14.4210
29	1.3345	1.5400	1.7758	2.3566	3.1187	4.1161	5.4184	7.1143	9.3173	12.1722	15.8631
30	1.3478	1.5631	1.8114	2.4273	3.2434	4.3219	5.7435	7.6123	10.0627	13.2677	17.4494

Note: For more detailed tables, see your reference booklet, the *Business Math Handbook.*

EXAMPLE   Pam Donahue deposits $8,000 in her savings account that pays 6% interest compounded quarterly. What will be the balance of her account at the end of 5 years?

Periods = 4 × 5 years = 20

Rate = 6% ÷ 4 = 1½%

| FIGURE | 12.2 |

Compounding (FV)

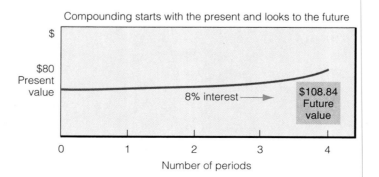

20 periods, $1\frac{1}{2}$%, in Table 12.1 = 1.3469 (table factor)

$8,000 × 1.3469 = $10,775.20

Next, let's look at bank rates and how they affect interest.

Bank Rates—Nominal versus Effective Rates (Annual Percentage Yield, or APY)

Banks often advertise their annual (nominal) interest rates and *not* their true or effective rate (annual percentage yield, or APY). This has made it difficult for investors and depos-

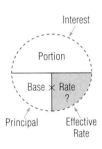

itors to determine the actual rates of interest they were receiving. The Truth in Savings law forced savings institutions to reveal their actual rate of interest. The APY is defined in the Truth in Savings law as the percentage rate expressing the total amount of interest that would be received on a $100 deposit based on the annual rate and frequency of compounding for a 365-day period. As you can see from the advertisement on the left, banks now refer to the effective rate of interest as the annual percentage yield.

Let's study the rates of two banks to see which bank has the better return for the investor. Blue Bank pays 8% interest compounded quarterly on $8,000. Sun Bank offers 8% interest compounded semiannually on $8,000. The 8% rate is the **nominal rate,** or stated rate, on which the bank calculates the interest. To calculate the **effective rate (annual percentage yield,** or **APY),** however, we can use the following formula:

$$\text{Effective rate (APY)}^6 = \frac{\text{Interest for 1 year}}{\text{Principal}}$$

Now let's calculate the effective rate (APY) for Blue Bank and Sun Bank.

Note the effective rates (APY) can be seen from Table 12.1 for $1:
1.0824 ← 4 periods, 2%
1.0816 ← 2 periods, 4%

Blue, 8% compounded quarterly	Sun, 8% compounded semiannually
Periods = 4 (4 × 1)	Periods = 2 (2 × 1)
Percent = $\frac{8\%}{4}$ = 2%	Percent = $\frac{8\%}{2}$ = 4%
Principal = $8,000	Principal = $8,000
Table 12.1 lookup: 4 periods, 2%	Table 12.1 lookup: 2 periods, 4%
$\begin{array}{r} 1.0824 \\ \times\ \$8,000 \\ \hline \$8,659.20 \end{array}$ Less principal $\begin{array}{r} -\ 8,000.00 \\ \hline \$\ \ \ 659.20 \end{array}$	$\begin{array}{r} 1.0816 \\ \times\ \$8,000 \\ \hline \$8,652.80 \\ -\ 8,000.00 \\ \hline \$\ \ \ 652.80 \end{array}$
Effective rate (APY) = $\frac{\$659.20}{\$8,000}$ = .0824	$\frac{\$652.80}{\$8,000}$ = .0816
= 8.24%	= 8.16%

Figure 12.3 (p. 302) illustrates a comparison of nominal and effective rates (APY) of interest. This comparison should make you question any advertisement of interest rates before depositing your money.

Before concluding this unit, we briefly discuss compounding interest daily.

Compounding Interest Daily

Although many banks add interest to each account quarterly, some banks pay interest that is **compounded daily,** and other banks use *continuous compounding.* Remember that

---

[6]Round to the nearest hundredth percent as needed. In practice, the rate is often rounded to the nearest thousandth.

FIGURE 12.3

Nominal and effective rates (APY) of interest compared

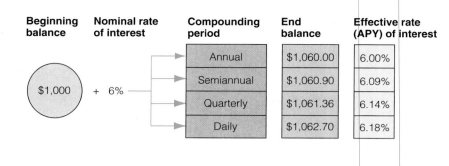

	Beginning balance	Nominal rate of interest	Compounding period	End balance	Effective rate (APY) of interest
	$1,000	+ 6%	Annual	$1,060.00	6.00%
			Semiannual	$1,060.90	6.09%
			Quarterly	$1,061.36	6.14%
			Daily	$1,062.70	6.18%

continuous compounding sounds great, but in fact, it yields only a fraction of a percent more interest over a year than daily compounding. Today, computers perform these calculations.

Table 12.2 is a partial table showing what $1 will grow to in the future by daily compounded interest, 360-day basis. For example, we can calculate interest compounded daily on $900 at 6% per year for 25 years as follows:

$900 × 4.4811 = $4,032.99 daily compounding

Now it's time to check your progress with the following Practice Quiz.

LU 12–1 PRACTICE QUIZ

Complete this **Practice Quiz** to see how you are doing

1. Complete the following without a table (round each calculation to the nearest cent as needed):

Principal	Time	Rate of compound interest	Compounded	Number of periods to be compounded	Total amount	Total interest
$200	1 year	8%	Quarterly	a.	b.	c.

2. Solve the previous problem by using compound value (FV) in Table 12.1.
3. Lionel Rodgers deposits $6,000 in Victory Bank, which pays 3% interest compounded semiannually. How much will Lionel have in his account at the end of 8 years?
4. Find the effective rate (APY) for the year: principal, $7,000; interest rate, 12%; and compounded quarterly.
5. Calculate by Table 12.2 what $1,500 compounded daily for 5 years will grow to at 7%.

TABLE 12.2 Interest on a $1 deposit compounded daily—360-day basis

Number of years	6.00%	6.50%	7.00%	7.50%	8.00%	8.50%	9.00%	9.50%	10.00%
1	1.0618	1.0672	1.0725	1.0779	1.0833	1.0887	1.0942	1.0996	1.1052
2	1.1275	1.1388	1.1503	1.1618	1.1735	1.1853	1.1972	1.2092	1.2214
3	1.1972	1.2153	1.2337	1.2523	1.2712	1.2904	1.3099	1.3297	1.3498
4	1.2712	1.2969	1.3231	1.3498	1.3771	1.4049	1.4333	1.4622	1.4917
5	1.3498	1.3840	1.4190	1.4549	1.4917	1.5295	1.5682	1.6079	1.6486
6	1.4333	1.4769	1.5219	1.5682	1.6160	1.6652	1.7159	1.7681	1.8220
7	1.5219	1.5761	1.6322	1.6904	1.7506	1.8129	1.8775	1.9443	2.0136
8	1.6160	1.6819	1.7506	1.8220	1.8963	1.9737	2.0543	2.1381	2.2253
9	1.7159	1.7949	1.8775	1.9639	2.0543	2.1488	2.2477	2.3511	2.4593
10	1.8220	1.9154	2.0136	2.1168	2.2253	2.3394	2.4593	2.5854	2.7179
15	2.4594	2.6509	2.8574	3.0799	3.3197	3.5782	3.8568	4.1571	4.4808
20	3.3198	3.6689	4.0546	4.4810	4.9522	5.4728	6.0482	6.6842	7.3870
25	4.4811	5.0777	5.7536	6.5195	7.3874	8.3708	9.4851	10.7477	12.1782
30	6.0487	7.0275	8.1645	9.4855	11.0202	12.8032	14.8747	17.2813	20.0772

✓ **Solutions**

1. **a.** 4 (4 × 1)   **b.** $216.48   **c.** $16.48 ($216.48 − $200)
    $200 × 1.02 = $204 × 1.02 = $208.08 × 1.02 = $212.24 × 1.02 = $216.48
2. $200 × 1.0824 = $216.48 (4 periods, 2%)
3. 16 periods, $1\frac{1}{2}\%$, $6,000 × 1.2690 = $7,614
4. 4 periods, 3%,
    $7,000 × 1.1255 = $7,878.50
                     − 7,000.00 $\dfrac{\$878.50}{\$7,000.00} = 12.55\%$
                     ─────────────
                     $ 878.50
5. $1,500 × 1.4190 = $2,128.50

Check out the plastic overlays that appear within Chapter 13 to review these concepts.

LU 12–1a **EXTRA PRACTICE QUIZ**

Need more practice? Try this **Extra Practice Quiz** (check figures in Chapter Organizer, p. 308)

1. Complete the following without a table (round each calculation to the nearest cent as needed):

Principal	Time	Rate of compound interest	Compounded	Number of periods to be compounded	Total amount	Total interest
$500	1 year	8%	Quarterly	a.	b.	c.

2. Solve the previous problem by using compound value (FV). See Table 12.1.
3. Lionel Rodgers deposits $7,000 in Victory Bank, which pays 4% interest compounded semiannually. How much will Lionel have in his account at the end of 8 years?
4. Find the effective rate (APY) for the year: principal, $8,000; interest rate, 6%; and compounded quarterly. Round to the nearest hundredth percent.
5. Calculate by Table 12.2 what $1,800 compounded daily for 5 years will grow to at 6%.

Learning Unit 12–2: Present Value—The Big Picture

Figure 12.1 (p. 296) in Learning Unit 12–1 showed how by compounding, the *future value* of $1 became $1.36. This learning unit discusses *present value*. Before we look at specific calculations involving present value, let's look at the concept of present value.

Figure 12.4 shows that if we invested 74 cents today, compounding would cause the 74 cents to grow to $1 in the future. For example, let's assume you ask this question: "If I need $1 in 4 years in the future, how much must I put in the bank *today* (assume an 8% annual interest)?" To answer this question, you must know the present value of that $1 today. From Figure 12.4, you can see that the present value of $1 is .7350. Remember that the $1 is only worth 74 cents if you wait 4 periods to receive it. This is one reason why so many athletes get such big contracts—much of the money is paid in later years when it is not worth as much.

FIGURE 12.4

Present value of $1 at 8% for four periods

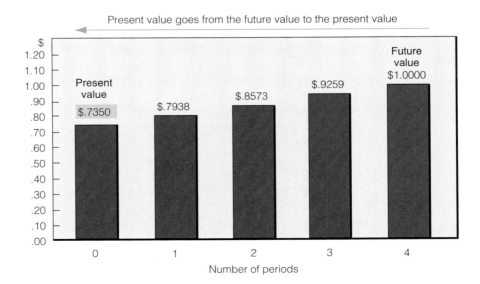

Present value goes from the future value to the present value

Number of periods

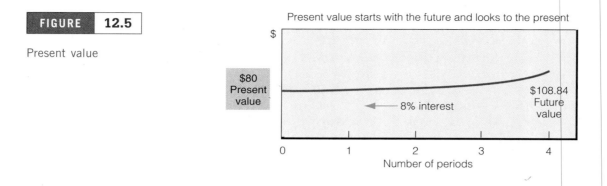

FIGURE	12.5

Present value

Present value starts with the future and looks to the present

RF/Corbis

Relationship of Compounding (FV) to Present Value (PV)—The Bill Smith Example Continued

In Learning Unit 12–1, our consideration of compounding started in the *present* ($80) and looked to find the *future* amount of $108.84. Present value (PV) starts with the *future* and tries to calculate its worth in the *present* ($80). For example, in Figure 12.5, we assume Bill Smith knew that in 4 years he wanted to buy a bike that cost $108.84 (future). Bill's bank pays 8% interest compounded annually. How much money must Bill put in the bank *today* (present) to have $108.84 in 4 years? To work from the future to the present, we can use a present value (PV) table. In the next section you will learn how to use this table.

How to Use a Present Value (PV) Table[7]

To calculate present value with a present value table, use the following steps:

CALCULATING PRESENT VALUE BY TABLE LOOKUP
Step 1. Find the periods: Years multiplied by number of times interest is compounded in 1 year.
Step 2. Find the rate: Annual rate divided by numbers of times interest is compounded in 1 year.
Step 3. Go down the Period column of the table to the number of periods desired; look across the row to find the rate. At the intersection of the two columns is the table factor for the compound value of $1.
Step 4. Multiply the table factor times the future value. This gives the present value.

Periods

$$4 \times 1 = 4$$

No. of years   No. of times compounded in 1 year

Table 12.3 is a present value (PV) table that tells you what $1 is worth today at different interest rates. To continue our Bill Smith example, go down the Period column in Table 12.3 to 4. Then go across to the 8% column. At 8% for 4 periods, we see a table factor of .7350. This means that $1 in the future is worth approximately 74 cents today. If Bill invested 74 cents today at 8% for 4 periods, Bill would have $1.

Since Bill knows the bike will cost $108.84 in the future, he completes the following calculation:

$$108.84 \times .7350 = \boxed{\$80.00}$$

This means that $108.84 in today's dollars is worth $80.00. Now let's check this.

---

[7]The formula for present value is $PV = \dfrac{A}{(1 + i)^N}$, where A equals future amount (compound amount), N equals number of compounding periods, and i equals interest rate per compounding period. The calculator sequence for Bill Smith would be as follows: 1 [+] .08 [y^x] 4 [=] [M+] 108.84 [÷] [MR] [=] 80.03.

TABLE	12.3	Present value of $1 at end period

Period	1%	1½%	2%	3%	4%	5%	6%	7%	8%	9%	10%
1	.9901	.9852	.9804	.9709	.9615	.9524	.9434	.9346	.9259	.9174	.9091
2	.9803	.9707	.9612	.9426	.9246	.9070	.8900	.8734	.8573	.8417	.8264
3	.9706	.9563	.9423	.9151	.8890	.8638	.8396	.8163	.7938	.7722	.7513
4	.9610	.9422	.9238	.8885	.8548	.8227	.7921	.7629	.7350	.7084	.6830
5	.9515	.9283	.9057	.8626	.8219	.7835	.7473	.7130	.6806	.6499	.6209
6	.9420	.9145	.8880	.8375	.7903	.7462	.7050	.6663	.6302	.5963	.5645
7	.9327	.9010	.8706	.8131	.7599	.7107	.6651	.6227	.5835	.5470	.5132
8	.9235	.8877	.8535	.7894	.7307	.6768	.6274	.5820	.5403	.5019	.4665
9	.9143	.8746	.8368	.7664	.7026	.6446	.5919	.5439	.5002	.4604	.4241
10	.9053	.8617	.8203	.7441	.6756	.6139	.5584	.5083	.4632	.4224	.3855
11	.8963	.8489	.8043	.7224	.6496	.5847	.5268	.4751	.4289	.3875	.3505
12	.8874	.8364	.7885	.7014	.6246	.5568	.4970	.4440	.3971	.3555	.3186
13	.8787	.8240	.7730	.6810	.6006	.5303	.4688	.4150	.3677	.3262	.2897
14	.8700	.8119	.7579	.6611	.5775	.5051	.4423	.3878	.3405	.2992	.2633
15	.8613	.7999	.7430	.6419	.5553	.4810	.4173	.3624	.3152	.2745	.2394
16	.8528	.7880	.7284	.6232	.5339	.4581	.3936	.3387	.2919	.2519	.2176
17	.8444	.7764	.7142	.6050	.5134	.4363	.3714	.3166	.2703	.2311	.1978
18	.8360	.7649	.7002	.5874	.4936	.4155	.3503	.2959	.2502	.2120	.1799
19	.8277	.7536	.6864	.5703	.4746	.3957	.3305	.2765	.2317	.1945	.1635
20	.8195	.7425	.6730	.5537	.4564	.3769	.3118	.2584	.2145	.1784	.1486
21	.8114	.7315	.6598	.5375	.4388	.3589	.2942	.2415	.1987	.1637	.1351
22	.8034	.7207	.6468	.5219	.4220	.3418	.2775	.2257	.1839	.1502	.1228
23	.7954	.7100	.6342	.5067	.4057	.3256	.2618	.2109	.1703	.1378	.1117
24	.7876	.6995	.6217	.4919	.3901	.3101	.2470	.1971	.1577	.1264	.1015
25	.7798	.6892	.6095	.4776	.3751	.2953	.2330	.1842	.1460	.1160	.0923
26	.7720	.6790	.5976	.4637	.3607	.2812	.2198	.1722	.1352	.1064	.0839
27	.7644	.6690	.5859	.4502	.3468	.2678	.2074	.1609	.1252	.0976	.0763
28	.7568	.6591	.5744	.4371	.3335	.2551	.1956	.1504	.1159	.0895	.0693
29	.7493	.6494	.5631	.4243	.3207	.2429	.1846	.1406	.1073	.0822	.0630
30	.7419	.6398	.5521	.4120	.3083	.2314	.1741	.1314	.0994	.0754	.0573
35	.7059	.5939	.5000	.3554	.2534	.1813	.1301	.0937	.0676	.0490	.0356
40	.6717	.5513	.4529	.3066	.2083	.1420	.0972	.0668	.0460	.0318	.0221

Note: For more detailed tables, see your booklet, the *Business Math Handbook.*

Comparing Compound Interest (FV) Table 12.1 with Present Value (PV) Table 12.3

We know from our calculations that Bill needs to invest $80 for 4 years at 8% compound interest annually to buy his bike. We can check this by going back to Table 12.1 and comparing it with Table 12.3. Let's do this now.

Compound value Table 12.1				Present value Table 12.3			
Table 12.1	Present value		Future value	Table 12.3	Future value		Present value
1.3605	×	$80.00	= $108.84	.7350	×	$108.84	= $80.00
(4 per., 8%)				(4 per., 8%)			
We know the present dollar amount and find what the dollar amount is worth in the future.				We know the future dollar amount and find what the dollar amount is worth in the present.			

FIGURE **12.6**

Present value

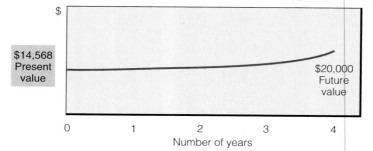

The present value is what we need *now* to have $20,000 in the future

Note that the table factor for compounding is over 1 (1.3605) and the table factor for present value is less than 1 (.7350). The compound value table starts with the present and goes to the future. The present value table starts with the future and goes to the present.

Let's look at another example before trying the Practice Quiz.

EXAMPLE Rene Weaver needs $20,000 for college in 4 years. She can earn 8% compounded quarterly at her bank. How much must Rene deposit at the beginning of the year to have $20,000 in 4 years?

Remember that in this example the bank compounds the interest *quarterly*. Let's first determine the period and rate on a quarterly basis:

$$\text{Periods} = 4 \times 4 \text{ years} = 16 \text{ periods} \qquad \text{Rate} = \frac{8\%}{4} = 2\%$$

Now we go to Table 12.3 and find 16 under the Period column. We then move across to the 2% column and find the .7284 table factor.

$$\$20,000 \times .7284 = \boxed{\$14,568}$$

(future value)   (present value)

We illustrate this in Figure 12.6.

We can check the $14,568 present value by using the compound value Table 12.1:

16 periods, 2% column = 1.3728 × $14,568 = $19,998.95[8]

Let's test your understanding of this unit with the Practice Quiz.

Complete this **Practice Quiz** to see how you are doing

Use the present value Table 12.3 to complete:

	Future amount desired	Length of time	Rate compounded	Table period	Rate used	PV factor	PV amount
1.	$ 7,000	6 years	6% semiannually	_____	_____	_____	_____
2.	$15,000	20 years	10% annually	_____	_____	_____	_____

3. Bill Blum needs $20,000 6 years from today to attend V.P.R. Tech. How much must Bill put in the bank today (12% quarterly) to reach his goal?

4. Bob Fry wants to buy his grandson a Ford Taurus in 4 years. The cost of a car will be $24,000. Assuming a bank rate of 8% compounded quarterly, how much must Bob put in the bank today?

✓ Solutions

1. 12 periods (6 years × 2)   3% (6% ÷ 2)   .7014 $4,909.80 ($7,000 × .7014)

2. 20 periods (20 years × 1)   10% (10% ÷ 1)   .1486 $2,229.00 ($15,000 × .1486)

3. 6 years × 4 = 24 periods $\dfrac{12\%}{4} = 3\%$ .4919 × $20,000 = $9,838

4. 4 × 4 years = 16 periods $\dfrac{8\%}{4} = 2\%$ .7284 × $24,000 = $17,481.60

[8]Not quite $20,000 due to rounding of table factors.

LU 12–2a EXTRA PRACTICE QUIZ

Need more practice? Try this **Extra Practice Quiz** (check figures in Chapter Organizer, p. 308)

Use the *Business Math Handbook* to complete:

Future amount desired	Length of time	Rate compounded	Table period	Rate used	PV factor	PV amount
1. $ 9,000	7 years	5% semiannually	_____	_____	_____	_____
2. $20,000	20 years	4% annually	_____	_____	_____	_____

3. Bill Blum needs $40,000 6 years from today to attend V.P.R. Tech. How much must Bill put in the bank today (8% quarterly) to reach his goal?

4. Bob Fry wants to buy his grandson a Ford Taurus in 4 years. The cost of a car will be $28,000. Assuming a bank rate of 4% compounded quarterly, how much must Bob put in the bank today?

CHAPTER ORGANIZER AND STUDY GUIDE
WITH CHECK FIGURES FOR EXTRA PRACTICE QUIZZES

Topic	Key point, procedure, formula	Example(s) to illustrate situation
Calculating compound amount without tables (future value),* p. 298	Determine new amount by multiplying rate times new balance (that includes interest added on). Start in present and look to future. $$\text{Compound interest} = \text{Compound amount} - \text{Principal}$$ ⊢—— Compounding ——⊣ PV →→→ FV	$100 in savings account, compounded annually for 2 years at 8%: $$\begin{array}{cc} \$100 & \$108 \\ \times\ 1.08 & \times\ 1.08 \\ \hline \$108 & \$116.64 \text{ (future value)} \end{array}$$
Calculating compound amount (future value) by table lookup, p. 299	$$\text{Periods} = \frac{\text{Number of times compounded}}{\text{per year}} \times \frac{\text{Years of}}{\text{loan}}$$ $$\text{Rate} = \frac{\text{Annual rate}}{\text{Number of times compounded per year}}$$ Multiply table factor (intersection of period and rate) times amount of principal.	*Example:* $2,000 @ 12% 5 years compounded quarterly: Periods = 4 × 5 years = 20 Rate = $\frac{12\%}{4} = 3\%$ 20 periods, 3% = 1.8061 (table factor) $2,000 × 1.8061 = $3,612.20 (future value)
Effective rate (APY), p. 301	$$\text{Effective rate (APY)} = \frac{\text{Interest for 1 year}}{\text{Principal}}$$ or Rate can be seen in Table 12.1 factor.	$1,000 at 10% compounded semiannually for 1 year. By Table 12.1: 2 periods, 5% 1.1025 means at end of year investor has earned 110.25% of original principal. Thus the interest is 10.25%. $$\begin{array}{r} \$1,000 \times 1.1025 = \$1,102.50 \\ -\ 1,000.00 \\ \hline \$\ \ \ 102.50 \end{array}$$ $\dfrac{\$102.50}{\$1,000} = 10.25\%$ effective rate (APY)

*$A = P(1 + i)^N$.

(continues)

CHAPTER ORGANIZER AND STUDY GUIDE
WITH CHECK FIGURES FOR EXTRA PRACTICE QUIZZES (concluded)

Topic	Key point, procedure, formula	Example(s) to illustrate situation
Calculating present value (PV) with table lookup*, p. 304	Start with future and calculate worth in the present. Periods and rate computed like in compound interest. ┌─── Present value ───┐ PV ←───────────── FV Find periods and rate. Multiply table factor (intersection of period and rate) times amount of loan.	*Example:* Want $3,612.20 after 5 years with rate of 12% compounded quarterly: Periods = 4 × 5 = 20; % = 3% By Table 12.3: 20 periods, 3% = .5537 $3,612.20 × .5537 = $2,000.08 Invested today will yield desired amount in future
KEY TERMS	Annual percentage yield (APY), *p. 301* Compound amount, *p. 296* Compounded annually, *p. 297* Compounded daily, *p. 297* Compounded monthly, *p. 297* Compounded quarterly, *p. 297* Compounded semiannually, *p. 297* Compounding, *p. 296* Compound interest, *p. 296* Effective rate, *p. 301* Future value (FV), *p. 296* Nominal rate, *p. 301* Number of periods, *p. 297* Present value (PV), *p. 296* Rate for each period, *p. 297*	
CHECK FIGURES FOR EXTRA PRACTICE QUIZZES WITH PAGE REFERENCES	LU 12–1a (p. 303) 1. 4 periods; Int. = $41.22; $541.21 2. $541.20 3. $9,609.60 4. 6.14% 5. $2,429.64	LU 12–2a (p. 307) 1. $6,369.30 2. $9,128 3. $24,868 4. $23,878.40

*$\frac{A}{(1 + i)^N}$ if table not used.

Critical Thinking Discussion Questions

1. Explain how periods and rates are calculated in compounding problems. Compare simple interest to compound interest.

2. What are the steps to calculate the compound amount by table? Why is the compound table factor greater than $1?

3. What is the effective rate (APY)? Why can the effective rate be seen directly from the table factor?

4. Explain the difference between compounding and present value. Why is the present value table factor less than $1?

Name _____ Date _____

DRILL PROBLEMS

Complete the following without using Table 12.1 (round to the nearest cent for each calculation) and then check by Table 12.1 (check will be off due to rounding).

	Principal	Time (years)	Rate of compound interest	Compounded	Periods	Rate	Total amount	Total interest
12–1.	$1,400	2	4%	Semiannually				

Complete the following using compound future value Table 12.1:

	Time	Principal	Rate	Compounded	Amount	Interest
12–2.	9 years	$10,000	3%	Annually		
12–3.	6 months	$10,000	8%	Quarterly		
12–4.	3 years	$2,000	12%	Semiannually		

Calculate the effective rate (APY) of interest for 1 year.

12–5. Principal: $15,500
Interest rate: 12%
Compounded quarterly
Effective rate (APY):

12–6. Using Table 12.2, calculate what $700 would grow to at $6\frac{1}{2}\%$ per year compounded daily for 7 years.

Complete the following using present value of Table 12.3 or *Business Math Handbook* Table.

	Amount desired at end of period	Length of time	Rate	Compounded	On PV Table 12.3		PV factor used	PV of amount desired at end of period
					Period used	Rate used		
12–7.	$4,500	7 years	2%	Semiannually				
12–8.	$8,900	4 years	6%	Monthly				
12–9.	$17,600	7 years	12%	Quarterly				
12–10.	$20,000	20 years	8%	Annually				

12–11. Check your answer in Problem 12–9 by the compound value Table 12.1. The answer will be off due to rounding.

WORD PROBLEMS

12–12. Savings plans and the cost of college attendance were discussed in the September 18, 2006 issue of *U.S. News & World Report*. Greg Lawrence anticipates he will need approximately $218,000 in 15 years to cover his 3 year old daughter's college bills for a 4 year degree. How much would he have to invest today, at an interest rate of 8 percent compounded semiannually?

12–13. Jennifer Toby, owner of a local Subway shop, loaned $25,000 to Mike Roy to help him open a Subway franchise. Mike plans to repay Jennifer at the end of 7 years with 4% interest compounded semiannually. How much will Jennifer receive at the end of 7 years?

12–14. Molly Slate deposited $35,000 at Quazi Bank at 6% interest compounded quarterly. What is the effective rate (APY) to the nearest hundredth percent?

12–15. Melvin Indecision has difficulty deciding whether to put his savings in Mystic Bank or Four Rivers Bank. Mystic offers 10% interest compounded semiannually. Four Rivers offers 8% interest compounded quarterly. Melvin has $10,000 to invest. He expects to withdraw the money at the end of 4 years. Which bank gives Melvin the better deal? Check your answer.

12–16. Brian Costa deposited $20,000 in a new savings account at 12% interest compounded semiannually. At the beginning of year 4, Brian deposits an additional $30,000 at 12% interest compounded semiannually. At the end of 6 years, what is the balance in Brian's account?

12–17. Lee Wills loaned Audrey Chin $16,000 to open a hair salon. After 6 years, Audrey will repay Lee with 8% interest compounded quarterly. How much will Lee receive at the end of 6 years?

12–18. *The Dallas Morning News* on June 12, 2006, reported on saving for retirement. Carl Hendrik is 56 years old and has worked for Texas Instruments Inc for 35 years. He has amassed a plump nest egg of $700,000. His bank compounds interest semiannually, at 6%. Carl plans to retire at 65, if he places his money in the bank, how much will his investment be worth at retirement?

12–19. John Roe, an employee of The Gap, loans $3,000 to another employee at the store. He will be repaid at the end of 4 years with interest at 6% compounded quarterly. How much will John be repaid?

12–20. On September 14, 2006 *USA Today* ran a story on funding for retirement. The average 65 year old woman can expect to live to nearly 87 according to the American Academy of Actuaries. Mary Tully is 40 years old. She expects to need at least $420,000 when she retires at age 65. How much money must she invest today, in an account paying 6% interest compounded annually, to have the amount of money she needs?

12–21. Security National Bank is quoting 1-year certificates of deposits with an interest rate of 5% compounded semiannually. Joe Saver purchased a $5,000 CD. What is the CD's effective rate (APY) to the nearest hundredth percent? Use tables in the *Business Math Handbook.*

12–22. Jim Jones, an owner of a Burger King restaurant, assumes that his restaurant will need a new roof in 7 years. He estimates the roof will cost him $9,000 at that time. What amount should Jim invest today at 6% compounded quarterly to be able to pay for the roof? Check your answer.

12–23. Tony Ring wants to attend Northeast College. He will need $60,000 4 years from today. Assume Tony's bank pays 12% interest compounded semiannually. What must Tony deposit today so he will have $60,000 in 4 years?

12–24. Could you check your answer (to the nearest dollar) in Problem 12–23 by using the compound value Table 12.1? The answer will be slightly off due to rounding.

12–25. Pete Air wants to buy a used Jeep in 5 years. He estimates the Jeep will cost $15,000. Assume Pete invests $10,000 now at 12% interest compounded semiannually. Will Pete have enough money to buy his Jeep at the end of 5 years?

12–26. Lance Jackson deposited $5,000 at Basil Bank at 9% interest compounded daily. What is Lance's investment at the end of 4 years?

12–27. Paul Havlik promised his grandson Jamie that he would give him $6,000 8 years from today for graduating from high school. Assume money is worth 6% interest compounded semiannually. What is the present value of this $6,000?

12–28. Earl Ezekiel wants to retire in San Diego when he is 65 years old. Earl is now 50. He believes he will need $300,000 to retire comfortably. To date, Earl has set aside no retirement money. Assume Earl gets 6% interest compounded semiannually. How much must Earl invest today to meet his $300,000 goal?

12–29. Lorna Evenson would like to buy a $19,000 car in 4 years. Lorna wants to put the money aside now. Lorna's bank offers 8% interest compounded semiannually. How much must Lorna invest today?

12–30. John Smith saw the following advertisement. Could you show him how $88.77 was calculated?

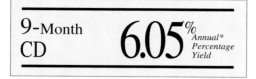

9-Month CD **6.05**% Annual* Percentage Yield

*As of January 31, 200X, and subject to change. Interest on the 9-month CD is credited on the maturity date and is not compounded. For example, a $2,000, 9-month CD on deposit for an interest rate of 6.00% (6.05% APY) will earn $88.77 at maturity. Withdrawals prior to maturity require the consent of the bank and are subject to a substantial penalty. There is $500 minimum deposit for IRA, SEP IRA, and Keogh CDs (except for 9-month CD for which the minimum deposit is $1,000). There is $1,000 minimum deposit for all personal CDs (except for 9-month CD for which the minimum deposit is $2,000). Offer not valid on jumbo CDs.

CHALLENGE PROBLEMS

12–31. Mary started her first job at 22. She began saving money immediately but stopped after five years. Mary invested $2,500 each year until age 27. She receives 10% interest compounded annually and plans to retire at 62. **(a)** What amount will Mary have when she reaches retirement age? Use the tables in the *Business Math Handbook*. **(b)** What is the total amount of interest she will have received?

12–32. You are the financial planner for Johnson Controls. Last year's profits were $700,000. The board of directors decided to forgo dividends to stockholders and retire high-interest outstanding bonds that were issued 5 years ago at a face value of $1,250,000. You have been asked to invest the profits in a bank. The board must know how much money you will need from the profits earned to retire the bonds in 10 years. Bank A pays 6% compounded quarterly, and Bank B pays $6\frac{1}{2}$% compounded annually. Which bank would you recommend, and how much of the company's profit should be placed in the bank? If you recommended that the remaining money not be distributed to stockholders but be placed in Bank B, how much would the remaining money be worth in 10 years? Use tables in the *Business Math Handbook*.* Round final answer to nearest dollar.

*Check glossary for unfamiliar terms.

1. Mia Kaminsky, owner of a Starbucks franchise, loaned $40,000 to Lee Reese to help him open a new flower shop online. Lee plans to repay Mia at the end of 5 years with 4% interest compounded semiannually. How much will Mia receive at the end of 5 years? *(p. 299)*

2. Joe Beary wants to attend Riverside College. Eight years from today he will need $50,000. If Joe's bank pays 6% interest compounded semiannually, what must Joe deposit today to have $50,000 in 8 years? *(p. 304)*

3. Shelley Katz deposited $30,000 in a savings account at 5% interest compounded semiannually. At the beginning of year 4, Shelley deposits an additional $80,000 at 5% interest compounded semiannually. At the end of 6 years, what is the balance in Shelley's account? *(p. 299)*

4. Earl Miller, owner of a Papa Gino's franchise, wants to buy a new delivery truck in 6 years. He estimates the truck will cost $30,000. If Earl invests $20,000 now at 5% interest compounded semiannually, will Earl have enough money to buy his delivery truck at the end of 6 years? *(pp. 299, 304)*

5. Minnie Rose deposited $16,000 in Street Bank at 6% interest compounded quarterly. What was the effective rate (APY)? Round to the nearest hundredth percent. *(p. 301)*

6. Lou Ling, owner of Lou's Lube, estimates that he will need $70,000 for new equipment in 7 years. Lou decided to put aside money today so it will be available in 7 years. Reel Bank offers Lou 6% interest compounded quarterly. How much must Lou invest to have $70,000 in 7 years? *(p. 304)*

7. Bernie Long wants to retire to California when she is 60 years of age. Bernie is now 40. She believes that she will need $900,000 to retire comfortably. To date, Bernie has set aside no retirement money. If Bernie gets 8% compounded semiannually, how much must Bernie invest today to meet her $900,000 goal? *(p. 304)*

8. Sam Slater deposited $19,000 in a savings account at 7% interest compounded daily. At the end of 6 years, what is the balance in Sam's account? *(p. 301)*

Personal Finance

A KIPLINGER APPROACH

CREDIT | Some card issuers offer help to the shopping-addicted and the savings-impaired.

Keep the CHANGE

AS A NATION, we're big spenders, not savers. So it figures that banks would invent a way for us to do both at once. Buy something using one of the new cards from American Express, Bank of America and a handful of other issuers, and the banks will stash a cash rebate into a savings account. Shopping and traveling won't replace your IRA contributions, but if you use plastic for gas and groceries, the money can add up.

American Express's One card funnels 1% of all purchases into a savings account that now pays 3.5%. At that rate, if you charge $2,000 a month, you'll have $6,000 in 18 years—not enough for your child's college tuition, but maybe enough for books. Amex will waive the $35 annual fee the first year and seed your account with $25.

Bank of America effec-tively puts your pocket change into an electronic piggy bank. Sign up for its Keep the Change program and the bank rounds up all purchases on your debit card to the nearest dollar and moves the difference into a savings account. For three months, the bank matches your deposits 100%. After that, it matches 5% per year up to $250. That's no windfall. But look at it this way: A penny spent becomes a penny saved. —**JOAN GOLDWASSER**

ALISON SEIFFER

BUSINESS MATH ISSUE

Keep the change is a gimmick that banks are using just to get new customers.

1. List the key points of the article and information to support your position.
2. Write a group defense of your position using math calculations to support your view.

Kiplinger © 2006

314

Slater's Business Math Scrapbook

with Internet Application

Putting Your Skills to Work

PROJECT A
Go to Web and find out the latest rates for 6 months, 1 year, and 5-year CDs along with the current rates for markets.

Interest Rates Lofty

Tim Foley

Interest Over Rising Interest

Rates offered by banks on various deposits over the past year

Yields	
5-Year CD	**3.90%**
1-Year CD	**3.29%**
6-Month CD	**2.84%**
Money–market account	**0.76%**

Note: Through Wed., Jan. 11
Source: Bankrate.com

Wall Street Journal © 2006

Internet Projects: See text Web site (www.mhhe.com/slater9e) and The Business Math Internet Resource Guide.

Additional Homework
by Learning Unit

Name _____   Date _____

Learning Unit 1–1:   Reading, Writing, and Rounding Whole Numbers

DRILL PROBLEMS

1. Express the following numbers in verbal form:
   a. 7,521 _____

   b. 160,501 _____

   c. 2,098,767 _____

   d. 58,003 _____

   e. 50,025,212,015 _____

2. Write in numeric form:
   a. Ninety thousand, two hundred eighty-one _____

   b. Fifty-eight thousand, three _____

   c. Two hundred eighty thousand, five _____

   d. Three million, ten _____

   e. Sixty-seven thousand, seven hundred sixty _____

3. Round the following numbers:
   a. To the nearest ten:

42	_____	379	_____	855	_____	5,981	_____	206	_____

   b. To the nearest hundred:

9,664	_____	2,074	_____	888	_____	271	_____	75	_____

   c. To the nearest thousand:

21,486	_____	621	_____	3,504	_____	9,735	_____

4. Round off each number to the nearest ten, nearest hundred, nearest thousand, and round all the way. (Remember that you are rounding the original number each time.)

		Nearest ten	Nearest hundred	Nearest thousand	Round all the way
a.	4,752	_____	_____	_____	_____
b.	70,351	_____	_____	_____	_____
c.	9,386	_____	_____	_____	_____
d.	4,983	_____	_____	_____	_____
e.	408,119	_____	_____	_____	_____
f.	30,051	_____	_____	_____	_____

5. Name the place position (place value) of the underlined digit.
   a. 8,<u>3</u>48 _____

   b. <u>9</u>,734 _____

   c. 3<u>4</u>7,107 _____

   d. 7<u>2</u>3 _____

e. 28,200,000,121 _____

f. 706,359,005 _____

g. 27,563,530 _____

WORD PROBLEMS

6. Ken Lawler was shopping for a computer. He went to three different Web sites and found the computer he wanted at three different prices. At Web site A the price was $2,115, at Web site B the price was $1,990, and at Web site C the price was $2,050. What is the approximate price Ken will have to pay for the computer? Round to the nearest thousand. (Just one price.)

7. Amy Parker had to write a check at the bookstore when she purchased her books for the new semester. The total cost of the books was $384. How will she write this amount in verbal form on her check?

8. Matt Schaeffer was listening to the news and heard that steel production last week was one million, five hundred eighty-seven thousand tons. Express this amount in numeric form.

9. Jackie Martin is the city clerk and must go to the aldermen's meetings and take notes on what is discussed. At last night's meeting, they were discussing repairs for the public library, which will cost three hundred seventy-five thousand, nine hundred eighty-five dollars. Write this in numeric form as Jackie would.

10. A government survey revealed that 25,963,400 people are employed as office workers. To show the approximate number of office workers, round the number all the way.

11. Bob Donaldson wished to present his top student with a certificate of achievement at the end of the school year in 2004. To make it appear more official, he wanted to write the year in verbal form. How did he write the year?

12. Nancy Morrissey has a problem reading large numbers and determining place value. She asked her brother to name the place value of the 4 in the number 13,542,966. Can you tell Nancy the place value of the 4? What is the place value of the 3?

   The 4 is in the _____ place.

   The 3 is in the _____ place.

Name _____   Date _____

Learning Unit 1-2: Adding and Subtracting Whole Numbers

DRILL PROBLEMS

1. Add by totaling each separate column:

| **a.** | 659
322 | **b.** | 43
58
96 | **c.** | 493
826 | **d.** | 36
76
43
24 | **e.** | 716
458
397
139
478 | **f.** | 535
107
778
215
391 | **g.** | 751
378
135
747
368 | **h.** | 75,730
48,531
15,797 |

2. Estimate by rounding all the way, then add the actual numbers:

| **a.** | 580
971
548
430
506 | **b.** | 1,470
7,631
4,383 | **c.** | 475
837
213
775
432 |

| **d.** | 442
609
766
410
128 | **e.** | 2,571
3,625
4,091
928 | **f.** | 10,928
9,321
12,654
15,492 |

3. Estimate by rounding all the way, then subtract the actual numbers:

| **a.** | 81
− 42 | **b.** | 91
− 33 | **c.** | 68
− 59 |

| **d.** | 981
− 283 | **e.** | 622
− 328 | **f.** | 1,125
− 913 |

4. Subtract and check:

| **a.** | 4,947
− 4,362 | **b.** | 3,724
− 2,138 | **c.** | 474,820
− 85,847 |

| **d.** | 50,000
− 21,762 | **e.** | 65,003
− 24,987 | **f.** | 15,715
− 3,503 |

5. In the following sales report, total the rows and the columns, then check that the grand total is the same both horizontally and vertically.

Salesperson	Region 1	Region 2	Region 3	Total
a. Becker	$ 5,692	$ 7,403	$ 3,591	
b. Edwards	7,652	7,590	3,021	
c. Graff	6,545	6,738	4,545	
d. Jackson	6,937	6,950	4,913	
e. Total				

WORD PROBLEMS

6. Joy Jill owes $6,500 on her car loan, plus interest of $499. How much will it cost her to pay off this loan?

7. Sales at Rich's Convenience Store were $3,587 on Monday, $3,944 on Tuesday, $4,007 on Wednesday, $3,890 on Thursday, and $4,545 on Friday. What were the total sales for the week?

8. Poor's Variety Store sold $5,000 worth of lottery tickets in the first week of August; it sold $289 less in the second week. How much were the lottery ticket sales in the second week of August?

9. A truck weighed 9,550 pounds when it was empty. After being filled with rubbish, it was driven to the dump where it weighed in at 22,347 pounds. How much did the rubbish weigh?

10. Lynn Jackson had $549 in her checking account when she went to the bookstore. Lynn purchased an accounting book for $62, the working papers for $28, a study guide for $25, and a mechanical pencil for $5. After Lynn writes a check for the entire purchase, how much money will remain in her checking account?

11. A new hard-body truck is advertised with a base price of $6,986 delivered. However, the window sticker on the truck reads as follows: tinted glass, $210; automatic transmission, $650; power steering, $210; power brakes, $215; safety locks, $95; air conditioning, $1,056. Estimate the total price, including the accessories, by rounding all the way and *then* calculating the exact price.

12. Four different stores are offering the same make and model of camcorder:

Store A	Store B	Store C	Store D
$1,285	$1,380	$1,440	$1,355

    Find the difference between the highest price and the lowest price. Check your answer.

13. A Xerox XC830 copy machine has a suggested retail price of $1,395. The net price is $649. How much is the discount on the copy machine?

Name _____   Date _____

Learning Unit 1–3:   **Multiplying and Dividing Whole Numbers**

DRILL PROBLEMS

1. In the following problems, first estimate by rounding all the way, then work the actual problems and check:

   Actual   **Estimate**   **Check**

   a.   160
       $\times$ 15

   b.   4,216
       $\times$ 45

   c.   52,376
       $\times$ 309

   d.   3,106
       $\times$ 28

2. Multiply (use the shortcut when applicable):

   a.   4,072   b.   5,100
       $\times$ 100 $\times$ 40

   c.   76,000   d. 93 $\times$ 100,000
       $\times$ 1,200

3. Divide by rounding all the way; then do the actual calculation and check showing the remainder as a whole number.

   Actual   **Estimate**   **Check**

   a. 8)7,709

   b. 26)5,910

	Actual	**Estimate**	**Check**

c. $151\overline{)3{,}783}$

d. $46\overline{)19{,}550}$

4. Divide by the shortcut method:

a. $200\overline{)5{,}400}$ b. $50\overline{)5{,}650}$

c. $1{,}200\overline{)43{,}200}$ d. $17{,}000\overline{)510{,}000}$

WORD PROBLEMS

5. Mia Kaminsky sells state lottery tickets in her variety store. If Mia's Variety Store sells 410 lottery tickets per day, how many tickets will be sold in a 7-day period?

6. Arlex Oil Company employs 100 people who are eligible for profit sharing. The financial manager has announced that the profits to be shared amount to $64,000. How much will each employee receive?

7. John Duncan's employer withheld $4,056 in federal taxes from his pay for the year. If equal deductions are made each week, what is John's weekly deduction?

8. Anne Domingoes drives a Volvo that gets 32 miles per gallon of gasoline. How many miles can she travel on 25 gallons of gas?

9. How many 8-inch pieces of yellow ribbon can be cut from a spool of ribbon that contains 6 yards (1 yard = 36 inches)?

10. The number of commercials aired per day on a local television station is 672. How many commercials are aired in 1 year?

11. The computer department at City College purchased 18 computers at a cost of $2,400 each. What was the total price for the computer purchase?

12. Net income for Goodwin's Partnership was $64,500. The five partners share profits and losses equally. What was each partner's share?

13. Ben Krenshaw's supervisor at the construction site told Ben to divide a load of 1,423 bricks into stacks containing 35 bricks each. How many stacks will there be when Ben has finished the job? How many "extra" bricks will there be?

Name _____   Date _____

Learning Unit 2–1:   Types of Fractions and Conversion Procedures

DRILL PROBLEMS

1. Identify the type of fraction—proper, improper, or mixed number:

   a. $9\dfrac{1}{5}$ **b.** $\dfrac{29}{28}$ **c.** $\dfrac{29}{27}$

   d. $9\dfrac{3}{11}$ **e.** $\dfrac{18}{5}$ **f.** $\dfrac{30}{37}$

2. Convert to a mixed number:

   a. $\dfrac{29}{4}$ **b.** $\dfrac{137}{8}$ **c.** $\dfrac{27}{5}$

   d. $\dfrac{29}{9}$ **e.** $\dfrac{71}{8}$ **f.** $\dfrac{43}{6}$

3. Convert the mixed number to an improper fraction:

   a. $7\dfrac{1}{5}$ **b.** $12\dfrac{3}{11}$ **c.** $4\dfrac{3}{7}$

   d. $20\dfrac{4}{9}$ **e.** $10\dfrac{11}{12}$ **f.** $17\dfrac{2}{3}$

4. Tell whether the fractions in each pair are equivalent or not:

   a. $\dfrac{3}{4}\quad\dfrac{9}{12}$ _____   **b.** $\dfrac{2}{3}\quad\dfrac{12}{18}$ _____   **c.** $\dfrac{7}{8}\quad\dfrac{15}{16}$ _____

   d. $\dfrac{4}{5}\quad\dfrac{12}{15}$ _____   **e.** $\dfrac{3}{2}\quad\dfrac{9}{4}$ _____   **f.** $\dfrac{5}{8}\quad\dfrac{7}{11}$ _____

   g. $\dfrac{7}{12}\quad\dfrac{7}{24}$ _____   **h.** $\dfrac{5}{4}\quad\dfrac{30}{24}$ _____   **i.** $\dfrac{10}{26}\quad\dfrac{12}{26}$ _____

5. Find the greatest common divisor by the step approach and reduce to lowest terms:

   a. $\dfrac{36}{42}$

   b. $\dfrac{30}{75}$

   c. $\dfrac{74}{148}$

   d. $\dfrac{15}{600}$

   e. $\dfrac{96}{132}$

f. $\dfrac{84}{154}$

6. Convert to higher terms:

a. $\dfrac{8}{10} = \dfrac{}{70}$

b. $\dfrac{2}{15} = \dfrac{}{30}$

c. $\dfrac{6}{11} = \dfrac{}{132}$

d. $\dfrac{4}{9} = \dfrac{}{36}$

e. $\dfrac{7}{20} = \dfrac{}{100}$

f. $\dfrac{7}{8} = \dfrac{}{560}$

WORD PROBLEMS

7. Ken drove to college in $3\frac{1}{4}$ hours. How many quarter-hours is that? Show your answer as an improper fraction.

8. Mary looked in the refrigerator for a dozen eggs. When she found the box, only 5 eggs were left. What fractional part of the box of eggs was left?

9. At a recent meeting of a local Boosters Club, 17 of the 25 members attending were men. What fraction of those in attendance were men?

10. By weight, water is two parts out of three parts of the human body. What fraction of the body is water?

11. Three out of 5 students who begin college will continue until they receive their degree. Show in fractional form how many out of 100 beginning students will graduate.

12. Tina and her friends came in late to a party and found only $\frac{3}{4}$ of a pizza remaining. In order for everyone to get some pizza, she wanted to divide it into smaller pieces. If she divides the pizza into twelfths, how many pieces will she have? Show your answer in fractional form.

13. Sharon and Spunky noted that it took them 35 minutes to do their exercise routine. What fractional part of an hour is that? Show your answer in lowest terms.

14. Norman and his friend ordered several pizzas, which were all cut into eighths. The group ate 43 pieces of pizza. How many pizzas did they eat? Show your answer as a mixed number.

Name _____   Date _____

Learning Unit 2–2: Adding and Subtracting Fractions

DRILL PROBLEMS

1. Find the least common denominator (LCD) for each of the following groups of denominators using the prime numbers:

   a. 8, 16, 32   **b.** 9, 15, 20

   c. 12, 15, 32   **d.** 7, 9, 14, 28

2. Add and reduce to lowest terms or change to a mixed number if needed:

   a. $\dfrac{1}{8} + \dfrac{4}{8}$ **b.** $\dfrac{5}{12} + \dfrac{8}{15}$

   c. $\dfrac{7}{8} + \dfrac{5}{12}$ **d.** $7\dfrac{2}{3} + 5\dfrac{1}{4}$

   e. $\dfrac{2}{3} + \dfrac{4}{9} + \dfrac{1}{4}$

3. Subtract and reduce to lowest terms:

   a. $\dfrac{5}{9} - \dfrac{2}{9}$ **b.** $\dfrac{14}{15} - \dfrac{4}{15}$ **c.** $\dfrac{8}{9} - \dfrac{5}{6}$ **d.** $\dfrac{7}{12} - \dfrac{9}{16}$

   e. $33\dfrac{5}{8} - 27\dfrac{1}{2}$ **f.** $9 - 2\dfrac{3}{7}$ **g.** $15\dfrac{1}{3} - 9\dfrac{7}{12}$

   h. $92\dfrac{3}{10} - 35\dfrac{7}{15}$ **i.** $93 - 57\dfrac{5}{12}$ **j.** $22\dfrac{5}{8} - 17\dfrac{1}{4}$

WORD PROBLEMS

4.   Dan Lund took a cross-country trip. He drove $5\frac{3}{8}$ hours on Monday, $6\frac{1}{2}$ hours on Tuesday, $9\frac{3}{4}$ hours on Wednesday, $6\frac{3}{8}$ hours on Thursday, and $10\frac{1}{4}$ hours on Friday. Find the total number of hours Dan drove in the first 5 days of his trip.

5.   Sharon Parker bought 20 yards of material to make curtains. She used $4\frac{1}{2}$ yards for one bedroom window, $8\frac{3}{5}$ yards for another bedroom window, and $3\frac{7}{8}$ yards for a hall window. How much material did she have left?

6.   Molly Ring visited a local gym and lost $2\frac{1}{4}$ pounds the first weekend and $6\frac{1}{8}$ pounds in week 2. What is Molly's total weight loss?

7.   Bill Williams had to drive $46\frac{1}{4}$ miles to work. After driving $28\frac{5}{6}$ miles he noticed he was low on gas and had to decide whether he should stop to fill the gas tank. How many more miles does Bill have to drive to get to work?

8.   Albert's Lumber Yard purchased $52\frac{1}{2}$ cords of lumber on Monday and $48\frac{3}{4}$ cords on Tuesday. It sold $21\frac{3}{8}$ cords on Friday. How many cords of lumber remain at Albert's Lumber Yard?

9.   At Arlen Oil Company, where Dave Bursett is the service manager, it took $42\frac{1}{3}$ hours to clean five boilers. After a new cleaning tool was purchased, the time for cleaning five boilers was reduced to $37\frac{4}{9}$ hours. How much time was saved?

Name _____   Date _____

Learning Unit 2–3:   Multiplying and Dividing Fractions

DRILL PROBLEMS

1. Multiply (use cancellation technique):

   a. $\dfrac{6}{13} \times \dfrac{26}{12}$

   b. $\dfrac{3}{8} \times \dfrac{2}{3}$

   c. $\dfrac{5}{7} \times \dfrac{9}{10}$

   d. $\dfrac{3}{4} \times \dfrac{9}{13} \times \dfrac{26}{27}$

   e. $6\dfrac{2}{5} \times 3\dfrac{1}{8}$

   f. $2\dfrac{2}{3} \times 2\dfrac{7}{10}$

   g. $45 \times \dfrac{7}{9}$

   h. $3\dfrac{1}{9} \times 1\dfrac{2}{7} \times \dfrac{3}{4}$

   i. $\dfrac{3}{4} \times \dfrac{7}{9} \times 3\dfrac{1}{3}$

   j. $\dfrac{1}{8} \times 6\dfrac{2}{3} \times \dfrac{1}{10}$

2. Multiply (do not use canceling; reduce by finding the greatest common divisor):

   a. $\dfrac{3}{4} \times \dfrac{8}{9}$

   b. $\dfrac{7}{16} \times \dfrac{8}{13}$

3. Multiply or divide as indicated:

   a. $\dfrac{25}{36} \div \dfrac{5}{9}$

   b. $\dfrac{18}{8} \div \dfrac{12}{16}$

   c. $2\dfrac{6}{7} \div 2\dfrac{2}{5}$

   d. $3\dfrac{1}{4} \div 16$

   e. $24 \div 1\dfrac{1}{3}$

   f. $6 \times \dfrac{3}{2}$

g. $3\frac{1}{5} \times 7\frac{1}{2}$

h. $\frac{3}{8} \div \frac{7}{4}$

i. $9 \div 3\frac{3}{4}$

j. $\frac{11}{24} \times \frac{24}{33}$

k. $\frac{12}{14} \div 27$

l. $\frac{3}{5} \times \frac{2}{7} \div \frac{3}{10}$

WORD PROBLEMS

4. Mary Smith plans to make 12 meatloafs to store in her freezer. Each meatloaf requires $2\frac{1}{4}$ pounds of ground beef. How much ground beef does Mary need?

5. Judy Carter purchased a real estate lot for $24,000. She sold it 2 years later for $1\frac{5}{8}$ times as much as she had paid for it. What was the selling price?

6. Lynn Clarkson saw an ad for a camcorder that cost $980. She knew of a discount store that would sell it to her for a markdown of $\frac{3}{20}$ off the advertised price. How much is the discount she can get?

7. To raise money for their club, the members of the Marketing Club purchased 68 bushels of popcorn to resell. They plan to repackage the popcorn in bags that hold $\frac{2}{21}$ of a bushel each. How many bags of popcorn will they be able to fill?

8. Richard Tracy paid a total of $375 for lumber costing $9\frac{3}{8}$ per foot. How many feet did he purchase?

9. While training for a marathon, Kristin Woods jogged $7\frac{3}{4}$ miles per hour for $2\frac{2}{3}$ hours. How many miles did Kristin jog?

10. On a map, 1 inch represents 240 miles. How many miles are represented by $\frac{3}{8}$ of an inch?

11. In Massachusetts, the governor wants to allot $\frac{1}{6}$ of the total sales tax collections to public education. The total sales tax collected is $2,472,000; how much will go to education?

Name _____   Date _____

Learning Unit 3–1:   Rounding Decimals; Fraction and Decimal Conversions

DRILL PROBLEMS

1. Write in decimal:
   a. Sixty-two hundredths _____

   b. Nine tenths _____

   c. Nine hundred fifty-three thousandths _____

   d. Four hundred one thousandths _____

   e. Six hundredths _____

2. Round each decimal to the place indicated:
   a. .4326 to the nearest thousandth _____

   b. .051 to the nearest tenth _____

   c. 8.207 to the nearest hundredth _____

   d. 2.094 to the nearest hundredth _____

   e. .511172 to the nearest ten thousandth _____

3. Name the place position of the underlined digit:
   a. .8$\underline{2}$6 _____

   b. .91$\underline{4}$ _____

   c. 3.$\underline{1}$169 _____

   d. 53.17$\underline{5}$ _____

   e. 1.017$\underline{4}$ _____

4. Convert to fractions (do not reduce):

   a. .83 _____   b. .426 _____   c. 2.516 _____

   d. .62$\frac{1}{2}$ _____   e. 13.007 _____   f. 5.03$\frac{1}{4}$ _____

5. Convert to fractions and reduce to lowest terms:

   a. .4   b. .44   c. .53

   d. .336   e. .096   f. .125

   g. .3125   h. .008   i. 2.625

   j. 5.75   k. 3.375   l. 9.04

6. Convert the following fractions to decimals and round your answer to the nearest hundredth:

   a. $\frac{1}{8}$ b. $\frac{7}{16}$

   c. $\frac{2}{3}$ d. $\frac{3}{4}$

5. Complete by the shortcut method:

    a. 6.87 × 1,000   **b.** 927,530 ÷ 100   **c.** 27.2 ÷ 1,000

    d. .21 × 1,000   **e.** 347 × 100   **f.** 347 ÷ 100

    g. .0021 ÷ 10   **h.** 85.44 × 10,000   **i.** 83.298 × 100

    j. 23.0109 ÷ 100

WORD PROBLEMS (Use Business Math Handbook Tables as Needed.)

6. Bill Blum noted his FJ cruiser odometer reading of 17,629.3 at the beginning of his vacation. At the end of his vacation the reading was 20,545.1. How many miles did he drive during his vacation?

7. Jeanne Allyn purchased 12.25 yards of ribbon for a craft project. The ribbon cost 37¢ per yard. What was the total cost of the ribbon?

8. Leo Green wanted to find out the gas mileage for his company truck. When he filled the gas tank, he wrote down the odometer reading of 9,650.7. The next time he filled the gas tank the odometer reading was 10,112.2. He looked at the gas pump and saw that he had taken 18.5 gallons of gas. Find the gas mileage per gallon for Leo's truck. Round to the nearest tenth.

9. At Halley's Rent-a-Car, the cost per day to rent a medium-size car is $35.25 plus 37¢ a mile. What would be the charge to rent this car for 1 day if you drove 205.4 miles?

10. A trip to Mexico costs 6,000 pesos. What is this in U.S. dollars? Check your answer.

11. If a commemorative gold coin weighs 7.842 grams, find the number of coins that can be produced from 116 grams of gold. Round to the nearest whole number.

Name _____   Date _____

Learning Unit 4–1:   The Checking Account; Credit Card Transactions

DRILL PROBLEMS

1. The following is a deposit slip made out by Fred Young of the F. W. Young Company.

   a. How much cash did Young deposit?   _____

   b. How many checks did Young deposit?   _____

   c. What was the total amount deposited?   _____

				ADDITIONAL CHECKS		
DESCRIPTION	DOLLARS	CENTS	DESCRIPTION	DOLLARS	CENTS	
BILLS	415	XX	7.			
COIN	15	64	8.			
LIST CHECKS 1. 53-1297	188	44	9.			
2. 51-1509	98	37	10.			
3. 53-1290	150	06	11.			
4.			12.			
5.			13.			
6.			14.			
SUB TOTAL ITEMS 1-6			SUB TOTAL ITEMS 7-14			
			TOTAL			

Fleet Bank — Checking Deposit — TO THE ACCOUNT OF — DATE 3/27/09 — This deposit is subject to: proof and verification, the Uniform Commercial Code, the collection and availability policy of this bank. — NAME (PLEASE PRINT) PLEASE ENDORSE ALL CHECKS — PLEASE ENTER CLEARLY YOUR ACCOUNT NUMBER

⑈5 2 ⑈ 2 0 0 0 ⑈ 7 ⑈:

2. Blackstone Company had a balance of $2,173.18 in its checking account. Henry James, Blackstone's accountant, made a deposit that consisted of 2 fifty-dollar bills, 120 ten-dollar bills, 6 five-dollar bills, 14 one-dollar bills, $9.54 in change, plus two checks they had accepted, one for $16.38 and the other for $102.50. Find the amount of the deposit and the new balance in Blackstone's checking account.

3. Answer the following questions using the illustration:

No. 113 $ 750 00/100
October 4   20 XX
To Neuner Realty
For real estate

	DOLLARS	CENTS
BALANCE	1,020	93
AMT. DEPOSITED	2,756	80
TOTAL	3,777	73
AMT. THIS CHECK	750	00
BALANCE FORWARD	3,027	73

Jones Company
22 Aster Road
Salem, MA 01970

No. 113

October 4   20 XX   5-13/110

PAY TO THE ORDER OF   Neuner Realty Company $ 750 00/100

Seven Hundred Fifty and 00/100 _____ DOLLARS

FLEET BANK OF MASSACHUSETTS, NATIONAL ASSOCIATION
Fleet Bank   BOSTON, MASSACHUSETTS

Kevin Jones

MEMO   real estate

⑈0 1 1 0 0 0 1 3 8⑈:   1 4   0 3 8 0   1 1 3

   a. Who is the payee?   _____

   b. Who is the drawer?   _____

   c. Who is the drawee?   _____

   d. What is the bank's identification number   _____

    e. What is Jones Company's account number? _____

    f. What was the balance in the account on September 30? _____

    g. For how much did Jones write Check No. 113? _____

    h. How much was deposited on October 1? _____

    i. How much was left after Check No. 113 was written? _____

4. Write each of the following amounts in verbal form as you would on a check:

    a. $25 _____

    b. $245.75 _____

    c. $3.98 _____

    d. $1,205.05 _____

    e. $3,013 _____

    f. $510.10 _____

Name _____ Date _____

Learning Unit 4–2: Bank Statement and Reconciliation Process; Trends in Online Banking

WORD PROBLEMS

1. Find the bank balance on January 31.

Date	Checks and payments			Deposits	Balance
January 1					401.17
January 2	108.64				_____
January 5	116.50			432.16	_____
January 6	14.92	150.00	10.00		_____
January 11	12.29			633.89	_____
January 18	108.64	18.60			_____
January 25	43.91	23.77		657.22	_____
January 26	75.00				_____
January 31	6.75 sc				_____

2. Joe Madruga, of Madruga's Taxi Service, received a bank statement for the month of May showing a balance of $932.36. His records show that the bank had not yet recorded two of his deposits, one for $521.50 and the other for $98.46. There are outstanding checks in the amounts of $41.67, $135.18, and $25.30. The statement also shows a service charge of $3.38. The balance in the check register is $1,353.55. Prepare a bank reconciliation for Madruga's as of May 31.

3. In reconciling the checking account for Nasser Enterprises, Beth Accomando found that the bank had collected a $3,000 promissory note on the company's behalf and had charged a $15 collection fee. There was also a service charge of $7.25. What amount should be added/subtracted from the checkbook balance to bring it up to date?

   Add: _____   Deduct: _____

4. In reconciling the checking account for Colonial Cleaners, Steve Papa found that a check for $34.50 had been recorded in the check register as $43.50. The bank returned an NSF check in the amount of $62.55. Interest income of $8.25 was earned and a service charge of $10.32 was assessed. What amount should be added/subtracted from the checkbook balance to bring it up to date?

   Add: _____   Deduct: _____

5. Matthew Stokes was completing the bank reconciliation for Parker's Tool and Die Company. The check register balance was $1,503.67. Matthew found that a $76.00 check had been recorded in the check register as $67.00; that a note for $1,500 had been collected by the bank for Parker's and the collection fee was $12.00; that $15.60 interest was earned on the account; and that an $8.35 service charge had been assessed. What should the check register balance be after Matthew updates it with the bank reconciliation information?

6. Consumers, community activists, and politicians are decrying the new line of accounts because several include a $3 service charge for some customers who use bank tellers for transactions that can be done through an automated teller machine. Bill Wade banks at a local bank that charges this fee. He was having difficulty balancing his checkbook because he did not notice this fee on his bank statement. His bank statement showed a balance of $822.18. Bill's checkbook had a balance of $206.48. Check No. 406 for $116.08 and Check No. 407 for $12.50 were outstanding. A $521 deposit was not on the statement. Bill has his payroll check electronically deposited to his checking account—the payroll check was for $1,015.12 (Bill's payroll checks vary each month). There are also a $1 service fee and a teller fee of $6. Complete Bill's bank reconciliation.

7. At First National Bank in San Diego, some customers have to pay $25 each year as an ATM card fee. John Levi banks at First National Bank and just received his bank statement showing a balance of $829.25; his checkbook balance is $467.40. The bank statement shows an ATM card fee of $25.00, teller fee of $9.00, interest of $1.80, and John's $880 IRS refund check, which was processed by the IRS and deposited to his account. John has two checks that have not cleared—No. 112 for $620.10 and No. 113 for $206.05. There is also a deposit in transit for $1,312.10. Prepare John's bank reconciliation.

Name _____ Date _____

Learning Unit 5–1: Solving Equations for the Unknown

DRILL PROBLEMS

1. Write equations for the following situations. Use N for the unknown number. Do not solve the equations.

  a. Three times a number is 90.

  b. A number increased by 13 equals 25.

  c. Seven less than a number is 5.

  d. Fifty-seven decreased by 3 times a number is 21.

  e. Fourteen added to one-third of a number is 18.

  f. Twice the sum of a number and 4 is 32.

  g. Three-fourths of a number is 9.

  h. Two times a number plus 3 times the same number plus 8 is 68.

2. Solve for the unknown number:

  a. $B + 12 = 38$ **b.** $29 + M = 44$ **c.** $D - 77 = 98$

  d. $7N = 63$ **e.** $\dfrac{X}{12} = 11$ **f.** $3Q + 4Q + 2Q = 108$

  g. $H + 5H + 3 = 57$ **h.** $2(N - 3) = 62$ **i.** $\dfrac{3R}{4} = 27$

  j. $E - 32 = 41$ **k.** $5(2T - 2) = 120$ **l.** $12W - 5W = 98$

m. $49 - X = \quad 37$ **n.** $12(V + 2) = \quad 84$ **o.** $7D + 4 = \quad 5D + 14$

p. $7(T - 2) = \quad 2T - 9$

Name _____ Date _____

Learning Unit 5–2: Solving Word Problems for the Unknown

WORD PROBLEMS

1. A blue denim shirt at the Old Navey was marked down $20. The sale price was $40. What was the original price?

Unknown(s)	Variables(s)	Relationship

2. Goodwin's Corporation found that $\frac{2}{3}$ of its employees were vested in their retirement plan. If 124 employees are vested, what is the total number of employees at Goodwin's?

Unknown(s)	Variables(s)	Relationship

3. Eileen Haskin's utility and telephone bills for the month totaled $180. The utility bill was 3 times as much as the telephone bill. How much was each bill?

Unknown(s)	Variables(s)	Relationship

4. Ryan and his friends went to the golf course to hunt for golf balls. Ryan found 15 more than $\frac{1}{3}$ of the total number of golf balls that were found. How many golf balls were found if Ryan found 75 golf balls?

Unknown(s)	Variables(s)	Relationship

5. Linda Mills and Sherry Somers sold 459 tickets for the Advertising Club's raffle. If Linda sold 8 times as many tickets as Sherry, how many tickets did each one sell?

6. Jason Mazzola wanted to buy a suit at Giblee's. Jason did not have enough money with him, so Mr. Giblee told him he would hold the suit if Jason gave him a deposit of $\frac{1}{5}$ of the cost of the suit. Jason agreed and gave Mr. Giblee $79. What was the price of the suit?

Unknown(s)	Variables(s)	Relationship

7. Peter sold watches ($7) and necklaces ($4) at a flea market. Total sales were $300. People bought 3 times as many watches as necklaces. How many of each did Peter sell? What were the total dollar sales of each?

Unknown(s)	Variables(s)	Price	Relationship

8. Peter sold watches ($7) and necklaces ($4) at a flea market. Total sales for 48 watches and necklaces were $300. How many of each did Peter sell? What were the total dollar sales of each?

Unknown(s)	Variables(s)	Price	Relationship

9. A 3,000 piece of direct mailing cost $1,435. Printing cost is $550, about $3\frac{1}{2}$ times the cost of typesetting. How much did the typesetting cost? Round to the nearest cent.

Unknown(s)	Variables(s)	Relationship

10. In 2009, Tony Rigato, owner of MRM, saw an increase in sales to $13.5 million. Rigato states that since 2006, sales have more than tripled. What were his sales in 2006?

Unknown(s)	Variables(s)	Relationship

Name _____   Date _____

Learning Unit 6–1:   Conversions

DRILL PROBLEMS

1. Convert the following to percents (round to the nearest tenth of a percent if needed):
   a. .07 _____ %   b. .645 _____ %   c. .009 _____ %
   d. 8.3 _____ %   e. 5.26 _____ %   f. 6 _____ %
   g. .0105 _____ %   h. .1180 _____ %   i. 5.0375 _____ %
   j. .862 _____ %   k. .2615 _____ %   l. .8 _____ %
   m. .025 _____ %   n. .06 _____ %

2. Convert the following to decimals (do not round):
   a. 46% _____   b. .09% _____
   c. 4.7% _____   d. 9.67% _____
   e. .2% _____   f. $\frac{1}{4}$% _____
   g. .76% _____   h. 110% _____
   i. $12\frac{1}{2}$% _____   j. 5% _____
   k. .004% _____   l. $7\frac{5}{10}$% _____
   m. $\frac{3}{4}$% _____   n. 1% _____

3. Convert the following to percents (round to the nearest tenth of a percent if needed):
   a. $\frac{7}{10}$ _____ %   b. $\frac{1}{5}$ _____ %
   c. $1\frac{5}{8}$ _____ %   d. $\frac{2}{7}$ _____ %
   e. 2 _____ %   f. $\frac{14}{100}$ _____ %
   g. $\frac{1}{6}$ _____ %   h. $\frac{1}{2}$ _____ %
   i. $\frac{3}{5}$ _____ %   j. $\frac{3}{25}$ _____ %
   k. $\frac{5}{16}$ _____ %   l. $\frac{11}{50}$ _____ %
   m. $4\frac{3}{4}$ _____ %   n. $\frac{3}{200}$ _____ %

4. Convert the following to fractions in simplest form:
   a. 40% _____   b. 15% _____
   c. 50% _____   d. 75% _____
   e. 35% _____   f. 85% _____
   g. $12\frac{1}{2}$% _____   h. $37\frac{1}{2}$% _____
   i. $33\frac{1}{3}$% _____   j. 3% _____
   k. 8.5% _____   l. $5\frac{3}{4}$% _____
   m. 100% _____   n. 10% _____

5. Complete the following table by finding the missing fraction, decimal, or percent equivalent:

	Fraction	Decimal	Percent		Fraction	Decimal	Percent
a.	_____	.25	25% _____	h.	$\frac{1}{6}$	$.16\overline{6}$	_____
b.	$\frac{3}{8}$	_____	$37\frac{1}{2}\%$	i.	_____	$.083\overline{3}$	$8\frac{1}{3}\%$
c.	$\frac{1}{2}$	.5	_____	j.	$\frac{1}{9}$	_____	$11\frac{1}{9}\%$
d.	$\frac{2}{3}$	_____	$66\frac{2}{3}\%$	k.	_____	.3125	$31\frac{1}{4}\%$
e.	_____	.4	40%	l.	$\frac{3}{40}$	.075	_____
f.	$\frac{3}{5}$	.6	_____	m.	$\frac{1}{5}$	_____	20%
g.	$\frac{7}{10}$	_____	70%	n.	_____	1.125	$112\frac{1}{2}\%$

WORD PROBLEMS

6. In 2009, Mutual of New York reported an overwhelming 60% of its new sales came from existing clients. What fractional part of its new sales came from existing clients? Reduce to simplest form.

7. Six hundred ninety corporations and design firms competed for the Industrial Design Excellence Award (IDEA). Twenty were selected as the year's best and received gold awards. Show the gold award winners as a fraction; then show what percent of the entrants received gold awards. Round to the nearest tenth of a percent.

8. In the first half of 2009, stock prices in the Standard & Poor's 500-stock index rose 17.5%. Show the increase in decimal.

9. In the recent banking crisis, many banks were unable to cover their bad loans. Citicorp, the nation's largest real estate lender, was reported as having only enough reserves to cover 39% of its bad loans. What fractional part of its loan losses was covered?

10. Dave Mattera spent his vacation in Las Vegas. He ordered breakfast in his room, and when he went downstairs to the coffee shop, he discovered that the same breakfast was much less expensive. He had paid 1.884 times as much for the breakfast in his room. What was the percent of increase for the breakfast in his room?

11. Putnam Management Company of Boston recently increased its management fee by .09%. What is the increase as a decimal? What is the same increase as a fraction?

12. Joel Black and Karen Whyte formed a partnership and drew up a partnership agreement, with profits and losses to be divided equally after each partner receives a $7\frac{1}{2}\%$ return on his or her capital contribution. Show their return on investment as a decimal and as a fraction. Reduce.

Name _____   Date _____

Learning Unit 6–2:   Application of Percents—Portion Formula

DRILL PROBLEMS

1. Fill in the amount of the base, rate, and portion in each of the following statements:
   a. The Johnsons spend $3,600 a month on food, which is 30% of their monthly income of $12,000.
      Base _____   Rate _____   Portion _____

   b. Rocky Norman got a $15 discount when he purchased a new camera. This was 20% off the sticker price of $75.
      Base _____   Rate _____   Portion _____

   c. Mary Burns got a 12% senior citizens discount when she bought a $7.00 movie ticket. She saved $0.84.
      Base _____   Rate _____   Portion _____

   d. Arthur Bogey received a commission of $13,500 when he sold the Brown's house for $225,000. His commission rate is 6%.
      Base _____   Rate _____   Portion _____

   e. Leo Davis deposited $5,000 in a certificate of deposit (CD). A year later he received an interest payment of $450 which was a yield of 9%.
      Base _____   Rate _____   Portion _____

   f. Grace Tremblay is on a diet that allows her to eat 1,600 calories per day. For breakfast she had 600 calories, which is $37\frac{1}{2}\%$ of her allowance.
      Base _____   Rate _____   Portion _____

2. Find the portion; round to the nearest hundredth if necessary:
   a. 7% of 74 _____
   b. 12% of 205 _____
   c. 16% of 630 _____
   d. 7.5% of 920 _____
   e. 25% of 1,004 _____
   f. 10% of 79 _____
   g. 103% of 44 _____
   h. 30% of 78 _____
   i. .2% of 50 _____
   j. 1% of 5,622 _____
   k. $6\frac{1}{4}\%$ of 480 _____
   l. 150% of 10 _____
   m. 100% of 34 _____
   n. $\frac{1}{2}\%$ of 27 _____

3. Find the rate; round to the nearest tenth of a percent as needed:

   a. 30 is what percent of 90? _____
   b. 6 is what percent of 200? _____
   c. 275 is what percent of 1,000? _____
   d. .8 is what percent of 44? _____
   e. 67 is what percent of 2,010? _____
   f. 550 is what percent of 250? _____
   g. 13 is what percent of 650? _____
   h. $15 is what percent of $455? _____
   i. .05 is what percent of 100? _____
   j. $6.25 is what percent of $10? _____

4. Find the base; round to the nearest tenth as needed:

   a. 63 is 30% of _____
   b. 60 is 33% of _____
   c. 150 is 25% of _____
   d. 47 is 1% of _____
   e. $21 is 120% of _____
   f. 2.26 is 40% of _____
   g. 75 is $12\frac{1}{2}\%$ of _____
   h. 18 is 22.2% of _____
   i. $37.50 is 50% of _____
   j. 250 is 100% of _____

5. Find the percent of increase or decrease. Round to nearest tenth percent as needed:

	Last year	This year	Amount of change	Percent of change
a.	5,962	4,378	_____	_____
b.	$10,995	$12,250	_____	_____
c.	120,000	140,000	_____	_____
d.	120,000	100,000	_____	_____

WORD PROBLEMS

6. A machine that originally cost $2,400 was sold for $600 at the end of 5 years. What percent of the original cost is the selling price?

7. Joanne Byrne invested $75,000 in a candy shop and is making 12% per year on her investment. How much money per year is she making on her investment?

8. There was a fire in Bill Porper's store that caused 2,780 inventory items to be destroyed. Before the fire, 9,565 inventory items were in the store. What percent of inventory was destroyed? Round to nearest tenth percent.

9. Elyse's Dress Shoppe makes 25% of its sales for cash. If the cash receipts on January 21 were $799, what were the total sales for the day?

10. The YMCA is holding a fund-raiser to collect money for a new gym floor. So far it has collected $7,875, which is 63% of the goal. What is the amount of the goal? How much more money must the YMCA collect?

11. Leslie Tracey purchased her home for $51,500. She sold it last year for $221,200. What percent profit did she make on the sale? Round to nearest tenth percent.

12. Maplewood Park Tool & Die had an annual production of 375,165 units this year. This is 140% of the annual production last year. What was last year's annual production?

Name _____   Date _____

Learning Unit 7–1: Trade Discounts—Single and Chain*

DRILL PROBLEMS

1. Calculate the trade discount amount for each of the following items:

Item	List price	Trade discount	Trade discount amount
a. Apple iPod	$ 300	40%	_____
b. Flat-screen TV	$1,200	30%	_____
c. Suit	$ 500	10%	_____
d. Bicycle	$ 800	$12\frac{1}{2}$	_____
e. David Yurman bracelet	$ 950	40%	_____

2. Calculate the net price for each of the following items:

Item	List price	Trade discount amount	Net price
a. Home Depot table	$600	$250	_____
b. Bookcase	$525	$129	_____
c. Rocking chair	$480	$ 95	_____

3. Fill in the missing amount for each of the following items:

Item	List price	Trade discount amount	Net price
a. Sears electric saw	_____	$19	$56.00
b. Electric drill	$90	_____	$68.50
c. Ladder	$56	$15.25	_____

4. For each of the following, find the percent paid (complement of trade discount) and the net price:

List price	Trade discount	Percent paid	Net price
a. $45	15%	_____	_____
b. $195	12.2%	_____	_____
c. $325	50%	_____	_____
d. $120	18%	_____	_____

5. In each of the following examples, find the net price equivalent rate and the single equivalent discount rate:

Chain discount	Net price equivalent rate	Single equivalent discount rate
a. 25/5	_____	_____
b. 15/15	_____	_____
c. 15/10/5	_____	_____
d. 12/12/6	_____	_____

*Freight problems to be shown in LU 7–2 material.

6. In each of the following examples, find the net price and the trade discount:

List price	Chain discount	Net price	Trade discount
a. $5,000	10/10/5	_____	_____
b. $7,500	9/6/3	_____	_____
c. $898	20/7/2	_____	_____
d. $1,500	25/10	_____	_____

7. The list price of a handheld calculator is $19.50, and the trade discount is 18%. Find the trade discount amount.

8. The list price of a silver picture frame is $29.95, and the trade discount is 15%. Find the trade discount amount and the net price.

9. The net price of a set of pots and pans is $65, and the trade discount is 20%. What is the list price?

10. Jennie's Variety Store has the opportunity to purchase candy from three different wholesalers; each of the wholesalers offers a different chain discount. Company A offers 25/5/5, Company B offers 20/10/5, and Company C offers 15/20. Which company should Jennie deal with? *Hint:* Choose the company with the highest single equivalent discount rate.

11. The list price of a television set is $625. Find the net price after a series discount of 30/20/10.

12. Mandy's Accessories Shop purchased 12 purses with a total list price of $726. What was the net price of each purse if the wholesaler offered a chain discount of 25/20?

13. Kransberg Furniture Store purchased a bedroom set for $1,097.25 from Furniture Wholesalers. The list price of the set was $1,995. What trade discount rate did Kransberg receive?

14. Susan Monk teaches second grade and receives a discount at the local art supply store. Recently she paid $47.25 for art supplies after receiving a chain discount of 30/10. What was the regular price of the art supplies?

Name _____ Date _____

Learning Unit 7–2: Cash Discounts, Credit Terms, and Partial Payments

DRILL PROBLEMS

1. Complete the following table:

	Date of invoice	Date goods received	Terms	Last day of discount period	End of credit period
a.	February 8		2/10, n/30		
b.	August 26		2/10, n/30		
c.	October 17		3/10, n/60		
d.	March 11	May 10	3/10, n/30, ROG		
e.	September 14		2/10, EOM		
f.	May 31		2/10, EOM		

2. Calculate the cash discount and the net amount paid.

	Invoice amount	Cash discount rate	Discount amount	Net amount paid
a.	$75	3%		
b.	$1,559	2%		
c.	$546.25	2%		
d.	$9,788.75	1%		

3. Use the complement of the cash discount to calculate the net amount paid. Assume all invoices are paid within the discount period.

	Terms of invoice	Amount of invoice	Complement	Net amount paid
a.	2/10, n/30	$1,125		
b.	3/10, n/30 ROG	$4,500		
c.	2/10, EOM	$375.50		
d.	1/15, n/45	$3,998		

4. Calculate the amount of cash discount and the net amount paid.

	Date of invoice	Terms of invoice	Amount of invoice	Date paid	Cash discount	Amount paid
a.	January 12	2/10, n/30	$5,320	January 22		
b.	May 28	2/10, n/30	$975	June 7		
c.	August 15	2/10, n/30	$7,700	August 26		
d.	March 8	2/10, EOM	$480	April 10		
e.	January 24	3/10, n/60	$1,225	February 3		

5. Complete the following table:

	Total invoice	Freight charges included in invoice total	Date of invoice	Terms of invoice	Date of payment	Cash discount	Amount paid
a.	$852	$12.50	3/19	2/10, n/30	3/29		
b.	$669.57	$15.63	7/28	3/10, EOM	9/10		
c.	$500	$11.50	4/25	2/10, n/60	6/5		
d.	$188	$9.70	1/12	2/10, EOM	2/10		

6. In the following table, assume that all the partial payments were made within the discount period.

Amount of invoice	Terms of invoice	Partial payment	Amount to be credited	Balance outstanding
a. $481.90	2/10, n/30	$90.00	_____	_____
b. $1,000	2/10, EOM	$500.00	_____	_____
c. $782.88	3/10, n/30, ROG	$275.00	_____	_____
d. $318.80	2/15, n/60	$200.00	_____	_____

WORD PROBLEMS

7. Northwest Chemical Company received an invoice for $12,480, dated March 12, with terms of 2/10, n/30. If the invoice was paid March 22, what was the amount due?

8. On May 27, Trotter Hardware Store received an invoice for trash barrels purchased for $13,650 with terms of 3/10, EOM; the freight charge, which is included in the price, is $412. What are (a) the last day of the discount period and (b) the amount of the payment due on this date?

9. The Glass Sailboat received an invoice for $930.50 with terms 2/10, n/30 on April 19. On April 29, it sent a payment of $430.50. (a) How much credit will be given on the total due? (b) What is the new balance due?

10. Dallas Ductworks offers cash discounts of 2/10, 1/15, n/30 on all purchases. If an invoice for $544 dated July 18 is paid on August 2, what is the amount due?

11. The list price of a DVD player is $299.90 with trade discounts of 10/20 and terms of 3/10, n/30. If a retailer pays the invoice within the discount period, what amount must the retailer pay?

12. The invoice of a sneakers supplier totaled $2,488.50, was dated February 7, and offered terms 2/10, ROG. The shipment of sneakers was received on March 7. What are (a) the last date of the discount period and (b) the amount of the discount that will be lost if the invoice is paid after that date?

13. Starburst Toy Company receives an invoice amounting to $1,152.30 with terms of 2/10, EOM and dated November 6. If a partial payment of $750 is made on December 8, what are (a) the credit given for the partial payment and (b) the balance due on the invoice?

14. Todd's Sporting Goods received an invoice for soccer equipment dated July 26 with terms 3/10, 1/15, n/30 in the amount of $3,225.83, which included shipping charges of $375.50. If this bill is paid on August 5, what amount must be paid?

Name _____   Date _____

Learning Unit 8–1: Markups Based on Cost (100%)

DRILL PROBLEMS

1. Fill in the missing numbers:

	Cost	Dollar markup	Selling price
a.	$11.80	$2.50	_____
b.	$8.32	_____	$11.04
c.	$25.27	_____	$29.62
d.	_____	$75.00	$165.00
e.	$86.54	$29.77	_____

2. Calculate the markup based on cost (round to the nearest cent).

	Cost	Markup (percent of cost)	Dollar markup
a.	$425.00	30%	_____
b.	$1.52	20%	_____
c.	$9.90	$12\frac{1}{2}$	_____
d.	$298.10	50%	_____
e.	$74.25	38%	_____
f.	$552.25	100%	_____

3. Calculate the dollar markup and rate of the markup as a percent of cost (round percents to nearest tenth percent). Verify your result, which may be slightly off due to rounding.

	Cost	Selling price	Dollar markup	Markup (percent of cost)	Verify
a.	$2.50	$4.50	_____	_____	____
b.	$12.50	$19.00	_____	_____	____
c.	$0.97	$1.25	_____	_____	____
d.	$132.25	$175.00	_____	_____	____
e.	$65.00	$89.99	_____	_____	____

4. Calculate the dollar markup and the selling price.

	Cost	Markup (percent of cost)	Dollar markup	Selling price
a.	$2.20	40%	_____	_____
b.	$2.80	16%	_____	_____
c.	$840.00	$12\frac{1}{2}$%	_____	_____
d.	$24.36	30%	_____	_____

5. Calculate the cost (round to the nearest cent).

	Selling price	Rate of markup based on cost	Cost
a.	$1.98	30%	_____
b.	$360.00	60%	_____
c.	$447.50	20%	_____
d.	$1,250.00	100%	_____

6. Find the missing numbers. Round money to the nearest cent and percents to the nearest tenth percent.

	Cost	Dollar markup	Percent markup on cost	Selling price
a.	$72.00	_____	40%	_____
b.	_____	$7.00	_____	$35.00
c.	$8.80	$1.10	_____	_____
d.	_____	_____	28%	$19.84
e.	$175.00	_____	_____	$236.25

WORD PROBLEMS

7. The cost of an recliner chair is $399 and the markup rate is 35% of the cost. What are **(a)** the dollar markup and **(b)** the selling price?

8. If Barry's Furniture Store purchased a floor lamp for $120 and plans to add a markup of $90, **(a)** what will the selling price be and **(b)** what is the markup as a percent of cost?

9. If Lesjardin's Jewelry Store is selling a gold bracelet for $349, which includes a markup of 35% on cost, what are **(a)** Lesjardin's cost and **(b)** the amount of the dollar markup?

10. Toll's Variety Store sells an alarm clock for $14.75. The alarm clock cost Toll's $9.90. What is the markup amount as a percent of cost? Round to the nearest whole percent.

11. Swanson's Audio Supply marks up its merchandise by 40% on cost. If the markup on a cassette player is $85, what are **(a)** the cost of the cassette player and **(b)** the selling price?

12. Brown's Department Store is selling a shirt for $55. If the markup is 70% on cost, what is Brown's cost (to the nearest cent)?

13. Ward's Greenhouse purchased tomato flats for $5.75 each. Ward's has decided to use a markup of 42% on cost. Find the selling price.

Name _____   Date _____

Learning Unit 8–2:   Markups Based on Selling Price (100%)

DRILL PROBLEMS

1. Calculate the markup based on the selling price.

Selling price	Markup (percent of selling price)	Dollar markup
a. $16.00	40%	_____
b. $230.00	25%	_____
c. $81.00	42.5%	_____
d. $72.88	$37\frac{1}{2}\%$	_____
e. $1.98	$7\frac{1}{2}\%$	_____

2. Calculate the dollar markup and the markup as a percent of selling price (to the nearest tenth percent). Verify your answer, which may be slightly off due to rounding.

Cost	Selling price	Dollar markup	Markup (percent of selling price)	Verify
a. $2.50	$4.25	_____	_____	_____
b. $16.00	$24.00	_____	_____	_____
c. $45.25	$85.00	_____	_____	_____
d. $0.19	$0.25	_____	_____	_____
e. $5.50	$8.98	_____	_____	_____

3. Given the *cost* and the markup as a percent of *selling price*, calculate the selling price.

Cost	Markup (percent of selling price)	Selling price
a. $5.90	15%	_____
b. $600	32%	_____
c. $15	50%	_____
d. $120	30%	_____
e. $0.29	20%	_____

4. Given the selling price and the percent markup on selling price, calculate the cost.

Cost	Markup (percent of selling price)	Selling price
a. _____	40%	$6.25
b. _____	20%	$16.25
c. _____	19%	$63.89
d. _____	$62\frac{1}{2}\%$	$44.00

5. Calculate the equivalent rate of markup (round to the nearest hundredth percent).

Markup on cost	Markup on selling price		Markup on cost	Markup on selling price
a. 40%	_____	**b.** 50%		_____
c. _____	50%	**d.** _____		35%
e. _____	40%			

WORD PROBLEMS

6. Fisher Equipment is selling a Wet/Dry Shop Vac for $49.97. If Fisher's markup is 40% of the selling price, what is the cost of the Shop Vac?

7. Gove Lumber Company purchased a 10-inch table saw for $225 and will mark up the price 35% on the selling price. What will the selling price be?

8. To realize a sufficient gross margin, City Paint and Supply Company marks up its paint 27% on the selling price. If a gallon of Latex Semi-Gloss Enamel has a markup of $4.02, find **(a)** the selling price and **(b)** the cost.

9. A Magnavox 20-inch color TV cost $180 and sells for $297. What is the markup based on the selling price? Round to the nearest hundredth percent.

10. Bargain Furniture sells a five-piece country maple bedroom set for $1,299. The cost of this set is $700. What are **(a)** the markup on the bedroom set, **(b)** the markup percent on cost, and **(c)** the markup percent on the selling price? Round to the nearest hundredth percent.

11. Robert's Department Store marks up its sundries by 28% on the selling price. If a 6.4-ounce tube of toothpaste costs $1.65, what will the selling price be?

12. To be competitive, Tinker Toys must sell the Nintendo Control Deck for $89.99. To meet expenses and make a sufficient profit, Tinker Toys must add a markup on the selling price of 23%. What is the maximum amount that Tinker Toys can afford to pay a wholesaler for Nintendo?

13. Nicole's Restaurant charges $7.50 for a linguini dinner that costs $2.75 for the ingredients. What rate of markup is earned on the selling price? Round to the nearest hundredth percent.

Name _____   Date _____

Learning Unit 8–3: Markdowns

DRILL PROBLEMS

1. Find the dollar markdown and the sale price.

	Original selling price	Markdown percent	Dollar markdown	Sale price
a.	$100	30%	_____	_____
b.	$2,099.98	25%	_____	_____
c.	$729	30%	_____	_____

2. Find the dollar markdown and the markdown percent on original selling price.

	Original selling price	Sale price	Dollar markdown	Markdown percent
a.	$19.50	$9.75	_____	_____
b.	$250	$175	_____	_____
c.	$39.95	$29.96	_____	_____

3. Find the original selling price.

	Sale price	Markdown percent	Original selling price
a.	$328	20%	_____
b.	$15.85	15%	_____

4. Calculate the final selling price.

	Original selling price	First markdown	Second markdown	Final markup	Final selling price
a.	$4.96	25%	8%	5%	_____
b.	$130	30%	10%	20%	_____

WORD PROBLEMS

5. Speedy King is having a 30%-off sale on their box springs and mattresses. A queen-size, back-supporter mattress is priced at $325. What is the sale price of the mattress?

6. Murray and Sons sell a personal fax machine for $602.27. It is having a sale, and the fax machine is marked down to $499.88. What is the percent of the markdown?

7. Coleman's is having a clearance sale. A lamp with an original selling price of $249 is now selling for $198. Find the percent of the markdown. Round to the nearest hundredth percent.

8. Johnny's Sports Shop has advertised markdowns on certain items of 22%. A soccer ball is marked with a sale price of $16.50. What was the original price of the soccer ball?

9. Sam Grillo sells seasonal furnishings. Near the end of the summer a five-piece patio set that was priced $349.99 had not been sold, so he marked it down by 12%. As Labor Day approached, he still had not sold the patio set, so he marked it down an additional 18%. What was the final selling price of the patio set?

10. Calsey's Department Store sells their down comforters for a regular price of $325. During its white sale the comforters were marked down 22%. Then, at the end of the sale, Calsey's held a special promotion and gave a second markdown of 10%. When the sale was over, the remaining comforters were marked up 20%. What was the final selling price of the remaining comforters?

Classroom Notes

Classroom Notes

Name _____   Date _____

Learning Unit 9–1:   Calculating Various Types of Employees' Gross Pay

DRILL PROBLEMS

1. Fill in the missing amounts for each of the following employees. Do not round the overtime rate in your calculations and round your final answers to the nearest cent.

Employee	Total hours	Rate per hour	Regular pay	Overtime pay	Gross pay
a. Ben Badger	40	$7.60	_____	_____	_____
b. Casey Guitare	43	$9.00	_____	_____	_____
c. Norma Harris	37	$7.50	_____	_____	_____
d. Ed Jackson	45	$12.25	_____	_____	_____

2. Calculate each employee's gross from the following data. Do not round the overtime rate in your calculation but round your final answers to the nearest cent.

Employee	S	M	Tu	W	Th	F	S	Total hours	Rate per hour	Regular pay	Overtime pay	Gross pay
a. L. Adams	0	8	8	8	8	8	0	_____	$8.10	_____	_____	_____
b. M. Card	0	9	8	9	8	8	4	_____	$11.35	_____	_____	_____
c. P. Kline	2	$7\frac{1}{2}$	$8\frac{1}{4}$	8	$10\frac{3}{4}$	9	2	_____	$10.60	_____	_____	_____
d. J. Mack	0	$9\frac{1}{2}$	$9\frac{3}{4}$	$9\frac{1}{2}$	10	10	4	_____	$9.95	_____	_____	_____

3. Calculate the gross wages of the following production workers.

Employee	Rate per unit	No. of units produced	Gross pay
a. A. Bossie	$0.67	655	_____
b. J. Carson	$0.87\frac{1}{2}$	703	_____

4. Using the given differential scale, calculate the gross wages of the following production workers.

Units produced	Amount per unit
From 1–50	$.55
From 51–100	.65
From 101–200	.72
More than 200	.95

Employee	Units produced	Gross pay
a. F. Burns	190	_____
b. B. English	210	_____
c. E. Jackson	200	_____

5. Calculate the following salespersons' gross wages.

   a. Straight commission:

Employee	Net sales	Commission	Gross pay
M. Salley	$40,000	13%	_____

b. Straight commission with draw:

Employee	Net sales	Commission	Draw	Commission minus draw
G. Gorsbeck	$38,000	12%	$600	_____

c. Variable commission scale:

Up to $25,000	8%
Excess of $25,000 to $40,000	10%
More than $40,000	12%

Employee	Net sales	Gross pay
H. Lloyd	$42,000	_____

d. Salary plus commission:

Employee	Salary	Commission	Quota	Net sales	Gross pay
P. Floyd	$2,500	3%	$400,000	$475,000	_____

WORD PROBLEMS

For all problems with overtime, be sure to round only the final answer.

6. In the first week of December, Dana Robinson worked 52 hours. His regular rate of pay is $11.25 per hour. What was Dana's gross pay for the week?

7. Davis Fisheries pays its workers for each box of fish they pack. Sunny Melanson receives $.30 per box. During the third week of July, Sunny packed 2,410 boxes of fish. What is Sunny's gross pay?

8. Maye George is a real estate broker who receives a straight commission of 6%. What would her commission be for a house that sold for $197,500?

9. Devon Company pays Eileen Haskins a straight commission of $12\frac{1}{2}\%$ on net sales. In January, Devon gave Eileen a draw of $600. She had net sales that month of $35,570. What was Eileen's commission minus draw?

10. Parker and Company pays Selma Stokes on a variable commission scale. In a month when Selma had net sales of $155,000, what was her gross pay based on the following schedule?

Net sales	Commission rate
Up to $40,000	5%
Excess of $40,000 to $75,000	5.5%
Excess of $75,000 to $100,000	6%
More than $100,000	7%

11. Marsh Furniture Company pays Joshua Charles a monthly salary of $1,900 plus a commission of $2\frac{1}{2}\%$ on sales over $12,500. Last month, Joshua had net sales of $17,799. What was Joshua's gross pay for the month?

12. Amy McWha works at Lamplighter Bookstore where she earns $7.75 per hour plus a commission of 2% on her weekly sales in excess of $1,500. Last week, Amy worked 39 hours and had total sales of $2,250. What was Amy's gross pay for the week?

Name _____ Date _____

Learning Unit 9–2: Computing Payroll Deductions for Employees' Pay; Employers' Responsibilities

DRILL PROBLEMS

Use tables in the *Business Math Handbook* (assume FICA rates in text).

Employee	Allowances and marital status	Cumulative earnings	Salary per week	Taxable earnings S.S.	Medicare
1. Pete Small	M—3	$97,000	$2,300	a. _____	b. _____
2. Alice Hall	M—1	$90,000	$1,100	c. _____	d. _____
3. Jean Rose	M—2	$100,000	$2,000	e. _____	f. _____

4. What is the tax for Social Security and Medicare for Pete in Problem 1?

5. Calculate Pete's FIT by the percentage method.

6. What would employees contribute for this week's payroll for SUTA and FUTA?

WORD PROBLEMS

7. Cynthia Pratt has earned $96,000 thus far this year. This week she earned $3,500. Find her total FICA tax deduction (Social Security and Medicare).

8. If Cynthia (Problem 7) earns $1,050 the following week, what will be her new total FICA tax deduction?

9. Roger Alley, a service dispatcher, has weekly earnings of $750. He claimed four allowances on his W-4 form and is married. Besides his FIT and FICA deductions, he has deductions of $35.16 for medical insurance and $17.25 for union dues. Calculate his net earnings for the third week in February. Use the percentage method.

10. Nicole Mariotte is unmarried and claimed one withholding allowance on her W-4 form. In the second week of February, she earned $707.35. Deductions from her pay included federal withholding, Social Security, Medicare, health insurance for $47.75, and $30.00 for the company meal plan. What is Nicole's net pay for the week? Use the percentage method.

11. Gerald Knowlton had total gross earnings of $97,200 in the last week of November. His earnings for the first week in December were $804.70. His employer uses the percentage method to calculate federal withholding. If Gerald is married, claims two allowances, and has medical insurance of $52.25 deducted each week from his pay, what is his net pay for the week?

Name _____ Date _____

Learning Unit 10–1: Calculation of Simple Interest and Maturity Value

DRILL PROBLEMS

1. Find the simple interest for each of the following loans:

	Principal	Rate	Time	Interest
a.	$6,000	4%	1 year	_____
b.	$3,000	12%	3 years	_____
c.	$18,000	$8\frac{1}{2}\%$	10 months	_____

2. Find the simple interest for each of the following loans; use the exact interest method. Use the days-in-a-year calendar in the text when needed.

	Principal	Rate	Time	Interest
a.	$900	4%	30 days	_____
b.	$4,290	8%	250 days	_____
c.	$1,500	8%	Made March 11 Due July 11	_____

3. Find the simple interest for each of the following loans using the ordinary interest method (Banker's Rule).

	Principal	Rate	Time	Interest
a.	$5,250	$7\frac{1}{2}\%$	120 days	_____
b.	$700	3%	70 days	_____
c.	$2,600	11%	Made on June 15 Due October 17	_____

WORD PROBLEMS

4. On October 17, Nina Verga borrowed $4,500 at a rate of 3%. She promised to repay the loan in 10 months. What are **(a)** the amount of the simple interest and **(b)** the total amount owed upon maturity?

5. Marjorie Folsom borrowed $5,500 to purchase a computer. The loan was for 9 months at an annual interest rate of $12\frac{1}{2}$%. What are **(a)** the amount of interest Marjorie must pay and **(b)** the maturity value of the loan?

6. Eric has a loan for $1,200 at an ordinary interest rate of 9.5% for 80 days. Julie has a loan for $1,200 at an exact interest rate of 9.5% for 80 days. Calculate **(a)** the total amount due on Eric's loan and **(b)** the total amount due on Julie's loan.

7. Roger Lee borrowed $5,280 at $13\frac{1}{2}$% on May 24 and agreed to repay the loan on August 24. The lender calculates interest using the exact interest method. How much will Roger be required to pay on August 24?

8. On March 8, Jack Faltin borrowed $10,225 at $9\frac{3}{4}$%. He signed a note agreeing to repay the loan and interest on November 8. If the lender calculates interest using the ordinary interest method, what will Jack's repayment be?

9. Dianne Smith's real estate taxes of $641.49 were due on November 1, 2007. Due to financial difficulties, Dianne was unable to pay her tax bill until January 15, 2008. The penalty for late payment is $13\frac{3}{8}$% ordinary interest. What is the penalty Dianne will have to pay, and what is Dianne's total payment on January 15?

10. On August 8, Rex Eason had a credit card balance of $550, but he was unable to pay his bill. The credit card company charges interest of $18\frac{1}{2}$% annually on late payments. What amount will Rex have to pay if he pays his bill 1 month late?

11. An issue of *Your Money* discussed average consumers who carry a balance of $2,000 on one credit card. If the yearly rate of interest is 18%, how much are consumers paying in interest per year?

12. AFBA Industrial Bank of Colorado Springs, Colorado, charges a credit card interest rate of 11% per year. If you had a credit card debt of $1,500, what would your interest amount be after 3 months?

Name _____   Date _____

Learning Unit 10–2: Finding Unknown in Simple Interest Formula

DRILL PROBLEMS

1. Find the principal in each of the following. Round to the nearest cent. Assume 360 days. *Calculator hint:* Do denominator calculation first, do not round; when answer is displayed, save it in memory by pressing [M+]. Now key in the numerator (interest amount), [÷], [MR], [=] for the answer. Be sure to clear memory after each problem by pressing [MR] again so that the M is no longer in the display.

	Rate	Time	Interest	Principal
a.	8%	70 days	$68	_____
b.	11%	90 days	$125	_____
c.	9%	120 days	$103	_____
d.	$8\frac{1}{2}$%	60 days	$150	_____

2. Find the rate in each of the following. Round to the nearest tenth of a percent. Assume 360 days.

	Principal	Time	Interest	Rate
a.	$7,500	120 days	$350	_____
b.	$975	60 days	$25	_____
c.	$20,800	220 days	$910	_____
d.	$150	30 days	$2.10	_____

3. Find the time (to the nearest day) in each of the following. Assuming ordinary interest, use 360 days.

	Principal	Rate	Interest	Time (days)	Time (years) (Round to nearest hundredth)
a.	$400	11%	$7.33	_____	_____
b.	$7,000	12.5%	$292	_____	_____
c.	$1,550	9.2%	$106.95	_____	_____
d.	$157,000	10.75%	$6,797.88	_____	_____

4. Complete the following. Assume 360 days for all examples.

	Principal	Rate (nearest tenth percent)	Time (nearest day)	Simple interest
a.	$345	_____	150 days	$14.38
b.	_____	12.5%	90 days	$46.88

c. $750	12.2%	_____	$19.06
d. $20,260	16.7%	110 days	_____

WORD PROBLEMS

Use 360 days.

5. In June, Becky opened a $20,000 bank CD paying 6% interest, but she had to withdraw the money in a few days to cover one child's college tuition. The bank charged her $600 in penalties for the withdrawal. What percent of the $20,000 was she charged?

6. Dr. Vaccarro invested his money at $12\frac{1}{2}\%$ for 175 days and earned interest of $760. How much money did Dr. Vaccarro invest?

7. If you invested $10,000 at 5% interest in a 6-month CD compounding interest daily, you would earn $252.43 in interest. How much would the same $10,000 invested in a bank paying simple interest earn?

8. Thomas Kyrouz opened a savings account and deposited $750 in a bank that was paying 7.2% simple interest. How much were his savings worth in 200 days?

9. Mary Millitello paid the bank $53.90 in interest on a 66-day loan at 9.8%. How much money did Mary borrow? Round to the nearest dollar.

10. If Anthony Lucido deposits $2,400 for 66 days and makes $60.72 in interest, what interest rate is he receiving?

11. Find how long in days David Wong must invest $23,500 of his company's cash at 8.4% in order to earn $652.50 in interest.

Name _____ Date _____

Learning Unit 10–3: U.S. Rule—Making Partial Note Payments Before Due Date

DRILL PROBLEMS

1. A merchant borrowed $3,000 for 320 days at 11% (assume a 360-day year). Use the U.S. Rule to complete the following table:

Payment number	Payment day	Amount paid	Interest to date	Principal payment	Adjusted balance
					$3,000
1	75	$500	_____	_____	_____
2	160	$750	_____	_____	_____
3	220	$1,000	_____	_____	_____
4	320	_____	_____	_____	_____

2. Use the U.S. Rule to solve for total interest costs, balances, and final payments (use ordinary interest).

   Given

   Principal, $6,000, 5%, 100 days
   Partial payments on 30th day, $2,000
          on 70th day, $1,000

WORD PROBLEMS

3. John Joseph borrowed $10,800 for 1 year at 14%. After 60 days, he paid $2,500 on the note. On the 200th day, he paid an additional $5,000. Use the U.S. Rule and ordinary interest to find the final balance due.

4. Doris Davis borrowed $8,200 on March 5 for 90 days at $8\frac{3}{4}$%. After 32 days, Doris made a payment on the loan of $2,700. On the 65th day, she made another payment of $2,500. What is her final payment if you use the U.S. Rule with ordinary interest?

5. David Ring borrowed $6,000 on a 13%, 60-day note. After 10 days, David paid $500 on the note. On day 40, David paid $900 on the note. What are the total interest and ending balance due by the U.S. Rule? Use ordinary interest.

Name _____   Date _____

Learning Unit 11–1:   Structure of Promissory Notes; the Simple Discount Note

DRILL PROBLEMS

1. Identify each of the following characteristics of promissory notes with an **I** for simple interest note, a **D** for simple discount note, or a **B** if it is true for both.
   ___ Interest is computed on face value, or what is actually borrowed.
   ___ A promissory note for a loan usually less than 1 year.
   ___ Borrower receives proceeds = Face value − Bank discount.
   ___ Maturity value = Face value + Interest.
   ___ Maturity value = Face value.
   ___ Borrower receives the face value.
   ___ Paid back by one payment at maturity.
   ___ Interest computed on maturity value, or what will be repaid, and not on actual amount borrowed.

2. Find the bank discount and the proceeds for the following (assume 360 days):

	Maturity value	Discount rate	Time (days)	Bank discount	Proceeds
a.	$8,000	3%	60	_____	_____
b.	$4,550	8.1%	110	_____	_____
c.	$19,350	12.7%	55	_____	_____
d.	$63,400	10%	90	_____	_____
e.	$13,490	7.9%	200	_____	_____
f.	$780	$12\frac{1}{2}\%$	65	_____	_____

3. Find the effective rate of interest for each of the loans in Problem 2. Use the answers you calculated in Problem 2 to solve these problems (round to the nearest tenth percent).

	Maturity value	Discount rate	Time (days)	Effective rate
a.	$8,000	.03	60	_____
b.	$4,550	8.1%	110	_____
c.	$19,350	12.7%	55	_____
d.	$63,400	10%	90	_____

e. $13,490	7.9%	200	_____
f. $780	$12\frac{1}{2}\%$	65	_____

WORD PROBLEMS

Assume 360 days.

4. Mary Smith signed a $9,000 note for 135 days at a discount rate of 4%. Find the discount and the proceeds Mary received.

5. The Salem Cooperative Bank charges an $8\frac{3}{4}\%$ discount rate. What are the discount and the proceeds for a $16,200 note for 60 days?

6. Bill Jackson is planning to buy a used car. He went to City Credit Union to take out a loan for $6,400 for 300 days. If the credit union charges a discount rate of $11\frac{1}{2}\%$, what will the proceeds of this loan be?

7. Mike Drislane goes to the bank and signs a note for $9,700. The bank charges a 15% discount rate. Find the discount and the proceeds if the loan is for 210 days.

8. Flora Foley plans to have a deck built on the back of her house. She decides to take out a loan at the bank for $14,300. She signs a note promising to pay back the loan in 280 days. If the note was discounted at 9.2%, how much money will Flora receive from the bank?

9. At the end of 280 days, Flora (Problem 8) must pay back the loan. What is the maturity value of the loan?

10. Dave Cassidy signed a $7,855 note at a bank that charges a 14.2% discount rate. If the loan is for 190 days, find **(a)** the proceeds and **(b)** the effective rate charged by the bank (to the nearest tenth percent).

11. How much money must Dave (Problem 10) pay back to the bank?

Name _____   Date _____

Learning Unit 11–2: Discounting an Interest-Bearing Note Before Maturity

DRILL PROBLEMS

1. Calculate the maturity value for each of the following promissory notes (use 360 days):

Date of note	Principal of note	Length of note (days)	Interest rate	Maturity value
a. April 12	$5,000	150	6%	_____
b. August 23	$15,990	85	13%	_____
c. December 10	$985	30	11.5%	_____

2. Find the maturity date and the discount period for the following; assume no leap years. *Hint:* See Exact Days-in-a-Year Calendar, Chapter 7.

Date of note	Length of note (days)	Date of discount	Maturity date	Discount period
a. March 11	200	June 28	_____	_____
b. January 22	60	March 2	_____	_____
c. April 19	85	June 6	_____	_____
d. November 17	120	February 15	_____	_____

3. Find the bank discount for each of the following (use 360 days):

Date of note	Principal of note	Length of note	Interest rate	Bank discount rate	Date of discount	Bank discount
a. October 5	$2,475	88 days	11%	9.5%	December 10	_____
b. June 13	$9,055	112 days	15%	16%	August 11	_____
c. March 20	$1,065	75 days	12%	11.5%	May 24	_____

4. Find the proceeds for each of the discounted notes in Problem 3.

   a. _____

   b. _____

   c. _____

WORD PROBLEMS

5. Connors Company received a $4,000, 90-day, 10% note dated April 6 from one of its customers. Connors Company held the note until May 16, when the company discounted it at a bank at a discount rate of 12%. What were the proceeds that Connors Company received?

6. Souza & Sons accepted a 9%, $22,000, 120-day note from one of its customers on July 22. On October 2, the company discounted the note at Cooperative Bank. The discount rate was 12%. What were **(a)** the bank discount and **(b)** the proceeds?

7. The Fargate Store accepted an $8,250, 75-day, 9% note from one of its customers on March 18. Fargate discounted the note at Parkside National Bank at $9\frac{1}{2}$% on March 29. What proceeds did Fargate receive?

8. On November 1, Marjorie's Clothing Store accepted a $5,200, $8\frac{1}{2}$%, 90-day note from Mary Rose in granting her a time extension on her bill. On January 13, Marjorie discounted the note at Seawater Bank, which charged a 10% discount rate. What were the proceeds that Majorie received?

9. On December 3, Duncan's Company accepted a $5,000, 90-day, 12% note from Al Finney in exchange for a $5,000 bill that was past due. On January 29, Duncan discounted the note at The Sidwell Bank at 13.1%. What were the proceeds from the note?

10. On February 26, Sullivan Company accepted a 60-day, 10% note in exchange for a $1,500 past-due bill from Tabot Company. On March 28, Sullivan Company discounted at National Bank the note received from Tabot Company. The bank discount rate was 12%. What are **(a)** the bank discount and **(b)** the proceeds?

11. On June 4, Johnson Company received from Marty Russo a 30-day, 11% note for $720 to settle Russo's debt. On June 17, Johnson discounted the note at Eastern Bank whose discount rate was 15%. What proceeds did Johnson receive?

12. On December 15, Lawlers Company went to the bank and discounted a 10%, 90-day, $14,000 note dated October 21. The bank charged a discount rate of 12%. What were the proceeds of the note?

Name _____   Date _____

Learning Unit 12–1:   Compound Interest (Future Value)—The Big Picture

DRILL PROBLEMS

1. In the following examples, calculate manually the amount at year-end for each of the deposits, assuming that interest is compounded annually. Round to the nearest cent each year.

	Principal	Rate	Number of years	Year 1	Year 2	Year 3	Year 4
a.	$530	4%	2	_____	_____		
b.	$1,980	12%	4	_____	_____	_____	_____

2. In the following examples, calculate the simple interest, the compound interest, and the difference between the two. Round to the nearest cent; do not use tables.

	Principal	Rate	Number of years	Simple interest	Compound interest	Difference
a.	$4,600	10%	2	_____	_____	_____
b.	$18,400	9%	4	_____	_____	_____
c.	$855	$7\frac{1}{5}\%$	3	_____	_____	_____

3. Find the future value and the compound interest using the Future Value of $1 at Compound Interest table or the Compound Daily table. Round to the nearest cent.

	Principal	Investment terms	Future value	Compound interest
a.	$10,000	6 years at 8% compounded annually	_____	_____
b.	$10,000	6 years at 8% compounded quarterly	_____	_____
c.	$8,400	7 years at 12% compounded semiannually	_____	_____
d.	$2,500	15 years at 10% compounded daily	_____	_____
e.	$9,600	5 years at 6% compounded quarterly	_____	_____
f.	$20,000	2 years at 6% compounded monthly	_____	_____

4. Calculate the effective rate (APY) of interest using the Future Value of $1 at Compound Interest table.

Investment terms	Effective rate (annual percentage yield)
a. 12% compounded quarterly	_____
b. 12% compounded semiannually	_____
c. 6% compounded quarterly	_____

WORD PROBLEMS

5. John Mackey deposited $5,000 in his savings account at Salem Savings Bank. If the bank pays 6% interest compounded quarterly, what will be the balance of his account at the end of 3 years?

6. Pine Valley Savings Bank offers a certificate of deposit at 12% interest, compounded quarterly. What is the effective rate (APY) of interest?

7. Jack Billings loaned $6,000 to his brother-in-law Dan, who was opening a new business. Dan promised to repay the loan at the end of 5 years, with interest of 8% compounded semiannually. How much will Dan pay Jack at the end of 5 years?

8. Eileen Hogarty deposits $5,630 in City Bank, which pays 12% interest, compounded quarterly. How much money will Eileen have in her account at the end of 7 years?

9. If Kevin Bassage deposits $3,500 in Scarsdale Savings Bank, which pays 8% interest, compounded quarterly, what will be in his account at the end of 6 years? How much interest will he have earned at that time?

10. Arlington Trust pays 6% compounded semiannually. How much interest would be earned on $7,200 for 1 year?

11. Paladium Savings Bank pays 9% compounded quarterly. Find the amount and the interest on $3,000 after three quarters. Do not use a table.

12. David Siderski bought a $7,500 bank certificate paying 16% compounded semiannually. How much money did he obtain upon cashing in the certificate 3 years later?

13. An issue of *Your Money* showed that the more frequently the bank compounds your money, the better. Just how much better is a function of time. A $10,000 investment for 6% in a 5-year certificate of deposit at three different banks can result in different interest being earned.
    a. Bank A (simple interest, no compounding)
    b. Bank B (quarterly compounding)
    c. Bank C (daily compounding)
       What would be the interest for each bank?

Name _____   Date _____

Learning Unit 12–2:   Present Value—The Big Picture

DRILL PROBLEMS

1. Use the *Business Math Handbook* to find the table factor for each of the following:

	Future value	Rate	Number of years	Compounded	Table value
a.	$1.00	10%	5	Annually	_____
b.	$1.00	12%	8	Semiannually	_____
c.	$1.00	6%	10	Quarterly	_____
d.	$1.00	12%	2	Monthly	_____
e.	$1.00	8%	15	Semiannually	_____

2. Use the *Business Math Handbook* to find the table factor and the present value for each of the following:

	Future value	Rate	Number of years	Compounded	Table value	Present value
a.	$1,000	14%	6	Semiannually	_____	_____
b.	$1,000	16%	7	Quarterly	_____	_____
c.	$1,000	8%	7	Quarterly	_____	_____
d.	$1,000	8%	7	Semiannually	_____	_____
e.	$1,000	8%	7	Annually	_____	_____

3. Find the present value and the interest earned for the following:

	Future value	Number of years	Rate	Compounded	Present value	Interest earned
a.	$2,500	6	8%	Annually	_____	_____
b.	$4,600	10	6%	Semiannually	_____	_____
c.	$12,800	8	10%	Semiannually	_____	_____
d.	$28,400	7	8%	Quarterly	_____	_____
e.	$53,050	1	12%	Monthly	_____	_____

4. Find the missing amount (present value or future value) for each of the following:

	Present value	Investment terms	Future value
a.	$3,500	5 years at 8% compounded annually	_____
b.	_____	6 years at 12% compounded semiannually	$9,000
c.	$4,700	9 years at 14% compounded semiannually	_____

WORD PROBLEMS

Solve for future value or present value.

5. Paul Palumbo assumes that he will need to have a new roof put on his house in 4 years. He estimates that the roof will cost him $18,000 at that time. What amount of money should Paul invest today at 8%, compounded semiannually, to be able to pay for the roof?

6. Tilton, a pharmacist, rents his store and has signed a lease that will expire in 3 years. When the lease expires, Tilton wants to buy his own store. He wants to have a down payment of $35,000 at that time. How much money should Tilton invest today at 6% compounded quarterly to yield $35,000?

7. Brad Morrissey loans $8,200 to his brother-in-law. He will be repaid at the end of 5 years, with interest at 10% compounded semiannually. Find out how much he will be repaid.

8. The owner of Waverly Sheet Metal Company plans to buy some new machinery in 6 years. He estimates that the machines he wishes to purchase will cost $39,700 at that time. What must he invest today at 8% compounded semiannually to have sufficient money to purchase the new machines?

9. Paul Stevens's grandparents want to buy him a car when he graduates from college in 4 years. They feel that they should have $27,000 in the bank at that time. How much should they invest at 12% compounded quarterly to reach their goal?

10. Gilda Nardi deposits $5,325 in a bank that pays 12% interest, compounded quarterly. Find the amount she will have at the end of 7 years.

11. Mary Wilson wants to buy a new set of golf clubs in 2 years. They will cost $775. How much money should she invest today at 9% compounded annually so that she will have enough money to buy the new clubs?

12. Jack Beggs plans to invest $30,000 at 10% compounded semiannually for 5 years. What is the future value of the investment?

13. Ron Thrift has a 2000 Honda that he expects will last 3 more years. Ron does not like to finance his purchases. He went to First National Bank to find out how much money he should put in the bank to purchase a $20,300 car in 3 years. The bank's 3-year CD is compounded quarterly with a 4% rate. How much should Ron invest in the CD?

14. The Downers Grove YMCA had a fund-raising campaign to build a swimming pool in 6 years. Members raised $825,000; the pool is estimated to cost $1,230,000. The money will be placed in Downers Grove Bank, which pays daily interest at 6%. Will the YMCA have enough money to pay for the pool in 6 years?

Classroom Notes

Check Figures

Odd-Numbered Drill and Word Problems for End-of-Chapter Problems.

Challenge Problems.

Summary Practice Tests (all).

Cumulative Reviews (all).

Odd-Numbered Additional Assignments by Learning Unit from Appendix A.

Check Figures to Drill and Word Problems (Odds), Challenge Problems, Summary Practice Tests, and Cumulative Reviews

Chapter 1

End-of-Chapter Problems

1–1. 104
1–3. 158
1–5. 13,580
1–7. 113,690
1–9. 38
1–11. 3,600
1–13. 1,074
1–15. 31,110
1–17. 340,531
1–19. 126,000
1–21. 90
1–23. 86 R4
1–25. 309
1–27. 1,616
1–29. 24,876
1–31. 17,989; 18,000
1–33. 80
1–35. 144
1–37. 216
1–39. 19 R21
1–41. 7,690; 6,990
1–43. 70,470; 72,000
I–45. 700
1–47. $500; $300; $497
1–49. $240; $200; $1,200; $1,080
1–51. $2,436; $3,056; $620 more
1–53. 905,600
1–55. 1,080
1–57. 106
1–59. $547,400
1–61. $1,872,000
1–63. $4,815; $250,380
1–65. $54,872
1–67. 200,000; 10,400,000
1–69. $1,486
1–71. No Avg. $33
1–73. $796
1–75. $600,000, $150,000
1–76. $2,974,400; $800,800
1–77. $12,000 difference

Summary Practice Test

1. 7,017,243
2. Nine million, six hundred twenty-two thousand, three hundred sixty-four
3. **a.** 70
   b. 900
   c. 8,000
   d. 10,000
4. 17,000; 17,672
5. 8,100,000 $8,011,758
6. 829,412,000
7. 379 R19
8. 100

9. $95
10. $500; no
11. $1,000

Chapter 2

End-of-Chapter Problems

2–1. Improper
2–3. Proper
2–5. $61\frac{2}{5}$
2–7. $\frac{59}{3}$
2–9. $\frac{11}{13}$
2–11. 60 ($2 \times 2 \times 3 \times 5$)
2–13. 96 ($2 \times 2 \times 2 \times 2 \times 2 \times 3$)
2–15. $\frac{13}{21}$
2–17. $15\frac{5}{12}$
2–19. $\frac{5}{6}$
2–21. $7\frac{4}{9}$
2–23. $\frac{5}{16}$
2–25. $\frac{3}{25}$
2–27. $\frac{1}{3}$
2–29. $\frac{7}{18}$
2–31. $408\frac{3}{4}$; $128\frac{1}{4}$
2–33. $35
2–35. $1,200
2–37. $63\frac{1}{4}$ inch; $11\frac{1}{12}$ inch remain
2–39. $119\frac{1}{8}$; $48\frac{7}{8}$
2–41. $6\frac{1}{2}$ gallons
2–43. $525
2–45. $\frac{23}{36}$
2–47. $25
2–49. $3\frac{3}{4}$ lb apple; $8\frac{1}{8}$ cups flour; $\frac{5}{8}$ cup marg.; $5\frac{15}{16}$ cups of sugar; 5 teaspoon cin.
2–51. 400 people
2–53. 92 pieces
2–55. 5,800 books
2–57. $200
2–59. $45\frac{3}{16}$ inch

2–61. $62,500,000; $37,500,000
2–63. $\frac{3}{8}$
2–65. $2\frac{3}{5}$ hours
2–67. 60 sandwiches
2–68. $103\frac{3}{4}$ inch; yes 39 inch left from board #2
2–69. **a.** 400 homes **b.** $320,000
   c. 3,000 people; 2,500 people
   d. $112.50
   e. $8,800,000

Summary Practice Test

1. Mixed number
2. Proper
3. Improper
4. $18\frac{1}{9}$
5. $\frac{65}{8}$
6. 9; $\frac{7}{10}$
7. 64
8. 24 ($2 \times 2 \times 3 \times 2 \times 1 \times 1 \times 1$)
9. $6\frac{17}{20}$
10. $\frac{1}{4}$
11. $6\frac{2}{21}$
12. $\frac{1}{14}$
13. $3\frac{5}{6}$ hours
14. 7,840 rolls
15. **a.** 60,000 veggie
    b. 30,000 regular
16. $39\frac{1}{2}$ hours
17. $26

Chapter 3

End-of-Chapter Problems

3–1. Thousandths
3–3. .8; .76; .758
3–5. 5.8; 5.83; 5.831
3–7. 6.6; 6.56; 6.556
3–9. $4,822.78
3–11. .09
3–13. .09
3–15. .64
3–17. 14.91
3–19. $\frac{62}{100}$

3-21. $\dfrac{125}{10,000}$

3-23. $\dfrac{825}{1,000}$

3-25. $\dfrac{7,065}{10,000}$

3-27. $28\dfrac{48}{100}$

3-29. .004
3-31. .0085
3-33. 818.1279
3-35. 3.4
3-37. 2.32
3-39. 1.2; 1.26791
3-41. 4; 4.0425
3-43. 24,526.67
3-45. 161.29
3-47. 6,824.15
3-49. .04
3-51. .63
3-53. 2.585
3-55. .0086
3-57. 486
3-59. 3.950
3-61. 7,913.2
3-63. .583
3-65. $17.00
3-67. $1.40
3-69. $119.47
3-71. $8.97
3-73. $116 savings
3-75. $399.16
3-77. $105.08
3-79. $210
3-81. $73.52
3-83. $1.58; $3,713
3-85. $6,465.60
3-87. $.90; 589,176,000
3-88. $560.45

Summary Practice Test
1. 767.849
2. .7
3. .07
4. .007
5. $\dfrac{9}{10}$
6. $6\dfrac{97}{100}$
7. $\dfrac{685}{1,000}$
8. .29
9. .13
10. 4.57
11. .08
12. 390.2702
13. 9.2
14. 118.67
15. 34,684.01
16. 62,940
17. 832,224,982.1
18. $24.56

19. $936.30
20. $385.40
21. A $.12
22. $441.35
23. $28.10

Chapter 4

End-of-Chapter Problems
4-1. $4,641.33
4-3. $4,626.33
4-5. $800.72
4-7. $540.82
4-9. $577.95
4-11. $998.86
4-12. $1,862.13
4-13. $3,061.67

Summary Practice Test
1. End Bal. $15,649.21
2. $8,730
3. $1,282.70
4. $10,968.50

Chapter 5

End-of-Chapter Problems
5-1. $D = 81$
5-3. $Q = 300$
5-5. $Y = 15$
5-7. $Y = 12$
5-9. $P = 25$
5-11. 2,325
5-13. Hugh 50; Joe 250
5-15. 50 shorts; 200 T-shirts
5-17. $D = 80$
5-19. $N = 63$
5-21. $Y = 7$
5-23. $P = 485.99
5-25. Pete = 90; Bill = 450
5-27. 48 boxes pens; 240 batteries
5-29. $A = 135$
5-31. $M = 60$
5-33. $3,750
5-35. $W = 129$
5-37. Shift 1: 3,360; shift 2: 2,240
5-39. 22 cartons of hammers 18 cartons of wrenches
5-40. 208 children; 229 women; 1,009 total homeless
5-41. $B = 10$; $6B = 30$

Summary Practice Test
1. $541.90
2. $84,000
3. Sears, 70; Buy 560
4. Abby 200; Jill 1,000
5. 13 dishes; 78 pots
6. Pasta 300; 1,300 pizzas

Chapter 6

End-of-Chapter Problems
6-1. 74%
6-3. 90%
6-5. 356.1%
6-7. .08
6-9. .643
6-11. 1.19
6-13. 8.3%
6-15. 87.5%
6-17. $\dfrac{1}{25}$
6-19. $\dfrac{19}{60}$
6-21. $\dfrac{27}{400}$
6-23. 10.5
6-25. 102.5
6-27. 156.6
6-29. 114.88
6-31. 16.2
6-33. 141.67
6-35. 10,000
6-37. 17,777.78
6-39. 108.2%
6-41. 110%
6-43. 400%
6-45. 59.40
6-47. 1,100
6-49. 40%
6-51. −6%
6-53. 75%
6-55. $10,000
6-57. $160
6-59. 677.78%
6-61. $28,175
6-63. 94%
6-65. 19.04%; $1.21; $8.74
6-67. 39.94%
6-69. 12.8%
6-71. 1,000
6-73. $400
6-75. 25%
6-77. $44,444,400
6-79. 1,747,758
6-81. 13.3%
6-83. 40%
6-85. $1,160,000
6-87. $24,000
6-89. 29.79%
6-91. $41,176
6-93. 40%
6-95. 585,000
6-96. $18.76; $11.73; 4.00%
6-97. $55,429

Summary Practice Test
1. 92.1%
2. 40%

3. 1,588%
4. 800%
5. .42
6. .0798
7. 4.0
8. .0025
9. 16.7%
10. 33.3%
11. $\dfrac{31}{160}$
12. $\dfrac{31}{500}$
13. $540,000
14. $2,330,000
15. 75%
16. 2.67%
17. $382.61
18. $639
19. $150,000

Chapter 7

End-of-Chapter Problems

7–1. .931; .069; $20.70; $279.30
7–3. .893079; .106921; $28.76; $240.24
7–5. $369.70; $80.30
7–7. $1,392.59; $457.41
7–9. June 28; July 18
7–11. June 15; July 5
7–13. July 10; July 30
7–15. $138; $6,862
7–17. $2; $198
7–19. $408.16; $291.84
7–21. $190; $285
7–23. $1,347.50; $67.38; $1,280.12
7–25. $576.06; $48.94
7–27. $5,100; $5,250
7–29. $5,850
7–31. $8,571.43
7–33. $8,173.20
7–35. $8,333.33; $11,666.67
7–37. $99.99
7–39. $489.90; $711.10
7–41. $4,658.97
7–43. $1,083.46; $116.54
7–45. $5,008.45
7–47. Save $4.27 with Verizon
7–49. $1,500; 8.34%; $164.95; $16,330.05; $1,664.95
7–50. $4,794.99

Summary Practice Test

1. $332.50
2. $211.11
3. $819.89; $79.11
4. a. Nov. 14; Dec. 4
   b. March 20; April 9
   c. June 10; June 30
   d. Jan. 10; Jan. 30
5. $15; $285
6. $7,120

7. B: 20.95%
8. $1,938.78; $6,061.22
9. $7,076.35

Chapter 8

End-of-Chapter Problems

8–1. $120; $420
8–3. $4,285.71
8–5. $6.90; 45.70%
8–7. $180; $270
8–9. $110.83
8–11. $34.20; 69.8%
8–13. 11%
8–15. $3,830.40; $1,169.60; 23.39%
8–17. $870
8–19. $49.30; 85%
8–21. 68.75%; 52.63%
8–23. $92.31
8–25. 18.91%
8–27. $558.60
8–29. $195
8–31. $129.99
8–33. $4,629.63; $370.37; $10,204.08; $5,204.08 savings
8–34. $94.98; $20.36; loss

Summary Practice Test

1. $126
2. 30.26%
3. $482.76; $217.24
4. $79; 37.97%
5. $133.33
6. $292.50
7. 27.27%
8. $160
9. 25.9%

Cumulative Review 6, 7, 8

1. 650,000
2. $296.35
3. $133
4. $2,562.14
5. $48.75
6. $259.26
7. $1.96; $1.89

Chapter 9

End-of-Chapter Problems

9–1. 39; $292.50
9–3. $12.00; $452
9–5. $1,071
9–7. $60
9–9. $13,000
9–11. $4,500
9–13. $11,900; $6,900; $138; $388
9–15. $465; $116
9–17. $152.54; $86.80; $20.30; $1,140.36
9–19. $752.60; $113.60

9–21. $520.00; $32.24; $7.54; $43.54; $436.68
9–23. $297
9–25. $825
9–27. $1,081.61
9–29. $357; $56
9–31. $233.38; $195.22; $38.16
9–32. Difference $143.34

Summary Practice Test

1. 49; $428
2. $790
3. $24,700
4. $465; $290
5. $293.46
6. $798 SUTA; $112 FUTA; no tax in quarter 2

Chapter 10

End-of-Chapter Problems

10–1. $960; $16,960
10–3. $978.75; $18,978.75
10–5. $28.23; $613.23
10–7. $20.38; $1,020.38
10–9. $73.78; $1,273.78
10–11. $1,904.76
10–13. $4,390.61
10–15. $595.83; $10,595.83
10–17. $2,377.70
10–19. 4.7 years
10–21. $21,596.11
10–23. $714.87; $44.87
10–25. $3,569.27; $3,540.10
10–27. $2,608.65
10–29. $18,720.12
10–31. 12.37%
10–33. 72 days
10–35. 5.6%
10–36. $6,815.10; $6,834.38; $19.28 saved
10–37. $7.82; $275.33

Summary Practice Test

1. $27.23; $2,038.11
2. $86,400
3. $14,901.25
4. $14,888.90
5. $32,516
6. $191.09; $10,191.09

Chapter 11

End-of-Chapter Problems

11–1. $637.50; $17,362.50
11–3. 25 days
11–5. $51,451.39; 57; $733.18; $50,718.21
11–7. 4.04%
11–9. $8,537.50; 9.8%
11–11. $8,937
11–13. 5.06%

11–15. $5,133.33; 56; $71.87; $5,061.46

11–17. $4,836.44

11–18. $329,955.64; $329,524.33; $431.31 more

11–19. $2,127.66; 9.57%

Summary Practice Test

1. $160,000
2. $302.22; $16,697.98; $17,000; 4.1%
3. $61,132.87
4. $71,264.84
5. $57,462.50; 7.6%
6. 5.58%

Chapter 12

End-of-Chapter Problems

12–1. 4; 2%; $1,515.40; $115.40

12–3. $10,404; $404

12–5. 12.55%

12–7. 14; 1%; .8700; $3,915.00

12–9. 28; 3%; .4371; $7,692.96

12–11. 2.2879 × $7,692.96

12–13. $32,987.50

12–15. Mystic $4,775

12–17. $25,734.40

12–19. $3,807

12–21. 5.06%

12–23. $37,644

12–25. Yes, $17,908 (compounding) or $8,376 (p. v.)

12–27. $3,739.20

12–29. $13,883.30

12–31. $471,813.71; $459,313.71 int.

12–32. $689,125; $34,125 Bank B

Summary Practice Test

1. $48,760
2. $31,160
3. $133,123.12
4. No, $26,898 (compounding) or $22,308 (p. v.)
5. 6.14%
6. $46,137
7. $187,470
8. $28,916.10

Check Figures (Odds) to Additional Assignments by Learning Unit from Appendix A

LU 1–1

1. **a.** Seven thousand, five hundred twenty-one
   d. Fifty-eight thousand, three
3. **a.** 40; 380; 860; 5,980; 210
   c. 21,000; 1,000; 4,000; 10,000
5. **a.** Hundreds place
   c. Ten thousands place
   e. Billions place
7. Three hundred eighty-four
9. $375,985
11. Two thousand, four

LU 1–2

1. **a.** 981
   c. 1,319
   d. 179
3. **a.** Estimated 40; 39
   c. Estimated 10; 9
5. $71,577
7. $19,973
9. 12,797 lbs
11. Estimated $9,400; $9,422
13. $746 discount

LU 1–3

1. **a.** Estimated 4,000; actual 2,400
   c. Estimated 15,000,000; actual 16,184,184
3. **a.** Estimated 1,000; actual 963 R5
   c. Estimated 20; actual 25 R8
5. 2,870
7. $78
9. 27
11. $43,200
13. 40 stacks and 23 "extra" bricks

LU 2–1

1. **a.** Mixed
   b. Improper

   c. Improper
   d. Mixed number
   e. Improper
   f. Proper
3. **a.** $\frac{36}{5}$　**c.** $\frac{31}{7}$　**f.** $\frac{53}{3}$
5. **a.** 6; $\frac{6}{7}$　**b.** 15; $\frac{2}{5}$　**e.** 12; $\frac{8}{11}$
7. $\frac{13}{4}$
9. $\frac{17}{25}$
11. $\frac{60}{100}$
13. $\frac{7}{12}$

LU 2–2

1. **a.** 32　**b.** 180　**c.** 480
   d. 252
3. **a.** $\frac{1}{3}$　**b.** $\frac{2}{3}$　**e.** $6\frac{1}{8}$　**h.** $56\frac{5}{6}$
5. $3\frac{1}{40}$ yards
7. $17\frac{5}{12}$ miles
9. $4\frac{8}{9}$ hours

LU 2–3

1. **a.** $\dfrac{\overset{1}{\cancel{6}}}{\underset{1}{13}} \times \dfrac{\overset{2}{\cancel{26}}}{\underset{1}{\cancel{12}}} = 1$
3. **a.** $1\frac{1}{4}$　**b.** 3　**g.** 24　**l.** $\frac{4}{7}$
5. $39,000
7. 714
9. $20\frac{2}{3}$ miles
11. $412,000

LU 3–1

1. **a.** .62　**b.** .9　**c.** .953
   d. .401　**e.** .06
3. **a.** Hundredths place
   d. Thousandths place
5. **a.** $\frac{2}{5}$　**b.** $\frac{11}{25}$
   g. $\frac{5}{16}$　**l.** $9\frac{1}{25}$
7. .286
9. $\frac{566}{1,000}$
11. .333
13. .0020507

LU 3–2

1. **a.** 33.226　**b.** 5.2281　**d.** 3.7736
3. **a.** .3　**b.** .1　**c.** 1,480.0　**d.** .1
5. **a.** 6,870　**c.** .0272
   e. 34,700　**i.** 8,329.8
7. $4.53
9. $111.25
11. 15

LU 4–1

1. **a.** $430.64　**b.** 3　**c.** $867.51
3. **a.** Neuner Realty Co.
   b. Kevin Jones
   h. $2,756.80

LU 4–2

1. $1,435.42
3. Add $3,000; deduct $22.25
5. $2,989.92
7. $1,315.20

LU 5–1

1. **a.** $3N = 90$　**e.** $14 + \dfrac{N}{3} = 18$
   h. $2N + 3N + 8 = 68$

LU 5–2

1. $60
3. $45 telephone; $135 utility
5. 51 tickets—Sherry;
   408 tickets—Linda
7. 12 necklaces ($48);
   36 watches ($252)
9. $157.14

LU 6–1

1. **a.** 7%   **b.** 64.5%
   i. 503.8%   **l.** 80%
3. **a.** 70%   **c.** 162.5%
   h. 50%   **n.** 1.5%
5. **a.** $\frac{1}{4}$ **b.** .375   **c.** 50%
   d. .66$\overline{6}$ **n.** 1$\frac{1}{8}$
7. 2.9%
9. $\frac{39}{100}$
11. $\frac{9}{10,000}$

LU 6–2

1. **a.** $12,000; 30%; $3,600
   c. $7.00; 12%; $.84
3. **a.** 33.3%   **b.** 3%
   c. 27.5%
5. **a.** −1,584; −26.6%
   d. −20,000; −16.7%
7. $9,000
9. $3,196
11. 329.5%

LU 7–1

1. **a.** $120   **b.** $360   **c.** $50
   d. $100   **e.** $380
3. **a.** $75   **b.** $21.50; $40.75
5. **a.** .7125; .2875   **b.** .7225; .2775
7. $3.51
9. $81.25
11. $315
13. 45%

LU 7–2

1. **a.** February 18; March 10
   d. May 20; June 9
   e. October 10; October 30
3. **a.** .98; $1,102.50
   c. .98; $367.99
5. **a.** $16.79; $835.21
7. $12,230.40
9. **a.** $439.29   **b.** $491.21
11. $209.45
13. **a.** $765.31   **b.** $386.99

LU 8–1

1. **a.** $14.30   **b.** $2.72
   c. $4.35   **d.** $90   **e.** $116.31

3. **a.** $2; 80%   **b.** $6.50; 52%
   c. $.28; 28.9%
5. **a.** $1.52   **b.** $225
   c. $372.92   **d.** $625
7. **a.** $139.65   **b.** $538.65
9. **a.** $258.52   **b.** $90.48
11. **a.** $212.50   **b.** $297.50
13. $8.17

LU 8–2

1. **a.** $6.40   **b.** $57.50
   c. $34.43   **d.** $27.33   **e.** $.15
3. **a.** $6.94   **b.** $882.35   **c.** $30
   d. $171.43
5. **a.** 28.57%   **b.** 33.33%
   d. 53.85%
7. $346.15
9. 39.39%
11. $2.29
13. 63.33%

LU 8–3

1. **a.** $30.00; $70
   b. $525; $1,574.98
3. **a.** $410   **b.** $18.65
5. $227.50
7. 20.48%
9. $252.55

LU 9–1

1. **a.** $304; 0; $304
   b. $360; $40.50; $400.50
3. **a.** $438.85   **b.** $615.13
5. **a.** $5,200   **b.** $3,960
   c. $3,740   **d.** $4,750
7. $723.00
9. $3,846.25
11. $2,032.48

LU 9–2

1. **a.** $500; $2,300
3. 0; $2,000
5. $352.12
7. $143.75
9. $604.79
11. $658.94

LU 10–1

1. **a.** $240   **b.** $1,080
   c. $1,275
3. **a.** $131.25   **b.** $4.08
   c. $98.51
5. **a.** $515.63   **b.** $6,015.63
7. **a.** $5,459.66
9. $659.36
11. $360

LU 10–2

1. **a.** $4,371.44   **b.** $4,545.45
   c. $3,433.33
3. **a.** 60; .17   **b.** 120; .33
   c. 270; .75   **d.** 145; .40
5. 3%
7. $250
9. $3,000
11. 119 days

LU 10–3

1. **a.** $2,568.75; $1,885.47;
   $920.04
3. $4,267.59
5. $4,715.30; $115.30

LU 11–1

1. I; B; D; I; D; I; B; D
3. **a.** 3%
   c. 13%
5. $15,963.75
7. $848.75; $8,851.25
9. $14,300
11. $7,855

LU 11–2

1. **a.** $5,125
   b. $16,480.80
   c. $994.44
3. **a.** $14.76
   b. $223.25
   c. $3.49
5. $4,031.67
7. $8,262.74
9. $5,088.16
11. $721.45

LU 12–1

1. **a.** $573.25 year 2
   b. $3,115.57 year 4
3. **a.** $15,869; $5,869
   b. $16,084; $6,084
5. $5,980
7. $8,881.20
9. $2,129.40
11. $3,207.09; $207.09
13. $3,000; $3,469; $3,498

LU 12–2

1. **a.** .6209   **b.** .3936   **c.** .5513
3. **a.** $1,575,50; $924.50
   b. $2,547.02; $2,052.98
5. $13,152.60
7. $13,356.98
9. $16,826.40
11. $652.32
13. $18,014.22

Classroom Notes

Classroom Notes

Classroom Notes

Classroom Notes

Classroom Notes

Classroom Notes

Classroom Notes

Glossary

The Glossary contains a comprehensive list of the key terms used in the text. In many cases, examples are also included in the definitions. Recall that key terms and their page references are listed in the Chapter Organizer and Study Guide for each chapter.

Accelerated Cost Recovery System (ACRS) (p. 418) Tax law enacted in 1981 for assets put in service from 1981 through 1986.

Accelerated depreciation method (p. 418) Computes more depreciation expense in the early years of the asset's life than in the later years.

Accounts payable (p. 385) Amounts owed to creditors for services or items purchased.

Accounts receivable (p. 385) Amount owed by customers to a business from previous sales.

Accumulated depreciation (p. 413) Amount of depreciation that has accumulated on plant and equipment assets.

Acid test (p. 396) Current assets less inventory less prepaid expenses divided by current liabilities.

Addends (p. 8) Numbers that are combined in the addition process. *Example:* 8 + 9 = 17, of which 8 and 9 are the addends.

Adjustable rate mortgage (p. 366) Rate of mortgage is lower than a fixed rate mortgage. Rates adjusted without refinancing. Caps available to limit how high rate can go for each adjustment period over term of loan.

Adjusted bank balance (p. 96) Current balance of checkbook after reconciliation process.

Amortization (p. 346) Process of paying back a loan (principal plus interest) by equal periodic payments (see **amortization schedule**).

Amortization schedule (p. 371) Shows monthly payment to pay back loan at maturity. Payment also includes interest. Note payment is fixed at same amount each month.

Amount financed (p. 342) Cash price less down payment.

Annual percentage rate (APR) (p. 343) True or effective annual interest rate charged by sellers. Required to be stated by Truth in Lending Act.

Annual percentage rate (APR) table (p. 343) Effective annual rate of interest on a loan or installment purchase as shown by table lookup.

Annual percentage yield (APY) (p. 301) Truth in savings law forced banks to report actual interest in form of APY. Interest yield must be calculated on actual number of days bank has the money.

Annuities certain (p. 318) Annuities that have stated beginning and ending dates.

Annuity (p. 317) Stream of equal payments made at periodic times.

Annuity due (p. 318) Annuity that is paid (or received) at the beginning of the time period.

Assessed value (p. 456) Value of a property that an assessor sets (usually a percent of property's market value) that is used in calculating property taxes.

Asset cost (p. 413) Amount company paid for the asset.

Assets (p. 384) Things of value owned by a business.

Asset turnover (p. 396) Net sales divided by total assets.

ATM (p. 89) Automatic teller machine that allows customers of a bank to transfer funds and make deposits or withdrawals.

Average daily balance (p. 352) Sum of daily balances divided by number of days in billing cycle.

Average inventory (p. 458) Total of all inventories divided by number of times inventory taken.

Balance sheet (p. 384) Financial report that lists assets, liabilities, and equity. Report reflects the financial position of the company as of a particular date.

Bank discount (p. 282) The amount of interest charged by a bank on a note. (Maturity value × Bank discount rate × Number of days bank holds note) ÷ 360.

Bank discount rate (p. 280) Percent of interest.

Banker's Rule (p. 260) Time is exact days/360 in calculating simple interest.

Bank reconciliation (p. 96) Process of comparing the bank balance to the checkbook balance so adjustments can be made regarding checks outstanding, deposits in transit, and the like.

Bank statement (p. 95) Report sent by the bank to the owner of the checking account indicating checks processed, deposits made, and so on, along with beginning and ending balances.

Bar graph (p. 515) Visual representation using horizontal or vertical bars to make comparison or to show relationship on items of similar makeup.

Base (p. 144) Number that represents the whole 100%. It is the whole to which something is being compared. Usually follows word *of*.

Beneficiary (p. 467) Person(s) designated to receive the face value of the life insurance when insured dies.

Biweekly (p. 236) Every 2 weeks (26 times in a year).

Biweekly mortgage (p. 367) Mortgage payments made every 2 weeks rather than monthly. This payment method takes years off the life of the mortgage and substantially reduces the cost of interest.

Blank endorsement (p. 91) Current owner of check signs name on back. Whoever presents checks for payment receives the money.

Bodily injury (p. 467) Auto insurance that pays damages to people injured or killed by your auto.

Bond discount (p. 496) Bond selling for less than the face value.

Bond premium (p. 496) Bond selling for more than the face value.

Bonds (p. 495) Written promise by a company that borrows money usually with fixed-interest payment until maturity (repayment time).

Bond yield (p. 496) Total annual interest divided by total cost.

Book value (p. 413) Cost less accumulated depreciation.

Breakeven point (p. 219) Point at which seller has covered all expenses and costs and has made no profit or suffered a loss.

Cancellation (p. 47) Reducing process that is used to simplify the multiplication and division of fractions. *Example:*

$$\frac{\overset{1}{\cancel{4}}}{8} \times \frac{1}{\underset{1}{\cancel{4}}}$$

Capital (p. 384) Owners' investment in the business.

Cash advance (p. 309) Money borrowed by holder of credit card. It is recorded as another purchase and is used in the calculation of the average daily balance.

Cash discount (p. 179) Savings that result from early payment by taking advantage of discounts offered by the seller; discount is not taken on freight or taxes.

Cash dividend (p. 493) Cash distribution of company's profit to owners of stock.

Cash value (p. 469) Except for term insurance, this indicates the value of the policy when terminated. Options fall under the heading of nonforfeiture values.

Centi- (Appendix D) Prefix indicating .01 of a basic metric unit.

Chain or series discount (p. 176) Two or more trade discounts that are applied to the balance remaining after the previous discount is taken. Often called a **series discount.**

Check register (p. 89) Record-keeping device that records checks paid and deposits made by companies using a checking account.

Checks (p. 89) Written documents signed by appropriate person that directs the bank to pay a specific amount of money to a particular person or company.

Check stub (p. 89) Provides a record of checks written. It is attached to the check.

Circle graph (p. 517) A visual representation of the parts to the whole.

Closing costs (p. 368) Costs incurred when property passes from seller to buyer such as for credit reports, recording costs, points, and so on.

CM (p. 97) Abbreviation for **credit memorandum.** The bank is adding to your account. The CM is found on the bank statement. *Example:* Bank collects a note for you.

Coinsurance (p. 474) Type of fire insurance in which the insurer and insured share the risk. Usually there is an 80% coinsurance clause.

Collision (p. 477) Optional auto insurance that pays for the repairs to your auto from an accident after deductible is met. Insurance company will only pay for repairs up to the value of the auto (less deductible).

Commissions (p. 238) Payments based on established performance criteria.

Common denominator (p. 40) To add two or more fractions, denominators must be the same.

Common stocks (p. 386) Units of ownership called shares.

Comparative statement (p. 387) Statement showing data from two or more periods side by side.

Complement (p. 174) 100% less the stated percent. *Example:* 18% → 82% is the complement (100% − 18%).

Compounding (p. 299) Calculating the interest periodically over the life of the loan and adding it to the principal.

Compound interest (p. 299) The interest that is calculated periodically and then added to the principal. The next period the interest is calculated on the adjusted principal (old principal plus interest).

Comprehensive insurance (p. 477) Optional auto insurance that pays for damages to the auto caused by factors other than from collision (fire, vandalism, theft, and the like).

Compulsory insurance (p. 476) Insurance required by law—standard coverage.

Constants (p. 116) Numbers that have a fixed value such as 3 or −7. Placed on right side of equation; also called *knowns.*

Contingent annuities (p. 318) Beginning and ending dates of the annuity are uncertain (not fixed).

Contingent liability (p. 282) Potential liability that may or may not result from discounting a note.

Contribution margin (p. 219) Difference between selling price and variable cost.

Conversion periods (p. 297) How often (a period of time) the interest is calculated in the compounding process. *Example:* Daily—each day; monthly—12 times a year; quarterly—every 3 months; semiannually—every 6 months.

Corporation (p. 384) Company with many owners or stockholders. Equity of these owners is called stockholders' equity.

Cost (p. 204) Price retailers pay to manufacturer or supplier to bring merchandise into store.

Cost of merchandise (goods) sold (p. 391) Beginning inventory + Net purchases − Ending inventory.

Credit card (p. 350) A piece of plastic that allows you to buy on credit.

Credit memo (CM) (p. 97) Transactions of bank that increase customer's account.

Credit period (end) (p. 179) Credit days are counted from date of invoice. Has no relationship to the discount period.

Cumulative preferred stock (p. 492) Holders of preferred stock must receive current year and any dividends in arrears before any dividends are paid out to the holders of common stock.

Current assets (p. 384) Assets that are used up or converted into cash within 1 year or operating cycle.

Current liabilities (p. 385) Obligations of a company due within 1 year.

Current ratio (p. 396) Current assets divided by current liabilities.

Daily balance (p. 352) Calculated to determine customer's finance charge: Previous balance + Any cash advances + Purchases − Payments.

Daily compounding (p. 299) Interest calculated on balance each day.

Debit card (p. 89) Transactions result in money being immediately deducted from customer's checking account.

Debit memo (DM) (p. 97) A debit transaction bank does for customers.

Deca- (Appendix D) Prefix indicating 10 times basic metric unit.

Deci- (Appendix D) Prefix indicating .1 of basic metric unit.

Decimal equivalent (p. 69) Decimal represents the same value as the fraction. *Example:*

$$.05 = \frac{5}{100}$$

Decimal fraction (p. 67) Decimal representing a fraction; the denominator has a power of 10.

Decimal point (p. 2, 65) Center of the decimal system—located between units and tenths. Numbers to left are *whole numbers;* to the right are *decimal numbers.*

Decimal system (p. 2) The U.S. base 10 numbering system that uses the 10 single-digit numbers shown on a calculator.

Decimals (p. 65) Numbers written to the right of a decimal point. *Example:* 5.3, 18.22.

Declining-balance method (p. 417) Accelerated method of depreciation. The depreciation each year is calculated by book value beginning each year times the rate.

Deductibles (p. 477) Amount insured pays before insurance company pays. Usually the higher the deductible, the lower the premium will be.

Deductions (p. 237) Amounts deducted from gross earnings to arrive at net pay.

Deferred payment price (p. 343) Total of all monthly payments plus down payment.

Denominator (p. 35) The number of a common fraction below the division line (bar). *Example:*

$\frac{8}{9}$, of which 9 is the denominator

Deposit slip (p. 90) Document that shows date, name, account number, and items making up a deposit.

Deposits in transit (p. 97) Deposits not received or processed by bank at the time the bank statement is prepared.

Depreciation (p. 413) Process of allocating the cost of an asset (less residual value) over the asset's estimated life.

Depreciation causes (p. 413) Normal use, product obsolescence, aging, and so on.

Depreciation expense (p. 413) Process involving asset cost, estimated useful life, and residual value (salvage or trade-in value).

Depreciation schedule (p. 414) Table showing amount of depreciation expense, accumulated depreciation, and book value for each period of time for a plant asset.

Difference (p. 9) The resulting answer from a subtraction problem. *Example:* Minuend less subtrahend equals difference.

$$215 − 15 = 200$$

Differential pay schedule (p. 238) Pay rate is based on a schedule of units completed.

Digit (p. 3) Our decimal number system of 10 characters from 0 to 9.

Discounting a note (p. 283) Receiving cash from selling a note to a bank before the due date of a note. Steps to discount include: (1) calculate maturity value, (2) calculate number of days bank waits for money, (3) calculate bank discount, and (4) calculate proceeds.

Discount period (p. 180, 283) Amount of time to take advantage of a cash discount.

Distribution of overhead (p. 439) Companies distribute overhead by floor space or sales volume.

Dividend (p. 14) Number in the division process that is being divided by another. *Example:* 5)15, in which 15 is the dividend.

Dividends (p. 495) Distribution of company's profit in cash or stock to owners of stock.

Dividends in arrears (p. 492) Dividends that accumulate when a company fails to pay dividends to cumulative preferred stockholders.

Divisor (p. 14) Number in the division process that is dividing into another. *Example:* 5)15, in which 5 is the divisor.

DM (p. 97) Abbreviation for **debit memorandum.** The bank is charging your account. The DM is found on the bank statement. *Example:* NSF.

Dollar markdown (p. 216) Original selling price less the reduction to price. Markdown may be stated as a percent of the original selling price. *Example:*

$$\frac{\text{Dollar markdown}}{\text{Original selling price}}$$

Dollar markup (p. 205) Selling price less cost. Difference is the amount of the markup. Markup is also expressed in percent.

Down payment (p. 342) Amount of initial cash payment made when item is purchased.

Drafts (p. 89) Written orders like checks instructing a bank, credit union, or savings and loan institution to pay your money to a person or organization.

Draw (p. 239) The receiving of advance wages to cover business or personal expenses. Once wages are earned, drawing amount reduces actual amount received.

Drawee (p. 90) One ordered to pay the check.

Drawer (p. 90) One who writes the check.

Due date (p. 180) Maturity date or when the note will be repaid.

Earnings per share (p. 493) Annual earnings ÷ Total number of shares outstanding.

Effective rate (p. 281, 301) True rate of interest. The more frequent the compounding, the higher the effective rate.

Electronic deposits (p. 98) Credit card run through terminal which approves (or disapproves) the amount and adds it to company's bank balance.

Electronic funds transfer (EFT) (p. 95) A computerized operation that electronically transfers funds among parties without the use of paper checks.

Employee's Withholding Allowance Certificate (W-4) (p. 241) Completed by employee to indicate allowance claimed to determine amount of FIT that is deducted.

End of credit period (p. 180) Last day from date of invoice when customer can take cash discount.

End of month—EOM (also **proximo**) **(p. 184)** Cash discount period begins at the end of the month invoice is dated. After the 25th discount period, one additional month results.

Endorse (p. 91) Signing the back of the check; thus ownership is transferred to another party.

Endowment life (p. 469) Form of insurance that pays at maturity a fixed amount of money to insured or to the beneficiary. Insurance coverage would terminate when paid—similar to term life.

Equation (p. 116) Math statement that shows equality for expressions or numbers, or both.

Equivalent (fractional) (p. 38) Two or more fractions equivalent in value.

Escrow account (p. 368) Lending institution requires that each month $\frac{1}{12}$ of the insurance cost and real estate taxes be kept in a special account.

Exact interest (p. 260) Calculating simple interest using 365 days per year in time.

Excise tax (p. 455) Tax that government levies on particular products and services. Tax on specific luxury items or nonessentials.

Expression (p. 116) A meaningful combination of numbers and letters called *terms.*

Extended term insurance (p. 470) Resulting from nonforfeiture, it keeps the policy for the full face value going without further premium payments for a specific period of time.

Face amount (p. 467) Dollar amount stated in policy.

Face value (p. 279) Amount of insurance that is stated on the policy. It is usually the maximum amount for which the insurance company is liable.

Fair Credit and Charge Card Disclosure Act of 1988 (p. 351) Act that tightens controls on credit card companies soliciting new business.

Fair Labor Standards Act (p. 237) Federal law has minimum wage standards and the requirement of overtime pay. There are many exemptions for administrative personnel and for others.

Federal income tax (FIT) withholding (p. 242) Federal tax withheld from paycheck.

Federal Insurance Contribution Act (FICA) (p. 241) Percent of base amount of each employee's salary. FICA taxes used to fund retirement, disabled workers, Medicare, and so on. FICA is now broken down into Social Security and Medicare.

Federal Unemployment Tax Act (FUTA) (p. 244) Tax paid by employer. Current rate is .8% on first $7,000 of earnings.

Federal withholding tax (p. 242) See **Income tax.**

Finance charge (p. 343) Total payments − Actual loan cost.

Fire insurance (p. 472) Stipulated percent (normally 80%) of value that is required for insurance company to pay to reimburse one's losses.

First-in, first-out (FIFO) method (p. 433) This method assumes the first inventory brought into the store will be the first sold. Ending inventory is made up of goods most recently purchased.

Fixed cost (p. 219) Costs that do not change with increase or decrease in sales.

Fixed rate mortgage (p. 367) Monthly payment fixed over number of years, usually 30 years.

FOB destination (p. 173) Seller pays cost of freight in getting goods to buyer's location.

FOB shipping point (p. 173) Buyer pays cost of freight in getting goods to his location.

Formula (p. 116) Equation that expresses in symbols a general fact, rule, or principle.

Fraction (p. 35) Expresses a part of a whole number. *Example:*

$\frac{5}{6}$ expresses 5 parts out of 6

Freight terms (p. 173) Determine how freight will be paid. Most common freight terms are **FOB shipping point** and **FOB destination.**

Frequency distribution (p. 515) Shows by table the number of times event(s) occurs.

Full endorsement (p. 91) This endorsement identifies the next person or company to whom the check is to be transferred.

Future value (FV) (p. 299) Final amount of the loan or investment at the end of the last period. Also called *compound amount.*

Future value of annuity (p. 318) Future dollar amount of a series of payments plus interest.

Graduated-payment mortgage (p. 367) Borrower pays less at beginning of mortgage. As years go on, the payments increase.

Graduated plans (p. 367) In beginning years, mortgage payment is less. As years go on, monthly payments rise.

Gram (Appendix D) Basic unit of weight in metric system. An ounce equals about 28 grams.

Greatest common divisor (p. 37) The largest possible number that will divide evenly into both the numerator and denominator.

Gross pay (p. 237) Wages before deductions.

Gross profit (p. 204) Difference between cost of bringing goods into the store and selling price of the goods.

Gross profit from sales (p. 392) Net sales − Cost of goods sold.

Gross profit method (p. 437) Used to estimate value of inventory.

Gross sales (p. 391) Total earned sales before sales returns and allowances or sales discounts.

Hecto- (Appendix D) Prefix indicating 100 times basic metric unit.

Higher terms (p. 38) Expressing a fraction with a new numerator and denominator that is equivalent to the original. *Example:*

$$\frac{2}{9} \to \frac{6}{27}$$

Home equity loan (p. 366) Cheap and readily accessible lines of credit backed by equity in your home; tax-deductible; rates can be locked in.

Horizontal analysis (p. 388) Method of analyzing financial reports where each total this period is compared by amount of percent to the same total last period.

Improper fraction (p. 35) Fraction that has a value equal to or greater than 1; numerator is equal to or greater than the denominator. *Example:*

$$\frac{6}{6}, \frac{14}{9}$$

Income statement (p. 389) Financial report that lists the revenues and expenses for a specific period of time. It reflects how well the company is performing.

Income tax or FIT (p. 242) Tax that depends on allowances claimed, marital status, and wages earned.

Indemnity (p. 474) Insurance company's payment to insured for loss.

Index numbers (p. 517) Express the relative changes in a variable compared with some base, which is taken as 100.

Individual retirement account (IRA) (p. 316) An account established for retirement planning.

Installment cost (p. 342) Down payment + (Number of payments × Monthly payment). Also called deferred payment.

Installment loan (p. 342) Loan paid off with a series of equal periodic payments.

Installment purchases (p. 342) Purchase of an item(s) that requires periodic payments for a specific period of time with usually a high rate of interest.

Insured (p. 467) Customer or policyholder.

Insurer (p. 467) The insurance company that issues the policy.

Interest (p. 259) Principal × Rate × Time.

Interest-bearing note (p. 279) Maturity value of note is greater than amount borrowed since interest is added on.

Interest-only mortgage (p. 366) Type of mortgage where in early years only interest payment is required.

Inventory turnover (p. 438) Ratio that indicates how quickly inventory turns:

$$\frac{\text{Cost of goods sold}}{\text{Average inventory at cost}}$$

Invoice (p. 171) Document recording purchase and sales transactions.

Just-in-time (JIT) inventory system (p. 435) System that eliminates inventories. Suppliers provide materials daily as manufacturing company needs them.

Kilo- (Appendix D) Prefix indicating 1,000 times basic metric unit.

Last-in, first-out (LIFO) method (p. 433) This method assumes the last inventory brought into the store will be the first sold. Ending inventory is made up of the oldest goods purchased.

Least common denominator (LCD) (p. 40) Smallest nonzero whole number into which all denominators will divide evenly. *Example:*

$$\frac{2}{3} \, and \, \frac{1}{4} \quad LCD = 12$$

Level premium term (p. 468) Insurance premium that is fixed, say, for 50 years.

Liabilities (p. 385) Amount business owes to creditors.

Liability insurance (p. 476) Insurance for bodily injury to others and damage to someone else's property.

Like fractions (p. 40) Proper fractions with the same denominators.

Like terms (p. 116) Terms that are made up with the same variable:

$$A + 2A + 3A = 6A$$

Limited payment life (20-payment life) (p. 469) Premiums are for 20 years (a fixed period) and provide paid-up insurance for the full face value of the policy.

Line graphs (p. 516) Graphical presentation that involves a time element. Shows trends, failures, backlogs, and the like.

Line of credit (p. 283) Provides immediate financing up to an approved limit.

Liquid assets (p. 384) Cash or other assets that can be converted quickly into cash.

List price (p. 172) Suggested retail price paid by customers.

Liter (Appendix D) Basic unit of measure in metric, for volume.

Loan amortization table (p. 346) Table used to calculate monthly payments.

Long-term liabilities (p. 385) Debts or obligations that company does not have to pay within 1 year.

Lowest terms (p. 37) Expressing a fraction when no number divides evenly into the numerator and denominator except the number 1. *Example:*

$$\frac{5}{10} \to \frac{1}{2}$$

Maker (p. 279) One who writes the note.

Margin (p. 204) Difference between cost of bringing goods into store and selling price of goods

Markdowns (p. 204) Reductions from original selling price caused by seasonal changes, special promotions, and so on.

Markup (p. 204) Amount retailers add to cost of goods to cover operating expenses and make a profit.

Markup percent calculation (p. 205) Markup percent on cost × Cost = Dollar markup; or Markup percent on selling price × Selling price = Dollar markup.

Maturity date (p. 259, 279) Date the principal and interest are due.

Maturity value (MV) (p. 259, 279) Principal plus interest (if interest is charged). Represents amount due on the due date.

Maturity value of note (p. 279) Amount of cash paid on the due date. If interest-bearing maturity, value is greater than amount borrowed.

Mean (p. 512) Statistical term that is found by:

$$\frac{\text{Sum of all figures}}{\text{Number of figures}}$$

Measure of dispersion (p. 520) Number that describes how the numbers of a set of data are spread out or dispersed.

Median (p. 512) Statistical term that represents the central point or midpoint of a series of numbers.

Merchandise inventory (p. 385) Cost of goods for resale.

Meter (Appendix D) Basic unit of length in metric system. A meter is a little longer than a yard.

Metric system (Appendix D) A decimal system of weights and measures. The basic units are meters, grams, and liters.

Mill (p. 457) $\frac{1}{10}$ of a cent or $\frac{1}{1,000}$ of a dollar.

In decimal, it is .001. *In application:*

$$\frac{\text{Property}}{\text{tax due}} = \frac{\text{Mills} \times .001 \times}{\text{Assessed valuation}}$$

Milli- (Appendix D) Prefix indicating .001 of basic metric unit.

Minuend (p. 9) In a subtraction problem, the larger number from which another is subtracted. *Example:*

$$50 - 40 = 10$$

Mixed decimal (p. 69) Combination of a whole number and decimal, such as 59.8, 810.85.

Mixed number (p. 36) Sum of a whole number greater than zero and a proper fraction:

$$2\frac{1}{4}, 3\frac{3}{9}$$

Mode (p. 513) Value that occurs most often in a series of numbers.

Modified Accelerated Cost Recovery System (MACRS) (p. 418) Part of Tax Reform Act of 1986 that revised depreciation schedules of ACRS. Tax Bill of 1989 updates MACRS.

Monthly (p. 236) Some employers pay employees monthly.

Mortgage (p. 367) Cost of home less down payment.

Mortgage note payable (p. 385) Debt owed on a building that is a long-term liability; often the building is the collateral.

Multiplicand (p. 13) The first or top number being multiplied in a multiplication problem. *Example:*

Product = Multiplicand × Multiplier
40 = 20 × 2

Multiplier (p. 13) The second or bottom number doing the multiplication in a problem. *Example:*

Product = Multiplicand × Multiplier
40 = 20 × 2

Mutual fund (p. 498) Investors buy shares in the fund's portfolio (group of stocks and/or bonds).

Net asset value (NAV) (p. 498) The dollar value of one mutual fund share; calculated by subtracting current liabilities from current market value of fund's investments and dividing this by number of shares outstanding.

Net income (p. 392) Gross profit less operating expenses.

Net pay (p. 237) See **Net wages.**

Net price (p. 172) List price less amount of trade discount. The net price is before any cash discount.

Net price equivalent rate (p. 176) When multiplied times the list price, this rate or factor produces the actual cost to the buyer. Rate is found by taking the complement of each term in the discount and multiplying them together (do not round off).

Net proceeds (p. 280) Maturity value less bank discount.

Net profit (net income) (p. 204) Gross profit − Operating expenses.

Net purchases (p. 392) Purchases − Purchase discounts − Purchase returns and allowances.

Net sales (p. 391) Gross sales − Sales discounts − Sales returns and allowances.

Net wages (p. 242) Gross pay less deductions.

Net worth (p. 384) Assets less liabilities.

No-fault insurance (p. 479) Involves bodily injury. Damage (before a certain level) that is paid by an insurance company no matter who is to blame.

Nominal rate (p. 301) Stated rate.

Nonforfeiture values (p. 471) When a life insurance policy is terminated (except term), it represents (1) the available cash value, (2) additional extended term, or (3) additional paid-up insurance.

Noninterest-bearing note (p. 280) Note where the maturity value will be equal to the amount of money borrowed since no additional interest is charged.

Nonsufficient funds (NSF) (p. 97) Drawer's account lacked sufficient funds to pay written amount of check.

Normal distribution (p. 521) Data is spread symmetrically about the mean.

Numerator (p. 35) Number of a common fraction above the division line (bar). *Example:*

$$\frac{8}{9}, \text{in which 8 is the numerator}$$

Omnibus Budget Reconciliation Act of 1989 (p. 420) An update of MACRS. Unless business use of equipment is greater than 50%, straight-line depreciation is required.

Open-end credit (p. 351) Set payment period. Also, additional credit amounts can be added up to a set limit. It is a revolving charge account.

Operating expenses (overhead) (p. 392) Regular expenses of doing business. These are not costs.

Ordinary annuities (p. 317) Annuity that is paid (or received) at end of the time period.

Ordinary dating (p. 182) Cash discount is available within the discount period. Full amount due by end of credit period if discount is missed.

Ordinary interest (p. 261) Calculating simple interest using 360 days per year in time.

Ordinary life insurance (p. 414) See **Straight life insurance.**

Outstanding balance (p. 351) Amount left to be paid on a loan.

Outstanding checks (p. 97) Checks written but not yet processed by the bank before bank statement preparation.

Overdraft (p. 95) Occurs when company or person wrote a check without enough money in the bank to pay for it (NFS check).

Overhead expenses (p. 439) Operating expenses *not* directly associated with a specific department or product.

Override (p. 237) Commission that managers receive due to sales by people that they supervise.

Overtime (p. 237) Time-and-a-half pay for more than 40 hours of work.

Owner's equity (p. 384) See **Capital.**

Paid-up insurance (p. 469) A certain level of insurance can continue, although the premiums are terminated. This results from the nonforfeiture value (except term). Result is a reduced paid-up policy until death.

Partial products (p. 13) Numbers between multiplier and product.

Partial quotient (p. 14) Occurs when divisor doesn't divide evenly into the dividend.

Partnership (p. 384) Business with two or more owners.

Payee (p. 90, 279) One who is named to receive the amount of the check.

Payroll register (p. 240) Multicolumn form to record payroll data.

Percent (p. 144) Stands for hundredths. *Example:*

4% is 4 parts of one hundred, or $\frac{4}{100}$

Percentage method (p. 242) A method to calculate withholdings. Opposite of wage bracket method.

Percent decrease (p. 149) Calculated by decrease in price over original amount.

Percent increase (p. 149) Calculated by increase in price over original amount.

Percent markup on cost (p. 205) Dollar markup divided by the cost; thus, markup is a percent of the cost.

Percent markup on selling price (p. 210) Dollar markup divided by the selling price; thus, markup is a percent of the selling price.

Periodic inventory system (p. 430) Physical count of inventory taken at end of a time period. Inventory records are not continually updated.

Periods (p. 297) Number of years times the number of times compounded per year (see **Conversion period**).

Perishables (p. 217) Goods or services with a limited life.

Perpetual inventory system (p. 430) Inventory records are continually updated; opposite of periodic.

Personal property (p. 456) Items of possession, like cars, home, furnishings, jewelry, and so on. These are taxed by the property tax (don't forget real property is also taxed).

Piecework (p. 238) Compensation based on the number of items produced or completed.

Place value (p. 3) The digit value that results from its position in a number.

Plant and equipment (p. 385) Assets that will last longer than 1 year.

Point of sale (p. 100) Terminal that accepts cards (like those used at ATMs) to purchase items at retail outlets. No cash is physically exchanged.

Points (p. 368) Percentage(s) of mortgage that represents an additional cost of borrowing. It is a one-time payment made at closing.

Policy (p. 467) Written insurance contract.

Policyholder (p. 467) The insured.

Portion (p. 144) Amount, part, or portion that results from multiplying the base times the rate. Not expressed as a percent; it is expressed as a number.

Preferred stock (p. 386) Type of stock that has a preference regarding a corporation's profits and assets.

Premium (p. 467) Periodic payments that one makes for various kinds of insurance protection.

Prepaid expenses (p. 385) Items a company buys that have not been used are shown as assets.

Prepaid rent (p. 385) Rent paid in advance.

Present value (PV) (p. 296) How much money will have to be deposited today (or at some date) to reach a specific amount of maturity (in the future).

Present value of annuity (p. 323) Amount of money needed today to receive a specified stream (annuity) of money in the future.

Price-earnings (PE) ratio (p. 492) Closing price per share of stock divided by earnings per share.

Price relative (p. 518) The quotient of the current price divided by some previous year's price—the base year—multiplied by 100.

Prime number (p. 41) Whole number greater than 1 that is only divisible by itself and 1. *Examples:* 2, 3, 5.

Principal (p. 259) Amount of money that is originally borrowed, loaned, or deposited.

Proceeds (p. 280) Maturity value less the bank charge.

Product (p. 13) Answer of a multiplication process, such as:

$$\text{Product} = \text{Multiplicand} \times \text{Multiplier}$$
$$50 = 5 \times 10$$

Promissory note (p. 279) Written unconditional promise to pay a certain sum (with or without interest) at a fixed time in the future.

Proper fractions (p. 35) Fractions with a value less than 1; numerator is smaller than denominator, such as $\frac{5}{9}$.

Property damage (p. 476) Auto insurance covering damages that are caused to the property of others.

Property tax (p. 457) Tax that raises revenue for school districts, cities, counties, and the like.

Property tax due (p. 457) Tax rate × Assessed valuation

Proximo (prox) (p. 184) Same as end of month.

Purchase discounts (p. 391) Savings received by buyer for paying for merchandise before a certain date.

Purchase returns and allowances (p. 391) Cost of merchandise returned to store due to damage, defects, and so on. An *allowance* is a cost reduction that results when buyer keeps or buys damaged goods.

Pure decimal (p. 69) Has no whole number(s) to the left of the decimal point, such as .45.

Quick assets (p. 396) Current assets − Inventory − Prepaid expenses.

Quick ratio (p. 396) (Current assets − Inventory − Prepaid expenses) ÷ Current liabilities.

Quotient (p. 14) The answer of a division problem.

Range (p. 520) Difference between the highest and lowest values in a group of values or set of data.

Rate (p. 144) Percent that is multiplied times the base that indicates what part of the base we are trying to compare to. Rate is not a whole number.

Rate of interest (p. 297) Percent of interest that is used to compute the interest charge on a loan for a specific time.

Ratio analysis (p. 395) Relationship of one number to another.

Real property (p. 456) Land, buildings, and so on, which are taxed by the property tax.

Rebate (p. 349) Finance charge that a customer receives for paying off a loan early.

Rebate fraction (p. 349) Sum of digits based on number of months to go divided by sum of digits based on total number of months of loan.

Receipt of goods (ROG) (p. 183) Used in calculating the cash discount period; begins the day that the goods are received.

Reciprocal of a fraction (p. 48) The interchanging of the numerator and the denominator. Inverted number is the reciprocal. *Example:*

$$\frac{6}{7} \rightarrow \frac{7}{6}$$

Reduced paid-up insurance (p. 470) Insurance that uses cash value to buy protection, face amount is less than original policy, and policy continues for life.

Remainder (p. 14) Leftover amount in division.

Repeating decimals (p. 67) Decimal numbers that repeat themselves continuously and thus do not end.

Residual value (p. 413) Estimated value of a plant asset after depreciation is taken (or end of useful life).

Restrictive endorsement (p. 91) Check must be deposited to the payee's account. This restricts one from cashing it.

Retail method (p. 437) Method to estimate cost of ending inventory. The cost ratio times ending inventory at retail equals the ending cost of inventory.

Retained earnings (p. 386) Amount of earnings that is kept in the business.

Return on equity (p. 396) Net income divided by stockholders' equity.

Revenues (p. 391) Total earned sales (cash or credit) less any sales discounts, returns, or allowances.

Reverse mortgage (p. 367) Federal Housing Administration makes it possible for older homeowners to live in their homes and get cash or monthly income.

Revolving charge account (p. 351) Charges for a customer are allowed up to a specified maximum, a minimum monthly payment is required, and interest is charged on balance outstanding.

ROG (p. 183) Receipt of goods; cash discount period begins when goods are received, not ordered.

Rounding decimals (p. 67) Reducing the number of decimals to an indicated position, such as $59.59 \rightarrow 59.6$ to the nearest tenth.

Rounding whole numbers all the way (p. 5) Process to estimate actual answer. When rounding all the way, only one nonzero digit is left. Rounding all the way gives the least degree of accuracy. *Example:* 1,251 to 1,000; 2,995 to 3,000.

Rule of 78 (p. 347) Method to compute rebates on consumer finance loans. How much of finance charge are you entitled to? Formula or table lookup may be used.

Safekeeping (p. 100) Bank procedure whereby a bank does not return checks. Canceled checks are photocopied.

Salaries payable (p. 385) Obligations that a company must pay within 1 year for salaries earned but unpaid.

Sales (not trade) discounts (p. 391) Reductions in selling price of goods due to early customer payment.

Sales returns and allowances (p. 391) Reductions in price or reductions in revenue due to goods returned because of product defects, errors, and so on. When the buyer keeps the damaged goods, an allowance results.

Sales tax (p. 454) Tax levied on consumers for certain sales of merchandise or services by states, counties, or various local governments.

Salvage value (p. 413) Cost less accumulated depreciation.

Selling price (p. 219) Cost plus markup equals selling price.

Semiannually (p. 236) Twice a year.

Semimonthly (p. 236) Some employees are paid twice a month.

Series discount (p. 176) See **chain discount.**

Short-rate table (p. 473) Fire insurance rate table used when insured cancels the policy.

Short-term policy (p. 472) Fire insurance policy for less than 1 year.

Signature card (p. 90) Information card signed by person opening a checking account.

Simple discount note (p. 283) A note in which bank deducts interest in advance.

Simple interest (p. 259) Interest is only calculated on the principal. In $I = P \times R \times T$, the interest plus original principal equals the maturity value of an interest-bearing note.

Simple interest formula (p. 262)

$$\text{Interest} = \text{Principal} \times \text{Rate} \times \text{Time}$$

$$\text{Principal} = \frac{\text{Interest}}{\text{Rate} \times \text{Time}}$$

$$\text{Rate} = \frac{\text{Interest}}{\text{Principal} \times \text{Time}}$$

$$\text{Time} = \frac{\text{Interest}}{\text{Principal} \times \text{Rate}}$$

Single equivalent discount rate (p. 177) Rate or factor as a single discount that calculates the amount of the trade discount by multiplying the rate times the list price. This single equivalent discount replaces a series of chain discounts. The single equivalent rate is $(1 - \text{Net price equivalent rate})$.

Single trade discount (p. 174) Company gives only one trade discount.

Sinking fund (p. 326) An annuity in which the stream of deposits with appropriate interest will equal a specified amount in the future.

Sliding scale commissions (p. 239) Different commission. Rates depend on different levels of sales.

Sole proprietorship (p. 384) A business owned by one person.

Specific identification method (p. 431) This method calculates the cost of ending inventory by identifying each item remaining to invoice price.

Standard deviation (p. 520) Measures the spread of data around the mean.

State unemployment tax (SUTA) (p. 244) Tax paid by employer. Rate varies depending on amount of unemployment the company experiences.

Stockbrokers (p. 492) People who with their representatives do the trading on the floor of the stock exchange.

Stockholder (p. 492) One who owns stock in a company.

Stockholders' equity (p. 384) Assets less liabilities.

Stocks (p. 492) Ownership shares in the company sold to buyers, who receive stock certificates.

Stock yield percent (p. 493) Dividend per share divided by the closing price per share.

Straight commission (p. 239) Wages calculated as a percent of the value of goods sold.

Straight life insurance (whole or ordinary) (p. 469) Protection (full value of policy) results from continual payment of premiums by insured. Until death or retirement, nonforfeiture values exist for straight life.

Straight-line method (p. 414) Method of depreciation that spreads an equal amount of depreciation each year over the life of the assets.

Straight-line rate (rate of depreciation) (p. 44) One divided by number of years of expected life.

Subtrahend (p. 9) In a subtraction problem smaller number that is being subtracted from another. *Example:* 30 in

$$150 - 30 = 120$$

Sum (p. 8) Total in the adding process.

Tax rate (p. 456) $\dfrac{\text{Budget needed}}{\text{Total assessed value}}$

Term life insurance (p. 468) Inexpensive life insurance that provides protection for a specific period of time. No nonforfeiture values exist for term.

Term policy (p. 468) Period of time that the policy is in effect.

Terms of the sale (p. 179) Criteria on invoice showing when cash discounts are available, such as rate and time period.

Time (p. 260) Expressed as years or fractional years, used to calculate the simple interest.

Trade discount (p. 171) Reduction off original selling price (list price) not related to early payment.

Trade discount amount (p. 171) List price less net price.

Trade discount rate (p. 171) Trade discount amount given in percent.

Trade-in (scrap) (p. 413) Estimated value of a plant asset after depreciation is taken (or end of useful life).

Treasury bill (p. 281) Loan to the federal government for 91 days (13 weeks), 182 days (26 weeks), or 1 year.

Trend analysis (p. 394) Analyzing each number as a percentage of a base year.

Truth in Lending Act (p. 343) Federal law that requires sellers to inform buyers, in writing, of (1) the finance charge and (2) the annual percentage rate. The law doesn't dictate what can be charged.

Twenty-payment life (p. 469) Provides permanent protection and cash value, but insured pays premiums for first 20 years.

Twenty-year endowment (p. 469) Most expensive life insurance policy. It is a combination of term insurance and cash value.

Unemployment tax (p. 244) Tax paid by the employer that is used to aid unemployed persons.

Units-of-production method (p. 415) Depreciation method that estimates amount of depreciation based on usage.

Universal life (p. 470) Whole life insurance plan with flexible premium and death benefits. This life plan has limited guarantees.

Unknown (p. 116) The variable we are solving for.

Unlike fractions (p. 40) Proper fractions with different denominators.

Useful life (p. 413) Estimated number of years the plant asset is used.

U.S. Rule (p. 264) Method that allows the borrower to receive proper interest credits when paying off a loan in more than one payment before the maturity date.

U.S. Treasury bill (p. 281) A note issued by federal government to investors.

Value of an annuity (p. 317) Sum of series of payments and interest (think of this as the maturity value of compounding).

Variable commission scale (p. 239) Company pays different commission rates for different levels of net sales.

Variable cost (p. 220) Costs that do change in response to change in volume of sales.

Variable rate (p. 367) Home mortgage rate is not fixed over its lifetime.

Variables (p. 116) Letters or symbols that represent unknowns.

Vertical analysis (p. 387) Method of analyzing financial reports where each total is compared to one total. *Example:* Cash is a percent of total assets.

W-4 (p. 241) See **Employee's Withholding Allowance Certificate.**

Wage bracket method (In Handbook) Tables used in Circular E to compute FIT withholdings.

Weekly (p. 236) Some employers pay employees weekly.

Weighted-average method (p. 432) Calculates the cost of ending inventory by applying an average unit cost to items remaining in inventory for that period of time.

Weighted mean (p. 512) Used to find an average when values appear more than once.

Whole life insurance (p. 470) See **Straight life insurance.**

Whole number (p. 2) Number that is 0 or larger and doesn't contain a decimal or fraction, such as 10, 55, 92.

Withholding (p. 242) Amount of deduction from one's paycheck.

Workers' compensation (p. 244) Business insurance covering sickness or accidental injuries to employees that result from on-the-job activities.

Classroom Notes

Index

Student DVD-ROM

This student DVD-ROM contains the following assets designed to help you succeed in the business math course:

- **Videos** bring the author to you, where Jeff Slater carefully walks you through a review of each of the Learning Unit Practice Quizzes, with brief real applications to introduce each chapter segment.

- **Video Cases** applying business math concepts to real companies tied to information and assignments in the text.

- **Excel Spreadsheet Templates** to assist in solving end-of-chapter exercises that are indicated by an Excel logo.

- **PowerPoint** lecture slides walk you through the chapter concepts.

- **Practice Quizzes** covering key concepts in each chapter and giving you quick feedback on your responses.

- **Internet Resource Guide** providing information on using the Internet and useful Web sites for use with each chapter.

- **Web Link** to the Practical Business Math Procedures text Web site, which contains additional material to help you.